PICTURE-WRITING
OF THE AMERICAN INDIANS

by GARRICK MALLERY

FOREWORD
by J. W. Powell

IN TWO VOLUMES

VOLUME

ONE

DOVER PUBLICATIONS, INC.
NEW YORK

Published in Canada by General Publishing Company, Ltd., 30 Lesmill Road, Don Mills, Toronto, Ontario.

Published in the United Kingdom by Constable and Company, Ltd.

This Dover edition, first published in 1972, is an unabridged republication of the Accompanying Paper, "Picture-Writing of the American Indians," of the *Tenth Annual Report of the Bureau of Ethnology to the Secretary of the Smithsonian Institution, 1888–'89, by J. W. Powell, Director*, originally published by the Government Printing Office, Washington, D. C., in 1893. The first section of the original volume, "Report of the Director," has been omitted in the present edition, except for a few pages referring directly to the Accompanying Paper.

The original edition (Report plus Accompanying Paper) was in one volume. The present edition (unabridged Accompanying Paper and excerpt from Report) is in two volumes.

The following plates, which appear in black and white in the present edition, were in color in the original edition: XVI, XX through XXIX, XXXIX, XLV, XLVI, XLVIII and XLIX.

International Standard Book Number: 0-486-22842-8
Library of Congress Catalog Card Number: 76-188815

Manufactured in the United States of America
Dover Publications, Inc.
180 Varick Street
New York, N. Y. 10014

FOREWORD.

By J. W. Powell, from his 1889 refort as Director of the Bureau of Ethnology

For the first time in the series of the Annual Reports of this Bureau a single paper is submitted to exhibit the character of the investigations undertaken and the facts collected by its officers, with the results of their studies upon such collections. But while the paper is single in form and in title, it includes, in its illustrations and the text relating to them, nearly all topics into which anthropology can properly be divided, and therefore shows more diversity than would often be contained in a volume composed of separate papers by several authors. Its subject-matter being essentially pictorial, it required a large number of illustrations, twelve hundred and ninety-five figures being furnished in the text, besides fifty-four full-page plates, which, with their explanation and discussion, expanded the volume to such size as to exclude other papers.

The papers accompanying the Fourth Annual Report of this Bureau, which was for the fiscal year 1882–'83, included one under the title "Pictographs of the North American Indians, a Preliminary Paper, by Garrick Mallery." Although that work was of considerable length and the result of much research and study, it was in fact as well as in title preliminary. The substance and general character of the information obtained at that time on the subject was published not only for the benefit of students already interested in it, but also to excite interest in that branch of study among active explorers in the field and, indeed, among all persons engaged in anthropologic researches. For the convenience of such workers as were invited in general terms to become collaborators, suggestions were offered for the examination, description, and study of the objects connected with this branch of investigation which might be noticed or discovered by them. The result of this preliminary publication has shown the wisdom of the plan adopted. Since the distribution of the Fourth Annual Report pictography in its various branches has become, far more than ever before, a prominent feature in the publications of learned societies, in the separate works of anthropologists, and in the notes of scientific explorers. The present paper includes, with proper credit to the authors quoted or cited, many contributions to this branch of study which obviously have been induced by the preliminary paper before mentioned.

The interest thus excited has continued to be manifested by the publication of new information of importance, in diverse shapes and in many languages, some of which has been received too late for proper attention in this paper.

Col. Mallery's studies in pictography commenced in the field. He was stationed with his military command at Fort Rice, on the upper Missouri river, in the autumn of 1876, and obtained a copy of the remarkable pictograph which he then called "A Calendar of the Dakota Nation," and published under that title, with interpretation and explanation, in Vol. III, No. 1, of the series of bulletins of the U. S. Geological and Geographical Survey of the Territories, issued April 9, 1877. This work attracted attention, and at the request of the Secretary of the Interior he was ordered by the Secretary of War, on June 13, 1877, to report for duty, in connection with the ethnology of the North American Indians, to the present Director of this Bureau, then in charge of the Geographical and Geological Survey of the Rocky Mountain Region. Upon the organization of the Bureau of Ethnology, in 1879, Col. Mallery was appointed ethnologist, and has continued in that duty without intermission, supplementing field explorations by study of all accessible anthropologic literature and by extensive correspondence. His attention has been steadily directed to pictography and to sign-language, which branches of study are so closely connected that neither can be successfully pursued to the exclusion of the other, but his researches have by no means been confined to those related subjects.

The plan and scope of the present work may be very briefly stated as follows:

After some introductory definitions and explanations general remarks are submitted upon the grand division of petroglyphs or pictures upon rocks as distinct from other exhibitions of pictography. This division is less susceptible of interpretation than others, but it claims special interest and attention because the locality of production is fixed, and also because the antiquity of workmanship may often be determined with more certainty than can that of pictures on less enduring and readily transportable objects. Descriptions, with illustrations, are presented of petroglyphs in North America, including those in several provinces of Canada, in many of the states and territories of the United States, in Mexico, and in the West Indies. A large number from Central and South America also appear, followed by examples from Australia, Oceanica, Europe, Africa, and Asia, inserted chiefly for comparison with the picture-writings in America, to which the work is specially devoted, and therefore styled extra-limital petroglyphs. The curious forms called cup sculptures are next discussed, followed by a chapter on pictographs considered generally, which condenses the results of much thought. The substances, apart from rocks, on which picture-writing is found are next considered, and afterwards the instruments and materials by which they are made. The subjects of pictography and the practices which elucidate it are classified under several headings, viz: *Mnemonic*, subdivided into (1) Knotted cords and objects tied, (2) Notched or marked sticks, (3) Wampum, (4) Order of songs, (5) Traditions, (6) Treaties, (7) Appointment, (8) Numeration, (9) Accounting; *Chronology*, in which the charts at first called calendars, but now, in correct translation of the Indian terms, styled winter-counts, are discussed and illustrated with the care required by their remarkable characteristics; *Notices*, which chapter embraces

(1) Notice of visit, departure, and direction, (2) Direction by drawing topographic features, (3) Notice of condition, (4) Warning and guidance; *Communications*, including (1) Declaration of war, (2) Profession of peace and friendship, (3) Challenge, (4) Social and religious missives, (5) Claim or demand; *Totems, titles, and names*, divided into (1) Pictorial tribal designations, (2) Gentile and clan designation, (3) Significance of tattoo marks, which topic is discussed at length, with ample illustration, and (4) Designations of individuals, subdivided into insignia or tokens of authority, signs of individual achievements, property marks, and personal names. Some of the facts presented are to be correlated with the antique forms of heraldry and others with proper names in modern civilization.

The topic *Religion*, considered in the popular significance of that term, is divided into (1) Symbols of the supernatural, (2) Myths and mythic animals, (3) Shamanism, (4) Charms and amulets, (5) Religious ceremonies, and (6) Mortuary practices. *Customs* are divided into (1) Cult associations, (2) Daily life and habits, (3) Games. The chapter entitled *Historic* presents (1) Record of expeditions, (2) Record of battle, which includes a highly interesting Indian pictured account of the battle of the Little Big Horn, commonly called the "Custer massacre," (3) Record of migration, (4) Record of notable events. The *Biographic* chapter gives too many minutiæ for particularization here, but is divided into (1) Continuous record of events in life and (2) Particular exploits or events. *Ideography* permeates and infuses all the matter under the other headings, but is discussed distinctively and with evidential illustrations in the sections of (1) abstract ideas expressed objectively, and (2) symbols and emblems. In the latter section the author suggests that the proper mode of interpretation of pictographs whose origin and significance are unknown is that they are to be primarily supposed to be objective representations, but may be, and often are, ideographic, and in a limited number of cases may have become symbolic, but that the strong presumption without extrinsic evidence is against the occult or esoteric symbolism often attributed to the markings under discussion. The significance of colors is connected with ideography and examples are given of the colors used in many parts of the world for mere decoration, in ceremonies, for death and mourning, for war and peace, and to designate social status. The depiction of gesture and posture signs is next discussed, showing the intimate relation between a thought as expressed without words by signs, and a thought expressed without words by pictures corresponding to those signs.

Conventionalizing is divided into conventional devices, which were the precursors of writing, and the syllabaries and alphabets evolved. The pictographic origin of all the current alphabets of the world, often before discussed, receives further explanation.

While comparison by the reader between all the illustrations and the facts recorded and the suggestions submitted about them is essential to the utility of the work, the author gives, as representing his own mode of study, found to be advantageous in use, a chapter on *Special Comparison*, divided into (1) Typical style, (2) Homomorphs and symmorphs, (3) Composite forms, (4) Artistic skill and methods. This chapter is followed by one with which it is closely connected, styled *Means of Interpretation*, divided into (1) Marked characters of known significance, (2) Distinctive costumes, weapons, and ornaments, (3) Ambiguous characters with known meanings, the latter being chiefly a collection of separate figures which would not be readily recognized without labels, but which are understood through reliable authority. Finally, under the rather noncommittal title of *Controverted Pictographs*, the subjects of fraud and error are discussed with striking examples and useful cautions.

From this brief paraphrase of the table of contents, it is obvious that nearly all branches of anthropology are touched upon. It is also to be remarked that the work is unique because it presents the several anthropologic topics recorded by the Indians themselves according to their unbiased conceptions, and in their own mode of writing. From this point of view the anonymous and generally unknown pictographers may be considered to be the primary authors of the treatise and Col.

Mallery a discoverer, compiler, and editor. But such deprecia-
tive limitation of his functions would ignore the originality of
treatment pervading the work and the systematic classification
and skillful analysis shown in it which enhance its value and
interest.

CONTENTS.

ILLUSTRATIONS.

20 ILLUSTRATIONS.

PICTURE-WRITING OF THE AMERICAN INDIANS.

BY GARRICK MALLERY.

INTRODUCTION.

An essay entitled "Pictographs of the North American Indians: A Preliminary Paper," appeared in the Fourth Annual Report of the Bureau of Ethnology. The present work is not a second edition of that essay, but is a continuation and elaboration of the same subject. Of the eighty-three plates in that paper not one is here reproduced, although three are presented with amendments; thus fifty-one of the fifty-four plates in this volume are new. Many of the text figures, however, are used again, as being necessary to the symmetry of the present work, but they are now arranged and correlated so as to be much more useful than when unmethodically disposed as before, and the number of text figures now given is twelve hundred and ninety-five as against two hundred and nine, the total number in the former paper. The text itself has been rewritten and much enlarged. The publication of the "Preliminary Paper" has been of great value in the preparation of the present work, as it stimulated investigation and report on the subject to such an extent that it is now impossible to publish within reasonable limits of space all the material on hand. Indeed, after the present work had been entirely written and sent to the Public Printer, new information came to hand which ought to be published, but can not now be inserted.

It is also possible to give more attention than before to the picture-writing of the aboriginal inhabitants of America beyond the limits of the United States. While the requirements of the acts of Congress establishing the Bureau of Ethnology have been observed by directing main attention to the Indians of North America, there is sufficient notice of Central and South America to justify the present title, in which also the simpler term "picture-writing" is used instead of "pictographs."

Picture-writing is a mode of expressing thoughts or noting facts by marks which at first were confined to the portrayal of natural or artificial objects. It is one distinctive form of thought-writing without

25

reference to sound, gesture language being the other and probably earlier form. Whether remaining purely ideographic, or having become
conventional, picture-writing is the direct and durable expression of
ideas of which gesture language gives the transient expression. Originally it was not connected with the words of any language. When
adopted for syllabaries or alphabets, which is the historical course of
its evolution, it ceased to be the immediate and became the secondary
expression of the ideas framed in oral speech. The writing common
in civilization may properly be styled sound-writing, as it does not
directly record thoughts, but presents them indirectly, after they have
passed through the phase of sound. The trace of pictographs in alphabets and syllabaries is discussed in the present work under its proper
heading so far as is necessary after the voluminous treatises on the topic,
and new illustrations are presented. It is sufficient for the present
to note that all the varied characters of script and print now current are derived directly or mediately from pictorial representations
of objects. Bacon well said that "pictures are dumb histories," and he
might have added that in the crude pictures of antiquity were contained the germs of written words.

The importance of the study of picture-writing depends partly upon
the result of its examination as a phase in the evolution of human
culture. As the invention of alphabetic writing is admitted to be the
great step marking the change from barbarism to civilization, the history of its earlier development must be valuable. It is inferred from
internal evidence, though not specifically reported in history, that picture-writing preceded and generated the graphic systems of Egypt,
Assyria, and China, but in America, especially in North America, its
use is still current. It can be studied here without any requirement
of inference or hypothesis, in actual existence as applied to records
and communications. Furthermore, the commencement of its evolution into signs of sound is apparent in the Aztec and the Maya
characters, in which transition stage it was arrested by foreign conquest. The earliest lessons of the genesis and growth of culture in
this important branch of investigation may, therefore, be best learned
from the western hemisphere. In this connection it should be noticed
that picture-writing is found in sustained vigor on the same continent
where sign language has prevailed and has continued in active operation to an extent historically unknown in other parts of the world.
These modes of expression, i. e., transient and permanent thought-
writing, are so correlated in their origin and development that neither
can be studied to the best advantage without including the other.
Unacquainted with these facts, but influenced by an assumption that
America must have been populated from the eastern hemisphere, some
enterprising persons have found or manufactured American inscriptions composed of characters which may be tortured into identity with
some of the Eurasian alphabets or syllabaries, but which sometimes

suggest letters of indigenous invention. This topic is discussed in its place.

For the purposes of the present work there is no need to decide whether sign-language, which is closely connected with picture-writing, preceded articulate speech. It is sufficient to admit the high antiquity of thought-writing in both its forms, and yet it is proper to notice a strong current of recent opinions as indicated by Prof. Sayce (a) in his address to the anthroplologic section of the British Association for the Advancement of Science, as follows:

I see no escape from the conclusions that the chief distinctions of race were established long before man acquired language. If the statement made by M. de Mortillet is true, that the absence of the mental tubercle, or bony excrescence in which the tongue is inserted, in a skull of the Neanderthal type found at La Naulette, indicates an absence of the faculty of speech, one race at least of palæolithic man would have existed in Europe before it had as yet invented an articulate language. Indeed it is difficult to believe that man has known how to speak for any very great length of time. * * * We can still trace through the thin disguise of subsequent modifications and growth the elements, both lexical and grammatical, out of which language must have arisen. * * * The beginnings of articulate language are still too transparent to allow us to refer them to a very remote era. * * * In fact the evidence that he is a drawing animal * * * mounts back to a much earlier epoch than the evidence that he is a speaking animal.

When a system of ideographic gesture signs prevailed and at the same time any form of artistic representation, however rude, existed, it would be expected that the delineations of the former would appear in the latter. It was but one more and an easy step to fasten upon bark, skins, or rocks the evanescent air pictures that still in pigments or carvings preserve their ideography or conventionalism in their original outlines. A transition stage between gestures and pictographs, in which the left hand is used as a supposed drafting surface, upon which the index draws lines, is exhibited in the Dialogue between Alaskan Indians in the First Annual Report of the Bureau of Ethnology (a). This device is common among deaf-mutes, without equal archeologic importance, as it may have been suggested by the art of writing, with which, even when not instructed in it, they are generally acquainted.

The execution of the drawings, of which the several forms of picture-writing are composed, often exhibits the first crude efforts of graphic art, and their study in that relation is of value.

When pictures are employed for the same purpose as writing, the conception intended to be presented is generally analyzed and only its most essential points are indicated, with the result that the characters when frequently repeated become conventional, and in their later form cease to be recognizable as objective portraitures. This exhibition of conventionalizing has its own historic import.

It is not probable that much valuable information will ever be obtained from ancient rock carvings or paintings, but they are important as indications of the grades of culture reached by their authors, and of the subjects which interested those authors, as is shown in the appropriate chapters following. Some portions of these pictures can be interpreted. With regard to others, which are not yet interpreted and perhaps never can be, it is nevertheless useful to gather together for synoptic study and comparison a large number of their forms from many parts of the world. The present collection shows the interesting psychologic fact that primitive or at least very ancient man made the same figures in widely separated regions, though it is not established that the same figures had a common significance. Indications of priscan habitat and migrations may sometimes be gained from the general style or type of the drawings and sculptures, which may be divided into groups, although the influence of the environing materials must always be considered.

The more modern specimens of picture-writing displayed on skins, bark, and pottery are far more readily interpreted than those on rocks, and have already afforded information and verification as to points of tribal history, religion, customs, and other ethnologic details.

A criticism has been made on the whole subject of picture-writing by the eminent anthropologist, Dr. Andree, who, in Ethnographische Parallelen und Vergleiche (a), has described and figured a large number of examples of petroglyphs, a name given by him to rock-drawings and now generally adopted. His views are translated as follows:

But if we take a connected view of the petroglyphs to which the rock pictures, generally made with red paint, are equivalent, and make a comparison of both, it becomes evident that they are usually made for mere pastime and are the first artistic efforts of rude nations. Nevertheless, we find in them the beginnings of writing, and in some instances their transition to pictography as developed among North American Indians becomes evident.

It appears, therefore, that Dr. Andree carefully excludes the picture-writings of the North American Indians from his general censure, his conclusion being that those found in other parts of the world usually occupy a lower stage. It is possible that significance may yet be ascertained in many of the characters found in other regions, and perhaps this may be aided by the study of those in America; but no doubt should exist that the latter have purpose and meaning. The relegation to a trivial origin of such pictographs as are described and illustrated in the present work will be abandoned after a thorough knowledge of the labor and thought which frequently were necessary for their production. American pictographs are not to be regarded as mere curiosities. In some localities they represent the only intellectual remains of the ancient inhabitants. Wherever found, they bear significantly upon the evolution of the human mind.

Distrust concerning the actual significance of the ancient American petroglyphs may be dispelled by considering the practical use of similar devices by historic and living Indians for purposes as important to them as those of alphabetic writing, these serving to a surprising extent the same ends. This paper presents a large number of conclusive examples. The old devices are substantially the same as the modern, though improved and established in the course of evolution. The ideography and symbolism displayed in these devices present suggestive studies in psychology more interesting than the mere information or text contained in the pictures. It must also be observed that when Indians now make pictographs it is with intention and care—seldom for mere amusement. Even when the labor is undertaken merely to supply the trade demand for painted robes or engraved pipes or bark records, it is a serious manufacture, though sometimes only imitative and not intrinsically significant. In all other known instances in which pictures are made without such specific intent as is indicated under the several headings of this work, they are purely ornamental; but in such cases they are often elaborate and artistic, not idle scrawls.

This paper is limited in its terms to the presentation of the most important known pictographs of the American Indians, but examples from other parts of the world are added for comparison. The proper classification and correlation of the matter collected has required more labor and thought than is apparent. The scheme of the work has been to give in an arrangement of chapters and sections some examples with illustrations in connection with each heading in the classification. This plan has involved a large amount of cross reference, because in many cases a character or a group of characters could be considered with reference to a number of different characteristics, and it was necessary to choose under which one of the headings it should be presented, involving reference to that from the other divisions of the work. Sometimes the decision was determined by taste or judgment, and sometimes required by mechanical considerations.

It may be mentioned that the limitation of the size of the present volume required that the space occupied by the text should be subordinated to the large amount of illustration. It is obvious that a work on picture-writing should be composed largely of pictures, and to allow room for them many pages of the present writer's views have been omitted. Whatever may be the disadvantage of this omission it leaves to students of the work the opportunity to form their own judgments without bias. Indeed, this writer confesses that although he has examined and studied in their crude shape, as they went to the printer, all the illustrations and descriptions now presented, he expects that after the volume shall be delivered to him in printed form with its synoptic arrangement he will be better able than now to make appropriate remarks on its subject-matter. Therefore he anticipates that careful readers will judiciously correct errors in the details of the work which may have escaped him and that they will extend and expand what is yet limited and partial. It may be proper to note that when the writer's observation has resulted in agreement with published authorities or contributors, the statements that could have been made on his own personal knowledge have been cited, when possible, from the printed or manuscript works of others. Quotation is still more requisite when there is disagreement with the authorities.

Thanks for valuable assistance are due and rendered to correspondents and to officers of the Bureau of Ethnology and of the United States Geological Survey, whose names are generally mentioned in connection with their several contributions. Acknowledgment is also made now and throughout the work to Dr. W. J. Hoffman, who has officially assisted in its preparation during several years, by researches in the field, in which his familiarity with Indians and his artistic skill have been of great value. Similar recognition is due to Mr. De Lancey W. Gill, in charge of the art department of the Bureau of Ethnology and the U. S. Geological Survey, and to Mr. Wells M. Sawyer, his assistant, specially detailed on the duty, for their work on the illustrations presented. While mentioning the illustrations, it may be noted that the omission to furnish the scale on which some of them are produced is not from neglect, but because it was impossible to ascertain the dimensions of the originals in the few cases where no scale or measurement is stated. This omission is most frequently noticeable in the illustrations of petroglyphs which have not been procured directly by the officers of the Bureau of Ethnology. The rule in that Bureau is to copy petroglyphs on the scale of one-sixteenth actual size. Most of the other classes of pictographs are presented without substantial reduction, and in those cases the scale is of little importance.

It remains to give special notice to the reader regarding the mode adopted to designate the authors and works cited. A decision was formed that no footnotes should appear in the work. A difficulty in observing that rule arose from the fact that in the repeated citation of published works the text would be cumbered with many words and numbers to specify titles, pages and editions. The experiment was tried of printing in the text only the most abbreviated mention, generally by the author's name alone, of the several works cited, and to present a list of them arranged in alphabetic order with cross references and catch titles. This list appears at the end of the work with further details and examples of its use. It is not a bibliography of the subject of picture-writing, nor even a list of authorities read and studied in the preparation of the work, but it is simply a special list, prepared for the convenience of readers, of the works and authors cited in the text, and gives the page and volume, when there is more than one volume in the edition, from which the quotation is taken.

CHAPTER I.

PETROGLYPHS.

In the plan of this work a distinction has been made between a petroglyph, as Andree names the class, or rock-writing, as Ewbank called it, and all other descriptions of picture-writing. The criterion for the former is that the picture, whether carved or pecked, or otherwise incised, and whether figured only by coloration or by coloration and incision together, is upon a rock either in situ or sufficiently large for inference that the picture was imposed upon it where it was found. This criterion allows geographic classification. In presenting the geographic distribution, prominence is necessarily (because of the laws authorizing this work) given to the territory occupied by the United States of America, but examples are added from various parts of the globe, not only for comparison of the several designs, but to exhibit the prevalence of the pictographic practice in an ancient form, though probably not the earliest form. The rocks have preserved archaic figures, while designs which probably were made still earlier on less enduring substances are lost.

Throughout the world in places where rocks of a suitable character appear, and notably in South America, markings on them have been found similar to those in North America, though until lately they have seldom been reported with distinct description or with illustration. They are not understood by the inhabitants of their vicinity, who generally hold them in superstitious regard, and many of them appear to have been executed from religious motives. They are now most commonly found remaining where the population has continued to be sparse, or where civilization has not been of recent introduction, with exceptions such as appear in high development on the Nile.

The superstitions concerning petroglyphs are in accord with all other instances where peoples in all ages and climes, when observing some phenomenon which they did not understand, accounted for it by supernatural action. The following examples are selected as of interest in the present connection.

It must be premised with reference to the whole character of the mythology and folk-lore of the Indians that, even when professed converts to Christianity, they seem to have taken little interest in the stories of the Christian church, whether the biblical narratives or the lives and adventures of the saints, which are so constantly dwelt upon throughout the Christian world that they have become folk-lore. The general character of the Christian legends does not seem to have suited the taste of Indians and has not at all impaired their affection for or their belief in the aboriginal traditions.

Among the gods or demigods of the Abnaki are those who particularly preside over the making of petroglyphs. Their name in the plural, for there are several personages, is Oonagamessok. They lived in caves by the shore and were never seen, but manifested their existence by inscriptions on the rocks. The fact that these inscribed rocks are now very seldom found is accounted for by the statement that the Oonagamessok have become angry at the want of attention paid to them since the arrival of the white people and have caused the pictures to disappear. There is no evidence to determine whether this tradition should be explained by the fact that the ingenious shamans of the last century would sometimes produce a miracle, carving the rocks themselves and interpreting the marks in their own way, or by the fact that the rock inscriptions were so old that their origin was not remembered and an explanation was, as usual, made by ascription to a special divinity, perhaps a chieftain famous in the old stage of mythology, or perhaps one invented for the occasion by the class of priests who from immemorial antiquity have explained whatever was inexplicable.

At a rock near the mouth of the Magiguadavic river, at the time immediately before the Passamaquoddy Indians chose their first governor after the manner of the whites, the old Indians say there suddenly appeared a white man's flag carved on the rocks. The old Indians interpreted this as a prophecy that the people would soon be abandoned to the white man's methods, and this came to pass shortly after. Formerly they had a "Mayouett" or chief. Many other rock carvings are said to have foretold what has since come to pass. Strange noises have also been heard near them.

The Omaha superstition is mentioned on pages 91–92 infra.

The Mandans had an oracle stone on which figures appeared on the morning after a night of public fasting. They were deciphered by the shaman, who doubtless had made them.

Mr. T. H. Lewis (a) gives the following tradition relating to the incised bowlders in the upper Minnesota valley:

In olden times there used to be an object that marked the bowlders at night. It could be seen, but its exact shape was indistinct. It would work making sounds like hammering, and occasionally emit a light similar to that of a firefly. After finishing its work it would give one hearty laugh like a woman laughing and then disappear. The next morning the Indians would find another pictured bowlder in the vicinity where the object had been seen the night previous.

Mr. J. W. Lynd (a) says of the Dakotas:

The deities upon which the most worship is bestowed, if, indeed, any particular one is nameable, are Tunkan (Inyan) the Stone God and Wakinyan, the Thunder Bird. The latter, as being the main god of war, receives constant worship and sacrifices; whilst the adoration of the former is an every-day affair. The Tunkan, the Dakotas say, is the god that dwells in stones or rocks, and is the oldest god. If asked why it is considered the oldest, they will tell you because it is the hardest.

Mr. Charles Hallock, on the authority of Capt. Ed. Hunter, First Cavalry, U. S. A., furnishes the following information respecting the Assiniboin, Montana, rock pictures, which shows the reverence of these Indians for the petroglyphs even when in ruins:

Some of the rocks of the sculptured cliff cleaved off and tumbled to the ground, whereupon the Indians assembled in force, stuck up a pole, hung up some buffalo heads and dried meat, had a song and dance, and carefully covered the detached fragments (which were sculptured or painted) with cotton cloth and blankets. Jim Brown, a scout, told Capt. Hunter that the Indians assembled at this station at stated times to hold religious ceremonies. The pictures are drawn on the smooth face of an outcrop or rocky projection.

Marcano (a) gives an account in which superstition is mixed with historic tradition. It is translated as follows:

The legend of the Tamanaques, transmitted by Father Gili, has also been invoked in favor of an ancient civilization. According to the beliefs of this nation, there took place in days of old a general inundation, which recalls the age of the great waters of the Mexicans, during which the scattered waves beat against the Encaramada. All the Tamanaques were drowned except one man and one woman, who fled to the mountain of Tamacu or Tamanacu, situated on the banks of Asiveru (Cuchivero). They threw above their heads the fruits of the palm tree, Mauritia, and saw arising from their kernels the men and women who repeopled the earth. It was during this inundation that Amalavica, the creator of mankind, arrived on a bark and carved the inscription of Tepumereme. Amalavica remained long among the Tamanaques, and dwelt in Amalavica-Jeutitpe (house). After putting everything in order he set sail and returned "to the other shore," whence he had come. "Did you perchance meet him there?" said an Indian to Father Gili, after relating to him this story. In this connection Humboldt recalls that in Mexico, too, the monk Sahagun was asked whether he came from the other shore, whither Quetzalcoatl had retired.

The same traveler adds: "When you ask the natives how the hieroglyphic characters carved on the mountains of Urbana and Encaramada could have been traced, they reply that this was done in the age of the great waters, at the time when their fathers were able to reach the heights in their canoes."

If these legends and these petroglyphs are proof of an extinct civilization, it is astonishing that their authors should have left no other traces of their culture. To come to the point, is it admissible that they were replaced by savage tribes without leaving a trace of what they had been, and can we understand this retrograde march of civilization when progress everywhere follows an ascending course? These destructions of American tribes in place are very convenient to prop up theories, but they are contrary to ethnologic laws.

The remarkable height of some petroglyphs has misled authors of good repute as well as savages. Petroglyphs frequently appear on the face of rocks at heights and under conditions which seemed to render their production impossible without the appliances of advanced civilization, a large outlay, and the exercise of unusual skill. An instance among many of the same general character is in the petroglyphs at Lake Chelan, Washington, where they are about 30 feet above the present water level, on a perpendicular cliff, the base of which is in the lake. On simple examination the execution of the pictographic work would seem to involve details of wharfing, staging, and ladders if operated from the base, and no less elaborate machinery if approached from the summit. Strahlenberg suggests that such elevated drawings were made by the ingenious use of stone wedges driven into the rock, thus affording support for ascent or descent, and reports that he actually saw such stone wedges in position on the Yenesei river. A very rough geological theory has been presented by others to account for the phenomena by the rise of the rocks to a height far above the adjacent surface at a time later than their carving.

But in the many cases observed in America it is not necessary to propose either the hypothesis involving such elaborate work as is suggested or one postulating enormous geological changes. The escarpment of cliffs is from time to time broken down by the action of the elements and the fragments fall to the base, frequently forming a talus of considerable height, on which it is easy to mount and incise or paint on the remaining perpendicular face of the cliff. When the latter adjoins a lake or large stream, the disintegrated débris is almost immediately carried off, leaving the drawings or paintings at an apparently inaccessible altitude. When the cliff is on dry land, the rain, which is driven against the face of the cliff and thereby increased in volume and force at the point in question, also sweeps away the talus, though more slowly. The talus is ephemeral in all cases, and the face of the cliff may change in a week or a century, as it may happen, so its aspect gives but a slight evidence of age. The presence, therefore, of the pictures on the heights described proves neither extraordinary skill in their maker nor the great antiquity which would be indicated by the emergence of the pictured rocks through volcanic or other dynamic agency. The age of the paintings and sculptures must be inferred from other considerations.

Pictures are sometimes found on the parts of rocks which at present are always, or nearly always, covered with water. On the sea shore at Machias bay, Maine, the peckings have been continued below the line of the lowest tides as known during the present generation. In such cases subsidence of the rocky formation may be indicated. At Kejim-koojik lake, Nova Scotia, incisions of the same character as those on the bare surface of the slate rocks can now be seen only by the aid of a water glass, and then only when the lake is at its lowest. This may be caused by subsidence of the rocks or by rise of the water through the substantial damming of the outlet. Some rocks on the shores of rivers, e. g., those on the Kanahwa, in West Virginia, show the same general result of the covering and concealment of petroglyphs by water, except in an unusual drought, which may more reasonably be attributed to the gradual elevation of the river through the rise of the surface near its mouth than to the subsidence of the earth's crust at the locality of the pictured rocks.

It must be admitted that no hermeneutic key has been discovered applicable to American pictographs, whether ancient on stone or modern on bark, skins, linen, or paper. Nor has any such key been found which unlocks the petroglyphs of any other people. Symbolism was of individual origin and was soon variously obscured by conventionalizing; therefore it requires separate study in every region. No interpreting laws of general application to petroglyphs so far appear, although types and tendencies can be classified. It was hoped that in some lands petroglyphs might tell of the characters and histories of extinct or emigrated peoples, but it now seems that knowledge of the people who were the makers of the petroglyphs is necessary to any clear understanding of their work. The fanciful hypotheses which have been formed without corroboration, wholly from such works as remain, are now generally discarded.

There is a material reason why the interpretation of petroglyphs is attended with special difficulty. They have often become so blurred by the elements and so much defaced where civilized man has penetrated that they cease to have any distinct or at least incontrovertible features. The remarks relating to Dighton rock, infra, Chap. XXII, are in point.

Rock-carving or picture-writing on rocks is so old among the American tribes as to have acquired a nomenclature. The following general remarks of Schoolcraft (a) are of some value, though they apply with any accuracy only to the Ojibwa and are tinctured with a fondness for the mysterious:

For their pictographic devices the North American Indians have two terms, namely, *Kekeewin*, or such things as are generally understood by the tribe, and *Kekeenowin*, or teachings of the *medas* or priests and *jossakeeds* or prophets. The knowledge of the latter is chiefly confined to persons who are versed in their system of magic medicine, or their religion, and may be deemed hieratic. The former consists of the common figurative signs, such as are employed at places of sepulture or by hunting or traveling parties. It is also employed in the *muzzinabiks*, or rock-writings. Many of the figures are common to both and are seen in the drawings generally; but it is to be understood that this results from the figure alphabet being precisely the same in both, while the devices of the nugamoons or medicine, wabino, hunting, and war songs are known solely to the initiates who have learned them, and who always pay high to the native professors for this knowledge.

In the Oglala Roster mentioned in Chapter XIII, Section 4, infra, one of the heads of families is called Inyanowapi, translated as Painted (or inscribed) rock. A blue object in the shape of a bowlder is connected with the man's head by the usual line, and characters too minute for useful reproduction appear on the bowlder. The name is interesting as giving the current Dakota term for rock-inscriptions. The designation may have been given to this Indian because he was an authority on the subject and skilled either in the making or interpretation of petroglyphs.

The name "Wikhegan" was and still is used by the Abnaki to signify portable communications made in daily life, as distinct from the rock carvings mentioned above, which are regarded by them as mystic.

One of the curious facts in connection with petroglyphs is the meager notice taken of them by explorers and even by residents other than the Indians, who are generally reticent concerning them. The present writer has sometimes been annoyed and sometimes amused by this indifference. The resident nearest to the many inscribed rocks at Ke jimkoojik Lake, Nova Scotia, described in Chapter II, Section 1, was a middle-aged farmer of respectable intelligence who had lived all his life about 3 miles from those rocks, but had only a vague notion of their character, and with difficulty found them. A learned and industrious priest, who had been working for many years on the shores of Lake Superior preparing not only a dictionary and grammar of the Ojibwa language, but an account of Ojibwa religion and customs, denied the present existence of any objects in the nature of petroglyphs in that region. Yet he had lived for a year within a mile of a very important and conspicuous pictured rock, and, on being convinced of his error by sketches shown him, called in his Ojibwa assistant and for the first time learned the common use of a large group of words which bore upon the system of picture-writing, and which he thereupon inserted in his dictionary, thus gaining from the visitor, who had come from afar to study at the feet of this supposed Gamaliel, much more than the visitor gained from him.

CHAPTER II.

PETROGLYPHS IN NORTH AMERICA.

SECTION I.

CANADA.

The information thus far obtained about petroglyphs in Canada is meager. This may be partly due to the fact that through the region of the Dominion now most thoroughly known the tribes have generally resorted for their pictographic work to the bark of birch trees, which material is plentiful and well adapted for the purpose. Indeed the same fact affords an explanation of the paucity of rock-carvings or paintings in the lands immediately south of the boundary line separating the United States from the British possessions. It must also be considered that the country on both sides of that boundary was in general heavily timbered, and that even if petroglyphs are there they may not even yet have been noticed. But that the mere plenty of birch bark does not evince the actual absence of rock-pictures in regions where there was also an abundance of suitable rocks, and where the native inhabitants were known to be pictographers, is shown by the account given below of the multitudes of such pictures lately discovered in a single district of Nova Scotia. It is confidently believed that many petroglyphs will yet be found in the Dominion. Others may be locally known and possibly already described in publications which have escaped the researches of the present writer. In fact, from correspondence and oral narrations, there are indications of petroglyphs in several parts of the Dominion besides those mentioned below, but their descriptions are too vague for presentation here. For instance, Dr. Boas says that he has seen a large number of petroglyphs in British Columbia, of which neither he nor any other traveler has made distinct report.

NOVA SCOTIA.

The only petroglyphs yet found in the peninsula of Nova Scotia are in large numbers within a small district in Queens county, and they comprise objects unique in execution and in interest. They were examined by the present writer in the field seasons of 1887 and 1888, and some were copied by him, but many more copies were taken in the last-mentioned year by Mr. George Creed, of South Rawdon, Nova Scotia, who had guided the writer to the locality. Attention was at first confined to Fairy lake and its rocks. This lake is really a bay of a larger lake which is almost exactly on the boundary line between Annapolis and Queens counties, one of those forming the chain through which the Liverpool river runs, and called Cegemacaga in More's History of Queens County (a), but according to Dr. Silas Rand in his Reading Book in the Micmac Language (a), Kejimkoojik, translated by him as "swelled parts," doubtless referring to the expansion of the Maitland river at its confluence with the Liverpool river.

The Fairy rocks, as distinct from others in the lake, are three in number, and are situated on the east side of Kejimkoojik lake and south of the entrance to Fairy lake. The northernmost of the three rocks is immediately at the entrance, the westernmost and central rock showing but a small surface at high water and at the highest stage of the water being entirely submerged. Three other inscribed rocks are about 2 miles south of these, at Piels (a corruption of Pierre's) point, opposite an island called Glodes or Gload island, so named from a well-known Micmac family. These rocks are virtually a continuation of the same formation with depressions between them. Two other localities in the vicinity where the rocks are engraved, as hereafter described, are at Fort Medway river and Georges lake. As they are all of the same character, on the same material, and were obviously made by the same people, they are all classed together, when referred to in this paper, as at Kejimkoojik lake. All of these rocks are of schistose slate of the Silurian formation, and they lie with so gentle a dip that their magnitudes vary greatly with a slight change in the height of the water. On August 27, 1887, when, according to the reports of the nearest residents, the water was one foot above the average summer level, the unsubmerged portion of the central rock then surrounded by water was an irregular oval, the dimensions of which were 47 by 60 feet. The highest points of the Fairy rocks at that date were no more than three and few were more than two feet above the surface of the water. The inclination near the surface is so small that a falling of the water of one foot would double the extent of that part of the surface which, by its smoothness and softness, is adapted to engraving. The inclination at Piels point is steeper, but still allows a great variation of exposed surface in the manner mentioned.

Mr. Creed first visited the Fairy rocks in July, 1881. His attention was directed exclusively to the northernmost rock, which was then more exposed than it was in September, 1887, and much of the inscribed portion seen by him in 1881 was under water in 1887. The submerged parts of the rocks adjoining those exposed are covered with incisions. Many inscriptions were seen in 1881 by Mr. Creed through the water, and others became visible through a water glass in 1887. His recollection of the inscribed dates seen in 1881 is that some with French names attached were of years near 1700, and that the worn appearance of the figures and names corresponded with the lapse of time indicated by those dates. A number of markings were noticed by him which are not found in the parts now exposed, and were evidently more ancient than most of the engravings on the latter. From other sources of information it is evident that either from a permanent rise in the water of the lake or from the sinking of the rocks, they formerly showed, within the period of the recollection of people now living, a much larger exposed surface than of late years, and that the parts long since permanently submerged were covered with engravings. The inference is that those engravings were made before Europeans had visited the locality.

It is to be specially remarked that the exposed surfaces where the rocks were especially smooth were completely marked over, no space of 3 inches square being unmarked, and over nearly all of those choice parts there were two, and in many cases three, sets of markings, above one another, recognizable by their differing distinctness. It also seemed that the second or third marking was upon plane surfaces where the earlier markings had been nearly obliterated by time. With pains and skill the earlier markings can be traced, and these are the outlines which from intrinsic evidence are Indian, whereas the later and more sharpely marked outlines are obviously made by civilized men or boys, the latest being mere initials or full names of persons, with dates attached. Warning must be given that the ancient markings, which doubtless were made by the Micmacs, will probably not only escape the attention of the casual visitor, but even that an intelligent expert observer who travels to the scene with some information on the subject, and for the express purpose of finding the incisions, may fail to see anything but names, ships, houses, and similar figures of obviously modern design. This actually occurred within the week when the present writer was taking copies of the drawings by a mode of printing which left no room for fancy or deception. Indeed, frequently the marks were not distinctly apparent until after they had been examined in the printed copies.

The mode in which the copies were taken was by running over and through their outlines a blue aniline pencil, and then pressing a wetted sheet of ordinary printing paper upon them, so that the impression was actually taken by the process of printing. During the two field seasons mentioned, with the aid of Mr. Creed, three hundred and fifty different engravings and groups of engravings were thus printed. Some of these prints were of large dimensions, and included from ten to fifty separate characters and designs.

On the parts exposed in 1887 there were dates from 1800 to the current year, the number for the last year being much the greatest, which was explained by the fact that the wonderfully beautiful lake had been selected for a Sunday-school excursion. Over the greater part of the surface visible in 1887 there were few levels specially favorable for marking, and when these were found the double or treble use was in some instances noticed.

After the writer had inspected the rocks and discovered their characteristics, and learned how to distinguish and copy their markings, it
seemed that, with the exception of a few designs recently dug or chipped
out by lumbermen or visitors, almost always initials, the only interesting or ancient portions were scratchings which could be made on the
soft slate by any sharp instrument. The faces of the rocks were immense soft and polished drawing-slates, presenting to any person who
had ever drawn or written before an irresistible temptation to draw or

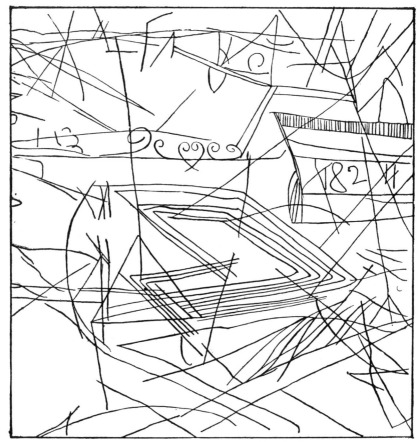

FIG. 1.—Palimpsest on Fairy rocks, Nova Scotia.

write. The writer, happening to have with him an Indian stone arrow
which had been picked up in the neighborhood, used its point upon the
surface, and it would make as good scratches as any found upon the
rocks except the very latest, which were obviously cut by the whites
with metal knives.

As is above suggested, the peculiar multiplication of the characters
upon the most attractive of the slates affords evidence as to their
relative antiquity superior to that generally found in petroglyphs.

The existence of two or three different sets of markings, all visible and of different degrees of obliteration or distinctness, is in itself important; but, in addition to that, it is frequently the case that the second and third in the order of time have associated with them dates, from which the relative antiquity of the faintest, the dateless, can be

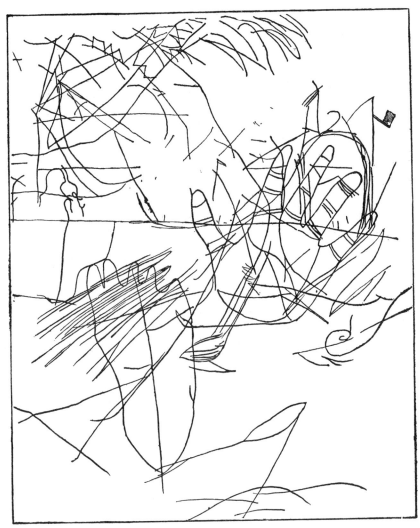

FIG. 2.—Palimpsest on Fairy rocks, Nova Scotia.

to some extent estimated. Dates of the third and most recent class are attached to English names and are associated with the forms of English letters; those of the second class accompany French names, and in some cases have French designs. Figs. 1 and 2, about one-fourth original size, are presented to give an idea of these peculiar palimpsests.

For examples of other copies printed from the rocks at Kejimkoojik lake, see Figs. 549, 550, 654, 655, 656, 657, 658, 717, 718, 739, 740, 741, 1254, 1255, and 1262. These offer intrinsic evidence of the Micmac origin of the early class of engravings.

The presence of French names and styles of art in the drawings is explained by a story which was communicated by Louis Labrador, whose great-grandfather, old Ledore, according to his account, guided a body of French Acadians who, at the time of the expulsion, were not shipped off with the majority. They escaped the English in 1756 and traveled from the valley of Annapolis to Shelbourne, at the extreme southeast of the peninsula. During that passage they halted for a considerable time to recruit in the beautiful valley along the Kejimkoojik lake, on the very ground where these markings appear, which also was on the ancient Indian trail. Another local tradition, told by a resident of the neighborhood, gives a still earlier date for the French work. He says that after the capture of Port Royal, now Annapolis, in 1710, a party of the defeated Frenchmen, with a number of Indians as guides, went with their cattle to the wide meadows upon Kejimkoojik lake and remained there for a long time. It is exceedingly probable that the French would have been attracted to scratch on this fascinating smooth slate surface whether they had observed previous markings or not, but it seems evident that they did scratch over such previous markings. The latter, at least, antedated the beginning of the eighteenth century.

A general remark may be made regarding the Kejimkoojik drawings, that the aboriginal art displayed in them did not differ in any important degree from that shown in other drawings of the Micmacs and the Abnaki in the possession of the Bureau of Ethnology. Also that the rocks there reveal pictographic tendencies and practices which suggest explanations of similar work in other regions where less evidence remains of intent and significance. The attractive material of the slates and their convenient situation tempted past generations of Indians to record upon them the images of their current thoughts and daily actions. Hence the pictographic practice went into operation at this locality with unusual vigor and continuity. Although at Kejimkoojik lake there is an exceptional facility for determining the relative dates of the several horizons of scratchings, the suggestion there evoked may help to ascertain similar data elsewhere.

ONTARIO.

Mr Charles Hallock kindly communicates information concerning pictographs on Nipigon bay, which is a large lake in the province of Ontario, 30 miles northwest of Lake Superior, with which it is connected by Nipigon river. He says:

The pictographs, which are principally of men and animals, occupy a zone some 60 feet long and 5 feet broad, about midway of the face of the rock; they are painted in blood-red characters, much darker than the color of the cliff itself.

He also, later, incloses a letter received by himself from Mr. Newton Flanagan, of the Hudson Bay Company, an extract from which is as follows:

About the dimensions of the red rock in Nipigon bay, upon which appear the Indian painted pictures, as near as I can give you at present, the face of the rock fronting the water is about 60 feet, rising to a greater height as it runs inland. The width along the water is something like 900 yards, depth quite a distance inland. The pictures are from 10 to 15 or perhaps 20 feet above the water; the pictures are representations of human figures, Indians in canoes, and of wild animals. They are supposed to have been painted ages ago, by what process or for what reason I am unable to tell you, nor do I know how the paint is made indelible.

As far as I can gather, the Indians here have no traditions in regard to those paintings, which I understand occur in several places throughout the country, and none of the Indians hereabouts nowadays practice any such painting.

MANITOBA.

Mr. Hallock also furnishes information regarding a petroglyph, the locality of which he gives as follows: Roche Percée, on the Souris river, in Manitoba, near the international boundary, 270 miles west of Dufferin, and nearly due north from Bismarck. This is an isolated rock in the middle of a plain, covered with pictographs of memorable events. It stands back from the river a half mile.

Mr. A. C. Lawson (a) gives an illustrated account of petroglyphs on the large peninsula extending into the Lake of the Woods and on an island adjacent to it. Strictly speaking this peninsula is in the district of Keewatin, but it is very near the boundary line of Manitoba, to which it is attached for administrative purposes. The account is condensed as follows:

On the north side of this peninsula, i. e., on the south shore of the northern half of the lake, about midway between the east and west shores, occurs one of the two sets of hieroglyphic markings. Lying off shore at a distance of a quarter to a half a mile, and making with it a long sheltered channel, is a chain of islands, trending east and west. On the south side of one of these islands, less than a mile to the west of the first locality, is to be seen the other set of inscriptions. The first set occurs on the top of a low, glaciated, projecting point of rock, which presents the characters of an ordinary roche moutonnée. The rock is a very soft, foliated, green, chloritic schist, into which the characters are more or less deeply carved. The top of the rounded point is only a few feet above the high-water mark of the lake, whose waters rise and fall in different seasons through a range of ten feet. The antiquity of the inscriptions is at once forced upon the observer upon a careful comparison of their weathering with that of the glacial grooves and striæ, which are very distinctly seen upon the same rock surface. Both the ice grooves and carved inscriptions are, so far as the eye can judge, identical in extent of weathering, though there was doubtless a considerable lapse of time between the disappearance of the glaciers and the date of the carving.

The island on which were found the other inscriptions is one of the many steep rocky islands known among the Indians as Ka-ka-ki-wa-bic min-nis, or Crow-rock island. The rock is a hard greenstone, not easily cut, and the inscriptions are not cut into the rock, but are painted with ochre, which is much faded in places. The surface upon which the characters are inscribed forms an overhanging wall protected from the rain, part of which has fallen down.

The Indians of the present day have no traditions about these inscriptions beyond the supposition that they must have been made by the "old people" long ago.

The sketches published as copies of these glyphs show spirals, concentric circles, crosses, horseshoe forms, arrow shapes, and other characters similar to those found on rocks in the southwestern part of the United States, and also to petroglyphs in Brazil, examples from both of which regions are presented in this work, under their appropriate headings.

BRITISH COLUMBIA.

Dr. Franz Boas (*a*) published an account of a petroglyph on Vancouver island (now presented as Fig. 3) which, slightly condensed, is translated as follows:

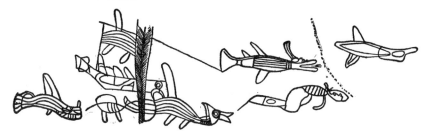

Fig. 3.—Petroglyph on Vancouver island.

The accompanying rock picture is found on the eastern shore of Sproat lake, near its southern outlet. Sproat lake lies about 10 kilometers north of the upper end of the Alberni fiord, which cuts deep into the interior of Vancouver island. In former times this region was the territory of the Hōpetschisāth, a tribe of the Nootka or Aht, who even now have a village some miles below the lake, at the entrance of Stamp river into the main river. That tribe, according to the statement of some of its older members, was a branch of the Kowitchin, who occupy the east side of Vancouver island, some kilometers northeast of the upper end of Alberni fiord. At that time the Ts'ēschāáth, another tribe of the Nootka, are said to have ascended the fiord and mixed with the Hōpetschisāth. The present inhabitants of the region know nothing concerning the origin of the rock picture. According to their legend, the rock on which it is carved was once the house of Kwótiath. Kwótiath is the wandering divinity in Nootka mythology, and corresponds approximately to the raven of the Tlinkit and Haida, the Qäls of the Kowitchin. The picture is found on a perpendicular rock wall about 7 meters high, which drops directly into the lake, so that it was necessary to make the copy while standing in the water. The rock is traversed in the middle by a broad cleft, narrowing below, from which blocks have fallen out which bore part of the drawing. To the north and south of the rock wall the shore rises gently, but rocky portions are found everywhere. The lines of the drawing are flat grooves, about two or three fingers' breadth, and in many places are so weathered as to be hardly recognizable. They have been scraped into the rock probably by the points of sticks rubbing moist sand against it. No marks of blows of any kind are found. The figures are here given in the same relative position in which they are found on the rock, except that the upper one on the right hand is at a distance from all the others, at the southern end of the rock. The objects represented are evidently fishes or marine monsters. The middle figure to the left of the cleft may be a manned boat, the fore part of which is probably destroyed.

Dr. Boas says that the copy as found in the Verhandlungen is incorrect. The design on the right hand is reversed and is now corrected.

Mr. G. M. Sproat (a) mentions this petroglyph:

It is rudely done and apparently not of an old date. There are half a dozen figures intended to represent fishes or birds—no one can say which. The natives affirm that Quawteaht made them. In their general character these figures correspond to the rude paintings sometimes seen on wooden boards among the Ahts, or on the sealskin buoys that are attached to the whale and halibut harpoons and lances. The meaning of these figures is not understood by the people; and I dare say if the truth were known, they are nothing but feeble attempts on the part of individual artists to imitate some visible objects which they had strongly in their minds.

SECTION 2.

UNITED STATES.

Drawings or paintings on rocks are distributed generally over the greater part of the territory of the United States.

They are found on bowlders formed by the sea waves or polished by ice of glacial epochs; on the faces of rock ledges adjoining lakes and streams; on the high walls of canyons and cliffs; on the sides and roofs of caves; in short, wherever smooth surfaces of rock appear. Yet, while they are so frequent, there are localities to be distinguished in which they are especially abundant and noticeable. They differ markedly in character of execution and apparent subject-matter.

An obvious division can be made between the glyphs bearing characters carved or pecked and those painted without incision. There is also a third, though small, class in which the characters are both incised and painted. This division seems to coincide to a certain extent with geographic areas and is not fully explained by the influence of materials; it may, therefore, have some relation to the idiosyncrasy or development of the several authors, and consequently to tribal habitat and migrations.

In examining a chart of the United States in use by the Bureau of Ethnology, upon which the distribution of the several varieties of petroglyphs is marked, two facts are noticeable: First, the pecked and incised characters are more numerous in the northern and those expressed in colors more numerous in the southern areas. Second, there are two general groupings, distinguished by typical styles, one in the north Atlantic states and the other in the south Pacific states.

The north Atlantic group is in the priscan habitat of the tribes of the Algonquian linguistic family, and extends from Nova Scotia southward to Pennsylvania, where the sculpturings are frequent, especially on the Susquehanna, Monongahela, and Alleghany rivers, and across Ohio from Lake Erie to the Kanawha river, in West Virginia. Isolated localities bearing the same type are found westward on the Mississippi river and a few of its western tributaries, to and including the Wind river mountains, in Wyoming, the former habitat of the Blackfeet Indians. All of these petroglyphs present typical characters, sometimes undefined and complicated. From their presumed authors, they have been termed the Algonquian type. Upon close study and comparison they show many features in common which are absent in extra-limital areas.

Immediately south of the Kanawha river, in West Virginia, and extending southward into Virginia, Tennessee, and North Carolina, the pecked or sculptured petroglyphs are replaced by painted figures of a style differing from the Algonquian. These are in the area usually designated as Cherokee territory, but there is no evidence that they are the work of that tribe; indeed, there is no indication of their authorship. The absence of pecked characters in this area is certainly not due to an absence of convenient material upon which to record them as the country is as well adapted to the mode of incision as is the northern Atlantic area.

Upon the Pacific slope a few pecked as well as colored petroglyphs occur scattered irregularly throughout the extreme northern area west of the Sierra Nevada, but on the eastern side of that range of mountains petroglyphs appear in Idaho, which have analogues extending south to New Mexico and Arizona, with remarkable groups at intervals between these extremes. All of these show sufficient similarity of form to be considered as belonging to a type which is here designated "Shoshonean." Tribes of that linguistic family still occupy, and for a long time have occupied, that territory. Most of this Shoshonean group consists of pecked or incised characters, though in the southern area unsculptured paintings predominate.

On the western side of the Sierra Nevada, from Visalia southward, at Tulare agency, and thence westward and southward along the Santa Barbara coast, are other groups of colored petroglyphs showing typical features resembling the Shoshonean. This resemblance may be merely accidental, but it is well known that there was intercourse between the tribes on the two sides of the Sierra Nevada, and the Shoshonean family is also represented on the Pacific slope south of the mountain range extending from San Bernardino west to Point Conception. In this manner the artistic delineation of the Santa Barbara tribes may have been influenced by contact with others.

Petroglyphs have seldom been found in the central area of the United

States.   In the wooded region of the Great lakes characters have been depicted upon birch bark for at least a century, while in the area between the Mississippi river and the Rocky mountains the skins of buffalo and deer have been used.   Large rocks and cliffs favorably situated are not common in that country, which to a great extent is prairie.

In the general area of these typical groups characters are frequently found which appear intrusive, i. e., they have a strong resemblance not only to those found in other American groups, but are nearly identical with characters in other parts of the world.   This fact, clearly established, prevents the adoption of any theory as to the authorship of many of the petroglyphs and thwarts attempts to ascertain their signification.

ALASKA.

Ensign Albert P. Niblack, U. S. Navy, (a) gives a brief account, with sketches, reproduced here as Fig. 4, of petroglyphs in Alaska, which were taken from rocks from the ancient village of Stikine, near Fort Wrangell.   Others were found on rocks just above high-water mark around the sites of ruined and abandoned villages.

FIG. 4.—Petroglyphs in Alaska.

In the upper character the Alaskan typical style of human faces is noticeable.   The lower gives a representation of the orca or whale killer, which the Haida believe to be a demon called Skana, about which there are many mythic tales.   Mr. Niblack remarks:

In their paintings the favorite colors used are black, light green, and dark red. Whether produced in painting, tattooing, or relief carving, the designs are some· what conventional.   However rude the outline, there are for some animals certain conventional signs that clearly indicate to the initiated what figure is meant.   With the brown bear it is the protruding tongue; with the beaver and wolf it is the character of the teeth; with the orca, the fin; with the raven, the sharp beak; with the eagle, the curved beak, etc.

ARIZONA.

Mr. G. K. Gilbert, of the U. S. Geological Survey, gives the following information concerning petroglyphs observed by him in the vicinity
of San Francisco mountain, Arizona:

The localities of the sketches Figs. 5, 6, and 7 are about 35 miles east and south-

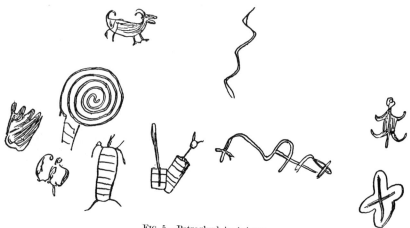

FIG. 5.—Petroglyph in Arizona.

east of San Francisco mountain, the material being a red sandstone, which stands
in low buttes upon the plain. About these are mealing stones, fragments of pottery
and chipped flints, giving evidence of the residence of sedentary Indians. So many
localities of petroglyphs were seen that I regard it as probable that a large number

FIG. 6.—Petroglyph in Arizona.

could be found by search. The drawings in every case but one were produced by
blows upon the surface of the rocks, breaking through the film of rock discolored by
weathering so as to reveal (originally) the color of the interior of the rock. The

single exception is the first pattern in Fig. 6, similar to the patterns on pottery and blankets, produced by painting with a white pigment on red rock. The original arrangement of the drawings upon the rock was not as a rule preserved, but they have approximately the original arrangement. I neglected to record the scale of the drawings, but the several pictures are drawn on approximately the same scale.

All of these figures partake of the general type designated as the Shoshonean, and it is notable that close repetitions of some of the characters appear in petroglyphs in Tulare valley and Owens valley, California, which are described and illustrated in this section.

The object resembling a centipede, in Fig. 6, is a common form in various localities in Santa Barbara county, California, as will be observed by comparing the illustrations given in connection with that locality. In other of the Arizona and New Mexican petroglyphs similar outlines are sometimes engraved to signify the maize stalk.

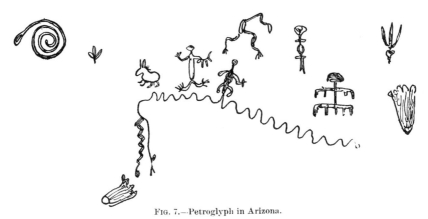

FIG. 7.—Petroglyph in Arizona.

Mr. Paul Holman, of the U. S. Geological Survey, reports that eight miles below Powers butte, on a mesa bordering on the Gila river and rising abruptly to the height of 150 feet, are pictographs covering the entire vertical face. Also on the summit of a spur of Oatman mountain, 200 yards from the Gila and 300 feet above it, are numbers of pictographs. Many of them are almost obliterated where they are on exposed surfaces.

Lieut. Col. Emory (a) reports that on a table-land near the Gila bend is a mound of granite bowlders, blackened by augite and covered with unknown characters, the work of human hands. On the ground near by were also traces of some of the figures, showing that some of the pictographs, at least, were the work of modern Indians. Others were of undoubted antiquity. He also reports in the same volume (b) that characters upon rocks of questionable antiquity occur on the Gila river at 32° 38′ 13″ N. lat. and 190° 7′ 30″ long. According to the plate, the figures are found upon bowlders and on the face of the cliff to the height of 30 feet.

Lieut. Whipple (*a*) remarks upon petroglyphs at Yampais spring, Williams river, as follows:

The spot is a secluded glen among the mountains. A high shelving rock forms a cave, within which is a pool of water and a crystal stream flowing from it. The lower surface of the rock is covered with pictographs. None of the devices seem to be of recent date.

Many of the country rocks lying on the Colorado plateau of northern Arizona, east of Peach springs, bear petroglyphs of considerable artistic workmanship. Some figures, observed by Dr. W. J. Hoffman in 1872, were rather elaborate and represented the sun, human beings in various styles approaching the grotesque, and other characters not understood. All of those observed were made by pecking the surface of basalt with a harder variety of stone.

Mr. Gilbert also obtained sketches of etchings in November, 1878, on Partridge creek, northern Arizona, at the point where the Beale wagon road comes to it from the east. He says: " The rock is cross-laminated Aubrey sandstone and the surfaces used are faces of the laminæ. All

Fig. 8.—Petroglyph in Arizona.

the work is done by blows with a sharp point. (Obsidian is abundant in the vicinity.) Some inscriptions are so fresh as to indicate that the locality is still resorted to. No Indians live in the immediate vicinity, but the region is a hunting ground of the Wallapais and Avasupais (Cosninos)."

Notwithstanding the occasional visits of the above named tribes, the characters submitted more nearly resemble those of other localities known to have been made by the Moki Pueblos.

Rock drawings are of frequent occurrence along the entire extent of the valley of the Rio Verde, from a short distance below Camp Verde to the Gila river.

Mr. Thomas V. Keam reports drawings on the rocks in Canyon Segy, and in Keam's canyon, northeastern Arizona. Some forms occurring at the latter locality are found also upon Moki pottery.

Petroglyphs are reported by Lieut. Theodore Mosher, Twenty-second Infantry, U. S. Army, to have been discovered by Lieut. Casey's party in December, 1887, on the Chiulee (or Chilalí) creek, 30 or 40 miles from its confluence with San Juan river, Arizona. A photograph made by the officer in charge of the party shows the characters to have been outlined by pecking, the designs resembling the Shoshonean type of pictographs, and those in Owens valley, California, a description of which is given below.

A figure, consisting of two concentric circles with a straight line running out from the larger circle, occurs, among other carvings, on one of the many sculptured bowlders seen by Mr. J. R. Bartlett (a) in the valley of the Gila river in Arizona. His representation of this bowlder is here copied as Fig. 8. His language is as follows:

I found hundreds of these bowlders covered with rude figures of men, animals, and other objects of grotesque forms, all pecked in with a sharp instrument. Many of them, however, were so much defaced by long exposure to the weather and by subsequent markings, that it was impossible to make them out. Among these rocks I found

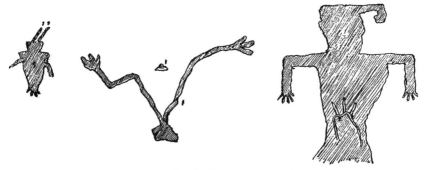

FIG. 9.—Petroglyph in Shinumo canyon, Arizona.

several which contained sculptures on the lower side, in such a position that it would be impossible to cut them where they then lay. Some weighed many tons each and would have required immense labor to place them there, and that, too, without an apparent object. The natural inference was that they had fallen down from the summit of the mountain after the sculptures were made on them. A few only seemed recent; the others bore the marks of great antiquity.

In the collections of the Bureau of Ethnology is an album or sketch book, which contains many drawings made by Mr. F. S. Dellenbaugh, from which the following sketches of petroglyphs in Arizona are selected, together with the brief references attached to each sheet.

Fig. 9 is a copy of characters appearing in Shinumo canyon, Arizona. They are painted, the middle and right hand figures being red, the human form having a white mark upon the abdomen; the left-hand figure of a man is painted yellow, the two plumes being red.

The petroglyphs in Fig. 10 are rather indistinct and were copied from the vertical wall of Mound canyon. The most conspicuous forms appear to be serpents.

CALIFORNIA.

In the foothills of California, wherever overhanging and rain-protected rocks occur, they are covered with paintings of various kinds made by Indians. Those on Rocky hill, some 15 miles east of Visalia, are especially interesting. The sheltered rocks are here covered with images of men, animals, and various inanimate objects, as well as curious figures. The paint used is red, black, and white, and wherever protected it has stood the ravages of time remarkably well. In many places the paintings are as vivid as the day they were laid on. Deer, antelope, coyotes, birds, and turtles are figured quite frequently, and may indicate either names of chiefs or tribes, or animals slain in the hunt. Here are also circles, spirals, crowns or bars, etc., signs the meaning of which is yet doubtful.

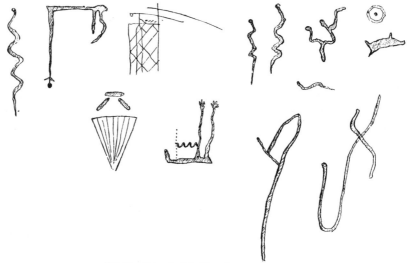

Fig. 10.—Petroglyph in Mound canyon, Arizona.

Mr. H. W. Turner, in a letter dated June 3, 1891, furnishes sketches (Fig. 11) from this locality, and a description of them as follows:

I send herewith a rough sheet of drawings of figures on the sheltered face of a huge granite cropping in Tulare county, California. One-half of the cropping had split off, leaving a nearly plane surface, on which the figures were drawn in red, white, and black pigments. The locality is known as Rocky point. They are now quarrying granite at the place. It lies about 12 miles nearly due east of Visalia, in the first foothills and south of Yokall creek. The figures appear to have been drawn many years ago, and numbers of them are now indistinct.

During the summer of 1882 Dr. Hoffman visited the Tule river agency, California, where he found a large rock painting, of which Fig. 983, infra, is a copy made by him. His description of it is as follows:

"The agency is upon the western side of the Sierra Nevada, in the headwater canyons of the branches of the south fork of Tule river. The country is at present occupied by several tribes of the Mariposan linguistic stock, and the only answer made to inquiries respecting the age or origin of the painting was that it was found there when the ancestors of the present tribes arrived. The local migrations of the various Indian tribes of this part of California are not yet known with sufficient certainty to determine to whom the records may be credited, but all appearances with respect to the weathering and disintegration of the rock upon which the record is engraved, the appearance of the coloring

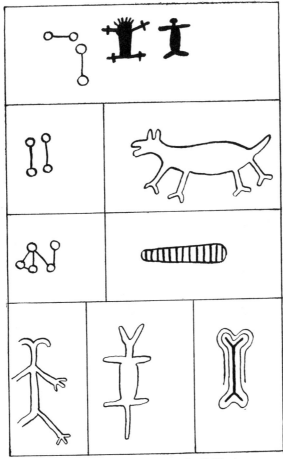

Fig. 11.—Petroglyphs near Visalia, California.

matter subsequently applied, and the condition of the small depressions made at the time for mixing the pigments with a viscous substance, indicate that the work was performed about a century ago.

"The Indians now at Tule river have occupied that part of the state for at least one hundred years, and the oldest now living state that the records were found by their ancestors, though whether more than two generations ago could not be ascertained.

"The drawings were outlined by pecking with a piece of quartz or other siliceous rock, the depth varying from a mere visible depression to a third of an inch. Having thus satisfactorily depicted the several ideas, colors were applied which appear to have penetrated the slight interstices between the crystalline particles of the rock, which had been bruised and slightly fractured by hammering with a piece of stone. It appears probable, too, that to insure better results the hammering was repeated after application of the colors.

"Upon a small bowlder, under the natural archway formed by the breaking of the large rock, small depressions were found which had been used as mortars for grinding and mixing the colors. These depressions average 2 inches in diameter and about 1 inch in depth.

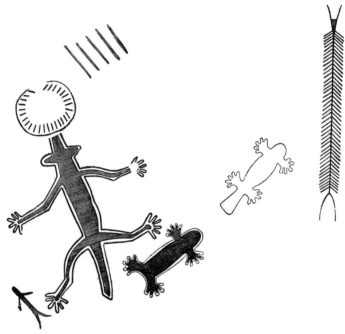

FIG. 12.—Petroglyph at Tule river, California.

Traces of color still remain, mixed with a thin layer of a shining substance resembling a coating of varnish and of flinty hardness. This coating is so thin that it can not be removed with a steel instrument, and appears to have become a part of the rock itself.

"From the animals depicted upon the ceiling it seems that both beaver and deer were found in the country, and as the beaver tail and the hoofs of deer and antelope are boiled to procure glue, it is probable that the tribe which made these pictographs was as far advanced in respect to the making of glue and preparing of paints as most other tribes throughout the United States.

"Examination shows that the dull red color is red ocher, found in various places in the valley, while the yellow was an ocherous clay, also found there. The white color was probably obtained there, and is evidently earthy, though of what nature can only be surmised, not sufficient being obtainable from the rock picture to make satisfactory analysis with the blow-pipe. The composition of the black is not known, unless it was made by mixing clay and powdered charcoal. The latter is a preparation common at this day among other tribes.

"An immense granite bowlder, about 20 feet in thickness and 30 in length, is so broken that a lower quarter is removed, leaving a large

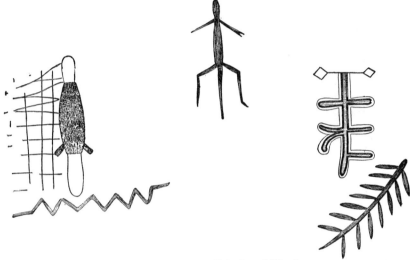

FIG. 13.—Petroglyph at Tule river, California.

square passageway through its entire diameter almost northwest and southeast. Upon the western wall of this passageway is a collection of the colored sketches of which Fig. 983 is a reduced copy. The entire face of the rock upon which the pictograph occurs measures about 12 or 15 feet in width and 8 in height. The largest human figure measures 6 feet in height, from the end of the toes to the top of the head, the others being in proportion as represented.

"Upon the ceiling are a number of well executed drawings of the beaver, bear, centipede (Fig. 12), and bald eagle (Fig. 13). Many of the other forms indicated appear to represent some variety of insects, several of which are drawn with exaggerated antennæ, as in Fig. 14, It is curious to note the gradual blending of forms, as, for instance, that of the bear with those resembling the human figure, often found among the Shoshonean types in Arizona and New Mexico, some of which are described and figured infra.

"Fig. 15 embraces a number of characters on the ceiling. The left hand upper figure is in black, with a narrow line of red surrounding it. The drawing is executed neatly and measures about 18 inches in length.

The remaining characters are in dull red, probably ocher, though the two on the left hand, beneath the one just mentioned, are more yellowish.

"The first three forms in Fig. 16 are copies of human-like figures painted on the ceiling. They are each about 12 inches in length. The other form in Fig. 16 is white and is on the southern vertical wall of the passageway facing the north. It resembles some of the human forms occurring elsewhere in the same series of petroglyphs."

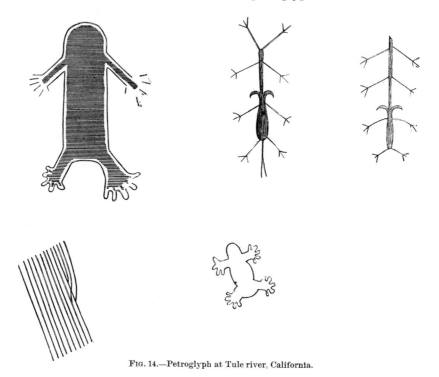

Fig. 14.—Petroglyph at Tule river, California.

OWENS VALLEY.

In the range of mountains forming the northwestern boundary of Owens valley are extensive groups of petroglyphs, apparently dissimilar to those found west of the Sierra Nevada. Dr. Hoffman, of the Bureau of Ethnology, hastily examined them in 1871 and more thoroughly in the autumn of 1884. They are now represented in Pls. I to XI. So large a space is given to these illustrations because of their intrinsic interest, and also because it is desirable to show for one locality what is true of some others, viz, the very large number of petroglyphs still to be found in groups and series. Even with the present illustrations, the petroglyphs in Owens valley are by no means exhaustively shown.

Dr. Hoffman's report is as follows:

PETROGLYPHS IN OWENS VALLEY, CALIFORNIA.

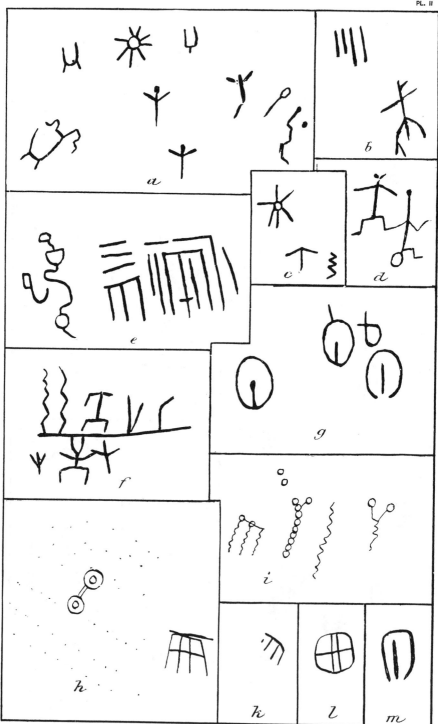

PETROGLYPHS IN OWENS VALLEY, CALIFORNIA.

PETROGLYPHS IN OWENS VALLEY, CALIFORNIA.

PETROGLYPHS IN OWENS VALLEY, CALIFORNIA.

PETROGLYPHS IN OWENS VALLEY, CALIFORNIA.

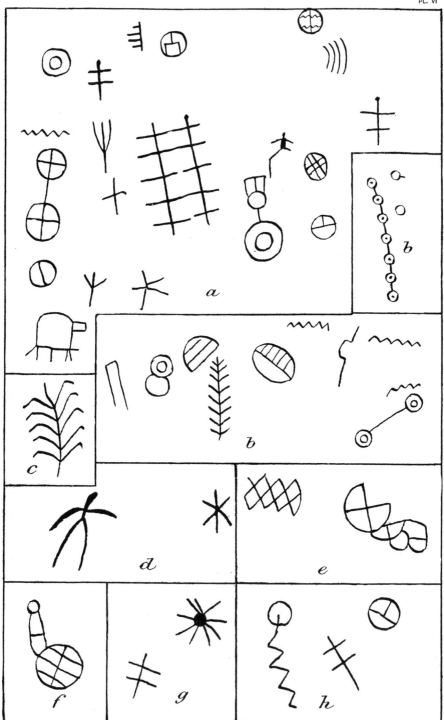

PETROGLYPHS IN OWENS VALLEY, CALIFORNIA.

PETROGLYPHS IN OWENS VALLEY, CALIFORNIA.

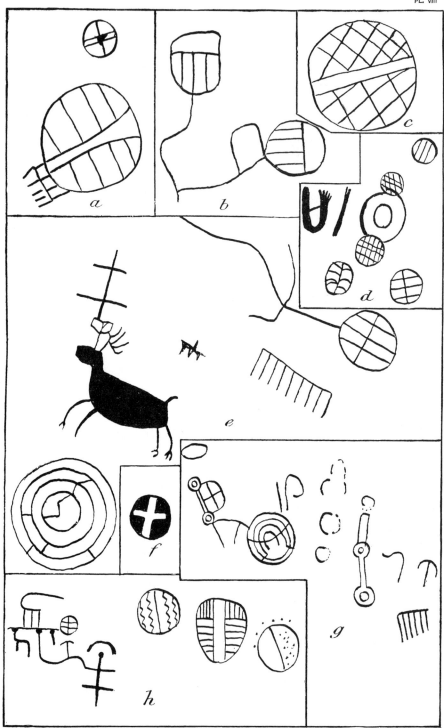

PETROGLYPHS IN OWENS VALLEY, CALIFORNIA.

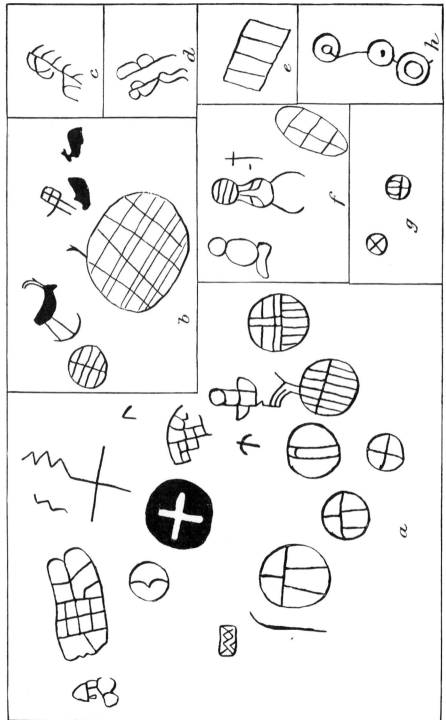

PETROGLYPHS IN OWENS VALLEY, CALIFORNIA.

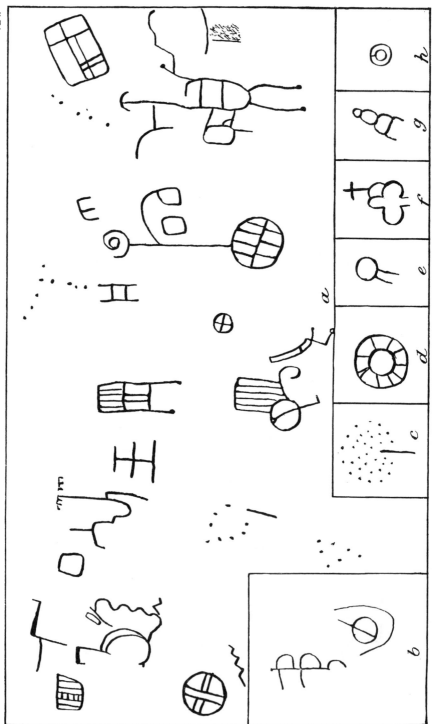

PETROGLYPHS IN OWENS VALLEY, CALIFORNIA.

PETROGLYPHS IN OWENS VALLEY, CALIFORNIA.

One of the most important series of groups is that in the northern portion of Owens valley, between the White mountains on the east and the Benton range on the west. On the western slope of the latter, at Watterson's ranch, is a detached low butte or mesa, upon the blackened basaltic bowlders and cliffs of which are

FIG. 15.—Petroglyph at Tule river, California.

numerous deeply cut characters, the most interesting of which are reproduced in Pls. I and II. The illustrations are, approximately, one-twelfth real size. The designs of footprints, in the lower left-hand corner of Pl. I, vary in depth from half an inch to 1½ inches. They appear to have been pecked and finally worked down to

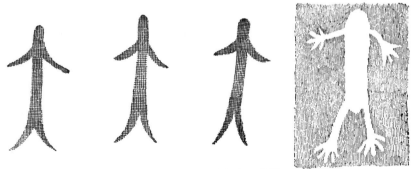

FIG. 16.—Petroglyph at Tule river, California.

a uniform and smooth surface by rubbing, as if with a piece of stone or with wood and sand.

In almost all, if not all, instances throughout the entire series referred to in this description the sculptured surfaces have assumed the same shining blackened luster as the original and undisturbed surface of the bowlder, caused by gradual oxidation of the iron present. This would seem to indicate considerable antiquity of the petroglyphs.

On the northeast angle of the mesa referred to were found the remains of an old camp, over which were scattered large quantities of arrowheads, knives, and flakes of obsidian. This in itself would be insignificant, but the fact that many of the specimens of this material have been lying exposed to the elements until the upper surface has undergone change in color, so as to become bleached and friable, in some instances to the depth of from one-tenth to one-fourth of an inch, warrants the inference that the relics may have been made by the same people who made the petroglyphs, as the worked relics generally differ from those of the present Indians by being larger and less elaborately finished.

At the lower end of the southeastern slope of the mesa are a number of flat rocks bearing mortar holes, which have no doubt been used in grinding grass seed and other grains.

In general type these petroglyphs correspond very closely to those of other areas, in which the so-called Shoshonian types occur, the most common, apart from those presented in Pls. I and II, consisting of concentric circles, rings, footprints of the bear and of man, and various outlines of the human form, beside numerous unintelligible forms.

Southeastward of this locality there is a low divide leading across the Benton range into the broad, arid, sloping sand desert of Owens valley proper, but it is not until a point 12 miles south of Benton, along the line of the old stage road, is reached that petroglyphs of any consequence are met with. From this point southward, for a distance of 6 miles, large exposures and bowlders of basalt are scattered, upon which are great numbers of petroglyphs, pecked into the rock to depths of from half an inch to 1½ inches, and representing circles, footprints, human forms, etc.

The first series of illustrations, selected from numerous closely-connected bowlders, are here presented on Pls. III to VII. The designs marked *a* on Pl. III resemble serpents, while that at *d* is obviously such. This device is on the horizontal surface, and is pecked to the depth of about 1 inch. The scale of the drawing is one-thirtieth of the original petroglyph. The characters indicating the human form in *e*, *g*, and *h* resemble the ordinary Shoshonian type, and are like those from various localities in Arizona and southern Utah and Colorado.

The upper characters in A on Pl. IV represent the trail of a grizzly bear—as indicated by the immense claws—followed by a human footprint. The original sculpturings are clearly cut, the toes of the man's foot being cup-like, as if drilled with a blunt piece of wood and sand. The tracks average 15 inches in length and vary in depth from half an inch to more than an inch. The course of direction of the tracks, which are cut upon a horizontal surface, is from north-northeast to south-southwest.

In E is the semblance of an apparently two-headed snake, as also in *a* on Pl. VII. It is possible that this was pecked into the rock to record the finding of such an anomaly. The occurrence of double-headed serpents is not unique, five or six instances having been recorded, one of which is from California, and a specimen may be seen in the collection of the U. S. National Museum.

In Pl. V, *c*, *e*, *g* are characters resembling some from the Canary islands [see Figs. 144 and 145], as well as many of the cupstones and dumb-bell forms from Scotland [see Figs. 149 and 150].

An interesting specimen is presented in *d*, on Pl. VI, resembling the Ojibwa thunder bird, as well as etchings of Innuit workmanship to denote man [as shown in Fig. 1159]. The figures presented in Pl. III are the northernmost of the series, of which those on Pl. VII form the southernmost examples, the distance between these two points being about 2 miles.

For the space of 4 miles southward there are a few scattered petroglyphs, to which reference will be made below, and the greatest number of characters are not found until the southernmost extremity of the entire series is reached. These are over the surface of immense bowlders lying on the east side of the road where it passes through a little valley known locally as the Chalk grade, probably on account of the whitened appearance of the sand and of some of the embankments. A general view of the faces of the bowlders upon which the chief sculpturings occur is presented in Fig. 17. The petroglyphs are represented in Pls. VIII to IX.

The figures presented in Pl. VIII are, with one exception, each about one-thirtieth the size of the original. The animal character in *e* is upon the top of the largest bowlder shown on Fig. 17, and is pecked to the depth of from one-fourth to one-half an inch. Portions of it are much defaced through erosion by sand blown by the strong summer winds. The characters in *g* are only one-tenth of the original size, but of depth similar to the preceding.

On Pl. IX, *a* is one-twentieth the size of the original, while the remaining sculpturings are about one-tenth size. The cross in *a* is singularly interesting because of the elaborateness of its execution. The surface within the circle is pecked out so as to have the cross stand out bold and level with the original surface. This is true also of *f* on Pl. VIII. Pl. IX, *b*, contains some animal forms like those reported from New Mexico and Arizona, and Brazil [and presented in this work], especially that

FIG. 17.—View of Chalk grade petroglyphs, Owens valley.

character to the right resembling a guanaco couchant, although, from its relationship to the figure of an antelope, in the same group, it no doubt is intended to represent one of the latter species.

On Pl. X, as well as on others of this collection, are found many forms of circles with interior decoration, such as lines arranged by pairs, threes, etc., zigzag and cross lines, and other seemingly endless arrangements. They are interesting from the fact of the occurrence of almost identical forms in remote localities, as in the Canary islands and in Brazil. [These are figured and described infra.]

It is probable that they are not meaningless, because the disposition of the Indian, as he is to-day, is such that no time would be spent upon such laborious work without an object, and only motives of a religious or ceremonial nature would induce him to expend the time and labor necessary to accomplish such results as are still presented. On Pl. XI, *a*, are more footprints and animal forms of the genus *cervus* or *antelocapra*. The figures in *b* and *d*, having an upright line with two crossing it at right angles, may signify either a lizard or man, the latter signification being probably the true one, as similar forms are drawn in petroglyphs of a Shoshonian type, as in Arizona. [See supra.]

The country over which these records are scattered is arid beyond description and destitute of vegetation. Watterson's ranch group is more favorably located, there being an abundance of springs and a stream running northward toward Black lake.

The only Indians found in this vicinity are Pai Utes, but they are unacquainted with the significance of the characters, and declare that they have no knowledge of the authors.

As to the age of the sculpturings nothing can be learned. The external surface of all the bowlders, as well as the surface of the deepest figures, is a glistening brownish black, due, possibly, to the presence of iron. The color of a freshly broken surface becomes lighter in tint as depth is attained, until at about one-half or three-fourths of an inch from the surface the rock is chocolate brown. How long it would take the freshly broken surface of this variety of rock to become thoroughly oxidized and blackened it is impossible even to conjecture, taking into consideration the physical conditions of the region and the almost entire absence of rainfall.

Upon following the most convenient course across the Benton range to reach Owen valley proper drawings are also found, though in limited numbers, and seem

Fig. 18.—Petroglyphs in Death valley, California.

to partake of the character of indicators as to course of travel. By this trail the northernmost of the several groups of drawings above mentioned is the nearest and most easily reached.

The pictures upon the bowlders at Watterson's are somewhat different from those found elsewhere. The number of specific designs is limited, many of them being reproduced from two to six or seven times, thus seeming to partake of the character of personal names.

In a communication dated Saratoga Springs, at the lower part of Death valley, California, February 5, 1891, Mr. E. W. Nelson says that about 200 yards from the springs, and on the side of a hill, he found several petroglyphs. He also furnished a sketch as an example of their general type, now presented as Fig. 18. The locality is in the lower end of Death valley. Mr. Nelson says:

The spring here is in a basin some 60 to 80 acres in extent in which are ponds and tule marsh. Close by is an extensive ancient Indian camping ground, over which are scattered very many "chips" made from manufacturing arrow points from quartz crystal, chert, chalcedony, flint, and other similar material.

The figures in the sketch inclosed are situated relatively, as to size and location, as they occur on the rock. The latter is cracked and slopes at different angles, but the figures are all visible from a single point of view. There are several other figures in this group that are too indistinct to copy owing to age, or weather wearing. The group copied is the most extensive one seen, but many smaller groups and single figures are to be found on the rocks near by.

The Shoshoni inhabit this region and a few families of Shoshoni live about the Panamint mountains at present.

FIG. 19.—Rattlesnake rock, Mojave desert, California.

Dr. C. Hart Merriam, of the Department of Agriculture, on his return from the exploration of Death valley, kindly furnished a photograph of a ledge in Emigrant canyon, Panamint mountains, which was received too late for insertion in this work. This is much regretted, as a large number of petroglyphs are represented in groups. The characters are of the Shoshonean type. Among them are "Moki goats," tridents, the Greek Φ, many crosses, and other figures shown in this chapter as found in the same general region.

In the Mojave desert, about 2 miles north of Daggett station, according to the Mining and Scientific Press (a) is a small porphyritic butte known as "Rattlesnake rock," "so named by reason of the immense number of these reptiles that find shelter in this mass of rock." The accompanying Fig. 19 is a reproduction of that given in the paper quoted. The author states that "the implement used in making these characters was evidently a dull-pointed stone, as the lines are not sharp, and the sides of the indentation show marks of striation."

Lieut. Whipple reports the discovery of pictographs at Piute creek, about 30 miles west of the Mojave villages. These are carved upon a rock, "are numerous, appear old, and are too confusedly obscured to be easily traceable." They bear great general resemblance to drawings scattered over northeast Arizona, southern Utah, and western New Mexico.

FIG. 20.—Petroglyph near San Marcos pass, California.

From information received from Mr. Alphonse Pinart, pictographic records exist in the hills east of San Bernardino, somewhat resembling those at Tule river in the southern spurs of the Sierra Nevada, Kern county.

FIG. 21.—Petroglyphs near San Marcos pass, California.

Mr. Willard J. Whitney, of Elmhurst, Lackawanna county, Pennsylvania, gives information regarding nearly obliterated pecked petroglyphs upon two flat granite rocks, or bowlders, on the summit of a mountain 4 miles directly west of Escondido, San Diego county, Cali-

fornia. The designs are not colored, and are not more than one-eighth
or one-fourth of an inch in depth. There is a good lookout from the

FIG. 22.—Petroglyphs near San Marcos pass, California.

eminence, but there are no indications of either trails or burials in the
vicinity.

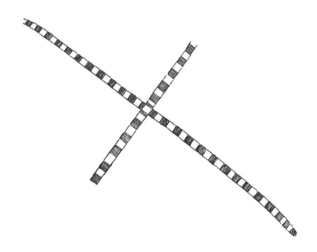

FIG. 23.—Petroglyphs in Najowe valley, California.

This may be the locality mentioned by Mr. Barnes, of San Diego, who furnished information relating to petroglyphs in San Diego county.

Dr. Hoffman reports the following additional localities in Santa Bar-

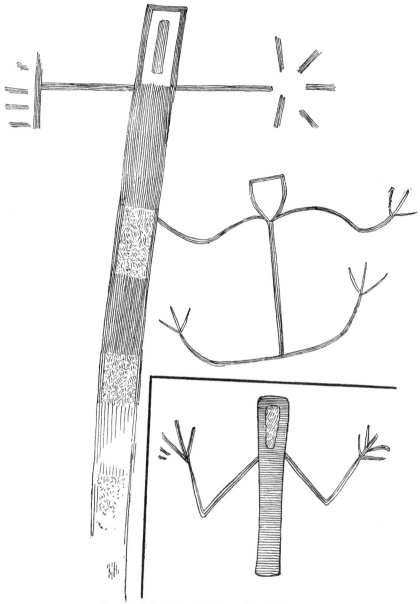

Fig. 24.—Petroglyphs in Najowe valley. California.

bara and Los Angeles counties. Fifteen miles west of Santa Barbara, on the northern summit of the Santa Ynez range, and near the San Marcos pass, is a group of paintings in red and black. Fig. 20 resembles a portion of a checker-board in the arrangement of squares.

Serpentine and zigzag lines occur, as also curved lines with serrations on the concave sides; figures of the sun; short lines and groups of short parallel lines, and figures representing types of insect forms also appear, as shown in Figs. 21 and 22.

These paintings are in a cavity near the base of an immense bowlder, over 20 feet in height. A short distance from this is a flat granitic bowlder, containing twenty-one mortar holes, which had evidently been

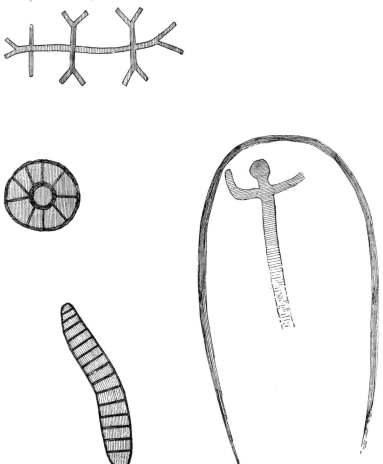

Fig. 25.—Petroglyphs, Najowe valley, California.

used by visiting Indians during the acorn season. Oaks are very abundant, and their fruit formed one of the sources of subsistence.

Three miles west-northwest of this locality, in the valley near the base of the mountain, are indistinct figures in faded red, painted upon a large rock. The characters appear similar, in general, to those above mentioned.

Forty-three miles west of Santa Barbara, in the Najowe valley, is a promontory, at the base of which is a large shallow cavern, the opening being smaller than the interior, upon the roof and back of which are

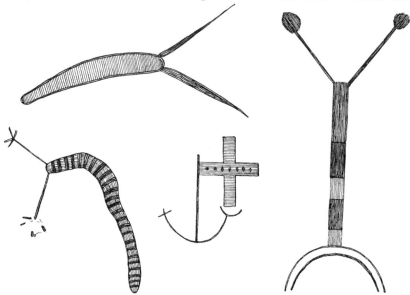

FIG. 26.—Petroglyphs in Najowe valley, California.

many designs, some of which are reproduced in Fig. 23, of forms similar to those observed at San Marcos pass. Several characters appear to

FIG. 27.—Petroglyphs in Najowe valley, California.

have been drawn at a later date than others, such as horned cattle, etc. The black used was a manganese compound, while the red pigments consist of ferruginous clays, abundant at numerous localities in the mountain canyons.

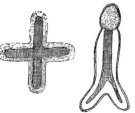

FIG. 28.—Petroglyphs in Najowe valley, California.

Some of the human figures are drawn with the hands and arms in the attitude of making the gestures for *surprise* or *astonishment*, and *negation*, as in Fig. 24.

FIG. 29.—Petroglyphs near Santa Barbara, California.

The characters in Fig. 25 resemble forms which occur at Tulare valley, and in Owens valley, respectively, and insect forms also occur as in Fig. 26.

Other designs abounding at this locality are shown in Figs. 27 and 28.

One of the most extensive groupings, and probably the most elaborately drawn, is in the Carisa plain, near Mr. Oreña's ranch, 60 or 70 miles due north of Santa Barbara. The most conspicuous figure is that of the sun, resembling a human face, with ornamental appendages at the cardinal points, and bearing striking resemblance to some Moki masks and pictographic work. Serpentine lines and anomalous forms also abound.

Four miles northeast of Santa Barbara, near the residence of Mr. Stevens, is an isolated sandstone bowlder measuring about 20 feet high

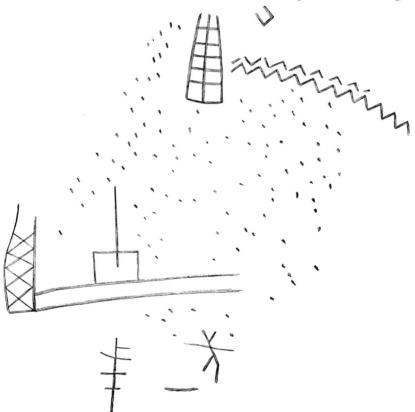

Fig. 30.—Petroglyphs near Santa Barbara. California.

and 30 feet in diameter, upon the western side of which is a slight cavity bearing designs shown in Fig. 29, which correspond in general form to others in Santa Barbara county. The gesture for negation appears in the attitude of the human figures.

Half a mile farther east, on Dr. Coe's farm, is another smaller bowlder, in a cavity of which various engravings appear shown in Fig. 30. Parts of the drawings have disappeared through disintegration of the rock, which is called "Pulpit rock," on account of the shape of the cavity, its position at the side of the narrow valley, and the echo observed upon speaking a little above the ordinary tone of voice.

Painted rocks also occur in the Azuza canyon, about 30 miles northeast of Los Angeles, of which Fig. 31 gives copies.

Just before his departure from the Santa Barbara region, Dr. Hoffman was informed of the existence of eight or nine painted records in that neighborhood, which up to that time had been observed only by a few sheep-herders and hunters.

FIG. 31.—Petroglyphs in Azuza canyon, California.

Mr. L. L. Frost, of Susanville, California, reports the occurrence of pictographs (undoubtedly petroglyphs) 15 miles south of that town, on Willow creek, and at Milford, in the lower end of the valley. No details were furnished as to their general type and condition.

On Porter creek, 9 miles southwest of Healdsburg, on a large bowlder of hornblende syenite, petroglyphs similar to those found in Arizona and Nevada are to be seen. They are generally oblong circles or ovals, some of which contain crosses.

Figs. 32 and 33 are reduced copies $\frac{1}{32}$ of original size of colored petroglyphs found by Dr. Hoffman in September, 1884, 12 miles west-northwest of the city of Santa Barbara, California. The locality is almost at the summit of the Santa Ynez range of mountains; the gray sand

stone rock on which they are painted is about 30 feet high and projects from a ridge so as to form a very marked promontory extending
into a narrow mountain canyon. At the base of the western side of
this bowlder is a rounded cavity, measuring on the inside about 15
feet in width and 8 feet in height. The floor ascends rapidly toward
the back of the cave, and the entrance is rather smaller in dimensions than the above measurements of the interior. About 40 yards
west of this rock is a fine spring of water. One of the four old Indian trails leading northward across the mountains passes by this
locality, and it is probable that this was one of the camping places of
the tribe which came south to trade, and that some of its members
were the authors of the paintings. The three trails beside the one
just mentioned cross the mountains at several points east of this, the
most distant being about 15 miles. Other trails were known, but

FIG. 32.—Petroglyph in Santa Barbara county, California.

these four were most direct to the immediate vicinity of the Spanish
settlement which sprang up shortly after the establishment of the Santa
Barbara mission in 1786. The appearance and position of these and
other pictographs in the vicinity appear to be connected with the several trails. The colors used in the paintings are red and black.

The circles figured in b and d of Fig. 32, and c, r, and w of Fig. 33,
together with other similar circular marks bearing cross lines upon the
interior, were at first unintelligible, as their forms among various tribes
have very different signification. The character in Fig. 32, above and
projecting from d, resembles the human form, with curious lateral bands
of black and white, alternately. Two similar characters appear, also,
in Fig. 33, a, b. In a the lines from the head would seem to indicate a
superior rank or condition of the person depicted.

At the private ethnologic collection of Mr. A. F. Coronel, of Los Angeles, California, Dr. Hoffman discovered a clue to the general import of the above petroglyphs, as well as the signification of some of their characters. In a collection of colored illustrations of old Mexican costumes he found blankets bearing borders and colors nearly identical with those shown in the circles in Fig. 32, *d*, and Fig. 33, *c, r, w*. It is probable that the circles represent bales of blankets which early became articles of trade at the Santa Barbara mission. If this supposition is correct, the cross lines would seem to represent the cords used in tying the blankets into bales, which same cross lines appear as cords in *l*, Fig. 33. Mr. Coronel also possesses small figures of Mexicans, of various conditions of life, costumes, trades, and professions,

Fig. 33.—Petroglyph in Santa Barbara county, California.

one of which, a painted statuette, is a representation of a Mexican lying down flat upon an outspread serape, similar in color and form to the black and white bands shown in the upper figure of *d*, Fig. 32, and *a, b*, of Fig. 33, and instantly suggesting the explanation of those figures. Upon the latter the continuity of the black and white bands is broken, as the human figures are probably intended to be in front, or on top, of the drawings of the blankets.

The small statuette above mentioned is that of a Mexican trader, and if the circles in the petroglyphs are considered to represent bales of blankets, the character in Fig. 32, *d*, is still more interesting, from the union of one of these circles with a character representing the trader, i.e., the man possessing the bales. Bales, or what appear to be bales, are represented to the top and right of the circle in *d*, in that figure. In Fig. 33, *l*, a bale is upon the back of what appears to be a horse, led in an upward direction by an Indian whose headdress and ends of the breechcloth are visible. To the right of the bale are three short lines, evidently showing the knot or ends of the cords used in tying a bale of blankets without colors, therefore of less importance, or of other goods. Other human forms appear in the attitude of making gestures, one also in *j*, Fig. 33, probably carrying a bale of goods. In the same figure *u* represents a centipede, an insect found occasionally south of the mountairs, but reported as extremely rare in the immediate northern regions. For remarks upon *x* in the same figure see Chapter XX, Section 2, under the heading The Cross.

Mr. Coronel stated that when he first settled in Los Angeles, in 1843, the Indians living north of the San Fernando mountains manufactured blankets of the fur and hair of animals, showing transverse bands of black and white similar to those depicted, which were sold to the inhabitants of the valley of Los Angeles and to Indians who transported them to other tribes.

It is probable that the pictographs are intended to represent the salient features of a trading expedition from the north. The ceiling of the cavity found between the paintings represented in the two figures has disappeared, owing to disintegration, thus leaving a blank about 4 feet long, and 6 feet from the top to the bottom between the paintings as now presented.

COLORADO.

Petroglyphs are reported by Mr. Cyrus F. Newcomb as found upon cliffs on Rock creek, 15 miles from Rio Del Norte, Colorado. Three small photographs, submitted with this statement, indicate the characters to have been pecked; they consist of men on horseback, cross-shaped human figures, animals, and other designs greatly resembling those found in the country of the Shoshonean tribes, examples of which are given infra.

Another notice of the same general locality is made by Capt. E. L. Berthoud (*a*) as follows:

The place is 20 miles southeast of Rio Del Norte, at the entrance of the canyon of the Piedra Pintada (Painted rock) creek. The carvings are found on the right of the canyon or valley and upon volcanic rocks. They bear the marks of age and are cut in, not painted, as is still done by the Utes everywhere. They are found for a quarter of a mile along the north wall of the canyon, on the ranches of W. M. Maguire and F. T. Hudson, and consist of all manner of pictures, symbols, and hieroglyphics done by artists whose memory even tradition does not now preserve. The fact that these are carvings done upon such hard rock invests them with additional interest, as they are quite distinct from the carvings I saw in New Mexico and Arizona on soft sandstone. Though some of them are evidently of much greater antiquity than others, yet all are ancient, the Utes admitting them to have been old when their fathers conquered the country.

Mr. Charles D. Wright, of Durango, Colorado, in a communication dated February 20, 1885, gives an account of some " hieroglyphs " on rocks and upon the walls of cliff houses near the boundary line between Colorado and New Mexico. He says:

The following were painted in red and black paints on the wall (apparently the natural rock wall) of a cliff house: At the head was a chief on his horse, armed with spear and lance and wearing a pointed hat and robe; behind this character were some twenty characters representing people on horses lassoing horses, etc. In fact the whole scene represented breaking camp and leaving in a hurry. The whole painting measured about 12 by 16 feet.

Mr. Wright further reports characters on rocks near the San Juan river. Four characters represent men as if in the act of taking an obligation, hands extended, and wearing a "kind of monogram on

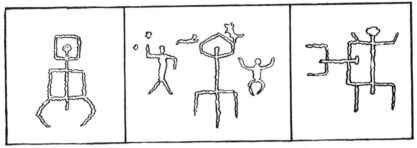

FIG. 34.—Petroglyphs on the Rio Mancos, Colorado.

breast, and at their right are some hieroglyphics written in black paint covering a space 3 by 4 feet."

The best discussed and probably the most interesting of the petroglyphs in the region are described and illustrated by Mr. W. H. Holmes (*a*), of the Bureau of Ethnology. The illustrations are here

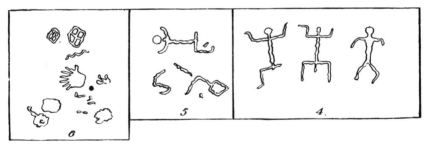

FIG. 35.—Petroglyphs on the Rio Mancos, Colorado.

reproduced in Figs. 34 to 37, and the remarks of Mr. Holmes, slightly condensed, are as follows:

The forms reproduced in Fig. 34 occur on the Rio Mancos, near the group of cliff houses. They are chipped into the rock evidently by some very hard implement and rudely represent the human figure. They are certainly not attempts to represent nature, but have the appearance rather of arbitrary forms, designed to symbolize some imaginary being.

The forms shown in Fig. 35 were found in the same locality, not engraved, but painted in red and white clay upon the smooth rocks. These were certainly done by the cliff-builders, and probably while the houses were in process of construction, since the material used is identical with the plaster of the houses. The sketches and notes were made by Mr. Brandegee. The reproduction is approximately one-twelfth the size of the original.

The examples shown in Fig. 36 occur on the Rio San Juan about 10 miles below the mouth of the Rio La Plata and are actually in New Mexico. A low line of bluffs, composed of light-colored massive sandstones that break down in great smooth-faced blocks, rises from the river level and sweeps around toward the north. Each of these great blocks has offered a very tempting tablet to the graver of the primitive artist, and many of them contain curious and interesting inscriptions. Drawings were made of such of these as the limited time at my disposal would permit. They are all engraved or cut into the face of the rock, and the whole body of each figure has generally been chipped out, frequently to the depth of one-fourth or one-half of an inch.

Fig. 36.—Petroglyphs on the Rio San Juan, New Mexico.

The work on some of the larger groups has been one of immense labor, and must owe its completion to strong and enduring motives. With a very few exceptions the engraving bears undoubted evidence of age. Such new figures as occur are quite easily distinguished both by the freshness of the chipped surfaces and by the designs themselves. The curious designs given in the final group have a very perceptible resemblance to many of the figures used in the embellishment of pottery.

The most striking group observed is given in Fig. 37 A, same locality. It consists of a great procession of men, birds, beasts, and fanciful figures. The whole picture as placed upon a rock is highly spirited and the idea of a general movement toward the right, skillfully portrayed. A pair of winged figures hover about the train as if to watch or direct its movements; behind these are a number of odd figures, followed by an antlered animal resembling a deer, which seems to be drawing a notched sledge containing two figures of men. The figures forming the main body of the procession appear to be tied together in a continuous line, and in form resemble one living creature about as little as another. Many of the smaller figures above and below are certainly intended to represent dogs, while a number of men are stationed about here and there as if to keep the procession in order.

As to the importance of the event recorded in this picture, no conclusions can be drawn; it may represent the migration of a tribe or family or the trophies of a victory. A number of figures are wanting in the drawing at the left, while some of those at the right may not belong properly to the main group. The reduction is, approximately, to one-twelfth.

Designs B and C of the same figure represent only the more distinct portions of two other groups. The complication of figures is so great that a number of hours would have been necessary for their delineation, and an attempt to analyze them here would be fruitless.

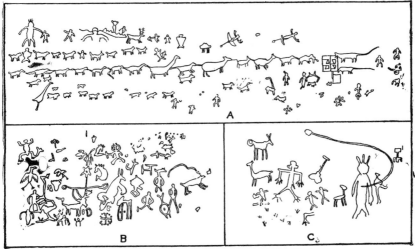

FIG. 37.—Petroglyphs on the Rio San Juan, New Mexico.

It will be noticed that the last two petroglyphs are in New Mexico, but they are so near the border of Colorado and so connected with the series in that state that they are presented under the same heading.

CONNECTICUT.

The following account is extracted from Rafn's Antiquitates Americanæ (a):

In the year 1789 Doctor Ezra Stiles, D. D., visited a rock situated in the Township of Kent in the State of Connecticut, at a place called Scaticook, by the Indians. He thus describes it: "Over against Scaticook and about one hundred rods East of Housatonic River, is an eminence or elevation which is called Cobble Hill. On the top of this stands the rock charged with antique unknown characters. This rock is by itself and not a portion of the Mountains; it is of White Flint; ranges North and South; is from twelve to fourteen feet long; and from eight to ten wide at base and top; and of an uneven surface. On the top I did not perceive any characters; but the sides all around are irregularly charged with unknown characters, made not indeed with the incision of a chisel, yet most certainly with an iron tool, and that by pecks or picking, after the manner of the Dighton Rock. The Lacunae or excavations are from a quarter to an inch wide; and from one tenth to two tenths of an inch deep. The engraving did not appear to be recent or new, but very old."

GEORGIA.

Charles C. Jones, jr., (*a*) describes a petroglyph in Georgia as follows:

In Forsyth county, Georgia, is a carved or incised bowlder of fine grained granite, about 9 feet long, 4 feet 6 inches high, and 3 feet broad at its widest point. The figures are cut in the bowlder from one-half to three-fourths of an inch deep. It is generally believed that they are the work of the Cherokees.

The illustration given by him is here reproduced in Fig. 38. It will be noted that the characters in it are chiefly circles, including plain, nucleated, and concentric, sometimes two or more being joined by straight lines, forming what is now known as the "spectacle shaped" figure. The illustrations should be compared with the many others presented in this paper under the heading of Cup Sculptures, see Chapter V, infra.

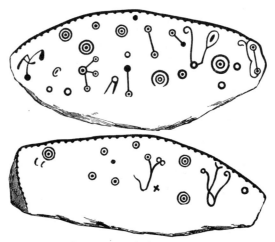

Fig. 38.—Petroglyphs in Georgia.

Dr. M. F. Stephenson (*a*) mentions sculptures of human feet, various animals, bear tracks, etc., in Enchanted mountain, Union county, Georgia. The whole number of sculptures is reported as one hundred and forty-six.

Mr. Jones (*b*) gives a different résumé of the objects depicted, as follows:

Upon the Enchanted mountain, in Union county, cut in plutonic rock, are the tracks of men, women, children, deer, bears, bisons, turkeys, and terrapins, and the outlines of a snake, of two deer, and of a human hand. These sculptures—so far as they have been ascertained and counted—number one hundred and thirty-six. The most extravagant among them is that known as the footprint of the "Great Warrior." It measures 18 inches in length and has six toes. The other human tracks and those of the animals are delineated with commendable fidelity.

IDAHO.

Mr. G. K. Gilbert, of the U. S. Geological Survey, has furnished a small collection of drawings of Shoshonean petroglyphs from Oneida, Idaho, shown in Fig. 39. Some of them appear to be totemic characters, and possibly were made to record the names of visitors to the locality.

Mr. Willard D. Johnson, of the U. S. Geological Survey, reports pictographic remains observed by him near Oneida, Idaho, in 1879. The figures represent human beings and were on a rock of basalt.

A copy of another petroglyph found in Idaho appears in Fig. 1092, infra.

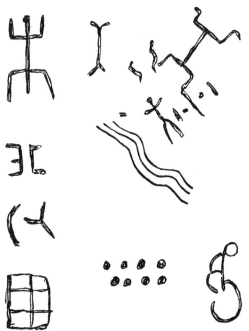

Fig. 39.—Petroglyphs in Idaho (Shoshonean).

ILLINOIS.

Petroglyphs are reported by Mr. John Criley as occurring near Ava, Jackson county, Illinois. The outlines of the characters observed by him were drawn from memory and submitted to Mr. Charles S. Mason, of Toledo, Ohio, through whom they were furnished to the Bureau of Ethnology. Little reliance can be placed upon the accuracy of such drawing, but from the general appearance of the sketches the originals of which they are copies were probably made by one of the middle Algonquian tribes of Indians.

The "Piasa" rock, as it is generally designated, was referred to by the missionary explorer Marquette in 1675. Its situation was immediately above the city of Alton, Illinois.

Marquette's remarks are translated by Dr. Francis Parkman (*a*) as follows:

On the flat face of a high rock were painted, in red, black, and green, a pair of monsters, each "as large as a calf, with horns like a deer, red eyes, a beard like a tiger, and a frightful expression of countenance. The face is something like that of a man, the body covered with scales; and the tail so long that it passes entirely round the body, over the head, and between the legs, ending like that of a fish."

Another version, by Davidson and Struvé (*a*), of the discovery of the petroglyph is as follows:

Again they (Joliet and Marquette) were floating on the broad bosom cf the unknown stream. Passing the mouth of the Illinois, they soon fell into the shadow of a tall promontory, and with great astonishment beheld the representation of two monsters painted on its lofty limestone front. According to Marquette, each of these frightful figures had the face of a man, the horns of a deer, the beard of a tiger, and the tail of a fish so long that it passed around the body, over the head, and between the legs. It was an object of Indian worship and greatly impressed the mind of the pious missionary with the necessity of substituting for this monstrous idolatry the worship of the true God.

A footnote connected with the foregoing quotation gives the following description of the same rock:

Near the mouth of the Piasa creek, on the bluff, there is a smooth rock in a cavernous cleft, under an overhanging cliff, on whose face, 50 feet from the base, are painted some ancient pictures or hieroglyphics, of great interest to the curious.

Fig. 40.—The Piasa petroglyph.

They are placed in a horizontal line from east to west, representing men, plants, and animals. The paintings, though protected from dampness and storms, are in great part destroyed, marred by portions of the rock becoming detached and falling down.

Mr. McAdams (*a*), of Alton, Illinois, says "The name Piasa is Indian and signifies, in the Illini, 'The bird which devours men.'" He furnishes a spirited pen-and-ink sketch, 12 by 15 inches in size and purporting to represent the ancient painting described by Marquette. On the picture is inscribed the following in ink: "Made by Wm. Dennis, April 3d, 1825." The date is in both letters and figures. On the top of the picture in large letters are the two words, "FLYING DRAGON." This picture, which has been kept in the old Gilham family of Madison county and bears the evidence of its age, is reproduced as Fig. 40.

He also publishes another representation (Fig. 41) with the following remarks:

One of the most satisfactory pictures of the Piasa we have ever seen is in an old German publication entitled "The Valley of the Mississippi Illustrated. Eighty illustrations from nature, by H. Lewis, from the Falls of St. Anthony to the Gulf of Mexico," published about the year 1839 by Arenz & Co., Düsseldorf, Germany. One of the large full-page plates in this work gives a fine view of the bluff at Alton, with the figure of the Piasa on the face of the rock. It is represented to have been taken on the spot by artists from Germany. We reproduce that part of the bluff (the whole picture being too large for this work) which shows the pictographs. In the German picture there is shown just behind the rather dim outlines of the second face a ragged crevice, as though of a fracture. Part of the bluff's face might have fallen and thus nearly destroyed one of the monsters, for in later years writers speak of but one figure. The whole face of the bluff was quarried away in 1846–'47.

FIG. 41.—The Piasa petroglyph.

Under Myths and Mythic Animals, Chapter XIV, Section 2, are illustrations and descriptions which should be compared with these accounts, and Chapter XXII gives other examples of errors and discrepancies in the description and copying of petroglyphs.

Mr. A. D. Jones (a) says of the same petroglyph:

After the distribution of firearms among the Indians, bullets were substituted for arrows, and even to this day no savage presumes to pass the spot without discharging his rifle and raising his shout of triumph. I visited the spot in June (1838) and examined the image and the ten thousand bullet marks on the cliff seemed to corroborate the tradition related to me in the neighborhood.

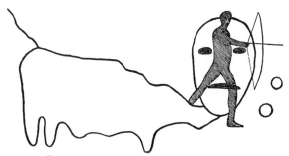

FIG. 42.—Petroglyph on the Illinois river.

Mr. McAdams, loc. cit., also reports regarding Fig. 42:

Some twenty-five or thirty miles above the mouth of the Illinois river, on the west bank of that stream, high up on the smooth face of an overhanging cliff, is another interesting pictograph sculptured deeply in the hard rock. It remains to-day probably in nearly the same condition it was when the French voyagers first descended the river and got their first view of the Mississippi. The animal-like body, with the human head, is carved in the rock in outline. The huge eyes are depressions like saucers, an inch or more in depth, and the outline of the body has been scooped out in the same way; also the mouth.

The figure of the archer with the drawn bow, however, is painted, or rather stained with a reddish brown pigment, over the sculptured outline of the monster's face.

Mr. McAdams suggests that the painted figure of the human form with the bow and arrows was made later than the sculpture.

The same author (*b*) says, describing Fig. 43:

Some 3 or 4 miles above Alton, high up beneath the overhanging cliff, which forms a sort of cave shelter on the smooth face of a thick ledge of rock, is a series of paintings, twelve in number. They are painted or rather stained in the rock with a reddish brown pigment that seems to defy the tooth of time. It may be said, however, that their position is so sheltered that they remain almost perfectly dry. We made sketches of them some thirty years ago and on a recent visit could see that they had changed but little, although their appearance denotes great age.

These pictographs are situated on the cliff more than a hundred feet above the river. A protruding ledge, which is easily reached from a hollow in the bluff, leads to the cavernous place in the rock.

FIG. 43.—Petroglyph near Alton, Illinois.

Mr. James D. Middleton, formerly of the Bureau of Ethnology, mentions the occurrence of petroglyphs on the bluffs of the Mississippi river, in Jackson county, about 12 miles below Rockwood. Also of others about 4 or 5 miles from Prairie du Rocher, near the Mississippi river.

IOWA.

Mr. P. W. Norris, of the Bureau of Ethnology, found numerous caves on the banks of the Mississippi river, in northeastern Iowa, 4 miles south of New Albion, containing incised petroglyphs. Fifteen miles south of this locality paintings occur on the cliffs. He also discovered painted characters upon the cliffs on the Mississippi river, 19 miles below New Albion.

KANSAS.

Mr. Edward Miller reports in Proceedings of the American Philosophical Society, vol. x, 1869, p. 383, the discovery of a petroglyph near the line of the Union Pacific railroad, 15 miles southeast of Fort Harker, formerly known as Fort Ellsworth, Kansas. The petroglyph is upon a formation belonging to No. 1, Lower Cretaceous group, according to the classification of Meek and Hayden.

The parts of the two plates VII and VIII of the work cited, which bear the inscriptions, are now presented as Fig. 44, being from two views of the same rock.

FIG. 44.—Petroglyphs in Kansas.

KENTUCKY.

Mr. James D. Middleton, formerly of the Bureau of Ethnology, in a letter dated August 14, 1886, reports that at a point in Union county, Kentucky, nearly opposite Shawneetown, Illinois, petroglyphs are found, and from the description given by him they appear to resemble those in Jackson county, Illinois, mentioned above.

Mr. W. E. Barton, of Wellington, Ohio, in a communication dated October 4, 1890, writes as follows:

At Clover Bottom, Kentucky, on a spur of the Big Hill, in Jackson county, about 13 miles from Berea, is a large rock which old settlers say was covered with soil and vegetation within their memory. Upon it are representations of human tracks, with what appear to be those of a bear, a horse, and a dog. These are all in the same direction, as though a man leading a horse, followed the dog upon the bear's track. Crossing these is a series of tracks of another and larger sort which I can not attempt to identify. The stone is a sandstone in the subcarboniferous. As I remember, the strata are nearly horizontal, but erosion has made the surface a slope of about 20°. The tracks ascending the slope cross the strata. I have not seen them for some years.

The crossing of the strata shows that the tracks are the work of human hands, if indeed it were not preposterous to think of anything else in rocks of that period. Still the tracks are so well made that one is tempted to ask if they can be real. They alternate right and left, though the erosion and travel have worn out some of the left tracks. A wagon road passes over the rock and was the cause of the present exposure of the stone. It can be readily found a fourth of a mile or less from the Pine Grove schoolhouse.

MAINE.

A number of inscribed rocks have been found in Maine and information of others has been obtained. The most interesting of them and the largest group series yet discovered in New England is shown in Pl. XII.

The rock upon which the glyphs appear is in the town of Machiasport, Maine, at Clarks point, on the northwestern side of Machias bay,

2 miles below the mouth of Machias river. The rock or ledge is about 50 feet long from east to west and about fifteen feet in width, nearly horizontal for two-thirds its length, from the bank or western end at high water, thence inclining at an angle of 15° to low-water mark. Its southern face is inclined about 40°. The formation is schistose slate, having a transverse vein of trap dike extending nearly across its section. Nearly the entire ledge is of blue-black color, very dense and hard except at the upper or western end, where the periodical formation of ice has scaled off thin layers of surface and destroyed many figures which are remembered by persons now living. The ebb and flow of tides, the abrasion of moving beach stones or pebble wash and of ice-worn bowlders, have also effaced many figures along the southern side, until now but one or two indentations are discernible. Visitors, in seeking to remove some portion of the rock as a curiosity or in striving to perpetuate their initials, have obscured several of the most interesting, and until recently the best defined figures. It was also evident to the present writer, who carefully examined the rock in 1888, that it lay much deeper in the water than once had been the case. At the lowest tides there were markings seen still lower, which could not readily have been made if that part of the surface had not been continuously exposed. The depression of a rock of such great size, which was so gradual that it had not been observed by the inhabitants of the neighboring settlement, is an evidence of the antiquity of the peckings.

The intaglio carving of all the figures was apparently made by repeated blows of a pointed instrument—doubtless of hard stone; not held as a chisel, but working by a repetition of hammerings or peckings. The deepest now seen is about three-eighths of an inch. The amount of patient labor bestowed upon these figures must have been great, considering the hardness of the rock and the rude implement with which they were wrought.

There is no extrinsic evidence of their age. The place was known to traders early in the seventeenth century, and much earlier was visited by Basque fishermen, and perhaps by the unfortunate Cortereals in 1500 and 1503. The descendants of the Mechises Indians, a tribal branch of the Abnaki, who once occupied the territory between the St. Croix and Narraguagus rivers, when questioned many years ago, would reply in substance that "all their old men knew of them," either by having seen them or by traditions handed down through many generations.

Several years ago Mr. H. R. Taylor, of Machias, who made the original sketch in 1868 and kindly furnished it to the Bureau of Ethnology, applied to a resident Indian there (Peter Benoit, then nearly 80 years old) for assistance in deciphering the characters. He gave little information, but pointed out that the figures must not all be read "from one side only," thus, the one near the center of the sketch, which seen from the south was without significance, became from the opposite

Pl. XII

PETROGLYPHS IN MAINE.

point a squaw with sea fowl on her head, denoting, as he said, "that squaw had smashed canoe, saved beaver-skin, walked one-half moon all alone toward east, just same as heron wading alongshore." Also that the three lines below the figure mentioned, which together resemble a bird track or a trident, represent the three rivers, the East, West, and Middle rivers of Machias, which join not far above the locality. The mark having a rough resemblance to a feather, next on the right of this river-sign, is a fissure in the rock. Most of the figures of human beings and other animals are easily recognizable.

Peckings of a character similar to those on the Picture rock at Clarks point, above described, were found and copied 600 feet south of it at high-water mark on a rock near Birch point. Others were discovered and traced on a rock on Hog island, in Holmes bay, a part of Machias bay. All these petroglyphs were without doubt of Abnaki origin, either of the Penobscot or the Passamaquoddy divisions of that body of Indians. The rocks lay on the common line of water communication between those divisions and were convenient as halting places.

MARYLAND.

In the Susquehanna river, about half a mile south of the state line, is a group of rocks, several of the most conspicuous being designated as the "Bald Friars." Near by are several mound-shaped bowlders of the so-called "nigger-head" rock, which is reported as a dark-greenish chlorite schist. Upon the several bowlders are deep sculpturings, apparently finished by rubbing the depression with stone, or wood and sand, thus leaving sharp and distinct edges to the outlines. Some of these figures are an inch in depth, though the greater number are becoming more and more eroded by the frequent freshets, and by the running ice during the breaking up in early spring of the frozen river.

The following account is given by Prof. P. Frazer (a):

Passing the Pennsylvania state line one reaches the southern barren serpentine rocks, which are in general tolerably level for a considerable distance.

About 700 yards, or 640 meters, south of the line, on the river shore, are rocks which have been named the Bald Friars. French's tavern is here, at the mouth of a small stream which empties into the Susquehanna. About 874 yards (800 meters) south of this tavern are a number of islands which have local names, but which are curious as containing inscriptions of the aborigines.

The material of which most of these islands are composed is chlorite schist, but as this rock is almost always distinguished by the quartz veins which intersect it, so in this case some of the islands are composed of this material almost exclusively, which gives them a very striking white appearance.

One of these, containing the principal inscriptions, is called Miles island.

The figures, which covered every part of the rocks that were exposed, were apparently of historical or at least narrative purport, since they seemed to be connected. Doubtless the larger portion of the inscription has been carried away by the successive vicissitudes which have broken up and defaced, and in some instances obliterated, parts of which we find evidence of the previous existence on the islands.

Every large bowlder seems to contain some traces of previous inscription, and in many instances the pictured side of the bowlder is on its under side, showing that it has been detached from its original place. The natural agencies are quite sufficient to account for any amount of this kind of displacement, for the rocks in their present condition are not refractory and offer no great resistance to the wear of weather and ice; but in addition to this must be added human agencies.

Amongst other things, they represent the conventional Indian serpent's head, with varying numbers of lines.

Some of the signs next frequently recurring were concentric circles, in some cases four and in other cases a lesser number.

Fig. 45 is a reproduction of Prof. Frazer's illustration.

FIG. 45.—Bald Friar rock, Maryland.

This region was also referred to by Dr. Charles Rau (*a*), his cut from the specimen in the collection of the Smithsonian Institution (Mus. No. 39010) being here reproduced as Fig. 46.

During the autumn of the years 1888 and 1889 Dr. Hoffman visited these rocks, securing sketches and measurements, the former of which are reproduced in Figs. 47 and 48. The figures are deeply cut, as if rubbed down with sand and a round stick of green wood. The deepest channels, varying from three-fourths to $1\frac{1}{4}$ inches across and almost as deep as they are wide, appear as if cut out with a gouge, and for this reason bear a strong resemblance to the petroglyphs in Owens valley, California. In whatever manner these sculpturings were made, it is evident that much time and great labor were expended upon them, as this variety of rock, locally termed "Nigger-head," is extremely hard.

Fig. 45 represents a bird's-eye view of the top of the rock, bearing the greater amount of workmanship. The petroglyphs cover a surface measuring about 5 feet by 4 feet 6 inches. The extreme ends of the figures extend beyond the irregular horizontal surface and project over the rounded edge of the rock, so that the line, at the left-hand lower part of the illustration, dips at an angle of about 45°. The two short lines at the extreme right are upon the side of the upper edge of the rock, where the surface inclines at an angle of 30°.

Some of the figures are indefinite, which is readily accounted for by the fact that the rock is in the river, a considerable distance from shore, and annually subjected to freshets and to erosion by floating logs and

FIG. 46.—Slab from Bald Friar rock, Maryland.

drift material. The characters at

FIG. 47.—Top of Bald Friar rock, Maryland.

the right end of the upper row resemble those near Washington, Lancaster county, Pennsylvania. (See Fig. 73.)

Fig. 48 presents three characters, selected from other portions of the rock, to illustrate the variety of designs found. They are like some found at Owens valley, California, as will be observed by comparing them with the descriptions and plates under that heading in this section. The left-hand figure is 4 inches in diameter, the middle one 6 inches wide and about 15 inches in height, and the third, or right-hand, is composed of concentric rings, measuring about 10 inches across.

FIG. 48.—Characters from Bald Friar rock, Maryland.

MASSACHUSETTS.

The following description of the much-discussed Dighton rock is taken from Schoolcraft (*b*), where it is accompanied with a plate, now reproduced as Fig. 49:

The ancient inscriptian on a bowlder of greenstone rock lying in the margin of the Assonet or Taunton river, in the area of ancient Vinland, was noticed by the New England colonists so early as 1680, when Dr. Danforth made a drawing of it. This outline, together with several subsequent copies of it, at different eras, reaching to 1830, all differing considerably in their details, but preserving a certain general resemblance, is presented in the Antiquatés Americanes [*sic*] (Tables XI, XII), and referred to the same era of Scandinavian discovery. The imperfections of the drawings (including that executed under the auspices of the Rhode Island Historical Society in 1839, Table XII), and the recognition of some characters bearing more or less resemblance to antique Roman letters and figures, may be considered to have misled Mr. Magnusen in his interpretation of it. From whatever cause, nothing could, it would seem, have been wider from the purport and true interpretation of it. It is of purely Indian origin, and is executed in the peculiar symbolic character of the Kekeewin.

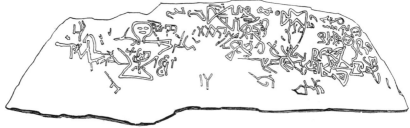

FIG. 49.—Dighton rock, Massachusetts.

A number of copies of the inscriptions on this rock, taken at different times by different persons, are given below in Chapter XXII, sec. 2, with remarks upon them.

Dr. Hoffman visited the locality in 1886, and found that the surface was becoming rapidly destroyed from the frequent use of scrubbing with broom and water to remove the film of sand and dirt which is

daily deposited by every tide, the rock being situated at a short distance inshore. Visitors are frequent, and the guide or ferryman does
not interfere with them so long as he can show his passengers the
famous inscription.

The resemblance between the characters on this rock and those found
in western Pennsylvania, near Millsboro, Fig. 75, and south of Franklin,
on the "Indian God rock," Fig. 74, will be noted.

In Rafn's Antiq. Amer. (*b*) is the following account:

A large stone, on which is a line of considerable length in unknown characters,
has been recently found in Rutland, Worcester county, Massachusetts; they are
regularly placed, and the strokes are filled with a black composition nearly as hard
as the rock itself. The Committee also adds that a similar rock is to be found in
Swanzy, county of Bristol and Commonwealth of Massachusetts, perhaps ten miles
from the Dighton Rock.

MINNESOTA.

The late Mr. P. W. Norris, who was connected with the Bureau of
Ethnology, reported large numbers of pecked totemic characters on the
horizontal faces of the ledges of rock at Pipestone quarry in Minnesota,
and presented some imitations of the peckings. There is a tradition
that it was formerly the custom for each Indian who gathered stone
(catlinite) for pipes, to inscribe his totem (whether clan or tribal or
personal totem is not specified) upon the rock before venturing to
quarry upon this ground. Some of the cliffs in the immediate vicinity
were of too hard a nature to admit of pecking or scratching, and upon
these the characters were placed in colors. Mr. Norris distinguished
bird tracks, the outline of a bird resembling a pelican, deer, turtle, a
circle with an interior cross, and a human figure.

Examples of so-called totemic designs from this locality are given in
Fig. 50, which are reproduced from the work of R. Cronau (*a*):

The same petroglyphs and also others at the Pipestone quarry are
described and illustrated by Prof. N. H. Winchell (*a*). A part of his
remarks is as follows:

On the glaciated surface of the quartzite about the "Three Maidens," which is
kept clean by the rebound of the winds, are a great many rude inscriptions, which
were made by pecking out the rock with some sharp-pointed instrument or by the
use of other pieces of quartzite. They are of different sizes and dates, the latter
being evinced by their manner of crossing and interfering and by the evident difference in the weight of the instruments used. They generally represent some animal,
such as the turtle, bear, wolf, buffalo, elk, and the human form. The "crane's foot"
is the most common; next is the image of men; next the turtle. It would seem as if
any warrior or hunter who had been successful and happened to pass here left his
tribute of thanks to the great spirit in a rude representation of his game and perhaps
a figure of himself on the rocks about these bowlders, or perhaps had in a similar
way invoked the good offices of the spirits of his clan when about to enter on some
expedition. In some cases there is a connection of several figures by a continuous
line, chipped in the surface of the rock in such a manner as if some legend or adventure were narrated, but for the most part the figures are isolated. This is the "sacred
ground" of the locality. Such markings can be seen at no other place, though there
is abundance of bare, smooth rock. (Similar inscriptions are found on the red

quartzite in Cottonwood county). The excavation of the surface of the rock is very slight, generally not exceeding a sixteenth of an inch, and sometimes only enough to leave a tracing of the designed form. The hardness of the rock was a barrier to deep sculpturing with the imperfect instruments of the aborigines; but it has effectually preserved the rude forms that were made. The fine glacial scratches that are abundantly scattered over this quartzite indicate the tenacity with which it retains all such impressions, and will warrant the assignment of any date to these inscriptions that may be called for within the human period. Yet it is probable that they date back to no very great antiquity. They pertain, at least, to the dynasty of the present Indian tribes. The totems of the turtle and the bear, which are known to have been powerful among the clans of the native races in America at the time of the earliest European knowledge of them, and which exist to this day, are the most frequent objects represented. The "crane's foot," or "turkey foot," or "bird track," terms which refer perhaps to the same totem sign—the snipe—is not only common on these rocks, but is seen among the rock inscriptions of Ohio, and was one of the totems of the Iroquois, of New York.

Fig. 50.—Petroglyphs at Pipestone, Minn.

In June, 1892, Mr. W. H. Holmes, of the Bureau of Ethnology, visited the Pipestone quarry and took a number of tracings of the petroglyphs, which unfortunately were received too late for insertion in the present work. Some of his remarks are as follows:

The trouble with the figures copied and published by Prof. Winchell is that they are not arranged in the original order. It will now be impossible to correct this entirely, as most of the stones have been taken up and removed. * * * The Winchell drawings were evidently drawn by eye and have a very large personal equation; besides, they are mixed up while appearing to be in some order. The few groups that I was able to get are, it seems to me, of more interest than all the single figures you could put in a book. There can be little doubt that in the main this

great group of pictures was arranged in definite order, agreeing with the arrangements of mythical personages and positions usual in the aboriginal ceremonials of
the region. It is a great pity that the original order has been destroyed, but the
inroads of relic hunters and inscription cranks made it necessary to take up the
stones. One large stone was taken to Minneapolis by Prof. Winchell. There are a
few pieces still in place. All were near the base of one of the great granite bowlders,
and it is said here that formerly, within the memory of the living, the place was
visited by Indians who wished to consult the gods.

The following description is extracted from the account of Mr. James
W. Lynd (b):

Numerous high bluffs and cliffs surround it; the Pipestone quarry and the alluvial
flat below these, in which the quarry is situated, contains a huge bowlder that rests
upon a flat rock of glistening, smooth appearance, the level of which is but a few
inches above the surface of the ground. Upon the portions of this rock not covered
by the bowlder above and upon bowlder itself are carved sundry wonderful figures—
lizards, snakes, otters, Indian gods, rabbits with cloven feet, muskrats with human
feet, and other strange and incomprehensible things—all cut into the solid granite,
and not without a great deal of time and labor expended in the performance. * * *

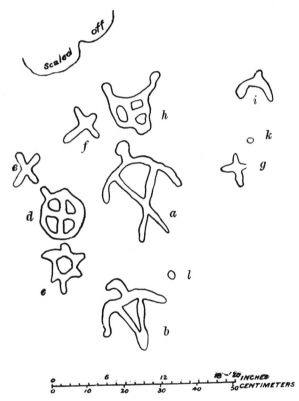

Fig. 51.—Petroglyphs in Brown's valley, Minnesota.

A large party of Ehanktonwanna and Teetonwan Dakotas, says the legend, had
gathered together at the quarry to dig the stone. Upon a sultry evening, just before
sunset, the heavens suddenly became overclouded by a heavy rumbling thunder and
every sign of an approaching storm, such as frequently arises on the prairie without

much warning. Each one hurried to his lodge, expecting a storm, when a vivid flash of lightning, followed immediately by a crashing peal of thunder, broke over them, and, looking towards the huge bowlder beyond their camp, they saw a pillar or column of smoke standing upon it, which moved to and fro, and gradually settled down into the outline of a huge giant, seated upon the bowlder, with one long arm extended to heaven and the other pointing down to his feet. Peal after peal of thunder, and flashes of lightning in quick succession followed, and this figure then suddenly disappeared. The next morning the Sioux went to this bowlder and found these figures and images upon it, where before there had been nothing, and ever since that the place has been regarded as wakan or sacred.

Mr. T. H. Lewis (b) gives a description of Fig. 51.

This bowlder is in the edge of the public park, on the north end of the plateau at Brown's valley, Minnesota. The bowlder has a flat surface with a western exposure, is irregular in outline, and is about 5 feet 8 inches in diameter, and firmly imbedded in the terrace.

The central figure, a, undoubtedly represents a man, although the form is somewhat conventional; b represents a bird; c represents a tortoise; d is a cross and circle combined, but the circle has a groove extending from it; e, f, and g, although somewhat in t e shape of crosses, probably represent bird tracks; h and i are nondescript in character, although there must be some meaning attached to them; k and l are small dots or cups cut into the bowlder.

The figures as illustrated are one-eighth of their natural size, and are also correct in their relative positions one to the other. The work is neatly done although the depth of the incisions is very slight.

MONTANA.

Mr. Charles Hallock, of Washington, D. C., reports the occurrence of pictured rocks near Fort Assiniboin, Montana, but does not mention whether they are colored or incised, and also fails to describe the general type of the characters found.

NEBRASKA.

The following (condensed) description of petroglyphs found in Dakota county, Nebraska, is furnished by Mr. J. H. Quick, of Sioux City, Iowa:

The petroglyphs are found upon the face of a sandstone cliff in a deep ravine at a point where two watercourses (dry for the most part), meet about 20 miles south of Sioux City, Iowa, but in Dakota county, in the State of Nebraska. At this point the range of bluffs which bounds the Missouri river bottom is deeply cut through by the above-mentioned ravine, which runs in a northerly direction towards the Missouri. Another ravine coming from the southwest leaves this narrow point of land between the two ravines, rising to a height of 50 to 75 feet above the bottom of the ravines. For some distance from the point this cape, if I may so term it, shows ledges of sandstone cropping out on both sides. And exactly at the point and for some rods back on the east side are found the pictographs under consideration.

The rocks are of two kinds, a few feet of hard jasperous sandstone superimposed on about the same thickness of sandstone so soft that it can be crumbled to pieces in the fingers. The lower soft strata have been worn away, leaving the upper harder layers jutting out to a distance of several feet over and completely sheltering them. And on the smooth surface of these lower soft strata, protected by the overhanging ledge above, shut in by bluffs 200 feet high on the east and sheltered from the winds by dense underwood and scrubby forest trees, are carved these pictographs. These safeguards, combined with the advantage of a very secluded situation, have combined to preserve them, very little marred by careless and mischievous hands.

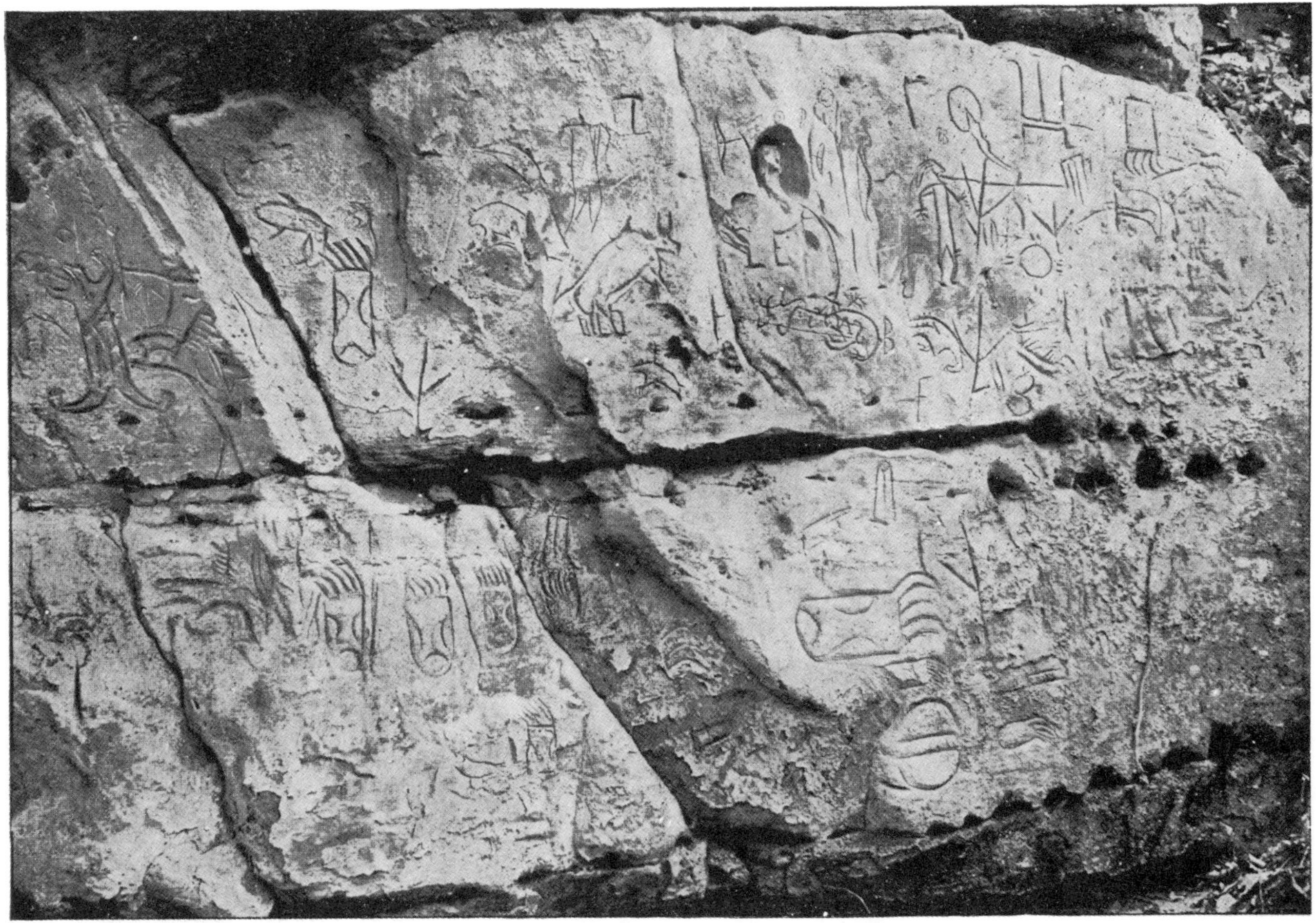

PETROGLYPHS IN NEBRASKA.

The eagle or "thunder-bird" figures are quite numerous. There are also many of the "buffalo track" and of the "turkey track" figures. I call them "turkey tracks" because they all show a spur and seem to represent some of the large *gallinaciæ*.

In one of the groups, which I will call the "bear-fight group," we are at a loss to determine whether the figure of the small animal was a part of the original design or a subsequent interpolation. It seemed genuine, but was not so deeply carved as the other figures. The same may be said of the diagonal bars across the figure of the bear.

In the other group, which I will term the "turkey-track group," there are some figures of which we could not even imagine the meaning. But they are undoubtedly genuine, and seem to belong to the same design as the other figure.

The "bear-track" figures are very numerous and of several different sizes. A cat-like figure, which we call a panther, shows faintly. It is about effaced by time. Other figures reminded us of a crab or crawfish, but we were unable to determine whether the line running back just below belongs to it or not.

I am informed by the same gentleman who saw these petroglyphs in 1857 that there were at one time many more some 3 or 4 miles from this place, near Homer, Nebraska, in the vicinity of a large spring, but he also said that as it is a favorite picnic ground for the country people the carvings are probably destroyed. I presume others may be found in these bluffs.

I surmise that the almost cave-like nature of the place where the carvings I have above attempted to describe are situated rendered it a favorite camping ground and resting place; and also that the ravines above mentioned made easy trails from the Missouri bottom up to the higher grounds farther from the river, because it obviated the ascent of the very steep bluffs.

The Winnebago Indian reservation is a few miles south of this locality, but they were placed here by the Government as late as from 1860 to 1865. Previous to that time I think this ground was occupied by the Omahas. I have been unable to gain any information as to the Indians who carved these figures or as to their meaning.

The most instructive of the petroglyphs, copies of which are kindly furnished by Mr. Quick, is presented as Pl. XIII, and selected sketches from that and the other petroglyphs copied are shown as Figs. 52 and 53.

FIG. 52.—Characters from Nebraska petroglyphs.

Frank La Flèche, of the Bureau of Indian Affairs, in February, 1886, communicated the following:

Ingna^{n}χe gikáχa-ina is the Omaha name of a rock ledge on the banks of the Missouri river, near the Santee agency, Nebraska. This ledge contains pictographs of men who passed to the happy hunting grounds, of life size, the sandstone being so soft that the engravings would be made with a piece of wood. They are represented with the special cause (arrow, gun, etc.), which sped them to hades. The souls themselves are said to make these pictographs before repairing "to the spirits."

FIG. 53.—Characters from Nebraska petroglyphs.

Rev. J. Owen Dorsey, of the Bureau of Ethnology, says that the probable rendering of the term when corrected is, "Spirit(s) they-made-themselves the (place where)."

NEVADA.

Petroglyphs have been found by members of the U. S. Geological Survey at the lower extremity of Pyramid lake, Nevada, though no accurate reproductions are available. These characters are mentioned as incised upon the surface of basalt rocks.

Petroglyphs also occur in considerable numbers on the western slope of Lone Butte, in the Carson desert. All of these appear to have been produced on the faces of bowlders and rocks by pecking and scratching with some hard mineral material like quartz.

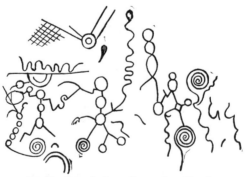

FIG. 54.—Petroglyphs on Carson river, Nevada.

A communication from Mr. R. L. Fulton, of Reno, Nevada, tells that the drawing now reproduced as Fig. 54 is a pencil sketch of curious petroglyphs on a rock on the Carson river, about 8 miles below old

Fort Churchill. It is the largest and most important one of a group of similar characters. It is basaltic, about 4 feet high and equally broad.

Mr. Fulton gives the following description:

The rock spoken of has an oblong hole about 2 inches by 4 and 16 inches deep at the left end, which has been chipped out before the lines were drawn, if it was not some form of the ancient mill which is so common, as it seems to be the starting point for the whole scheme of the artist. The rock lies with a broad, smooth top face at an angle towards the south, and its top and southeast side are covered with lines and marks that convey to the present generation no intelligence whatever, so far as I can learn.

A line half an inch wide starts at the hole on the left and sweeping downward forms a sort of border for the work until it reaches midway of the rock, when it suddenly turns up and mingles with the hieroglyphics above. Two or three similar lines cross at the top of the stone, and one runs across and turns along the north side, losing itself in a coating of moss that seems as hard and dry and old as the stone itself. From the line at the bottom a few scallopy looking marks hang that may be a part of the picture, or it may be a fringe or ornament. The figures are not pictures of any animal, bird, or reptile, but seem to be made up of all known forms and are connected by wavy, snake-like lines. Something which might be taken for a dog with a round and characterless head at each end of the body, looking towards you, occupies a place near the lower line. The features are all plain enough. A deer's head is joined to a patchwork that has something that might be taken for 4 legs beneath it. Bird's claws show up in two or three places, but no bird is near them. Snaky figures run promiscuously through the whole thing. A circle at the right end has spokes joining at the center which run out and lose themselves in the maze outside.

The best known and largest collection of marks that I know of covers a large smooth ledge at Hopkins Soda Springs, 12 miles south of the summit on the Central Pacific railroad. The rock is much the same in character as those I have described, but the groundwork in this case is a solid ledge 10 feet one way and perhaps 40 the other, all closely covered with rude characters, many of which seem to point to human figures, animals, reptiles, etc. The ledge lies at an angle of 45°, and must have been a tempting place for a lazy artist who chanced that way.

Many other places on the Truckee river have such rocks all very much alike, and yet each bearing its own distinct features in the marking. Near a rock half a mile east of Verdi, a station on the Central Pacific railroad, 10 miles east of Reno, lie two others, the larger of which has lines originating in a hole at the upper right-hand corner, all running in tangents and angles, making a double-ended kind of an arrangement of many-headed arrows, pointing three ways. A snail-like scroll lies between the two arms, but does not touch them. Below are blotches, as if the artist had tried his tools.

This region has been roamed over by the Washoe Indians from a remote period, but none of them know anything of these works. One who has gray hair and more wrinkles than hairs, who is bent with age and who is said to be a hundred years old, was led to the spot. He said he saw them a heap long time ago, when he was only a few summers old, and they looked then just as they do now.

Mr. Lovejoy, a well-known newspaper man, took up, in 1854, the ranche where the rocks lie, and said just before his death that they were in exactly the same condition when he first saw them as they are to-day. Others say the same, and they are certainly of a date prior to the settlement of this coast by Americans and probably by the Spanish.

They are very peculiar in many respects, and the rock is wonderfully adapted to the uses to which it has been put. Wherever the surface has been broken the color has changed to gray, and no amount of wear or weather seems to turn it back. The indentation is so shallow as to be imperceptible to sight or touch, and yet the marks are as plain as they could be made, and can be seen as far as the rock can be distinguished from its fellows.

It is hardly likely that the work was done without some motive besides the simple love of doing it, and it was well and carefully done, too, showing much patience and doubtless consumed a good deal of time, as the tools were poor.

A large ledge is marked near Meadow lake in Nevada county, and in the state of Nevada the petroglyphs cover a route extending from the southeast to the north-

FIG. 55.—Petroglyphs at Reveillé, Nevada.

west corner of the state, crossing the line into California in Modoc county, and leaving a string of samples clear across the Madeline plains.

Eight miles below Belmont, in Nye county, Nevada, an immense rock which at some time has fallen into the canyon from the porphyry ledge above it has a patch of marks nearly 20 feet square. It is so high that a man on horseback can not reach the top.

A number at Reveillé, in the same county, are also marked. On the road to Tybo every large rock is marked, one of the figures being a semicircle with a short vertical spoke within the curve. At Reno a heavy black rock a couple of feet across is beautifully engraved to represent a bull's eye of 4 rings, an arrow with a very large feather, and one which may mean a man. In a steep canyon 15 miles northeast of Reno, in Spanish Spring mountains, several cliffs are well marked, and an exposed ledge, where the Carson river has cut off the point of a hill below Big Bend, is covered with rings and snakes by the hundred. Several triangles, a well-formed square and compass, a woman with outstretched arms holding an olive branch, etc., are there.

Humboldt county has its share, the best being on a bluff below the old Sheba mine. Ten miles south of Pioche are about 50 figures cut into the rock, many of them designed to represent mountain sheep. Eighty miles farther south, near Kane's Spring, the most numerous and perfect specimens of this prehistoric art are found. Men on horseback engaged in the pursuit of animals are among the most numerous, best preserved, and carefully executed.

The region I have gone over is of immense size, and must impress everyone with the importance of a set of symbols which extends in broken lines from Arizona far into Oregon.

Fig. 55 exhibits engravings at Reveillé, Nevada. Great numbers of incised characters of various kinds are also reported from the walls of rocks flanking Walker river, near Walker lake, Nevada. Waving lines, rings, and what appear to be vegetable forms are of frequent occurrence. The human form and footprints are also depicted.

Fig. 56 is a copy of a drawing made by Lieut. A. G. Tassin, Twelfth U. S. Infantry, in 1877, of an ancient rock-carving at the base and in the recesses of Dead mountain and the abode of dead bad Indians according to the Mohave mythology. This drawing and its description is from a manuscript report on the Mohave Indians, in the library of the of the Bureau of Ethnology, prepared by Lieut. Tassin.

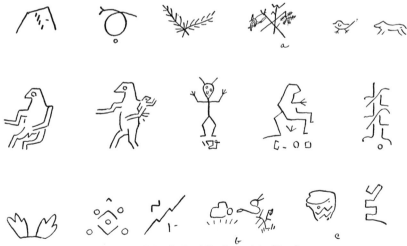

FIG. 56.—Petroglyphs at Dead mountain, Nevada.

He explains some of the characters as follows:

(a) Evidently the two different species of mesquite bean.

(b) Would seem to refer to the bite of the cidatus, and to the use of a certain herb for its cure.

(c) Presumably the olla or water cooler of the Mohaves.

The whole of this series of petroglyphs is regarded as being Shinumo or Moki. They show a general resemblance to drawings in Arizona, known to have been made by the Moki Indians. The locality is within the territory of the Shoshonean linguistic division, and the drawings are in all probability the work of one or more of the numerous tribes comprised within that division.

NEW MEXICO.

On the north wall of Canyon de Chelly, one-fourth of a mile east of its mouth, are several groups of petroglyphs, consisting chiefly.of various grotesque forms of the human figure, and also numbers of animals, circles, etc. A few of them are painted black, the greater portion consisting of rather shallow lines, which are in some places considerably weathered. Further up the canyon, in the vicinity of the cliff dwellings, are numerous small groups of pictographic characters, consisting of men and animals, waving or zigzag lines, and other odd figures.

Lieut. James H. Simpson (a), in his Journal of a Military Reconnoissance, etc., presents a number of plates bearing copies of inscriptions on rocks in the northwestern part of New Mexico, among which are those on the so-called "Inscription rock" at El Moro, here reproduced as Fig. 57. The petroglyphs are selected from the south face of the rock. Lieut. Simpson states that most of the characters are no higher than a man's head, and that some of them are undoubtedly of Indian origin.

Fig. 57.—Inscription rock, New Mexico.

Among the many colored etchings and paintings on rock discovered by the Pacific railroad expedition in 1853–'54, Lieut. Whipple (e) notes those at Rocky dell creek, New Mexico, which were found between the edge of the Llano Estacado and the Canadian river. The stream flows through a gorge, upon one side of which a shelving sandstone rock forms a sort of cave. The roof is covered with paintings, some evidently ancient, and beneath are innumerable carvings of footprints, animals, and symmetrical lines. He also remarks (d) that figures cut upon a rock at Arch spring, near Zuñi, present some faint similarity to those at Rocky dell creek.

Near Ojo Pescado, in the vicinity of the ruins, are petroglpyhs, also reported by Lieut. Whipple (d), which are very much weather-worn and have "no trace of a modern hand about them."

Mr. Edwin A. Hill, of Indianapolis, in a letter, notes petroglyphs on the Denver and Rio Grande railroad, between Antonite and Espanola. Below Tres Piedras and near Espanola are rude sculptures, lining the valley on both sides of the road for a long distance, at least several miles. The canyon has a slope of about 45° and contains many bowlders, and on every available face pictographs are cut. Figures of arrows, hatchets, circles, triangles, bows, spears, turtles, etc., are outlined as if with some cutting-tool. The country had two years before been occupied by Apaches, but far greater age is attributed to the petroglyphs.

Other petroglyphs actually within the geographical area of New Mexico are so near the border that they are treated of in connection with those of Colorado.

Prof. E. D. Cope (a) gives a copy of figures which he found on the side of a ravine near Abiquiu, on the river Chama. They are cut in Jurassic sandstone of medium hardness, and are quite worn and overgrown with the small lichen which is abundant on the face of the rock.

Mr. Gilbert Thompson, of the U. S. Geological Survey, reports his observation of petroglyphs at San Antonio springs, 30 miles east of Fort Wingate, New Mexico. The human figure, in various forms, occurs,

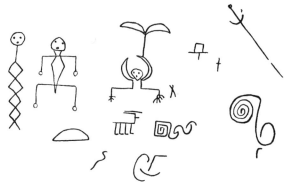

FIG. 58.—Petroglyphs at Ojo de Benado, New Mexico.

as well as numerous other characters, strikingly similar to those frequent in the country farther west occupied by the Moki Indians. The peculiarity of these figures is that the outlines are incised and that the depressions thus formed are filled with red, blue or white pigments. The interior of the figures is simply painted with one or more of the same colors.

Figs. 58 and 59 are reproductions of drawings of petroglyphs from Ojo de Benado, south of Zuñi, New Mexico. The manuscripts which once accompanied them, and which were forwarded to the Bureau of

Ethnology in the usual official manner, have become separated from the sketches, and on those there are no indications of the collectors' names.

The characters are very like others from several localities in the territory and in the adjacent region. The type is that of the Pueblos generally.

FIG. 59.—Petroglyphs at Ojo de Benado, New Mexico.

Mr. Bandelier, in conversation, reported having seen and sketched a petroglyph at Nambe, in a canyon about 2 miles east of the pueblo, also another at Cueva Pintada, about 17 miles by the trail northwest of Cochiti.

NEW YORK.

The following is extracted from Schoolcraft (c):

There is a pictographic Indian inscription [now obliterated] in the valley of the Hudson, above the Highlands, which from its antiquity and character appears to

FIG. 60.—Petroglyph at Esopus, New York.

denote the era of the introduction of firearms and gunpowder among the aboriginal tribes of that valley. This era, from the well-known historical events of the contemporaneous settlement of New Netherlands and New France, may be with general accuracy placed between the years 1609, the date of Hudson's ascent of that stream above the Highlands, and the opening of the Indian trade with the Iroquois at the present site of Albany, by the erection of Fort Orange, in 1614.   *   *   *

In a map published at Amsterdam, in Holland, in 1659, the country, for some distance both above and below Esopus creek, is delineated as inhabited by the Waranawankongs, who were a totemic division or enlarged family clan of the Mohikinder. They spoke a well-characterized dialect of the Mohigan, and have left numerous geographical names on the streams and physical peculiarities of that part of the river coast quite to and above Coxsackie. The language is Algonquin.

Esopus itself appears to be a word derived from Seepu, the Minsi-Algonquin name for a river.

*   *   *   The inscription may be supposed, if the era is properly conjectured, to have been made with metallic tools. The lines are deeply and plainly impressed. It is in double lines. The plumes from the head denote a chief or man skilled in the Indian medico-magical art. The gun is held at rest in the right hand; the left appears to support a wand. [The position of the arm may be merely a gesture.]

The reproduction here as Fig. 60 is from a rock on the western bank of the Hudson, at Esopus landing. It is presented mainly on account of the frequent allusions to it in literature.

NORTH CAROLINA.

Mr. James Mooney, of the Bureau of Ethnology, reports petroglyphs upon a gray gneissoid rock, a short distance east of Caney river, on the north side of the road from Asheville to Burnsville, North Carolina. The face of the surface is at an angle of 30° toward the south, and the sculptured area covers about 10 feet square. The characters consist chiefly of cup-shaped depressions, some about 2 inches deep, some being also connected. There are a few markings which appear to have been intended to represent footprints. The characters resemble, to some extent, those at Trap Rock gap, Georgia, and at the Juttaculla rock, North Carolina, on a branch of the Tuckasegee river, above Webster.

The above-described sculptured rock is on the property of Ellis Gardner, and is known as Gardner's, or the " Garden rock."

Mr. Mooney also reports that at Webster, North Carolina, there is one large rock bearing numerous petroglyphs, rings, cup-shaped depressions, fish-bone patterns, etc. He further states, upon the authority of Dr. J. M. Spainhour, of Lenoir, that upon a light gray rock measuring 4 feet by 30 are numerous cup-shaped petroglyphs, he having counted 215. The rock is on the Yadkin river, 4 miles below Wilkesboro, and is at times partly under water.

Dr. Hoffman, who in 1886 visited western North Carolina, gives the following account of colored pictographs found there by him.

" The locality known as ' Paint rock' is situated on the east or right bank of the French Broad river, about 100 yards above the Tennessee and North Carolina state line. The limestone cliff, which terminates abruptly near the river, measures about 100 feet in height and covers an area from side to side of exposure of at least 100 yards. The accompanying view (Fig. 61), taken from across the river, presents the wall of limestone rock and the position of the petroglyph, which is delineated in proper proportion nearly in the center of the illustration.

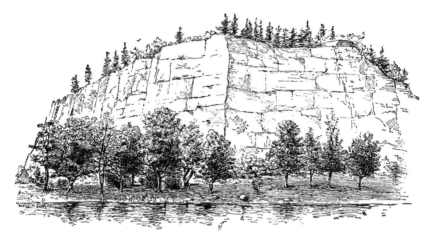

FIG. 61.—Paint rock, North Carolina.

" The property belongs to Mr. J. W. Chockley, who has been living in the vicinity for about fifteen years. He states that during this time the pictograph has undergone some change on account of gradual disintegration or fracture of the rock. The first knowledge of the pictograph, according to local tradition, dates back about sixty years, and no information as to its import could be learned, either from the white residents, who are few in number, or the straggling Cherokee Indians who visit the railway station at odd intervals."

The pictograph is peculiar in design, no animal forms being apparent but an indefinite number of short, straight lines at right angles to one another, as shown in Fig. 62. One-thirty-sixth actual size.

FIG. 62.—Petroglyphs on Paint rock, North Carolina.

The characters are in dark red, probably a ferrous oxide, quantities of which are found in the neighborhood. The color appears to have penetrated the softer portions of the limestone, though upon the harder surfaces it has been removed by exposure to the elements. The lowermost figure appears to resemble a rude outline of a human form, with one arm lowered and reaching forward, though this is only a suggestion.

Upon the face of the rock, a few yards to the right of the above, are indistinct outlines of circles, several of which indicate central spots, and one, at least, has a line extending from the center downward for about 8 inches.

OHIO.

A large number of petroglyphs are reported from this state. It is sufficient to present the following examples extracted, with reproduced illustrations and abbreviated descriptions, from the Report of the Committee of the State Archæological Society, published in the Report of the Ohio State Board of Centennial Managers.

Fig 63 is a copy of the petroglyph on the Newark Track rock.

Fig. 63.—Newark Track rock, Ohio.

It is described in the volume cited, pages 94, 95, as follows:

The inscriptions near Newark, in Licking county, Ohio, originally covered a vertical face of conglomerate rock, 50 or 60 feet in length, by 6 and 8 feet in height. This rock is soft and, therefore, the figures are easily erased * * *. About the year 1800 it became a place where white men sought to immortalize themselves by cutting their names across the old inscription * * *

On the rock faces and detached sandstone blocks of the banks of the Ohio river there are numerous groups of intaglios, but in them the style is quite different from those to which I have referred, and which are located in the interior. Those on the Ohio river resemble the symbolical records of the North American Indians, such as the Kelley Island stone, described in Schoolcraft by Capt. Eastman, the Dighton rock, the Big Indian rock of the Susquehanna, and the "God rock" of the Allegheny river. In those the supposed bird track is generally wanting. The large sculptured rock near Wellsville, which is only visible at low water of the Ohio, has among the figures one that is prominent on the Barnesville stones. This is the fore foot of the bear, with the outside toe distorted and set outward at right angles.

Other sculptured rocks of a similar character have been found in Fairfield, Belmont, Cuyahoga, and Lorain counties.

That the ancient bird-track character belonged to the mound-builders is evident from the fact that it is found among their works, constructed of soil on a large scale.

One of these bird-track mounds occurs in the center of the large circular inclosure near Newark, Ohio, now standing in the Licking county fair grounds. Among the characters will be noticed the human hand. In one instance the hand is open, the palm facing the observer, and in the other the hand is closed, except the index finger which points downward to the base of the cliff. Of the bird-track characters there are many varieties. There is also a character resembling a cross and another bearing some resemblance to an arrow.

Fig. 64 is an illustration of the Independence stone, which is described in the same volume, pp. 98, 99, as follows:

Great care has been taken to obtain a correct sketch of what remains of this inscription. A very rude drawing of it was published in Schoolcraft's great work upon the Indian tribes, in 1854.

The rock here described only contains a portion of the inscription. The balance was destroyed in quarrying. The markings on the portion of the rock preserved consist of the human foot, clothed with something like a moccasin or stocking; of the naked foot; of the open hand; of round markings one in front of the great toe, of each representation of the clothed foot; the figure of a serpent, and a peculiar character which might be taken for a rude representation of a crab or crawfish, but which bears a closer resemblance to an old-fashioned spearhead used in capturing fish.

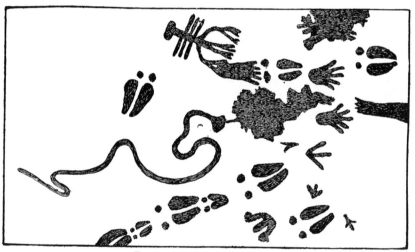

FIG. 64.—Independence stone, Ohio.

Fig. 65 is a copy of the drawings on the Track rock, near Barnsville, Belmont county, Ohio, the description of which is in the same volume, pp. 89–93.

The rude cuts of the human faces, part of the human feet, the rings, stars, serpents, and some others, are evidently works of art, as in the best of them the marks of the engraving instrument are to be seen. In all cases, whether single or in groups, the relative dimensions of the figures are preserved. The surface of this block is 8 by 11 feet.

At the south end of the petroglyphs occurs a figure of several concentric rings, a design by no means confined to Ohio. The third figure right of this resembles others in the same group, and evidently indicates

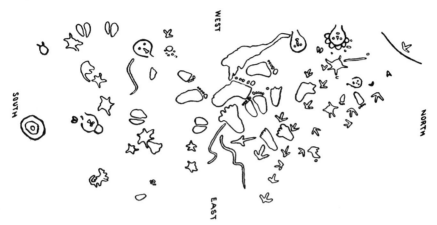

FIG. 65.—Barnesville Track rock, Ohio.

the footprints of the buffalo. Human footprints are generally indicated by the pronounced toe marks, either detached as slight depressions or attached to the foot, and are thus recognized as different from bear tracks, which frequently have but slight indications of toes or perhaps claw marks, and in which also the foot is shorter or rounder. The arrow-shaped figures are no doubt intended for turkey tracks, characters common to many petroglyphs of the middle and eastern Algonquian area.

Fig. 66 gives several of the above characters enlarged from the preceding figure.

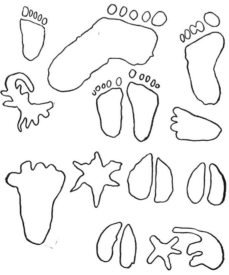

FIG. 66.—Characters from Barnesville Track rock.

In Fig. 67, referring to another block mentioned in the same report, lying 20 feet south of the one first mentioned, there is a duplication of the characters before noted—human footprints, bear and turkey tracks, and the indication of what may be intended to represent a serpent.

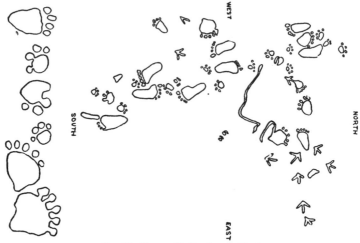

FIG. 67.—Barnesville Track rock, No. 2.

Fig. 68, from p. 105 of the same volume, gives copies of sketches from the rocks near Wellsville, Ohio, with remarks as follows:

On the Ohio side of the river, 1 mile above Wellsville, there is a large group of sculptures on a flat sand rock of the coal series, scarred by floating ice and flood wood. They are only visible in low water, as they are only 2 or 3 feet above the extreme low stage of the river. " * * They are made in double outline and not by a single deep channel. The outlines are a series of dots made with a round-pointed instrument, seldom more than half an inch deep.

The upper design is a rattlesnake with a fancy head and tail. Its length is 4½ feet, a very clumsy affair, but intended for the common yellow rattlesnake of the West.

The head of the snake, which occupies a space 6 inches square, is represented in the second character, which is reduced from a tracing size of nature. It brings to mind the horned snake of the Egyptians, which was an object of worship by them.

The character at the left hand of the lower line may be an uncouth representation of a demon or evil spirit. The right-hand character is probably an otter carrying a vine or string in his mouth.

FIG. 68.—Petroglyphs, Wellsville, Ohio.

It is more probable that the lines from the mouth of the animal indicate magic or supernatural power, of which many examples appear in this paper, as also of the device in the region of the animal's heart, from which a line extends to the mouth. These characteristics connect the glyph with the Ojibwa drawings on bark.

OREGON.

Many bowlders and rock escarpments at and near the Dalles of the Columbia river, Oregon, are covered with incised or pecked glyphs.

Some of them are representations of human figures, but characters of other forms predominate.

Mr. Albert S. Gatschet, of the Bureau of Ethnology, reports the discovery by him, in 1878, of rock etchings 4 miles from Gaston, Oregon, and 2½ miles from the ancient settlement of the Tuálati (or Atfálati) Indians. These etchings are about 100 feet above the valley bottom on six rocks of soft sandstone, projecting from the grassy hillside of Patten's valley, opposite Darling Smith's farm, and are surrounded with timber on two sides.

This sandstone ledge extends for one-eighth of a mile horizontally along the hillside, upon the projecting portions of which the inscriptions are found. These rocks differ greatly in size, and slant forward so that the inscribed portions are exposed to the frequent rains of that region. The first rock, or that one nearest the mouth of the canyon, consists of horizontal zigzag lines and a detached straight line, also horizontal. On another side of the same rock is a series of oblique parallel lines. Some of the most striking characters found upon other exposed portions of the rock appear to be human figures, i. e., circles to which radiating lines are attached, and bear indications of eyes and mouth, long vertical lines running downward as if to represent the body, and terminating in a furcation, as if intended for legs, toes, etc. To the right of one figure is an arm and three-fingered hand (similar to some of the Moki characters), bent downward from the elbow, the humerus extending at a right angle from the body. Horizontal rows of short vertical lines are placed below and between some of the figures, probably numerical marks of some kind.

Other characters occur of various forms, the most striking being an arrow pointing upward, with two horizontal lines drawn across the shaft, and with vertical lines having short oblique lines attached thereto.

Mr. Gatschet remarks that the Tuálati tell a trivial story to explain the origin of these pictures, the substance of which is as follows: The Tillamuk warriors living on the Pacific coast were often at variance with the several Kalapuya tribes. One day, passing through Patten's valley to invade the country of the Tuálati, they inquired of a woman how far they were from their camp. The woman, desirous not to betray her own countrymen, said they were yet at a distance of one (or two?) days' travel. This made them reflect over the intended invasion, and, holding a council, they decided to withdraw. In commemoration of this the inscription, with its numeration marks, was incised by the Tuálati.

Dr. Charles Rau received from Dr. James S. Denison, physician at the Klamath agency, Lake county, Oregon, a communication relative to the practice of painting figures on rocks in the territory of the Klamath Indians in Oregon. There are in that neighborhood many rocks bearing painted figures; but Dr. Rau's (b) description refers specially to a single rock, called Ktá-i Tupákshi (standing rock), situated about 50 yards north of Sprague river and 150 yards from the junction of Sprague and Williamson rivers. It is about 10 feet high, 14 feet long, and 12 or 14 feet deep. Fig. 69, drawn one-twelfth of the natural size, illustrates the character of the paintings seen on the smooth southern surface of this rock. The most frequent designs are single or concentric circles, like Fig. 69, *a*, which consists of a dark red circle surrounded by a white one, the center being formed by a round red spot. Fig. 69, *b*, painted in dark red and white colors, exhibits a somewhat Mahadeo-like shape; the straight appendage of the circle is provided on each side with short projecting lines, alternately red and white, and almost producing the effect of the so-called herring-bone ornament.

FIG. 69.—Petroglyphs in Lake county, Oregon.

Fig. 69, *c* and *d*, executed in dark red, are other designs seen on the standing rock above mentioned. The colors, which, as the informant thinks, are rubbed in with grease, appear quite distinct on the dark surface of the rock.

PENNSYLVANIA.

Along the river courses in northern and western Pennsylvania many rocks are found bearing traces of carvings, though, on account of the character of the geological formations, some of them are nearly obliterated.

In 1875 Mr. P. W. Shafer published in a historical map of Pennsylvania several groups of pictographs. These had before appeared in a rude and crowded form in the Transactions of the Anthropological Institute of New York, 1871–'72, page 66, where the localities are mentioned as "Big" and "Little" Indian rocks, respectively. One of these rocks is in the Susquehanna river, below the dam at Safe harbor, and the drawing clearly shows its Algonquian origin. The characters are nearly all either animals or various forms of the human body. Birds, bird tracks, and serpents also occur. A part of this pictograph is presented below, Fig. 1089.

Dr. W. J. Hoffman visited this place during the autumn of 1889 and made sketches of the petroglyphs. The Algonquian type of delineation of objects is manifest.

The rock known as "Big Indian rock" is in the Susquehanna river, three-fourths of a mile below the mouth of Conestoga creek and about 400 yards from the eastern bank of the Susquehanna. It is one of many, but larger than any other in the immediate vicinity, measuring about 60 feet in length, 30 feet in width, and an average height of about 20 feet. The upper surface is uneven, though smoothly worn, and upon this are pecked the characters, shown in Fig. 70.

FIG. 70.—Big Indian rock, Pennsylvania.

The characters, through exposure to the elements, are becoming rather indistinct, though a few of them are pecked so deep that they still present a depression of from one-fourth to one-half an inch in depth. The most conspicuous objects consist of human figures, thunder birds, and animals resembling the panther.

"Little Indian rock" is also situated in the Susquehanna river, one-fourth of a mile from the eastern bank and a like distance below the mouth of Conestoga creek. This rock, also of hard micaceous schist, is not so large as the one above mentioned, but bears more interesting characters, the most conspicuous being representations of the thunder bird, serpents, deer and bird tracks, etc.

Prof. Persifor Frazer, jr., (b) remarks upon the gradual obliteration of these pictographs, and adds:

In addition to these causes of obliteration it is a pity to have to record another, which is the vandalism of some visitors to the locality who have thought it an excellant practical joke to cut spurious figures alongside of and sometimes over those made by the Indians. It is not unlikely, too, that the "fish pots" here, as in the case of the Bald Friar's inscriptions, a few miles below the Maryland line, may have been constructed in great part out of fragments of rock containing these hieroglyphics, so that the parts of the connected story which they relate are separated and the record thus destroyed.

FIG. 71.—Little Indian rock, Pennsylvania.

Others have cut their initials or full names in these rocks, thus for an obscure record whose unriddling would award the antiquarian, substituting one, the correct deciphering of which leads to obscurity itself.

At McCalls ferry, on the Susquehanna river, in Lancaster county, and on the right shore near the water's edge, is a gray gneissoid flat rock, bearing petroglyphs that have been pecked upon the surface. It is irregular in shape, measuring about 3½ by 4 feet in superficial area, upon which is a circle covering nearly the entire surface, in the middle of which is a smaller circle with a central point. On one side of the inner space, between the outer and inner circles, are a number of characters resembling human figures and others of unintelligible form. The petroglyph is represented in Fig. 72.

FIG. 72.—Petroglyph at McCalls ferry, Pennsylvania.

The resemblance between these drawings and those on Dighton rock is to be noted, as well as that between both of them and some in Ohio. All those localities are within the area formerly occupied by tribes of the Algonquian stock.

Near Washington, Lancaster county, Pennsylvania, on "Mill stream," one-fourth of a mile above its junction with the Susquehanna river, is a large bowlder of gray sandstone (Fig. 73), the exposed portion of which bears several deeply incised lines which appear to have served as topographic indicators, as several others of like kind occur farther down-stream. The longest incision is about 28 inches in length, the next one parallel to it, about 14 inches, while the third character is V-shaped, one arm of which is about 10 inches in length and the other 12. The apex of this character points in a southeast direction.

One-eighth of a mile farther down is another bowlder, also near the water, which bears shorter lines than the preceding, but in general pointing almost southeast and northwest.

The workmanship is similar to that at Conowingo, Maryland, at the site of the Bald Friar rocks. The marks appear to have been chipped to a considerable depth and then rubbed with sand and some hard substance so as to present a smooth and even surface, removing all or nearly all of the pecked surface.

FIG. 73.—Petroglyph near Washington, Pennsylvania.

Mr. P. W. Shafer, on the same historical map of Pennsylvania before mentioned, presents also a group of pictures copied from the originals on the Alleghany river, in Venango county, 5 miles south of Franklin, on what is known as the Indian God rock. There are but six characters furnished in his copy, three of which are variations of the human form, while the others are undetermined.

This rock was visited in 1886 by Dr. Hoffman, who made a number of drawings of objects represented, of which only those in Fig. 74 are here reproduced. The face of the bowlder bearing the original petro-glyphs has been much disfigured by visitors who, in endeavoring to display their skill by pecking upon the surface names, dates, and other designs, have so injured it that it is difficult to trace the original characters.

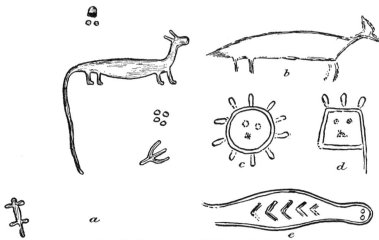

FIG. 74.—Petroglyphs on "Indian God rock."

Fig. 74, *a*, represents, apparently, a panther. Above and beneath it are markings resembling wolf tracks, while farther down is a turkey track, and in the left-hand lower corner is a human form, such as is usually found upon rocks in the areas represented by Shoshonian tribes.

The design at *b* is much mutilated and eroded, and may originally have been a character like *a*, the first of this series.

The characters at *c* and *d* are evidently human faces, the former representing that of the sun, the latter being very much like a mask. That at *e* is found upon other Algonquian rocks, notably those called "Bald Friar," Maryland, in the Susquehanna river, immediately below the state line of Pennsylvania.

The bowlder upon which these petroglyphs are engraved lies at the water's edge, and during each freshet the lower half of the surface and sometimes even more is under water. At these times floating logs, impelled according to the curve in the river immediately above, are directed toward this rock, which may explain the worn surface and the eroded condition of the sculpture.

Mr. J. Sutton Wall, of Monongahela city, describes in correspondence a rock bearing pictographs opposite the town of Millsboro, in Fayette county, Pennsylvania. This rock is about 390 feet above the level of the Monongahela river, and belongs to the Waynesburg stratum of sandstone. It is detached and rests somewhat below its true horizon. It is about 6 feet in thickness, and has vertical sides; only two figures are carved on the sides, the principal inscriptions being on the top, and all are now considerably worn. Mr. Wall mentions the outlines of animals and some other figures formed by grooves or channels cut from an inch to a mere trace in depth. No indications of tool marks were discovered. The footprints are carved depressions. The character marked z, near the lower left-hand corner, is a circular cavity 7 inches deep. A copy of the inscription made in 1882 by Mr. Wall and Mr. William Arison is reproduced as Fig. 75

FIG. 75.—Petroglyph at Millsboro, Pennsylvania.

Again the resemblance between these drawings, those on Dighton rock, and some of those in Ohio, introduced above, is to be noted, and the fact that all these localities are within the area formerly occupied by tribes of the Algonquian stock.

Mr. Wall also contributes a group of glyphs on what is known as the "Geneva Picture rock," in the Monongahela valley, near Geneva. These are footprints and other characters similar to those from Hamilton farm, West Virginia, which are shown in Fig. 1088.

Mr. L. W. Brown, of Redstone, Fayette county, Pennsylvania, mentions a rock near Layton, in that county, which measures about 15 by 25 feet in area, upon the surface of which occur a number of petroglyphs consisting of the human figure, animals, and footprints, some

of which are difficult to trace.   From a rough sketch reproduced as
Fig. 76, made by Mr. Brown, these appear to be Algonquian in type.

FIG. 76.—Petroglyphs near Layton, Pennsylvania.

Mr. Brown also submitted for examination two pieces of chocolate-
colored, smooth, fine grained slate, of hard texture, bearing upon the
several sides outlines of incised figures.   The specimens were found in
Indian graves in Fayette county, Pennsylvania.   The outline of the

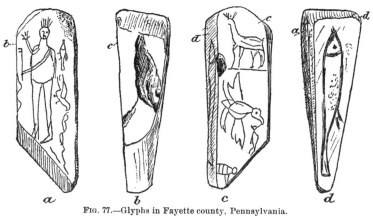

FIG. 77.—Glyphs in Fayette county, Pennsylvania.

incisions, although they are not strictly petroglyphs, are reproduced in Figs. 77 and 78.

The designs are made in delicate lines, as if scratched with a sharply pointed piece of quartz, or possibly metal. The character *d* on Fig. 78 is the representation of a fish, which has been accentuated by additional cutting since found. The characters resemble the Algonquian type, many of them being frequently found among those tribes living along the Great Lakes.

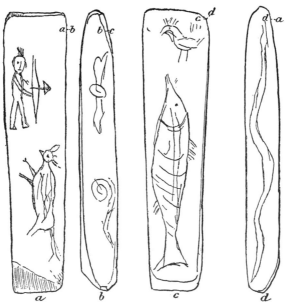

FIG. 78.—Glyphs in Fayette county, Pennsylvania.

RHODE ISLAND.

In C. C. Rafn's Antiq. Amer. (*c*), is the following account:

Portsmouth rocks.—The rocks, for there are several of them, are situated on the western side of the island of Rhode Island, in the town of Portsmouth, on the shore, about 7 miles from Newport, taking the western road, and 4 miles from Bristol ferry. * * * They are partially, if not entirely, covered by water at high tide; and such was the state of the tide and the lateness of the hour when the location was ascertained, that I was unable to make a thorough examination of them. I saw sufficient. however, to satisfy me that they were formerly well covered with characters, although a large portion of them have become obliterated by the action of air and moisture, and probably still more by the attrition of masses of stone against them in violent storms and gales, and by the ruthless ravages of that most destructive power of all, the hand of man.

Tiverton rocks [op. cit. *d*].—Their situation may be thus known: by tracing along the east side of the map of Rhode Island until you strike Tiverton, and then following along to the southwest extremity of that town, the Indian name Puncoteast, also the English names Almy and High Hill, will be seen. The inscriptions are on masses of Graywacke. * * * We can only state they were occupied with some kind of characters.

These two inscriptions are pictured, op. cit., Table XIII.

SOUTH DAKOTA.

Mr. T. H. Lewis (c), gives a description of Fig. 79 as follows:

This bowlder is on a high terrace on the west side of the Minnesota river, 1½ miles south of Browns valley, and is in Roberts county, South Dakota. It is oblong in form, being 3½ feet in length, 2 feet in width, and is firmly imbedded in the ground.

Of the characters a and b are undoubtedly tortoises; c is probably intended to represent a bird track; d represents a man, and is similar to the one at Browns valley, Minnesota, [Fig. 51, supra;] e is a nondescript of unusual form; f is apparently intended to represent a headless bird, in that respect greatly resembling certain earthen effigies in the regions to the southeast.

The figures are about one-fourth of an inch in depth and very smooth, excepting along their edges, which roughness is caused by a slight unevenness of the surface of the bowlder.

The same authority, op. cit., describes Fig. 79, g.

This bowlder, 4 miles northwest of Browns valley, Minnesota, is in Roberts county, South Dakota.

The figures here represented are roughly pecked into the stone, and were never finished; for the grooves that form the pictograph on other bowlders in this region have been rubbed until they are perfectly smooth. The face of the bowlder upon which these occur is about 2 feet long and 1½ feet in width.

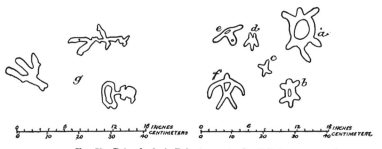

FIG. 79.—Petroglyphs in Roberts county, South Dakota.

TENNESSEE.

Mr. John Haywood (a) gives the following account:

About 2 miles below the road which crosses the Harpeth river from Nashville to Charlotte is a large mound 30 or 40 feet high. About 6 miles from it is a large rock, on the side of the river, with a perpendicular face of 70 or 80 feet altitude. On it, below the top some distance and on the side, are painted the sun and moon in yellow colors, which have not faded since the white people first knew it. The figure of the sun is 6 feet in diameter; that of the moon is of the old moon. The sun and moon are also painted on a high rock on the side of the Cumberland river, in a spot which several ladders placed upon each other could not reach, and which is also inaccessible except by ropes let down the summit of the rock to the place where the painting was performed. * * * The sun is also painted on a high rock on the side of the Cumberland river, 6 or 7 miles below Clarksville; and it is said to be painted also at the junction of the Holston and French Broad rivers, above Knox-ville, in East Tennessee; also on Duck river, below the bend called the Devil's Elbow, on the west side of the river, on a bluff; and on a perpendicular flat rock facing the river, 20 feet below the top of the bluff and 60 above the water, out of which the rock rises, is the painted representation of the sun in red and yellow colors, 6 feet in circumference, yellow on the upper side and a yellowish red on the lower. The colors are very fresh and unfaded. The rays, both yellow and red, are represented as darting from the center. It has been spoken of ever since the river was navigated and has been there from time immemorial.   *   *   *

The painting on Big Harpeth, before spoken of, is more than 80 feet from the water and 30 or 40 below the summit. All these paintings are in unfading colors, and on parts of the rock inaccessible to animals of every description except the fowls of the air. The painting is neatly executed, and was performed at an immense hazard of the operator.

Mr. W. M. Clarke, in Smithsonian Report for 1877, page 275, says:

On the bluffs of the Big Harpeth many pictures of Indians, deer, buffalo, and bows and arrows are to be seen. These pictures are rudely drawn, but the coloring is as perfect now as when first put on.

Haywood (b) says:

At a gap of the mountains and near the head of Brasstown creek, which is toward the head of the Hiawassee, and among the highlands, is a large horizontal rock on which are engraved the tracks of deer, bears, horses, wolves, turkeys, and barefooted human beings of all sizes. Some of the horses' tracks appear to have slipped forward. The direction of them is westward. Near them are signs of graves.

He also (c) gives the following account:

On the south bank of the Holston, 5 miles above the mouth of French Broad, is a bluff of limestone opposite the mounds and a cave in it. The bluff is 100 feet in height. On it are painted in red colors, like those on the Paint rock, the sun and moon, a man, birds, fishes, etc. The paintings have in part faded within a few years. Tradition says these paintings were made by the Cherokees, who were accustomed in their journeys to rest at this place. Wherever on the rivers of Tennessee are perpendicular bluffs, on the sides, and especially if caves be near, are often found mounds near them, inclosed in intrenchments, with the sun and moon painted on the rocks, and charcoal and ashes in the smaller mounds. These tokens seem to be evincive of a connection between the mounds, the charcoal and ashes, the paintings and the caves.

TEXAS.

Mr. J. R. Bartlett (b) gives the following account:

About 30 miles from El Paso del Norte, in Texas, very near the boundary line of Mexico, there is an overhanging rock, extending for some distance, the whole surface of which is covered with rude paintings and sculptures, representing men, animals, birds, snakes, and fantastic figures. The colors used are black, red, white, and a brownish yellow. The sculptures are mere peckings with a sharp instrument just below the surface of the rock. The accompanying engravings [reproduced in Fig. 80] show the character of the figures and the taste of the designers. Hundreds of similar ones are painted on the rocks at this place. Some of them, evidently of great age, had been partly defaced to make room for more recent devices.

The overhanging rock, beneath which we encamped, seemed to have been a favorite place of resort for the Indians, as it is at the present day for all passing travelers. The recess formed by this rock is about 15 feet in length by 10 in width. Its entire surface is covered with paintings, one laid on over the other, so that it is difficult to make out those which belong to the aborigines. I copied a portion of these figures, about which there can be no doubt as to the origin. They represent Indians with shields and bows, painted with a brownish earth; horses, with their riders; uncouth looking animals, and a large rattlesnake. Similar devices cover the rock in every part, but are much defaced. Near this overhanging rock is the largest and finest tank or pool of water to be found about here. It is only reached by clambering on the hands and knees 15 or 20 feet up a steep rock. Over it projects a gigantic bowlder, which, resting on or wedged between other rocks, leaves a space of about 4 feet above the surface of the water. On the under side of this bowlder are fantastic designs in red paint, which could only have been made by persons lying on their backs in this cool and sheltered spot.

Mr. Charles Hallock, of Washington, District of Columbia, gives information that there is a locality termed the Painted caves, "on the Rio Grande, near Devil's river, in Crockett county, Texas, on the line of the 'Sunset' railroad. Here the rock is gray limestone and the petroglyphs are for the most part sculptured. They are in great variety, from a manifest antiquity to the most recent date; for these cliff caverns have been from time immemorial the refuge and resort of all sorts of wayfarers, marauders, and adventurers, who have painted, cut, and carved in every geometrical and grotesque form imaginable."

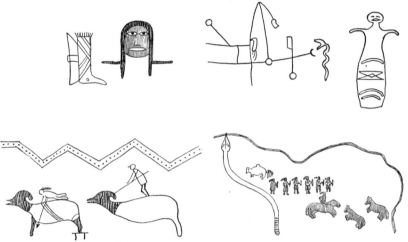

FIG. 80.—Petroglyphs near El Paso, Texas.

UTAH.

Carvings and paintings on rocks are found in such numbers in the southern interior of Utah that a locality there has been named Pictograph rocks.

Mr. G. K. Gilbert, of the U. S. Geological Survey, collected in 1875 a number of copies of inscriptions in Temple creek canyon, southeastern Utah, and noted their finding as follows:

The drawings were found only on the northeast wall of the canyon, where it cuts the Vermillion cliff sandstone. The chief parts are etched, apparently by pounding with a sharp point. The outline of a figure is usually more deeply cut than the body. Other marks are produced by rubbing or scraping, and still others by laying on colors. Some, not all, of the colors are accompanied by a rubbed appearance, as though the material had been a dry chalk.

I could discover no tools at the foot of the wall, only fragments of pottery, flints, and a metate.

Several fallen blocks of sandstone have rubbed depressions that may have been ground out in the sharpening of tools. There have been many dates of inscriptions, and each new generation has unscrupulously run its lines over the pictures already made. Upon the best protected surfaces, as well as the most exposed, there are drawings dimmed beyond restoration and others distinct. The period during which the work accumulated was longer by far than the time which has passed since the last. Some fallen blocks cover etchings on the wall, and are themselves etched.

Colors are preserved only where there is almost complete shelter from rain. In two places the holes worn in the rock by swaying branches impinge on etchings, but the trees themselves have disappeared. Some etchings are left high and dry by a diminishing talus (15 to 20 feet), but I saw none partly buried by an increasing talus (except in the case of the fallen block already mentioned).

The painted circles are exceedingly accurate, and it seems incredible that they were made without the use of a radius.

In the collection contributed by Mr. Gilbert there are at least fifteen series or groups of figures, most of which consist of the human form (from the simplest to the most complex style of drawing), animals, either singly or in long files—as if driven—bird tracks, human feet and hands, etc. There are also circles, parallel lines, and waving or undulating lines, spots, and other characters.

Mr. Gilbert also reports the discovery, in 1883, of a great number of pictographs, chiefly in color, though some are only incised, in a canyon of the Book cliff containing Thompson's spring, about 4 miles north of Thompson's station, on the Denver and Colorado Railroad, Utah. He has also furnished a collection of drawings of pictographs at Black rock spring, on Beaver creek, north of Milford, Utah. A number of fallen blocks of basalt at a low escarpment are filled with etchings upon the vertical faces. The characters generally are of an "unintelligible" nature, though the human figure is drawn in complex forms. Footprints and circles abound.

Mr. I. C. Russell, of the U. S. Geological Survey, furnished rude drawings of pictographs at Black rock spring, Utah (see Fig. 1093). Mr. Gilbert Thompson also discovered pictographs at Fool creek canyon, Utah (see Fig. 1094).

Mr. Vernon Bailey, in a letter dated January 18, 1889, reports that in the vicinity of St. George "all along the sandstone cliffs are strange figures like hieroglyphics and pictures of animals cut in the rocks, but now often worn dim."

Mr. George Pope, of Provo city, Utah county, in a letter, kindly gives an account of an inscription on a rock in a canyon at the mouth of Provo river, about 7 miles from the city named. There is no paint seen, the inscription being cut. A human hand is conspicuous, being cut (probably pecked) to a depth of at least one-third of an inch, and so with representations of animals.

Dr. Rau (c) gives the design of a portion of a group carved on a cliff in the San Pete valley at the city of Manti, Utah, now reproduced as Fig. 81. He says:

A line drawn horizontally through the middle of the parallel lines connecting the concentric circles would divide the figure into two halves, each bearing a close resemblance to Prof. Simpson's fifth type of cup stones. A copy of the group in question was made and published by Lieut. J. W. Gunnison, in The Mormons or Latter-Day Saints, etc., Philadelphia, 1853, p. 63. The illustration is taken from Bancroft's Native Races (Vol. IV, p. 717). In accordance with Lieut. Gunnison's design, the position of the grotesque human figure is changed to the left of the concentric circle. He also says that the Mormon leaders made this aboriginal inscription subservient to their religion by giving the following translation of it: "I, Mahanti, the second king of the Lamanites, in five valleys of the mountains, make this record in the twelve hundredth year since we came out of Jerusalem. And I have three sons gone to the south country to live by hunting antelope and deer." * * * Schoolcraft attempts (Vol. III, p. 494) something like an interpretation which appears to me fanciful and unsatisfactory.

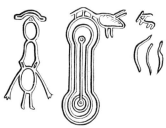

FIG. 81.—Petroglyphs near Manti, Utah.

The following extract is made from The Shinumos by F. S. Dellenbaugh (a).

Some of the least disintegrated ruins are situated on the Colorado river, only only a short distance below the mouth of the Dirty Devil river. * * * A level shelf varying from about 6 to 10 feet in width ran along for 150 feet or more. In most places the rocks above protruded as far as the edge of the lower rocks, sometimes farther, thus leaving a sort of gallery, generally 7 or 8 feet high. Walls that extended to the roof had been built along the outer edge of the natural floor, and the inclosed space being subdivided by stone partitions to suit the convenience of the

FIG. 82.—Petroglyphs on Colorado river, Utah.

builders, the whole formed a series of rather comfortable rooms or houses. The back walls of the houses—the natural rock—had on them many groups of hieroglyphics, and farther along where there was no roof rock at all the vertical faces had been inscribed with seeming great care. Some of the sheltered groups were painted in various dull colors, but most of them were chiseled.

The figure [82] gives a chiseled group. It is easy to see that these are signs of no low order. Considering their great age, their exposure, many of the delicate touches must be obliterated.

The inscriptions on this ruin might possibly be the history of the defense of the crossing, the stationing of the garrison, the death of officers of rank, etc.

The following sketches of petroglyphs, with the references attached, are taken from the sketch book of Mr. F. S. Dellenbaugh, before referred to.

The petroglyph, of which Fig. 83 is a copy, appears on a horizontal rock 5 miles below the mouth of the Dirty Devil river, Utah.

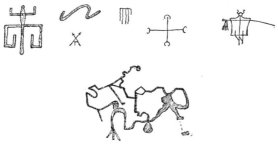

FIG. 83.—Petroglyphs on Colorado river, Utah.

The characters in Fig. 84 from rocks near the preceding group are painted red, with the imprint of a hand (on the larger figure) in white.

FIG. 84.—Petroglyphs on Colorado river, Utah.

The petroglyphs reproduced in Fig. 85 are copied from the vertical walls near the two groups immediately before mentioned.

The characters presented in Fig. 86 are copied from a vertical surface 10 by 16 feet in area and halfway up the ascent to the geodetic point west of "Windsor castle," Pipe Spring. The human forms are similar in general design to the greater number of such representations made by the Shinumo Indians.

The human forms represented in Fig. 87 are from the vicinity of Colorado river, 5 miles below the mouth of the Dirty Devil river. **Mr.**

Dellenbaugh notes that the darkest portions of the figures indicate a chiseled surface.

FIG. 85.—Petroglyphs on Colorado river, Utah.

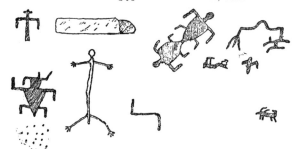

FIG. 86.—Petroglyphs at Pipe Spring, Utah.

FIG. 87.—Petroglyphs on Colorado river, Utah.

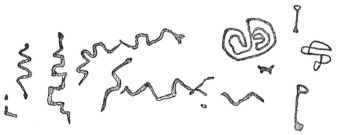

FIG. 88.—Petroglyphs on Colorado river, Utah.

Fig. 88 represents a number of petroglyphs obtained at the same locality as the one last mentioned. The greater number of the characters appear to represent snakes.

Fig. 89 shows characters from the Shinumo canyon, which, according to the draftsman's general notes, are painted.

FIG. 89.—Petroglyphs in Shinumo canyon, Utah.

VIRGINIA.

In 1886 Dr. Hoffman visited a local field 9 miles southwest of Tazewell, Tazewell county, Virginia, which can be designated as follows: The range of hills bounding the western side of the valley presents at various points low cliffs and exposures of Silurian sandstone. About 4 miles below the village, known as Knob post-office, there is a narrow ravine leading up toward a depression in the range, forming a pass to the valley beyond, near the summit of which is a large irregular exposure of rock facing west-southwest, upon the eastern extremity of which are a number of pictographs, many of which are still in good preservation. Fig. 90 is a representation. The westernmost object, i. e., the one on the extreme left, appears to be a circle about 16 inches in diameter, from the outer side of which are short radiating lines giving the whole the appearance of a sun. Beneath and to the right of this is the outline of an animal resembling a doe.

Other figures, chiefly human, follow in close succession to the eastern

FIG. 90.—Petroglyphs in Tazewell county, Virginia.

edge of the vertical face of the rock, nearly all of which present the arms in various attitudes, i. e., extended or raised as in extreme surprise or adoration. Concentric rings appear at one point, while a thunder-bird is shown not far away. About 12 feet east of this place are several figures resembling the thunder-bird.

All of the characters, with one exception, are drawn in heavy or solid lines of dark red paint, presumably a ferruginous coloring material prepared in the neighborhood, which abounds in iron compounds. The exception is one object which appears to have been black, but is now so faded or eroded as to seem dark gray.

The following account of the Tazewell county, Virginia, pictographs is taken from Coale's Life, etc., of Waters: (*a*)

In August, 1871, the writer went to visit Tazewell county by way of the salt-works. Upon this place are found those stangely painted rocks which have been a wonder and a mystery to all who have seen them. The grandfather of Gen. Bowen settled the cove in 1766, one hundred and ten years ago, and the paintings were there then, and as brilliant to-day as they were when first seen by a white man. They consist of horses, elk, deer, wolves, bows and arrows, eagles, Indians, and various other devices. The mountain upon which these rocks are based is about 1,000 feet high, and they lie in a horizontal line about half way up and are perhaps 75 feet broad upon their perpendicular face.

When it is remembered that the rock is hard, with a smooth white surface, incapable of absorbing paint, it is a mystery how the coloring has remained undimmed under the peltings of the elements for how much longer than a hundred years no one can tell. This paint is found near the rocks, and Gen. Bowen informed the writers that his grandmother used it for dyeing linsey, and it was a fadeless color.

As there was a battle fought on a neighboring mountain, between 1740 and 1750, between the Cherokees and Shawnees for the possession of a buffalo lick, the remains of the rude fortifications being still visible, it is supposed the paintings were hieroglyphics conveying such intelligence to the red man as we now communicate to each other through newspapers.

It was a perilous adventure to stand upon a narrow, inclined ledge without a shrub or a root to hold to, with from 50 to 75 feet of sheer perpendicular descent below to a bed of jagged bowlders and the home of innumerable rattlesnakes, but I didn't make it. I crawled far enough along that narrow slanting ledge with my fingers inserted in the crevices of the rocks to see most of the paintings, and then "coon'd" it back with equal care and caution.

Five miles east of the last-noted locality and 7 west of Tazewell, high up against a vertical cliff of rock, is visible a lozenge-shaped group of red and black squares, known in the locality as the " Handkerchief rock," because the general appearance of the colored markings suggests the idea of an immense bandana handkerchief spread out. The pictograph is on the same range of hills as the preceding, but neither is visible from any place near the other. The objects can not be viewed upon Handkerchief rock excepting from a point opposite to it and across the valley, as the locality is so overgrown with large trees as to obscure it from any position immediately beneath. The lozenge or diamond-shaped figure appears to cover an area about 3 feet in diameter.

WASHINGTON.

Capt. Charles Bendire, U. S. Army, in a letter dated Fort Wallawalla, Washington, May 18, 1881, mentions a discovery made by Col. Henry C. Merriam, then lieutenant-colonel Second United States Infantry, as thus quoted:

While encamped at the lower end of Lake Chelan, lat. 48° N., he made a trip to the upper end of said lake, where he found a perpendicular cliff of granite with a perfectly smooth surface, from 600 to 1,000 feet high, rising out of the lake. On the cliff he found Indian picture-writings, painted evidently at widely different periods, but evidently quite old. The oldest was from 25 to 30 feet above the present water level, and could at the time they were executed only be reached by canoe. The paintings are figures, black and red in color, and represent Indians with bows and arrows, elk, deer, bear, beaver, and fish, and are from 1 foot to 18 inches in size. There are either four or five rows of these figures, quite a number in each row. The Indians inhabiting this region know nothing of the origin of these pictures, and say that none of their people for the past four generations knew anything about them.

Since the preceding letter was written a notice of the same rock has been published, together with an illustration, by Mr. Alfred Downing, of Seattle, Washington, in "The Northwest," VII, No. 10, October, 1889, pp. 3, 4. The description, condensed, is as follows:

In that part of Washington territory until recent years known as the Moses Indian reservation lies the famous Lake Chelan, 70 miles in length with an average width of 2 miles.

About half a mile from its head, on the western shore and rising from the water, as an abrupt and precipitous wall of granite, stands "Pictured rock."

The most remarkable feature of the Chelan picture is that the figures representing Indians, bear, deer, birds, etc., are painted upon the surface of the smooth granite, nearly horizontal, but about 17 feet above the lake; the upper portion of the picture being about 2 feet higher. The figures depicted are 5 to 10 inches long.

The difference between high and low stage of water at any period during the year does not exceed 4 feet, and this high-water mark being well defined along the shore, it becomes self-evident that these signs were placed there ages ago, when the water was 17 feet higher than it is now. The granite bluff or walls in this instance are smooth, being weather and water worn, and afford no hold for hand or foot either from above or below, and from careful observation it would appear to be a physical impossibility for either a white or red man to show his artistic skill on those rocks unless at the ancient stage of water and with the aid of a canoe or a "dugout."

The paint or color used was black and red, the latter resembling venetian. How wonderfully the color has stood the test in the face of the storms to which the lake is subject is apparent; only in one or two instances does it to-day show any signs of fading or weather-wearing. The signs impressed me as intending to convey the idea of the prowess of an Indian chief in the hunt, or as being a page in the history of a a tribe, the small perpendicular strokes seen in the lower portion indicating probably the number of bear, deer, or other animals slain.

When referring, in Pacific Railroad Report, vol. I, page 411, to a locality on the Columbia river in Washington, between Yakima and Pisquouse counties, Mr. George Gibbs mentioned pecked and colored petroglyphs which he found there as follows:

It was a perpendicular rock, on the face of which were carved sundry figures, most of them intended for men. They were slightly sunk into the sandstone and colored, some black, others red, and traces of paint remained more less distinctly on all of them. These also, according to their [the Indians'] report, were the work of the ancient race; but from the soft nature of the rock, and the freshness of some of the paint, they were probably not of extreme antiquity.

For another example of petroglyphs from Washington see Fig. 679.

Mr. John Haywood (*d*) gives the following account:

In the county of Kenhaway [Kanawha] about 4 miles below the Burning spring, and near the mouth of Campbell's creek, in the state of Virginia, is a rock of great size, on which, in ancient times, the natives engraved many representations. There is the figure of almost every indigenous animal—the buffalo, the bear, the deer, the fox, the hare, and other quadrupeds of various kinds; fish of the various productions of the western waters, fowls of different descriptions, infants scalped, scalps alone, and men as large as life. The rock is in the river Kenhaway, near its northern shore, accessible only at low water unless by the aid of water craft.

The following notice of the same locality, but perhaps not of the same rock, was published by James Madison (*a*), bishop of Virginia, in 1804:

I cannot conclude this letter without mentioning another curious specimen of Indian labour, and of their progress in one of the arts. This specimen is found within 4 miles of the place whose latitude I endeavoured to take, and within 2 of what are improperly called Burning springs, upon a rock of hard freestone, which sloping to the south, touching the margin of the river, presents a flat surface of above 12 feet in length and 9 in breadth, with a plane side to the east of 8 or 9 feet in thickness.

Upon the upper surface of this rock, and also upon the side, we see the outlines of several figures, cut without relief, except in one instance, and somewhat larger than the life. The depth of the outline may be half an inch; its width three-quarters, nearly, in some places. In one line ascending from the part of the rock nearest the river there is a tortoise; a spread eagle, executed with great expression, particularly the head, to which is given a shallow relief, and a child, the outline of which is very well drawn. In a parallel line there are other figures, but among them that of a woman only can be traced. These are very indistinct. Upon the side of the rock there are two awkward figures which particularly caught my attention. One is that of a man with his arms uplifted, and hands spread out as if engaged in prayer. His head is made to terminate in a point, or rather, he has the appearance of something upon the head of a triangular or conical form; near to him is another similar figure suspended by a cord fastened to his heels. I recollected the story which Father Hennepin relates of one of the missionaries from Canada who was treated in a somewhat similar manner, but whether this piece of seemingly historical sculpture has reference to such an event can be only a matter of conjecture. A turkey, badly executed, with a few other figures may also be seen. The labour and the perseverance requisite to cut those rude figures in a rock so hard that steel appeared to make but little impression upon it, must have been great; much more so than making of enclosures in a loose and fertile soil.

Another petroglyph, a copy of which is presented in Fig. 1088, is thus described in a letter from Morgantown, West Virginia:

The famous pictured rocks on the Evansville pike, about 4 miles from this place, have been a source of wonder and speculation for more than a century, and have attracted much attention among the learned men of this country and Europe. The cliff upon which these drawings exist is of considerable size and within a short distance of the highway above mentioned. The rock is a white sandstone, which wears little from exposure to the weather, and upon its smooth surface are delineated the outlines of at least fifty [?] species of animals, birds, reptiles, and fish, embracing in the number panthers, deer, buffalo, otters, beavers, wildcats, foxes, wolves, raccoons, opossums, bears, elk, crows, eagles, turkeys, eels, various sorts of fish, large and small, snakes, etc. In the midst of this silent menagerie of specimens of the animal kingdom is the full length outline of a female form, beautiful and perfect in every respect. Interspersed among the drawings of animals, etc., are imitations of the footprints of each sort, the whole space occupied being 150 feet long by 50 feet wide. To what race the artist belonged or what his purpose was in making these rude portraits must ever remain a mystery, but the work was evidently done ages ago.

The late P. W. Norris, of the Bureau of Ethnology, reported that he found petroglyphs in many localities along the Kanawha river, West Virginia. Engravings are numerous upon smooth rocks, covered during high water, at the prominent fords in the river, as well as in the niches or long shallow caves high in the rocky cliffs of this region. Rude representations of men, animals, and some characters deemed symbolic were found, but none were observed superior to, or essentially differing from those of modern Indians.

On the rocky walls of Little Coal river, near the mouth of Big Horse creek, are cliffs which display many carvings. One of the rocks upon which a mass of characters appear, is 8 feet in length and 5 feet in height.

About 2 miles above Mount Pleasant, Mason county, on the north side of the Kanawha river, are numbers of characters, apparently totemic. These are at the foot of the hills flanking the river.

On the cliffs near the mouth of the Kanawha river, opposite Mount Carbon, Nicholas county, are numerous pictographs. These appear to be cut into the sandstone rock.

Pictographs were lately seen at various points on the banks of the Kanawha river, both above and below Charleston, but since the construction of the Chesapeake and Ohio railroad some of the rocks bearing them have been destroyed. About 6 miles above Charleston there was formerly a rock lying near its water's edge upon which, it is reported by old residents, were depicted the outline of a bear, turkey tracks, and other markings. Tradition told that this was a boat or canoe landing, used by the Indians in their travels when proceeding southward. The tribe was not designated. From an examination of the locality it was learned that this rock had been broken and used in the construction of buildings. It is said that a trail passing there led southward, and at a point 10 miles below the Kanawha river stood several large trees upon which were marks of red ocher or some similar pigment, at which point the trail spread or branched out in two directions, one leading southward into Virginia, the other southwest toward Kentucky.

On a low escarpment of sandstone facing Little Coal river, 6 or 8 miles above its confluence with Coal river and about 18 miles south of the Kanawha river, are depicted the outlines of animals, such as the deer, panther (?), etc., and circles, delineated in dark red, but rather faint from disintegration of the surface. The characters are similar in general appearance to those in Tazewell county, Virginia, and appear as if they might have been made by the same tribe. There are no peculiarities in the topography of the surrounding region that would suggest the idea of their having served as topographic indications, but they rather appear to be a record of a hunting party, and to designate the kinds of game abounding in the region.

Mr. L. V. McWhorter reports pictographs in a cave near Berlin, Lewis county, West Virginia. No details are given.

A petroglyph found in a rock shelter in West Virginia is also presented in Pl. XXXI.

WISCONSIN.

A large number of glyphs are incised on the face of a rock near Odanah, now a village of the Ojibwa Indians, 12 miles northeast from Ashland, on the south shore of lake Superior, near its western extremity. The characters were easily cut on the soft stone, so were also easily worn by the weather, and in 1887 were nearly indistinguishable. Many of them appeared to be figures of birds. An old Ojibwa Indian in the vicinity told the present writer that the site of the rock was

Fig. 91.—Petroglyphs in Brown's cave, Wisconsin.

formerly a well-known halting place and rendezvous, and that on the arrival of a party, or even of a single individual, the appropriate totemic mark or marks were cut on the rock, much as white men register their names at a hotel.

The Pictured cave of La Crosse valley, called Brown's cave, is described by Rev. Edward Brown (*a*) as follows:

This curious cavern is situated in the town of Barre, 4 miles from West Salem and 8 miles from La Crosse.   *   *   *

Before the landslide it was an open shelter cavern, 15 feet wide at the opening and 7 feet at the back end; greatest width, 16 feet; average, 13; length, 30 feet; height, 13 feet, and depth of excavation after clearing out the sand of the landslide, 5 feet. The pictures are mostly of the rudest kind, but differing in degree of skill. Except several bisons, a lynx, rabbit, otter, badger, elk, and heron, it is perhaps impossible to determine with certainty what were intended or whether they represented large or small animals, no regard being had to their relative sizes.

[Examples of the figures are here presented as Fig. 91.]

Perhaps *a* indicates a bison or buffalo, and is the best executed picture of the collection. Its size is 19 inches long by 15½ inches from tip of the horns to the feet.

b represents a hunter, with a boy behind him, in the act of shooting an animal with his bow and arrow weapon. The whole representation is 25 inches long; the animal from tip of tail to end of horn or proboscis 12 inches, and from top of head to feet 7 inches; the hunter 11 inches high, the boy 4½.

c represents a wounded animal, with the arrow or weapon near the wound. This figure is 21¾ inches from the lower extremity of the nose to the tip of the tail, 8¾ inches from fore shoulders to front feet, and 8 inches from the rump to the hind feet. The weapon is 4½ inches long by 5 inches broad from the tip of one prong or barb to that of the other.

d represents a chief with eight plumes and a war club, 11 inches from top of head to the lower extremity, and 6¾ inches from the tip of the upper finger to the end of the opposite arm; the war club 6½ inches long.

Dr. Hoffman made a visit to this cave in August, 1888, to compare the pictographic characters with others of apparently similar outline and of known signification. He found but a limited number of the figures distinct, and these only in part, owing to the rapid disintegration of the sandstone upon which they were drawn. Many names and inscriptions had been incised in the soft surface by visitors, who also, by means of the smoke of candles, added grotesque and meaningless figures over and between the original paintings, so as to seriously injure the latter.

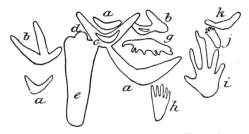

Fig. 92.—Petroglyphs at Trempealeau, Wisconsin.

Mr. T. H. Lewis (*d*) describes the petroglyphs, a part of which is reproduced in Fig. 92, as follows:

Last November my attention was called to some rock sculptures located about 2½ miles northwest from Trempealeau, Wisconsin. There is at the point in question an exposed ledge of the Potsdam sandstone extending nearly one-eighth of a mile along the east side of the lower mouth of the Trempealeau river, now known as the bay. Near its north end there is a projection extending out about 7 feet from the top of the ledge and overhanging the base about 10 feet. The base of the ledge is 40 feet back from the shore, and the top of the cliff at this point is 30 feet above the water. On the face of the projection, and near the top, are the sculpture figures referred to.

The characters designated *a a* are two so-called canoes, somewhat crescent-shaped, but with some variation in outline; *b* has the same form, but the additional upright portion overlaps it; *c* and *d* are also of the same form as *a*, but *c* is cut in the bottom of *d; e* probably represents a fort, and its length is 18½ inches; *f* is a nondescript, and it partly overlaps *d; g* is a nondescript four-legged animal, its length in a straight line from the end of the nose to the tip of the tail being 10½ inches; *h* may be intended to represent a foot, but possibly it may be a hand; it is 7¼ inches in length; *i* is an outspread hand, a little over 13 inches long; *j* undoubtedly represents a foot and is 4½ inches long; *k k* are of the same class as *a*.

The figures are not mere outlines, but intaglio, varying in depth from a quarter of an inch to fully 1 inch. Although the surface of the rock is rough the intaglios were rubbed perfectly smooth after they had been engraved by pecking or cutting.

WYOMING.

Several pictographs in Wyoming are described by Capt. William A. Jones, U. S. Army (a). They are reproduced here as Figs. 93, 94, and 95.

Fig. 93, found in the Wind river valley, Wyoming, was interpreted by members of a Shoshoni and Banak delegation to Washington in 1880 as "an Indian killed another." The latter is very roughly delineated in the horizontal figure, but is also represented by the line under the hand of the upright figure, meaning the same dead person. At the right is the scalp taken and the two feathers showing the dead warrior's rank. The arm nearest the prostrate foe shows the gesture for killed; concept, to put down, flat.

FIG. 93.—Petroglyph in Wind river valley, Wyoming.

The same gesture appears in Fig. 94, from the same authority and locality. The scalp is here held forth, and the numeral (1) is indicated by the lowest stroke.

FIG. 94.—Petroglyph in Wind river valley, Wyoming.

Fig. 95, from the same locality and authority, was also interpreted by the Shoshoni and Banak. It appears from their description that a Blackfoot had attacked the habitation of some of his own people. The right-hand upper figure represents his horse, with the lance suspended from the side. The lower figure illustrates the log house built against a stream. The dots are the prints of the horse's hoofs, while the two lines running outward from the upper inclosure show that two thrusts of the lance were made over the wall of the house, thus killing the occupant and securing two bows and five arrows, as represented in the left-hand group. The right-hand figure of that group shows the hand raised in the attitude of making the gesture for kill.

The Blackfeet, according to the interpreters, were the only Indians in the locality mentioned who constructed log houses, and therefore the drawing becomes additionally interesting, as an attempt appears to have been made to illustrate the crossing of the logs at the corners, the gesture for which (log house) is as follows:

Both hands are held edgewise before the body, palms facing, spread the fingers, and place those of one hand into the spaces between those of the other, so that the tips of each protrude about an inch beyond.

Fig. 95.—Petroglyphs in Wind river valley. Wyoming.

Another and more important petroglyph was discovered on Little Popo-Agie, northwestern Wyoming, by members of Capt. Jones's party in 1873. The glyphs are upon a nearly vertical wall of the yellow sandstone in the rear of Murphy's ranch, and appear to be of some antiquity. Further remarks, with specimens of the characters, are presented below in this paper. (See Fig. 1091.)

Dr. William H. Corbusier, U. S. Army, in a letter to the writer, mentions the discovery of drawings on a sandstone rock near the headwaters of Sage creek, in the vicinity of Fort Washakie, Wyoming, and gives a copy which is presented as Fig. 96. Dr. Corbusier remarks that neither the Shoshoni nor the Arapaho Indians know who made the drawings. The two chief figures appear to be those of the human form, with the hands and arms partly uplifted the whole being inclosed above and on either side by an irregular line.

FIG. 96.—Petroglyph near Sage creek, Wyoming.

The method of grouping, together with various accompanying appendages, as irregular lines, spirals, etc., observed in Dr. Corbusier's drawing, show great similarity to the Algonquian type, and resemble

FIG. 97.—Petroglyph near Sage creek, Wyoming.

some engravings found near the Wind river mountains, which were the work of Blackfeet (Satsika) Indians, who, in comparatively recent times, occupied portions of the country in question, and probably also sketched the designs near Fort Washakie.

Fig. 97 is also reported from the same locality.

SECTION 3.

MEXICO.

No adequate attention can be given in the present paper to the distribution and description of the petroglyphs of Mexico. In fact very little accurate information is accessible regarding them. The distinguished explorer, Mr. A. Bandelier, in a conversation mentioned that he had sketched but not published two petroglyphs in Sonora. One, very large and interesting, was at Cara Pintada, 3 miles southwest of Huassavas, and a smaller one was at Las Flechas, 1 mile west of Huassavas. He also sketched one in Chihuahua on the trail from Casas Grandes to the Cerro de Montezuma. From the accounts of persons met in his Mexican travels he gave it as his opinion that a large number of petroglyphs still remained in the region of the Sierra Madre.

The following mention of the paintings of the ancient inhabitants of Lower California is translated from an anonymous account, in Documentos para la Historia de Mexico (*a*), purporting to have been written in 1790:

Throughout civilized California, from south to north, and especially in the caves and smooth rocks, there remain various rude paintings. Notwithstanding their disproportion and lack of art, the representations of men, fish, bows and arrows, can be distinguished and with them different kind of strokes, something like characters. The colors of these paintings are of four kinds; yellow, a reddish color, green and black. The greater part of them are painted in high places, and from this it is inferred by some that the old tradition is true, that there were giants among the ancient Californians. Be this as it may, in the Mission of Santiago, which is at the south, was discovered on a smooth rock of great height, a row of hands stamped in red. On the high cliffs facing the shore are seen fish painted in various shapes and sizes, bows, arrows, and some unknown characters. In other parts are Indians armed with bows and arrows, and various kinds of insects, snakes, and mice, with lines and characters of other forms. On a flat rock about 2 yards in length were stamped insignia or escutcheons of rank and inscriptions of various characters.

Towards Purmo, about 30 leagues beyond the Mission of Santiago del Sur, is a bluff 8 yards in height and on the center of it is seen an inscription which resembles Gothic letters interspersed with Hebrew and Chaldean characters [?].

Though the Californian Indians have often been asked concerning the significance of the figures, lines, and characters, no satisfactory answer has been obtained. The most that has been established by their information is that the paintings were their predecessors, and that they are absolutely ignorant of the signification of them. It is evident that the paintings and drawings of the Californians are significant symbols and landmarks by which they intended to leave to posterity the memory, either of their establishment in this country, or of certain wars or political or natural triumphs. These pictures are not like those of the Mexicans, but might have the same purpose.

Several petroglyphs in Sonora are described and illustrated infra in Chapter XX on Special Comparisons. The following copies of petroglyphs are presented here as specimens and are markedly different from those in the northwestern states of Mexico, which represent the Aztec culture.

The description of Fig. 98 is extracted from Viages de Guillelmo Dupaix (a):

Going from the town of Tlalmanalco to that of Mecamecan, at a distance of a league to the east of the latter and in the confines of the estate of Señor Don José Tepatolco, is an isolated rock of granitic stone artificially cut into a conical form with a series of six steps cut in the solid rock itself on the eastern side, the summit forming a platform or horizontal section suitable for the purpose of observing the stars at all points of the compass. It is, therefore, most evident that this ancient

FIG. 98.—Petroglyphs in Mexico.

monument or observatory was employed solely for astronomical observations, and it is further proved by various hieroglyphs cut in the south side of the cone; but the most interesting feature of this side is the figure of a man standing upright and in profile directing his gaze to the east with the arms raised, holding in the hands a tube or species of optical instrument. Beneath his feet is seen a carved frieze with six compartments or squares and other symbols of a celestial nature are engraved on their surfaces, evidently the product of observation and calculation. Some of them have connection with those found symmetrically arranged in circles on the ancient Mexican calendar, exposed in this capital to general admiration. In front of the observer is a rabbit seated and confronted by two parallel rows of numerical figures; lastly two other symbols relating to the same science are seen at the back.

Prof. Daniel G. Brinton (*a*), gives an account of the illustration here produced on Pl. xiv A, which may be thus condensed:

The "Stone of the Giants" at Escamela near the city of Orizaba, Mexico, has been the subject of much discussion. Father Damaso Sotomayor sees in the inscribed figures a mystical allusion to the coming of Christ to the Gentiles and to the occurrences supposed in Hebrew myth to have taken place in the Garden of Eden. This stone was examined by Capt. Dupaix in the year 1808 and is figured in the illustrations to his voluminous narrative. The figure he gives [now presented as B on Pl. xiv] is, however, so erroneous that it yields but a faint idea of the real character and meaning of the drawing. It omits the ornament on the breast and also the lines along the right of the giant's face, which as I shall show are distinctive traits. It gives him a girdle where none is delineated, and the relative size and proportions of all the three figures are quite distorted.

The rock on which the inscription is found is roughly triangular in shape, presenting a nearly straight border of 30 feet on each side. It is hard and uniform in texture and of a dark color. The length or height of the principal figure is 27 feet, and the incised lines which designate the various objects are deeply and clearly cut.

I now approach the decipherment of the inscriptions. Any one versed in the signs of the Mexican calendar will at once perceive that it contains the date of a certain year and day. On the left of the giant is seen a rabbit surrounded with ten circular depressions. These depressions are the well-known Aztec marks for numerals, and the rabbit represents one of the four astronomic signs by which they adjusted their chronologic cycles of fifty-two years. The stone bears a carefully dated record, with year and day clearly set forth. The year is represented to the left of the figure and is that numbered "ten" under the sign of the rabbit; the day of the year is number "one" under the sign of the fish.

These precise dates recurred once, and only once, every fifty-two years, and had recurred only once between the year of our era, 1450, and the Spanish conquest of Mexico in 1519–'20. Within the period named the year "ten rabbit" of the Aztec calendar corresponded with the year 1502 of the Gregorian calendar. It is more difficult to fix the day, but it is, I think, safe to say that, according to the most probable computations, the day, "one fish," occurred in the first month of the year 1502, which month coincided in whole or in part with our February.

Such is the date on the inscription. Now, what is intimated to have occurred on that date? The clew to this is furnished by the figure of the giant. It represents an ogre of horrid mien with a death's-head grin and formidable teeth, his hair wild and long, the locks falling down upon the neck. Suspended on the breast as an ornament is the bone of a human lower jaw, with its incisor teeth. The left leg is thrown forward as in the act of walking, and the arms are uplifted, the hands open, and the fingers extended as at the moment of seizing the prey or the victim. The lines about the umbilicus represent the knot of the girdle which supported the *maxtli* or breechcloth.

There is no doubt as to which personage of the Aztec pantheon this fear-inspiring figure represents. It is *Tzontemoc Mictlantecutli*, "the Lord of the Realm of the Dead, He of the Falling Hair," the dread god of death and the dead. His distinctive marks are there, the death's-head, the falling hair, the jaw bone, the terrible aspect, the giant size.

We possess several chronicles of the empire before Cortes destroyed it, written in the hieroglyphs which the inventive genius of the natives had devised. Taking two of these chronicles, one known as the Codex Telleriano-Remensis, the other as the Codex Vaticanus, I turn to the year numbered "ten" under the sign of the rabbit and I find that both present the same record which I copy in the following figure.

The figure so copied is entitled "Extract from the Vatican Codex," which is a slight error. It is a copy from the Codex Telleriano-Remensis, Kingsborough, I, Pt. 4, p. 23, year 1502, which is here reproduced as Fig. 99. The record in the Vatican Codex, Kingsborough, II, p. 130, differs in some unimportant details. It may also be noted that in the text relating to the Codex Telleriano-Remensis, Kingsborough, VI, p. 141, the word Ahuitzotl is given as "the name of an aquatic animal famous in Mexican mythology." The present opportunity is embraced to recognize the acumen displayed by Prof. Brinton in his interpretation of the petroglyph. He proceeds as follows:

FIG. 99.—The Emperor Ahuitzotzin.

The sign of the year (the rabbit) is shown merely by his head for brevity. The ten dots, which give its number, are beside it. Immediately beneath is a curious quadruped, with what are intended as water-drops dripping from him. The animal is the hedgehog, and the figure is to be constructed *iconomatically;* that is, it must be read as a rebus through the medium of the Nahuatl language. In that language water is *atl,* in composition *a,* and hedgehog is *uitzotl.* Combine these and you get *ahuitzotl,* or, with the reverential termination, *ahuitzotzin.* This was the name of the ruler or emperor, if you allow the word, of ancient Mexico before the accession to the throne of that Montezuma whom the Spanish *conquistador,* Cortes, put to death.

Returning to the page from the chronicle, we observe that the hieroglypn of Ahuitzotzin is placed immediately over a corpse swathed in its mummy cloths, as was the custom of interment with the highest classes in Mexico. This signifies that the death of Ahuitzotzin took place in that year. Adjacent to it is the figure of his

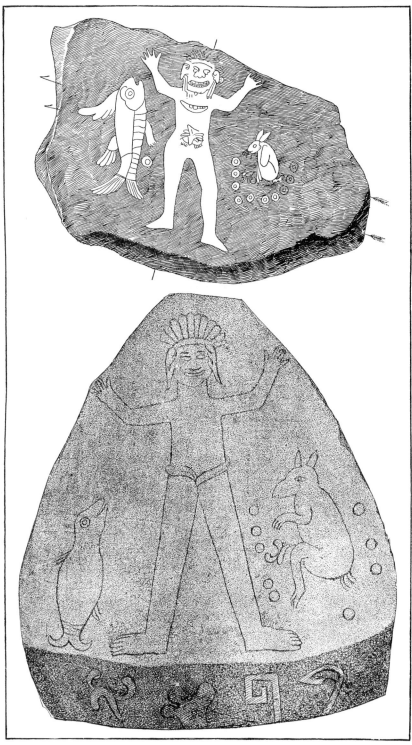

THE STONE OF THE GIANTS, MEXICO.

successor, his name iconomatically represented by the headdress of the nobles, the *tecuhtli*, giving the middle syllables of "*Mo-tecuh-zoma*." No doubt is left that *La Piedra de los Gigantes* of Escamela is a necrologic tablet commemorating the death of the Emperor Ahuitzotzin, some time in February, 1502.

Mr. Eugene Boban (*a*) mentions manuscript copies, dating from the beginning of the century, of various sculptured stones in Mexico. These sculpturings represent native ideographic characters, among them the *teocalli*, the *tepetl*, the sign *ollin*, etc.

On several of the plates which compose this collection are notes indicating the place where the monument, fragment, or ruin is found, from which the characters are copied; for example, one of them bears the note: "de la calle R¹ de la villa de Cuernabaca." Several others bear annotations which show that they have been copied in the cemetery, in the streets of that town, or in its environs.

Aside from these notes the plates are not accompanied by any information which could give a trace of the person who drew them, or the purpose for which they were intended.

The same author (*b*) describes a large sculptured stone of Mexico, the designs on which have been reproduced in paintings on deerskin. After giving a detailed description of the copied MS. he speaks of the stone as follows:

We deem it of interest to give some notes concerning the famous cylindrical stone, both sculptured and painted, known by the name *Teocuauhxicalli* (the sacred drinking vase of the eagles) on which are found the themes of all the designs which have been above described. This stone, buried at the time of the Spanish Conquest, was discovered in the first half of this century at the close of a series of excavations made in the soil of the Place d'Armes, Mexico. The director of the national museum, who was then M. Rafael Gondra, contented himself with taking the dimensions and making a hurried sketch of it. It was then reinterred, as the necessary funds were lacking to exhume it entirely and transport it to the museum.

The name Teocuauhxicalli is composed of: *Teotl*, god; *cuauhtli*, eagle, and *xicalli*, hemispherical vase formed from the half of a gourd. It may be translated by, "The vase of god and the eagles," or, rather, "The sacred drinking cup of the eagles."

"The Mexican monarch Axayacatl, jealous of his predecessor Motecuhzoma I, took down the Teocuauhxicalli which was in the upper part of the Great Temple of Mexico, and replaced it by another, sculptured by his order;" so says the eminent Mexican archæologist and historian, Don Manuel Orozco y Berra, in his excellent work, Historia Antigua y de la Conquesta de Mexico (t. III, p. 348). This monument was also dedicated to the god of war, Huitzilopochtli.

According to Duran and Tezozomoc, those stones on which gods were represented were designated by the name Teocuauhxicalli; i. e., divine cuauhxicalli. They belonged to the class of painted stones, for they were covered with several colors.

Orozco y Berra adds the following: "It is evident that the figures sculptured and painted do not represent armed warriors preparing for combat. On the contrary, we see that they represent gods. Among them is found Huitzilopochtli (god of war) with his arms and attributes, having before him another deity or high priest who holds in his hands the emblems of the holocaust.

"The figures of the upper part are not fighting and could not have known how to fight, if we judge by their positions; the chest is turned back, the face raised toward the sky, in which appears an object which resembles the astronomical sign *cipactli*.

"Everywhere on the surface of this stone are noticed symbols, birds, quadrupeds, fantastic reptiles, signs of the sun, days, months, and a quantity of objects whose character is imitated in manuscripts and rituals. There can be no doubt that we are in the presence of a monument devoted to the gods and bearing legends relative to their worship. M. the minister of Fomento, D. Vicente Rivera Palacio, in 1877 made several attempts at excavation in the Plaza Mayor of Mexico, to recover this important monument, but all search remained unfruitful."

This stone is supposed to be buried beneath the Place d'Armes at Mexico.

Mexican petroglyphs are also discussed and figured by Chavero (*a*).

It would seem from these and other descriptions of and allusions to petroglyphs in Mexico, that at the time of the Spanish conquest they were extant in large numbers, though now seldom found. Perhaps the Spaniards destroyed them in the same spirit which led them to burn up many of the Mexican pictographs on paper and other substances.

A number of illustrations of the Mexican pictographic writings are given below under various headings.

SECTION 4.

WEST INDIES.

The valuable paper of A. L. Pinart (*a*), giving a description of the petroglyphs found by him in the Greater and Lesser Antilles, is received too late for reproduction of the illustrations. He explored a number of the groups of the West Indies with varying success, but found that the island of Puerto Rico was the one which now furnishes the greatest amount of evidence of development in the pictographic art. His marks translated with condensation appear below.

PUERTO RICO.

The first petroglyph to be mentioned is found at la Cueva del Islote, on Punta Braba, about 5 leagues east from Arecibo and on the north side of the island of Puerto Rico. The grotto is found in an immense blackish mass of igneous rock, forming a point projecting into the sea, which beats furiously against it; it communicates with the sea at the foot, and the water entering this passage, which is quite narrow, produces a terrific roaring followed soon after by veritable thunder claps. The people of the neighborhood have a superstitious fear of it, and it is only with great difficulty that anyone can be found to accompany one there. The entrance on the land side is toward the east—a yawning crevasse, filled partly with rubbish and partly by the stunted vegetation of the coast. On penetrating to the interior we find, after following a short but wide passage, a pyriform chamber 20 meters in diameter. In the ceiling a very narrow crack admits a ray of light which, reflected in the water of the sea, filling the bottom of the cave, produces a bluish twilight. Notwithstanding this twilight, we are obliged to carry torches to distinguish objects. All around us, but especially over the point where the sea enters in, are to be seen the inscriptions represented here. The incisions are very deep, and the edges are generally dulled by the blows of the hammer; in certain spots, toward the lower part of the grotto, several inscriptions are partially effaced by the action of the sea, but those of the upper part are in a remarkable state of preservation. Beneath certain principal figures of the groups are little circular basin-like depressions cut in the rock with a trench running down toward the bottom.

I will not attempt here to give a formal explanation of these inscriptions, but may we not regard the spot in which they are found as having served for a rendezvous for the ancient Borrinqueños where they performed their sacrifices or the ceremonies of their religion? On the other hand, the appearance of these inscriptions is very peculiar. One of them might be considered a representation of those little figurines and statuettes of stone found in Mexico, in Mixteca, and in the country to the south. In another a head is curiously decorated with a diadem of feathers, and apparently represents one presiding at a feast served in the small circular basin set before him. The most noticeable thing in this group of inscriptions is the frequency of the grinning faces in a circle, often alone, often accompanied by two others placed at the sides, which are universally met with in every inscription found in the Greater and Lesser Antilles. The same may be said of the human figure apparently swaddled in cloths like a very young infant, the head and body more or less decorated, which is also very frequently found.

Following these petroglyphs of Islote, we present a list of others discovered at Puerto Rico, hastily describing them and giving a particular description only of those which are of the greatest interest.

In the above-mentioned grotto of Cueva de los Archillas, near the village of Ciales, we observed the curious figures bearing traces of a crown and peculiar ear ornaments. In la Cueva de los Conejos, some distance from Arecibo, on the road from Utauado, we found a figure partly incised and partly painted in a dark red; it is very artistically fashioned, and represents the famous "guava," the monster spider of the Greater Antilles, of which the natives have a great dread. It is probable that the ancient Borrinqueños also considered it with a certain awe, and we find images of the same animal in la Cueva del Templo on the coast of Haiti, at Santo Domingo. A solitary rock of a reddish color, in a field of the hacienda of Don Pedro Pavez at la Carolina, a short distance from the Rio Pedras, bears a series of grimacing faces in circles. On a granitic rock of large dimensions, superimposed on a heap of rocks of the same character, in the midst of a grove of Indian trees and at the entrance of the Cano del Indio into Rio la Ceiba, near Fajardo, on the east side, are found three swaddled human figures, the heads decorated with various ornaments. On a black rock in the Rio Arriba, one of the branches of the Rio de la Ceiba, is a petroglyph which presents but little that is of interest.

On the Loma Muñoz, near the Rio Arriba above mentioned, and on the summit of the hill, stands a dark rock with smooth face protected by another mass of rock, forming a sort of shelter on which is an inscription composed of a number of incised grinning faces. At the confluence of the Rio Blanco and the Rio de la Ceiba, in the district of Fajardo, is a series of violent rapids formed by immense rocks of a granitic character, on which are cut a large number of other grimacing faces and also some swaddled figures, and other incisions which are not of interest.

BAHAMA ISLANDS.

Lady Edith Blake, wife of Sir Henry Arthur Blake, formerly governor of the Bahama islands, has kindly furnished the following information and sketches (Figs. 100, 101, and 102), relating to petroglyphs in the Bahama islands. Lady Blake says:

The carvings are on the walls of an "Indian hole," also called Hartford cave, in the northern shore of a small island in Rum Cay, one of the Bahama group. Rum Cay measures 5 miles from north to south and about 8 or 9 from east to west. It lies 20 miles northwest of Watlings island, the San Salvador of Columbus.

The cave is situated on the seashore about a mile and a half from the western point of the island to the eastward of a bluff, close to which is a "puffing hole," through which the waves blow when the seas roll in from the north. The cave is semicircular in shape and about 20 yards in depth, and is partially filled with debris of rocks, earth, and sand.

Like all rocks of which the Bahamas are formed, those in Hartford cave are a mixture of coral, detritus, and shell, very rough and full of cracks and indentations, and in this cave, from the constant damp of filtration and spray, the walls were coated with a deposit of lime and salt, so that it would be impossible to say if the carvings had been colored. If ever they had been, any traces of coloring must long have

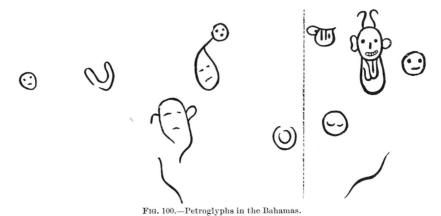

FIG. 100.—Petroglyphs in the Bahamas.

disappeared. Besides the markings copied there were others scattered over the walls of the cave, most of which were circles apparently resembling human faces. Unfortunately, we neglected to measure the carvings, but I should judge the circles or faces to be 10 inches or more across, while others of the figures must have been a foot

FIG. 101.—Petroglyphs in the Bahamas.

and a half in length, and the markings must have been nearly half an inch in depth, cut into the face of the rock, and seemed to us such as might have been made with a sharp stone implement. Although we visited numerous caves in the various islands of the Bahamas, in no other did we find any appearance of markings or carvings on the walls, nor could we hear of any reported to have such markings.

The absence of any traces of carvings in other caves whose situation was better adapted for the preservation of markings, had such ever existed, and the proof that their contents afforded that most of those caves had been known to the Lucayans and used by them as burying places or otherwise, and the close proximity of Hartford cave to the sea, taken in connection with the great number of markings on its walls, led me to think that possibly this cave had been the resort of the marauding tribes whom the Lucayans gave Columbus to understand were their enemies, and who were in the habit of making war upon them; and if so, the Caribs, or whatever tribe it may have been, had left these rock markings as mementos of their various expeditions and guides to succeeding ones.

The above-mentioned petroglyphs bear a remarkable similarity to those in British Guiana figured and described below, and the authorship would seem to relate to the same group of natives, the Caribs.

Fɪɢ. 102.—Petroglyphs in the Bahamas.

GUADELOUPE.

In the Guesde collection of antiquities, described in the Smithsonian report for 1884, p. 834, Fig. 208, here reproduced as Fig. 103, is an inscribed slab found in Guadeloupe. It weighs several tons and it is impossible to remove it. In the vicinity are to be seen many other rocks bearing inscriptions, but this is the most elaborate of the group.

The inscriptions may be compared with those from Guiana presented in this work.

ARUBA.

Pinart (*b*) gives the following account, translated and condensed:

The island of Aruba forms one of the group of the islands of Curaçao, on the north coast of Venezuela. This group consists of three principal islands, Curaçao, Buen Ayre, Aruba, and some isolated rocks. It belongs to Holland.

Aruba is the most western island of the group and is situated opposite the peninsula of Paraguana, on the mainland. The distance between the two is about 10 leagues, and from the island the shores of the continent can be seen very distinctly.

These islands, at the time of the discovery by the Spaniards, were inhabited by an Indian race which has left numerous traces of its occupancy; pottery, stone objects, petroglyphs, etc., are met with in large numbers in Oruba and in a less quantity on Buen Ayre and Curaçao. * * * These petroglyphs are quite different in character from those which I have recently described in a brief study of the Greater and Lesser Antilles, and their appearance brings to mind those found in Orinoco, in Venezuela, in the peninsula of Paraguana, on the border of the Magdalena river, and as far as Chiriqui. They differ from these, however, in several respects, and especially in that they are almost always multi-colored. The colors usually employed are red, blue, a yellowish white, and black.   They are, moreover, painted and not cut in the rock: They show the same degree of variance as I have already noticed in North America—in Sonora, Arizona, and Chihuahua—between the petroglyphs which I have designated as Pimos, which are always incised, and those in the mountains which I designated as Comanche, and which are always painted and in many colors.   The petroglyphs are, as has already been said, very numerous on the island of Aruba.   I have personal knowledge of thirty, but, according to my friend Père van Kolwsjk, there must be more than fifty.   The most important groups are as follows:

(1) *Avikok.*   An enormous dark rock forms the summit of a wooded knob, and in this rock are two large cavities, one above the other, on the walls of which are the petroglyphs represented.

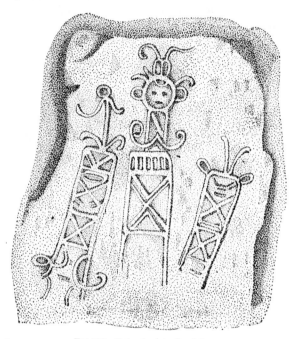

Fig. 103.—Petroglyph in Guadeloupe.

(2) *Fontein.*   On the border of a fresh-water lagoon, a short distance from the northeast part of the island, near the sea, is a grotto of coralline origin, whose walls are of remarkable whiteness.   This grotto is composed of a principal passage, quite wide, cut off toward the lower end by a row of stalactites and stalagmites, which, joining together, form a curious grimacing figure.   On the wall to the left, as we look toward the bottom of the grotto, are found some petroglyphs.   They are well preserved, thanks to their situation and the shelter from inclement weather, and they show no indication of painting, being distinctly traced on the walls.

(3) *Chiribana.*   On some granitic spurs of a hill of the same name are found curious petroglyphs.

(4) At Lero de Wajukan, near Avikok, and at the foot of a hill, petroglyphs are found on some blocks of granite.   I notice specially the human figure which in the original is outlined in red and bears on the shoulder a hatchet of the Carib type with a haft.

(5) At Ayo I discovered petroglyphs with figures in blue and red.

(6) At Woeboeri inscriptions are found on the wall of an immense mass of granite.

(7) Some petroglyphs on the walls of a grotto at Karasito.

CHAPTER III.

PETROGLYPHS IN CENTRAL AND SOUTH AMERICA.

Some writers have endeavored to draw definite ethnic distinctions between the pre-Columbian inhabitants of North America and those farther south. The opinions and theories which have favored such discriminations have originated in error and ignorance. Until lately there has been but scanty scientific investigation of the peoples of Central and South America and but a limited exploration of the regions now or formerly occupied by them. The latest opinion of the best ethnologists is that no sufficient reason can be shown for separate racial classification of the aborigines of the three Americas. The examples of petroglyphs now presented from Central and South America, all of which are selected as typical, show remarkable similarity to some of those above illustrated and described, especially to those in California, New Mexico, and Arizona. This topic is further discussed under the heading of Special Comparison, Chapter xx, infra.

SECTION I.

PETROGLYPHS IN CENTRAL AMERICA.

NICARAGUA.

Dr. J. F. Bransford (*a*) gives the following account:

On a hillside on the southern end of the island of Ometepec, Nicaragua, about 1½ miles east of Point San Ramon, are many irregular blocks of basalt with marks and figures cut on them. The hillside faces east, and is about half a mile from the lake. There were similar markings on many of the shore rocks, which, in May, were partially covered with water, notwithstanding that that was about the driest season. These markings were excavated about half an inch in depth and a little more in width. Human faces and spiral lines predominated. There was also a crown, a representation of a monkey, and many irregular figures.

Fig. 104.—Petroglyphs in Nicaragua.

Several illustrations from these rocks are presented, infra, in Figs. 1102 and 1103, and one is reproduced in this connection as Fig. 104.

141

GUATEMALA.

The following extract is taken from the work of Dr. S. Habel (*a*):

Santa Lucia is a village in the Republic of Guatemala, in the Department of Esquintla, near the base of the Volcano del Fuego, at the commencement of the inclined plane which extends from the mountain range to the coast of the Pacific Ocean.   *   *   *

The sculptured slabs are in the vicinity of the village.   The greater number of them form an extended heap, rendering it probable that there are others hidden from view that more extended researches would reveal.   *   *   *   All the sculptures, with the exception of three statues, are in low relief, nearly all being in cavo-relievo, that is, surrounded by a raised border, the height of which indicates the elevation of the relief.   The same kind of relief was practiced by the ancient Assyrians and Egyptians.

In seven instances the sculpture represents a person adoring a deity of a different theological conception in each case.   One of these seems to represent the sun, another the moon, while in the remaining five it is impossible to define their character.   All these deities are represented by a human figure, of which only the head, arms, and breast are correctly portrayed, proving that the religious conceptions had risen to anthropomorphism, while the idols of the nations of Central America and Mexico, which have previously come to our knowledge, are represented by disfigured human forms or grotesque images.

Four of the other sculptures represent allegorical subjects; two of them the myth of the griffin, the bird of the sun.

The slabs on which the low reliefs are sculptured are of various sizes; the greater number of these, like those representing the deities, are 12 feet in length, 3 feet in width, and 2 feet in thickness.   Nine feet of the upper part of these stones are occupied by the sculptures, while the lower 3 feet appear to have served as a base.

Several illustrations of these rock sculptures are presented, infra, as Figs. 1235 and 1236.   It is evident that these very large slabs received their markings when they were in the locality in which they are now found so can be classed geographically.

SECTION 2.

SOUTH AMERICA.

Alexander von Humboldt (*a*) gives general remarks, now condensed, upon petroglyphs in South America:

In the interior of South America, between the second and fourth degrees of north latitude, a forest-covered plain is inclosed by four rivers, the Orinoco, the Atabapo, the Rio Negro, and the Cassiquiare.   In this district are found rocks of granite and of syenite, covered with colossal symbolical figures of crocodiles and tigers, and drawings of household utensils, and of the sun and moon.   The tribes nearest to its boundaries are wandering naked savages, in the lowest stages of human existence, and far removed from any thoughts of carving hieroglyphics on rocks.   One may trace in South America an entire zone, extending through more than 8° of longitude, of rocks so ornamented, viz, from the Rupuniri, Essequibo, and the mountains of Pacaraima, to the banks of the Orinoco and of the Yupura.   These carvings may belong to very different epochs, for Sir Robert Schomburgk even found on the Rio Negro representations of a Spanish galiot, which must have been of a later date that the beginning of the sixteenth century; and this in a wilderness where the natives were probably as rude then as at the present time.   Some miles from Encaramada there rises in the middle of the savannah the rock Tepu-Mereme, or painted rock. It shows several figures of animals and symbolical outlines which resemble much those observed by us at some distance above Encaramada, near Caycara. Rocks thus marked are found between the Cassiquiare and the Atabapo and, what is particularly remarkable, 560 geographical miles farther to the east, in the solitudes of Parime. Nicholas Hortsmann found on the banks of the Rupunuri, at the spot where the river winding between the Macarana mountains forms several small cascades, and before arriving at the district immediately surrounding lake Amucu, "rocks covered with figures," or, as he says in Portuguese, "de varias letras." We were shown at the rock of Culimacari, on the banks of the Cassiquiare, signs which were called characters, arranged in lines, but they were only ill-shaped figures of heavenly bodies, boa-serpents, and the utensils employed in preparing manioc meal. I have never found among these painted rocks (piedras pintadas) any symmetrical arrangement or any regular even-spaced characters. I am therefore disposed to think that the word "letras," in Hortsmann's journal, must not be taken in the strictest sense.

Schomburgk saw and described other petroglyphs on the banks of the Essequibo, near the cascade of Warraputa. Neither promises nor threats could prevail on the Indians to give a single blow with a hammer to these rocks, the venerable monuments of the superior mental cultivation of their predecessors. They regard them as the work of the Great Spirit, and the different tribes whom we met with, though living at a great distance, were nevertheless acquainted with them. Terror was painted on the faces of my Indian companions, who appeared to expect every moment that the fire of heaven would fall on my head. I saw clearly that my endeavors to detach a portion of the rock would be fruitless, and I contented myself with bringing away a complete drawing of these memorials. Even the veneration everywhere testified by the Indians of the present day for these rude sculptures of their predecessors show that they have no idea of the execution of similar works. There is another circumstance which should be mentioned. Between Encaramada and Caycara, on the banks of the Orinoco, a number of these hieroglyphical figures are sculptured on the face of precipices at a height which could now be reached only by means of extraordinarily high scaffolding. If one asks the natives how these figures have been cut, they answer, laughing, as if it were a fact of which none but a white man could be ignorant, that "in the days of the great waters their fathers went in canoes at that height."

UNITED STATES OF COLOMBIA.

Mr. W. H. Holmes (*b*), of the Bureau of Ethnology, gives this account of petroglyphs in the province of Chiriqui, state of Panama:

Pictured rocks.—Our accounts of these objects are very meager. The only one definitely described is the "piedra pintal." A few of the figures engraved upon it are given by Seemann, from whom the following paragraph is quoted:

"At Caldera, a few leagues (north) from the town of David, lies a granite block known to the country people as the piedra pintal or painted stone. It is 15 feet high, nearly 50 feet in circumference, and flat on the top. Every part, especially the eastern side, is covered with figures. One represents a radiant sun; it is followed by a series of heads, all with some variations, scorpions, and fantastic figures. The top and the other side have signs of a circular and oval form, crossed by lines. The sculpture is ascribed to the Dorachos (or Dorasques), but to what purpose the stone was applied no historical account or tradition reveals."

These inscriptions are irregularly placed and much scattered. They are thought to have been originally nearly an inch deep, but in places are almost effaced by weathering, thus giving a suggestion of great antiquity. Tracings of these figures made recently by Mr A. L Pinart show decided differences in detail, and Mr. McNiel gives still another transcript.

In Fig. 105 Mr. McNiel's sketch of the southwest face of the rock is presented.

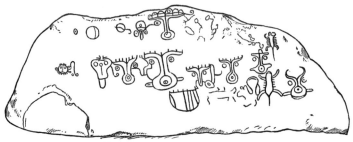

FIG. 105.—Petroglyphs in Colombia.

Other illustrations from Colombia appear as Figs. 151 and 1166, infra.

GUIANA.

The name of Guiana has been applied to the territory between the rivers Amazon, Orinoco, Negro, and Cassiquiare. It was once divided into the French, British, Dutch, Portuguese, and Spanish Guianas. The Portuguese Guiana now belongs to Brazil and Spanish Guiana is part of Venezuela. Many petroglyphs have been found in the several Guianas. They appear throughout the whole of the part belonging to Venezuela, but they are more thickly grouped in parts of the valley of the Orinoco.

The subject is well discussed in the following extract from Among the Indians of Guiana, by im Thurn (a):

The pictured rocks of Guiana are not all of one kind. In all cases various figures are rudely depicted on larger or smaller surfaces of rocks. Sometimes these figures are painted, though such cases are few and of but little moment; more generally they are graven on the rock, and these alone are of great importance. Rock sculptures may, again, be distinguished into two kinds, differing in the depth of incision, the apparent mode of execution, and, most important of all, the character of the figures represented.

Painted rocks in British Guiana are mentioned by Mr. C. Barrington Brown. He says that in coming down past Amailah fall, on the Cooriebrong river, he passed "a large white sandstone rock ornamented with figures in red paint." * * * Mr. Wallace, in his account of his Travels on the Amazons, mentions the occurrence of similar drawings in more than one place near the Amazons. * * *

The engraved rocks must be of some antiquity; that is to say, they must certainly date from a time before the influence of Europeans was much felt in Guiana. As has already been said, the engravings are of two kinds and are probably the work of two different people; nor is there even any reason to suppose that the two kinds were produced at one and the same time.

These two kinds of engravings may, for the sake of convenience, be distinguished as "deep" and "shallow," respectively, according as the figures are deeply cut into the rock or are merely scratched on the surface. The former vary from one-eighth to one-half of an inch, or even more, in depth; the latter are of quite inconsiderable depth. This difference probably corresponds with a difference in the means by which they were produced. The deep engravings seem cut into the rock with an edged tool, probably of stone; the shallow figures were apparently formed by long continued friction with stones and moist sand. The two kinds seem never to occur in the same place or even near to each other; in fact, a distinct line may almost be drawn between the districts in which the deep and shallow kinds occur, respectively; the deep form occurs at several spots on the Mazeruni, Essequibo, Ireng, Cotinga, Potaro, and Berbice rivers. The shallow form has as yet only been reported from the Corentyn river and its tributaries, where, however, examples occur in consider-able abundance. But the two kinds differ not only in the depth of incision, in the apparent mode of their production, and in the place of their occurrence, but also—and this is the chief difference between the two—in the figures represented.

Fig. 106 is a typical example of the shallow carvings.

FIG. 106.—Shallow carvings in Guiana.

Fig 1104, infra, is a similar example of the deep carvings.

The shallow engravings seem always to occur on comparatively large and more or less smooth surfaces of rock, and rarely, if ever, as the deep figures, on detached blocks of rock, piled one on the other. The shallow figures, too, are generally much larger, always combinations of straight or curved lines in figures much more elabor-ate than those in the deep engravings; and these shallow pictures always represent not animals, but greater or less variations of the figure which has been described. Lastly, though I am not certain that much significance can be attributed to this, all the examples that I have seen face more or less accurately eastward.

The deep engravings, on the other hand, consist not of a single figure but of a greater or less number of rude drawings. * * * These depict the human form, monkeys, snakes, and other animals, and also very simple combinations of two or three straight or curved lines in a pattern, and occasionally more elaborate combinations. The individual figures are small, averaging from 12 to 18 inches in height, but a considerable number are generally represented in a group.

Some of the best examples of this latter kind are at Warrapoota cataracts, about six days' journey up the Essequibo.

* * * The commonest figures at Warrapoota are figures of men or perhaps sometimes monkeys. These are very simple and generally consist of one straight line, representing the trunk, crossed by two straight lines at right angles to the body line; one about two-thirds of the distance from the top, represents the two arms as far as the elbows, where upward lines represent the lower part of the arms; the other, which is at the lower end, represent the two legs as far as the knees, from which point downward lines represent the lower part of the legs. A round dot, or a small circle, at the top of the trunk line, forms the head; and there are a few radiating lines where the fingers, a few more where the toes, should be. Occasionally the trunk line is produced downwards as if to represent a long tail. Perhaps the tailless figures represent men, the tailed monkeys. In a few cases the trunk, instead of being indicated by one straight line, is formed by two curved lines, representing the rounded outlines of the body; and the body thus formed is bisected by a row of dots, almost invariably nine in number, which seem to represent vertebræ.

Most of the other figures at Warrapoota are very simple combinations of two, three, or four straight lines similar to the so-called "Greek meander pattern," which is of such widespread occurrence. Combinations of curved and simple spiral lines also frequently occur. Many of these combinations closely resemble the figures which the Indians of the present day paint on their faces and naked bodies.

The same author (pp. 368, 369) gives the following account of the superstitious reverence entertained for the petroglyphs by the living Indians of Guiana:

Every time a sculptured rock or striking mountain or stone is seen, Indians avert the ill will of the spirits of such places by rubbing red peppers (*Capsicum*) each in his or her own eyes. * * * Though the old practitioners inflict this self-torture with the utmost stoicism, I have again and again seen that otherwise rare sight of Indians children, and even young men, sobbing under the infliction. Yet the ceremony was never omitted. Sometimes, when by a rare chance no member of the party had had the forethought to provide peppers, lime juice was used as a substitute; and once, when neither peppers nor limes were at hand, a piece of blue indigo-dyed cloth was carefully soaked, and the dye was then rubbed into the eyes.

The same author (*b*) adds:

It may be as well briefly to sum up the few facts that can be said, with any probability, of these rock pictures in Guiana. The engravings are of two kinds, which may or may not have had different authors and different intention. They were still produced after the first arrival of Europeans, as is shown by the sculptured ship. They were, therefore, probably made by the ancestors of the Indians now in the country; for, from the writings of Raleigh and other early explorers, as well as from the statements of early colonists, it is to be gathered that the present tribes were already in Guiana at the time of the first arrival of Europeans, though not perhaps in the same relative positions as at present. The art of stone-working being destroyed by the arrival of Europeans, the practice of rock-engraving ceased. Possibly the customary figures were for a time painted instead of engraved; but this degenerated habit was also soon relinquished. As to the intention of the figures, that they had some seems certain, but what kind this was is not clear. Finally, these figures really seem to indicate some very slight connection with Mexican civilization.

The following extract from a paper on the Indian picture-writing in

British Guiana, by Mr. Charles B. Brown (*a*), gives views and details somewhat different from the foregoing:

These writings or markings are visible at a greater or less distance in proportion to the depth of the furrows. In some instances they are distinctly visible upon the rocks on the banks of the river at a distance of 100 yards; in others they are so faint that they can only be seen in certain lights by reflected rays from their polished surfaces. They occur upon greenstone, granite, quartz-porphyry, gneiss, and jasperous sandstone, both in a vertical and horizontal position, at various elevations above the water. Sometimes they can only be seen during the dry season when the rivers are low, as in several instances on the Berbice and Cassikytyn rivers. In one instance, on the Corentyn river, the markings on the rock are so much above the level of the river when at its greatest height, that they could only have been made by erecting a staging against the face of the rock, unless the river was at the time much above its usual level. The widths of the furrows vary from half an inch to 1 inch, while the depth never exceeds one-fourth of an inch. * * * The furrows present the same weather-stained aspect as the rocks upon which they are cut. * * *

The Indians of Guiana know nothing about the picture-writing by tradition. They scout the idea of their having been made by the hand of man, and ascribe them to the handiwork of the Makunaima, their great spirit. * * *

As these figures were evidently cut with great care and at much labor by a former race of men, I conclude that they were made for some great purpose, probably a religous one, as some of the figures give indications of phallic worship.

VENEZUELA.

Prof. R. Hartmann (*a*) presented a pencil drawing of a South American rock, covered with sculptures, sketched by Mr. Anton Goering, a painter in Leipzig, which is here reproduced as Fig. 107. The rock is situated not far from San Esteban, a village in the vicinity of Puerto

Fig. 107.—Sculptured rock in Venezuela.

Cabello, in Venezuela. C. F. Appun, in Unter den Tropen, I, p. 82, remarks as follows in reference to this "Piedra de los Indios" (Indians' stone), a large granite block lying by the side of the road:

These drawings, cut in the stone to a depth of half an inch, mostly represent snakes and other animal forms, human heads and spiral lines, and differ from those which I afterward saw in Guiana, on the Essequibo and Rupununi, in characters and forms, but their execution, like that of the latter, is rude. Though greatly weathered by the influence of rain and the atmosphere, the figures can still be perfectly distinguished and gigantic patience, such as none but Indians possess, was surely needed to carve them in the hard granite mass by means of a stone.

Dr. G. Marcano (*a*) gives an account translated as follows, which is connected with Fig. 108:

FIG. 108.—Rock near Caïcara, Venezuela.

A tradition, the legend of the rock of Tepumereme, has been preserved by Father Gili. Some old writers, adhering to the Tamanak acceptation of the word, say indifferently tepumeremes or rocas pintadas (painted rocks). Usage has converted Tepumereme into a proper noun. At the present day it is applied exclusively to the rock situated some leagues from Encaramada, in the midst of the savanna, this rock having been the Mount Ararat of the Tamanaks.

Supposing that it is authentic, this legend, which we will relate further on [see page 33, supra], yields no information that might aid us in interpreting hieroglyphs, and so we are reduced to describing its principal characters.

Not all our pictographs correspond to the region of the Raudals, but in our ignorance of the peoples who carved them we see no harm in bringing them together so long as they all come from the banks of the Orinoco, and so long as the localities where they exist are indicated. The copies which we give of them have been very carefully made and reduced to one-tenth.

The first thing that strikes one on looking at them is that, despite differences in detail, the design presents a general common character. In fact, there is question not of figures with undecided forms, but with sure lines perfectly traced and combined in one and the same style. They are geometric designs rather than objective representations. The illustration [Fig. 108] came from a rock in the vicinity of Caïcara, a town situated on the right bank of the Orinoco, close to its last great bend. It represents three jaguars, one large and two small, the former being separated from the latter by an ornamented sun placed at the level of their feet. The spotting of their hides is rendered by means of angular lines arranged in so regular a manner that one might take them to be tigers did he not know that these felines never existed in these regions. The jaguars differ in insignificant details which, however, must have a purpose, in view of the general regularity. The largest shows six radiating lines on the muzzle and a circle in one of the ears. The second shows two hooks on the lower part of the body. The third is preceded by an isolated head, which is unfinished, without ears, inclined differently from the others. Some differences are also noted in the limbs.

Placed in the attitude of marching, these animals seem to descend from a height and to follow the same direction. Perhaps there is question here of a mnemonic whole, and, we might add, of a totem, if we knew that that system had been employed by the Indians of the region.

The same author (p. 205) gives a description of the petroglyphs of the rapids of Chicagua, here presented as Fig. 109.

This interesting collection includes the most varied ideographs.

Alongside of representations analogous to the preceding there appear new characters and partial groupings which we had not yet found. On running over them one passes successively from simple points to figures made up of tangled lines, to objective representations, and even to letters of the alphabet, a resemblance which, of course, is fortuitous.

The first group begins by three points similar to those in Fig. 19 [of Marcano, occurring in Fig. 1105 in this paper], followed by two circles with central dots, and terminates below in a plexus of broken lines. The second group, placed at the right, is composed of regular figures of great variety. Among them we note the two lowest, one of which resembles a K and the other a reversed A. A spiral, two circles, one of which has two appendices, and a figure in broken lines make up the third group. Below is seen a coiled serpent. Its head is characteristic; it is found in other pre-Columbian carvings of the Orinoco. As regards design *e*, we will merely call attention to the sign analogous to the E of our alphabet. It is found at times in the United States of America. [For this remark the author refers to the ideograph for pain, in Figs. 824 and 872, infra.]

FIG. 109.—Petroglyphs of Chicagua rapids, Venezuela.

Design *f* is an animal difficult to characterize; its head and tail may be guessed at. The body is covered with ornaments and the legs, very incomplete, are in the attitude of running. Design *g* represents probably a tree with an appendix of undulating lines; design *h*, a head surmounted by a complicated headgear. This is the first distinctly human representation that we have found in the country. The strange combinations of designs *j*, *k*, and *l* exhibit the dots at the end of the lines which we have already spoken of. Design *m* resembles an M; design *n* shows a circle with plane face.

Thus we see that the statements of some travelers concerning mysterious hieroglyphic combinations are far from being realized. As regards the exaggerations of

Humboldt, they arise from the fact that he did not content himself with describing what he had seen. This is illustrated by the following sentence: "There is even seen on a grassy plain near Uruana an isolated granite rock on which, according to the account of *trustworthy people*, there are seen at a height of 80 feet deeply carved images which appear arranged in rows and represent the sun, the moon, and different species of animals, especially crocodiles and boas." Elsewhere he speaks of kitchen and household utensils and of a number of objects which he can only have seen with the eyes of his imagination.

Other illustrations of pictographs in Venezuela are presented as Figs. 152, 153, 1105 and 1106, infra.

BRAZIL.

Remarks of general applicability to this region are made by Mr. J. Whitfield (*a*), an abstract of which follows:

The rock inscriptions were visited in August, 1865. Several similar inscriptions are said to exist in the interior of the province of Ceará, as well as in the provinces of Pernambuco and Piauhy, especially in the Sertaõs, that is, in the thinly-wooded parts of the interior, but no mention is ever made of their having been seen near the coast.

In the margin and bed only of the river are the rocks inscribed. On the margin they extend in some instances to 15 or 20 yards. Except in the rainy season the stream is dry. The rock is a silicious schist of excessively hard and flinty texture. The marks have the appearance of having been made with a blunt, heavy tool, such as might be made with an almost worn-out mason's hammer. The situation is about midway between Serra Grande or Ibiapaba and Serra Merioca, about 70 miles from the coast and 40 west of the town Sobral. The native population attribute all the "Letreiros" (inscriptions), as they do everything else of which they have no information, to the Dutch, as records of hidden wealth. The Dutch, however, only occupied the country for a few years in the early part of the seventeenth century. Along the coast numerous forts, the works of the Dutch, still remain; but there are no authentic records of their ever having established themselves in the interior of the country, and less probability still of their amusing themselves with inscribing puzzling hiero-glyphics, which must have been a work of time, on the rocks of the far interior, for the admiration of wandering Indians.

Mr. Franz Keller (*a*) narrates as follows regarding Fig. 110:

I found a "written rock" covered with spiral lines and concentric rings, evenly carved in the black gneiss-like material, and similar to those of the Caldeirão. Looking about for more, I discovered a perfect inscription, whose straight orderly lines can hardly be thought the result of lazy Indians' "hours of idleness." These characters were incised on a very hard smooth block 3 feet 4 inches in length, and 3¼ feet in height and breadth. It lay at an angle of 45°, only 8 feet above low water, and close to the water's edge of the second smaller rapid, the Cachoeira do Ribeirão. The transverse section of the characters is not very deep, and their surface is as worn as that of the inscription farther down. In some places they are almost effaced by time and are to be seen distinctly only with a favorable light. A dark brown coat of glaze, found everywhere on the surface of the stones, laved at times by the water, covers the block so uniformly well on the concave glyphs as on the parts untouched by instrument, that many ages must have elapsed since some patient Indian spent long hours in cutting them out with his quartz chisel. As the lines of the inscription run almost perfectly horizontally, and as the figures near the Caldeirão and the Cachoeira and the Cachoeira das Lages are so little above low-water mark, the present position of the block seems to have been the original one. * * * On the rocky shores of the Araguaya, that huge tributary of the Tocantino, there are similar rude outlines of animals near a rapid called Martirios, from the first Portuguese explorers fancying they recognized the instruments of the Passion in the clumsy representation.

FIG. 110.—Petroglyphs on the Cachoeira do Ribeirão, Brazil.

Dr. Ladisláu Netto (a) gives the illustration, reproduced as Fig. 111, of an inscription discovered by Domingos S. Ferreira Penna on the rock

FIG. 111.—The rock Itamaraca, Brazil.

called Itamaraca, on the Rio Xingu. Dr. Netto's description is translated as follows:

This whole inscription seems to represent one idea, figuring a collection of villages of vast proportions, inclosed by fortifications on two sides, at which it seems most accessible. On these same sides this collection of villages has external constructions or means of security, a kind of meanders or symbolic figures, which perhaps signify difficulties besetting the communication of the inhabitants with the surrounding fields.

In the lower part of the left-hand side there is a group of figures which seem to represent residences of chiefs, war houses, or redoubts, built near the principal entrance to the villages or to the city for its defense. There are found three figures of saurians, one with a large tail, on the side of the redoubts or fortified houses, as if representing the population, and two with small tails, which seem strange, and which walk toward the first.

This inscription is evidently the most perfect and the most notable of those found till now in all America [?], not only by its perfect condition and dimensions, but also by the mode in which a series of ideas has here been brought together.

The same author, on p. 552, furnishes copies of inscriptions carved on stones in the valley of the Rio Negro, and remarks: "In this series there are notable the two crowned personages [represented here in Fig. 112], one of whom holds a staff in the right hand, and below and under them there are two figures of capibars (sea-hogs) facing each other, and whose representation in black color resembles some figures from the inscriptions of North America."

Fig. 112.—Petroglyphs on the Rio Negro, Brazil.

The following account is in Dr. E. R. Heath's (a) Exploration of the River Beni:

Hieroglyphics were found on rocks at the falls and rapids of the rivers Madeira and Mamoré. * * * By accident we found some at the rapids at the foot of Caldierāo do Inferno. Designs d and b are figures on the same rock side by side. a is another face of the same rock 10 feet across. e and f are on the upper surface of a rock, and c on one of its sides near the bottom; g is upon a rock 15 feet above the surface of the river. Many more were on the other rocks, but our time did not permit further copying. Mr. T. M. Fetterman, my companion, and myself sketched as fast as possible.

Fig. 113 is a reproduction of the illustration given.

Fig. 113.—Petroglyphs at the Caldierāo do Inferno, Brazil.

The moment we arrived at the falls of Girāo we searched for stone carvings, finding a few, and several repetitions of circles similar to those already found. Designs a and d are on the west and east side of the same rock, which is 9 feet in length. The figure is 21 inches high, the five circles 1 foot across. The east side was almost obliterated. Designs b and c are on loose stones; b, facing west, is 16 inches long; the rock is 50 inches long and 35 wide; c is 22 inches long; the rock 70 inches long by 27 inches broad, and was 30 feet above the river at date. The rocks are basaltic, dipping north at an angle of 86°. Many small stones, 1 and 2 feet in diameter, lie about, with marks on them nearly defaced.

Fig. 114 is a reproduction of the illustration.

FIG. 114.—Petroglyphs at the falls of Girão, Brazil.

At Pederneira all the rocks on the right side at the foot of the rapids are literally covered with figures. Fig. 115 *a* is on a large bowlder facing the south; *b* has joined to its right side, *c*; *d*, *e*, and *f* are on the same stone. Most of these rocks are only a few feet above low water and are covered at least eight months each year.

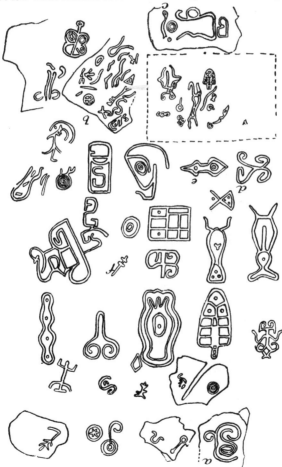

FIG. 115.—Petroglyphs at Pederneira, Brazil.

At Araras rapids the river is very wide, [containing] two islands and a rocky ledge crossing the river from the rapid. Nearly all the rocks on the right bank are covered with figures.

These are reproduced in Fig. 116.

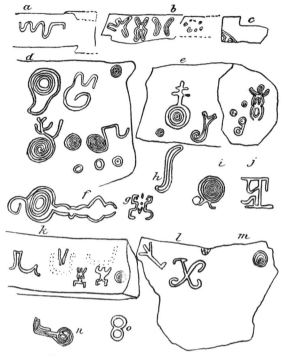

Having no small canoe we could not pass a small channel so as to gather copies of the figures we could see at a distance. The approaches both above and below the rapids and falls are many times as difficult to pass as the rapid or fall itself, giving rise to the division into "head," "body," and "tail." Some not only have these divisions, but also have these subdivided into "head, body, and tail." One is constantly hearing "el rabo," "el rabo del rabo," "el rabo del cuerpo," or "cabeza," and so on.

Ribeirão.—The tail of the rapid is 3 miles in length, a continuous broken current and fields of rocks. It is here, on a rock but a foot or two above the river, that the hieroglyphic shown in F. Keller's "Amazon and Madeira" is found.

FIG. 116.—Petroglyphs at Araras rapids, Brazil.

As both Mr. Fetterman and myself made copies of it, unknown to the other till finished, our copies may be relied on, although differing from Keller's. The length

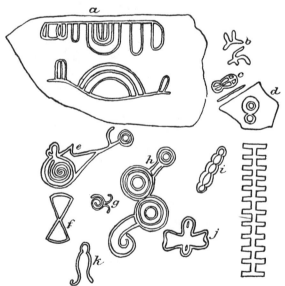

FIG. 117.—Petroglyphs at Ribeirão, Brazil.

of the upper part is 45 inches and of the lower 36 inches, with 13 inches depth of each.

The copy mentioned is given here as Fig. 117.

The character of the lower right-hand corner was at one time as clearly cut as we represent it, some of the edges being yet clear and distinct.

At the rapid of Madeira there were a number of circles similar to 15 and 16 at Ribeirão. On a ridge of rocks in the middle of the river, just above Larges rapids, are figures, and we had only time to sketch one, Fig. 118.

At Pao Grande we had a better harvest, showing evidently a later period than the former. One could easily believe these were made at the time of the Spanish conquest, the anchors, shields, and hearts being so often found in Spanish religious rites. Without doubt these were notices for navigators, as they were only out of water and seen when that passage was dangerous. Where projecting points of rock gave a face both up and down stream the same figure was on both faces. These rocks are syenitic granite and are cut to a depth of a half inch.

Fig. 119 is a reproduction of the copy published.

Senhor Tristão de Alencar Araripe (a) gives a large number of descriptions with illustrations, a selection of which, with translations, is as follows:

In the province of Ceará, district of Inhamun, on the plantation of Carrapateira, is a small hill (or mound). On the face of one of its rocks, on the eastern side, near the edge of the road, is the inscription given in Fig. 120 painted in red.

In the district of Inhamun, on the plantation of Carrapateira, in Morcego, on the top of a mound, is a semicircular

FIG. 118.—Character at Madeira rapid, Brazil.

stone bearing on the face toward the mound the four characters which appear in Fig. 121.

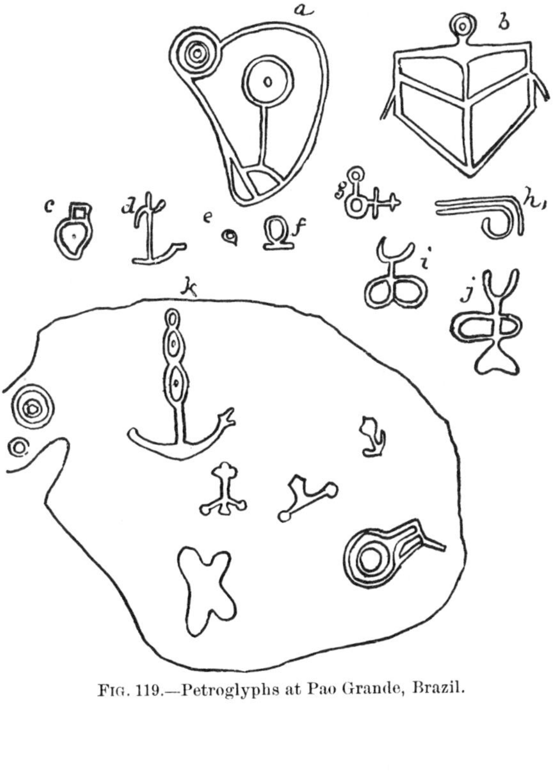

FIG. 119.—Petroglyphs at Pao Grande, Brazil.

In Inhamun, on the plantation of Carrapateira, in Morcego, is a large stone mound, the stones being piled up in a form of a tower; and in the inside of this tower, on the south or southwest side, are the characters given in Fig. 122 painted in bright, cochineal color.

FIG. 120.—Petroglyph in Ceará, Brazil.

Near the road from Cracara to Favelas, Inhamun, is a large rock, on the face of which, at the top of the western side, is the inscription [given on the upper part of Fig. 123,] all in red paint, as is also that following.

FIG. 121.—Petroglyph in Morcego, Brazil.

Fig. 122.—Petroglyphs in Morcego, Brazil.

The under part of this rock forms a shelter, and on the roof of this shelter are all the remaining characters of the figure.

To the right or south of the shelter containing the inscription is a stone, with the form of the figure represented in the third place in the lower row of characters, counting from left to right, on a small heap, with the rear end raised up and the sharp point toward the east, its side inclining toward the west, in such a way that it can be climbed to the end which is erect.

On the same side, at the south, but beyond this, on the top of a rise, is a mound in sight, which is represented by the figure [delineated in the lower part of Fig. 123 at the extreme right,] resembling an inclosure (corral) with the 21 small lines before it.

Fig. 123.—Petroglyphs in Inhamun, Brazil.

Fig. 124 is a copy of an inscription at Pedra Lavrada, Province of Parahiba, published loc. cit., but the description by Senhor de Alencar Araripe is very meager, amounting in substance to the following:

This is an inscription of vast proportions on a large rock in the town of Pedra Lavrada, which takes its name from that of the rock.

Other petroglyphs in Brazil are copied in Figs. 1107, 1108, 1109, 1110, 1111, 1113, 1114, and also under the heading of Cup Sculptures, Chapter V, infra.

ARGENTINE REPUBLIC.

F. P. Moreno (a), Museo de La Plata, Catamarca, gives an illustration of an inscribed rock at Bajo de Canota, Mendoza, reproduced as Fig. 125.

PERU.

The following account is furnished by Messrs. de Rivero and Von Tschudi (a):

Eight leagues north of Arequipa there exist a multitude of engravings on granite which represent figures of animals, flowers, and fortifications, and which doubtless tell the story of events anterior to the dynasty of the Incas.

Fig. 124.—Petroglyphs at Pedra Lavrada, Brazil.

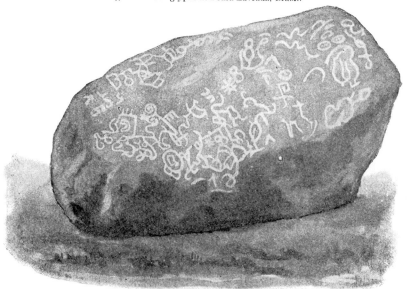

Fig. 125.—Inscribed rock at Bajo de Canota, Argentine Republic.

The illustration presented is copied here as Fig. 126.

The account is continued as follows:

In the province of Castro-Vireyna, in the town of Huaytara. there is found in the ruins of a large edifice, of similar construction to the celebrated palace of old Huanuco,

Fig. 126.—Petroglyphs near Arequipa, Peru.

a mass of granite many square yards in size, with coarse engravings like those last mentioned near Arequipa. None of the most trustworthy historians allude to these inscriptions or representations, or give the smallest direct information concerning the Peruvian hieroglyphics, from which it may possibly be inferred that in the times of the Incas there was no knowledge of the art of writing in characters and that all of these sculptures are the remains of a very remote period. * * * In many parts of Peru, chiefly in situations greatly elevated above the sea are vestiges of inscriptions very much obliterated by time.

The illustration is copied here as Fig. 127.

Fig. 127.—Petroglyph in Huaytara, Peru.

Charles Wiener (*a*), in Pérou et Bolivie, gives another statement, viz:

The archeologists of Peru have only found a single point—Tiahuanaco—where there were a limited number, though very interesting, of signs on rocks or stones which seemed to all observers to be symbolic. While there are a few petroglyphs found in Peru there are a large number of inscriptions properly so called on the tissues which cover or are found in connection with remains in the graves.

A number of pictographs from Peru are described and illustrated infra (see Figs. 688, 720, and 1167).

CHILE.

Prof. Edwyn C. Reed, of Valparaiso, Chile, presented through A. P. Niblack, ensign U. S. Navy, a photograph of a large bowlder bearing numerous sculpturings. No information pertaining to the locality at which the rock is situated or details respecting the characters upon it were furnished. The photograph is reproduced in Fig. 128.

Mr. R. A. Philippi, of Santiago, a corresponding member, made a communication to the Berliner Gesellschaft für Anthropologie, session

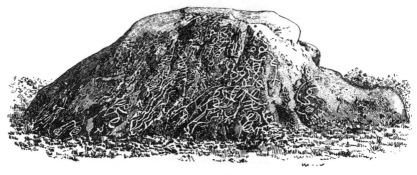

FIG. 128.—Sculptured bowlder in Chile.

of January 19, 1876, page 38, from which the following is extracted and translated:

I made a visit to the valley "Cajon de los Cipreses" in order to see the glacier giving rise to the Rio de los Cipreses, a tributary of the Cachapoal, and on that occasion had a cursory view of a rock with some pictures. I send you herewith a drawing of the rock and some of the figures cut on it. The rock, a kind of greenstone, lies at an altitude of about 5,000 feet above sea level, and the surface covered with figures, gently inclined down to the ground, may be 8 feet long and 5 or 6 feet high. The lines are about 4 mm. broad and 1 to ½ mm. deep. The carved figures on the stone are without any sort of order. When I spoke before a meeting of our faculty of physical and mathematical sciences concerning this stone which the shepherds of the region called piedra marcada, I learned that similar stones with carved figures are found in various places.

The figure mentioned is here reproduced as Fig. 129.

FIG. 129.—Petroglyph in Cajon de los Cipreses, Chile.

CHAPTER IV.

EXTRA-LIMITAL PETROGLYPHS.

The term "extra-limital," familiar to naturalists, refers in its present connection to the sculptures, paintings, and drawings on rocks beyond the continents of North and South America, which are now introduced for comparison and as evidence of the occurrence throughout the world of similar forms in the department of work now under examination.

SECTION 1.

AUSTRALIA.

Mr. Edward G. Porter (a), in "The Aborigines of Australia," says: "Their rock carvings are only outline sketches of men, fish, animals, etc., sometimes seen on the top of large flat rocks. Two localities are mentioned, one on Sydney common and another on a rock between Brisbane water and Hawkesbury river."

Much more detailed information is given by Thomas Worsnop, viz:

At Chasm island, which lies 1½ miles from "Groote Eylandt," in the steep sides of the chasms, were deep holes or caverns undermining the cliffs, upon the walls of which are found rude drawings, made with charcoal and something like red paint, upon the white ground of the rock. These drawings represented porpoises, turtle, kangaroos, and a human hand, and Mr. Westall found the representations of a kangaroo with a file of thirty-two persons following after it.

In the MacDonnell ranges, 6 miles from Alice springs, in a large cave, there were paintings made by the aborigines, well defined parallel lines, intersected with footprints of the emu, kangaroo rat, and birds, with the outlines of iguana, hands of men, well sketched and almost perfect.

The parallel lines were of deep red and yellow colors, with brown and white borders; the footprints of light red, light yellow, and black; the outlines of the animals and hands were of red, yellow, white, black, wonderfully (considering it was done by savages) displayed and blended. All the paintings were in good preservation and evidently touched up occasionally, as they looked quite fresh.

I can only conjecture that these paintings were left as a record, a life-long charm, against the total destruction of the above animals. The paintings were seen by Mr. S. Gason, of Beltana, in the year 1873.

Very interesting groups of native drawings are to be seen in the caves of the Emily gorge in the MacDonnell ranges. Many of these drawings represent life-size objects.

The same author, page 20, describes the petroglyph copied in Fig. 130 as follows:

Mr. Arthur John Giles in the year 1873 discovered, at the junction of Sullivan's creek with the Finke river, carvings on rocks. The sketch represents a smooth-faced rock, portion of a rock cliff about 45 feet high, composed of hard metamorphic slate. The lower portion of the sculptured face has been worn and broken away, forming a sort of cave. From the level of the creek to the lower edge of the sculptured rock is about 15 feet. The perpendicular lines are cut out, forming semicircular grooves about 1½ inches in diameter, cut in to a depth of nearly half an inch; all remaining figures are also carved into the solid rock to a depth of one-fourth of an inch.

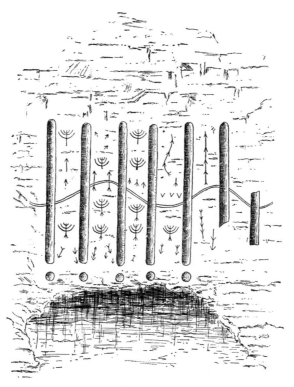

Fig. 130.—Petroglyph on Finke river, Australia.

The same author, page 14, gives the following description of some pictures discovered between 1831 and 1840 by Capt. Stokes on Depuch island, one of the Forestier group in Dampier archipelago, on the western coast of Australia:

Depuch island would seem to be their favorite resort, and we found several of their huts still standing. The natives are doubtless attracted to the place partly by the reservoirs of water they find among the rocks after rain; partly that they may enjoy the pleasure of delineating the various objects that attract their attention on the smooth surface of the rocks. This they do by removing the hard red outer coating and baring to view the natural color of the greenstone, according to the outline they have traced. Much ability is displayed in many of these representations, the subject of which could be discovered at a glance. The number of specimens are immense, so that the natives must have been in the habit of amusing themselves in this innocent manner for a long period of time.

These savages of Australia, who have adorned the rocks of Depuch island with their drawings, have in one thing proved themselves superior to the Egyptian and the Etruscan, whose works have elicited so much admiration and afforded food to so many speculations, namely, there is not in them to be observed the slightest trace of indecency.

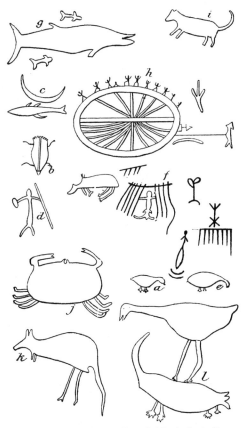

FIG. 131.—Petroglyphs in Depuch island, Australia.

Fig. 131 shows a number of the characters drawn on these rocks. They are supposed to represent objects as follows:

a, a goose or duck; *b*, a beetle; *c*, a fish, with a quarter moon over, considered to have some reference to fishing by moonlight; *d*, a native, armed with spear and wommera or throwing stick, probably relating his adventures, which is usually done by song and accompanied with great action and flourishing of weapons, particularly when boasting of his powers; *e*, a duck and a gull; *f*, a native in a hut, with portion of the matting with which they cover their habitations; *g*, shark and pilot fish; *h*, a corroboreeo or native dance; *i*, a native dog; *j*, a crab; *k*, a kangaroo; *l*, appears to be a bird of prey, having seized upon a kangaroo rat.

The same author, page 5, describes another locality as follows:

In New South Wales, in the neighborhood of Botany bay and port Jackson, the figures of animals, of shields and weapons, and even of men, have been found carved upon the rocks, roughly, indeed, but sufficiently well to ascertain very fully what was the object intended. Fish were often represented, and in one place the form of a large lizard was sketched out with tolerable accuracy. On top of one of the hills the figure of a man, in the attitude usually assumed by them when they begin to dance, was executed in a still superior style.

The figure last mentioned was probably the god Daramŭlŭn, see Howitt, Australian Customs of Initiation (a).

A special account of the aboriginal rock carvings at the head of Bantry bay is furnished by R. Etheridge, jr. (a), as follows, the illustration referred to being presented here as Fig. 132:

Of the numerous traces of aboriginal rock carvings to be seen on the shores of Port Jackson, none probably equal in extent or completeness of detail those on the heights at the head and on the eastern side of Bantry bay, Middle harbor, Australia.

The table of sandstone over which the carvings are scattered measures 2 chains in one direction by 3 in the contrary, and has a gentle slope of 7 degrees to the southwest. The high road as now laid out passes over a portion of them.   *   *   *

FIG. 132.—Petroglyphs at Bantry bay, Australia.

The figures are represented in their present state in outline by a continuous indentation or groove from 1 to 1½ inches broad by half an inch to 1 inch in depth. Some are single subjects scattered promiscuously over the surface; others form small groups, illustrating compound subjects, but all appear to have been executed about one and the same time.   *   *   *

An advance on the other sculptures existing at this place seems to be made in the originals of the designs a and b, from the fact that an attempt was apparently made to represent a compound idea in the form of a single combat between two warriors. The figures are quite contiguous to one another. The individual marked a seems to be holding in his right hand a body similar to that represented as c, and the position in which it is held would lend color to the belief in its shield-like nature. In the opposite hand are a bundle of rods which have been suggested to be spears, and this explanation for the want of a better may be accepted. On the other hand, we are confronted with the fact that these weapons of offense and defense are held in the wrong hands, unless the holder be regarded as sinistral; otherwise it must be conceived that the warrior's back is presented to the observer, which is contrary to the other evidence existing in the carving. The opponent, marked as b, with legs astride and arms outstretched much in the position of an aboriginal when throwing the boomerang, is equally definitive. I conceive it quite possible that the position of the boomerang close to the right hand conveys the idea that this man has just thrown the missile at the subject of *a*, allowing, of course, for the want of a knowledge of perspective on the part of the aboriginal artist.   *   *   *

In several other figures the head is a mere rounded outline, but in *b* it is presented with a rather bird-like appearance. Another peculiarty is the great angularity given to the kneecap: this is visible both in *a* and *b*. It is further exemplified in the elbow of the left arms of both *a* and *b*.

SECTION 2.

OCEANICA.

The term "Oceanica" is used here without geographic precision, to include several islands not mentioned in other sections of the present work, in different parts of the globe, where specially interesting petroglyphs have been found and made known in publications. Although more such localities are known than are now mentioned, the pictographs from them are not of sufficient importance to justify description or illustration, but it may be remarked that they show the universality of the pictographic practice.

NEW ZEALAND.

Dr. Julius von Haast (*a*) published notes, condensed as follows, descriptive of the illustration produced here as Fig. 133:

The most remarkable petroglyphs found in New Zealand are situated about 1 mile on the western side of the Weka Pass road in a rock shelter, which is washed out of a vertical wall of rock lining a small valley for about 300 feet on its right or southern side. The whole length of the rock below the shelter has been used for painting, and it is evident that some order has been followed in the arrangement of the subjects and figures. The paint consists of kokowai (red oxide of iron), of which the present aborigines of New Zealand make still extensive use, and of some fatty substance, such as fish oil, or perhaps some oily bird fat. It has been well fixed upon the somewhat porous rock and no amount of rubbing will get it off.

Some of the principal objects evidently belong to the animal kingdom, and represent animals which either do not occur in New Zealand or are only of a mythical or fabulous character. The paintings occur over a face of about 65 feet, and the upper end of some reaches 8 feet above the floor, the average height, however, being 4 to 5 feet. They are all of considerable size, most of them measuring several feet, and one of them even having a length of 15 feet.

Beginning at the eastern end in the left-hand corner is the representation *a* of what might be taken for a sperm whale with its mouth wide open diving downward. This figure is 3 feet long. Five feet from it is another figure *c*, which might also represent a whale or some fabulous two-headed marine monster. This painting is 3 feet 4 inches long. Below it, a little to the right in *d*, we have the representation of a large snake possessing a swollen head and a long protruding tongue. This figure is nearly 3 feet long, and shows numerous windings.

It is difficult to conceive how the natives in a country without snakes could not only have traditions about them but actually be able to picture them, unless they had received amongst them immigrants from tropical countries who had landed on the coasts of New Zealand.

Between the two fishes or whales is *b*, which might represent a fishhook, and below the snake *d* a sword *e* with a curved blade.

Advancing toward the right is a group which is of special interest, the figure *i*, which is nearly a foot long, having all the appearance of a long-necked bird carrying the head as the cassowary and emu do, and as the moa has done. If this design should represent the moa, I might suggest that it was either a conventional way of drawing that bird or that it was already extinct when this representation was painted according to tradition; in which latter case *k* might represent the taniwha or gigantic fabulous lizard which is said to have watched the moa. *h* is doubtless a quadruped, probably a dog, which was a contemporary of the moa and was used also as food by the moa hunters. *j* is evidently a weapon, probably an adz or tomahawk, and might, being close to the supposed bird, indicate the manner in which the latter was killed during the chase. The post, with the two branches near the top

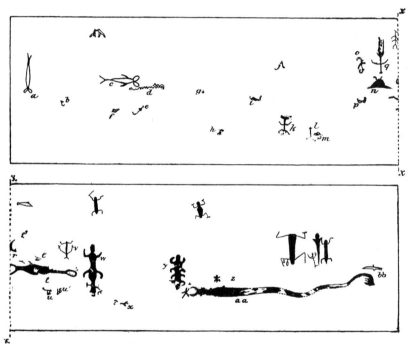

Fig 133.—Petroglyph in New Zealand.

l, finds a counterpart in the remnant of a similar figure *g* between the figures *c* and *i*. They might represent some of the means by which the moa was caught or indicate that it existed in open country between the forest. *m*, under which the rock in the central portion has scaled off, is like *f*, one of the designs which resemble ancient oriental writing.

Approaching the middle portion of the wall we find here a well-shaped group of paintings, the center of which *n* has all the appearance of a hat ornamented on the crown. The rim of this broad-brimmed relic measures 2 feet across. The expert of ancient customs and habits of the Malayan and South Indian countries might perhaps be able to throw some light upon this and the surrounding figures, *o* to *r*.

From *q*, which is altogether 3 feet high, evidently issues fire or smoke; it therefore might represent a tree on fire, a lamp or an altar with incense offering.   *   *   *
The figure *o* is particularly well painted, and the outlines are clearly defined, but I

can make no suggestion as to its meaning. In *s* we have, doubtless, the picture of a human being who is running away from *q*, the object from the top of which issues fire or smoke. I am strengthened in my conviction that it is meant for a man by observing a similar figure running away from the monster *aa*. *p*, which has been placed below that group, might be compared to a pair of spectacles, but is probably a letter or an imitation of such a sign.

A little more to the right a figure 6 feet long is very prominent. It is probably the representation of a right whale in the act of spouting. Above it, in *r*, the figure of a mantis is easily recognizable, whilst *u* and the characters to the right below the supposed right whale again resemble cyphers or letters. *w* and *y*, although in many respects different, belong doubtless to the same group, and represent large lizards or crocodiles. * * * *w* is 4 feet long; it is unfortunately deficient in its lower portion, but it is still sufficiently preserved to show that besides four legs it possesses two other lower appendages, of which one is forked and the other has the appearance of a trident. I wish also to draw attention to the unusual form of the head. *y* is a similar animal 3 feet long, but it has eight legs, and head and tail are well defined. The head is well rounded off, and both animals represent, without doubt, some fabulous animal, such as the taniwha, which is generally described as a huge crocodile, of which the ancient legends give so many accounts.

aa, a huge snake-like animal 15 feet long, is probably a representation of the tuna tuoro, a mythical monster. It is evident that the tuna tuoro is in the act of swallowing a man, who tries to save himself by running away from it.

KEI ISLANDS.

Mr. A. Langen (*a*) made a report on the Kei islands and their Ghost grottoes, with a plate now reproduced as Fig. 134. He says:

The group of the small Kei islands, more correctly Arue islands [southwest from New Guinea], is a sea bottom raised by volcanic forces and covered with corals and shells. The corals appear but at a few points. They are in the main covered with a layer of shells cemented together, whose cement is so hard and firm that it offers resistance to the influence of time even after the shell has been weathered away.

On the whole, all the figures in similar genre are represented in thousands of specimens. [They may be divided into three series, the first including letters *a* to *k*; the second, letters *l* to *t*; the third, letters *u* to *cc*.] Many are effaced and unrecognizable, only letter *k*, series 1; letters *n*, *o*, *s*, *t*, series 2; and letters *cc*, series 3, stand isolated and seem to have a peculiar meaning. The popular legend ascribes the greatest age to the characters of series 1 and series 2, and it is said that the signs record a terrible fight in which the islanders lost many dead, but yet remained victors. It is stated that the signs were produced by the ghosts of the fallen. The signs of series 3 are said to be the work of a woman named Tewaheru, who was able to converse with ghosts as well as with the living. But, when on one occasion she helped a living man to recover his dead wife by betraying to him the secret of making the spirit return to the body, she is said to have been destroyed by the ghosts and changed into a blackbird, whose call even at this day indicates death. Since that time no medium is said to exist between the living and the dead, nor do any new signs appear on the rock.

Investigation in place showed me that the color of series 3 consists of ocher made up with water. The very oldest drawings seem to have been made with water color, as the color has nowhere penetrated into the rock. Most of the figures are painted on overhanging rocks in such a way as to be protected as much as possible against wind and weather; whether they bear any relation to the signs on the rocks of Papua, and what that relation may be, I am not yet able to judge.

It may safely be assumed that the caves as abodes of spirits were sacred, but did not serve as places of burial.   The lead rings and pieces of copper gongs found in

Fig. 134.—Petroglyphs in Kei islands.

small number before some of the caves seem to be derived from sacrifices offered to the spirits.   At the present day no more sacrifices are offered there, and the islanders knew nothing of the existence of these things.

EASTER ISLAND.

In this island carved human figures of colossal size have been frequently noticed in various publications, with and without illustrations, but apart from those statues ancient stone houses remain in which have been found large stone slabs bearing painted figures. Paymaster William J. Thompson, U. S. Navy (a) says of the Orongo houses, that the "smooth slabs lining the walls and ceilings were ornamented with mythological figures and rude designs painted in white, red, and black pigments." The figures partake of the form of fish and bird-like animals, the exaggerated outlines clearly indicating mythologic beings, the type of which does not exist in nature. Fig. 135 is pre-

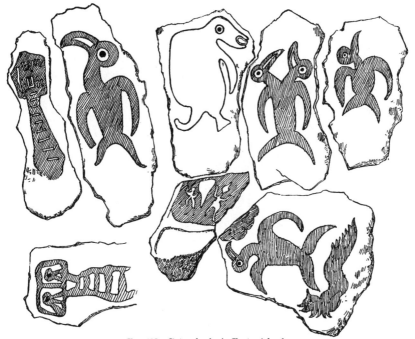

FIG. 135.—Petroglyphs in Easter island.

sented here, extracted by permission from the work above cited, and it may be of interest to know that nearly all, if not all, of the original specimens are now deposited in the U. S. National Museum.

While the curious carvings on the wooden tablets which are discussed in the work of Paymaster Thompson are not petroglyphs, it seems proper to mention them in this connection. Fig. 136 is taken from Mittheilungen der Anthropologischen Gesellschaft, in Wien (a), and shows one of the tablets, which does not appear to be presented in this exact form in the work before mentioned.

The following remarks by Prof. de Lacouperie (*b*) are quoted on account of the eminence of his authority, though the subject is still under discussion:

The character of eastern India, the Vengi-Châlukya, was also carried to north Celebes islands. The people have not remained at the level required for the practical use of a phonetic writing. It is no more used as an alphabet. Curiously enough, it is employed as pictorial ornaments on the MSS. they now write in a pictographic style of the lowest scale. This I have seen on the facsimile (Bilderschriften des Ostindischen Archipels, Pl. I, 1, 11) published by Dr. A. B. Meyer, of Dresden, in his splendid album on the writings of this region.

In the Easter island, or Vaihu, some fourteen inscriptions have been found incised on wooden boards, perhaps of driftwood. The characters are peculiar. Most of them display strange shapes, in which, with a little imagination, forms of men, fishes, trees, birds, and many other things have been fancied. A curious characteristic is that the upper part of the signs are shaped somewhat like the head of the herronia

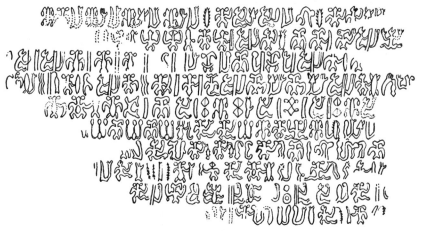

FIG. 136.—Tablet from Easter island.

or albatross. A pictorial tendency is obvious in all of these. Some persons in Europe have taken them for hieroglyphics, and have ventured to find a connection with the flora and fauna of the island. The knowledge of this writing is now lost; and it is not sure that the few priests and other men of the last generation who boasted of being able to read them could do so thoroughly. Anyhow, in 1770, some chiefs were still able to write down their names on a deed of gift when the island was taken in the name of Carlos III of Spain.

In examining carefully the characters I was struck by the forked heads of many of them, which reminded me of the forked matras of the Vengi-Châlukya inscriptions. A closer comparison with Pls. i to viii of the Elements of South Indian Paleography (A. C. Burnell, Elements of South Indian Paleography, from the fourth to the seventeenth century A. D., being An Introduction to the Study of South Indian Inscriptions and MSS., 2d edit., London and Mangalore, 1878; Pls. i, vii, viii are specially interesting for the forked matras) soon showed me that I was on the right track, and a further study of the Vaihu characters, and their analysis by comparing the small differences (vocalic notation) existing between several of them, convinced me that they are nothing else than a decayed form of the above writing of southern India returning to the hieroglyphical stage. With this clue, the inscriptions of Easter island are no more a sealed text. They can easily be read after a little training. Their language is Polynesian, and I can say that the vocabulary of the Samoan dialect has proved very useful to me for the purpose.

SECTION 3.

EUROPE.

In the more settled and civilized parts of Europe petroglyphs are now rarely found. This is, perhaps, accounted for in part by the many occasions for use of the inscribed rocks or by their demolition during the long period after the glyphs upon them had ceased to have their original interest and significance and before their value as now understood had become recognized. Yet from time to time such glyphs have been noticed, and they have been copied and described in publications.

But few of the petroglyphs in the civilized portions of Europe not familiar by publication have that kind of interest which requires their reproduction in the present paper. It may be sufficient to state in general terms that Europe is no exception to the rest of the world in the presence of petroglyphs.

A number of these extant in the British islands and in the Scandinavian peninsula, besides the few examples presented in this chapter, are described and illustrated in other parts of this work, and brief accounts of others recently noted in France, Spain, and Italy are also furnished.

GREAT BRITAIN AND IRELAND.

Nearly all of the petroglyphs found in the British islands, accounts of which have been published, belong to the class of cup sculptures discussed in Chapter v, infra, but several inscriptions showing characters not limited to that category are mentioned in "Archaic Rock Inscriptions," (a) from which the following condensed extract referring to cairn in county Meath, Ireland, is taken:

The ornamentation may be thus described: Small circles, with or without a central dot; two or many more concentric circles; a small circle with a central dot, surrounded by a spiral line; the single spiral; the double spiral, or two spirals starting from different centers; rows of small lozenges or ovals; stars of six to thirteen rays; wheels of nine rays; flower ornaments, sometimes inclosed in a circle or wide oval; wave-like lines; groups of lunette-shaped lines; pothooks; small squares attached to each other side by side, so as to form a reticulated pattern; small attached concentric circles; large and small hollows; a cup hollow surrounded by one or more circles; lozenges crossed from angle to angle (these and the squares produced by scrapings); an ornament like the spine of a fish with ribs attached, or the fiber system of some leaf; short equiarmed crosses, starting sometimes from a dot and small circle; a circle with rays round it, and the whole contained in a circle; a series of compressed semicircles like the letters ∩∩∩ inverted; vertical lines far apart, with ribs sloping downwards from them like twigs; an ornament like the fiber system of a broad leaf, with the stem attached; rude concentric circles with short rays extending from part of the outer one; an ornament very like the simple Greek fret, with dots in the center of the loop; five zigzag lines and two parallel lines, on each of which, and pointing toward each other, is a series of cones ornamented by lines radiating from the apex, crossed by others parallel to the base—this design has been produced by scraping, and I propose to call it the Patella ornament, as it strikingly resembles the large species of that shell so common on our coasts, and which shell Mr. Conwell discovered in numbers in some of the cists, in connection with fragments of pottery and human bones; a semicircle with three or four straight lines proceeding from it, but not touching it; a dot with several lines radiating from it; combinations of short straight lines arranged either at right angles to or sloping from a central line; an ∽-shaped curve, each loop inclosing concentric circles; and a vast number of other combinations of the circle, spiral, line, and dot, which can not be described in writing.

Some of the ancient "Turf-Monuments" of England are to be classed as petroglyphs. The following extracts from the work of Rev. W. A. Plenderleath (b) give sufficient information on these curious pictures:

Although all the White Horses, except one, are in Wiltshire, that one exception is the great sire and prototype of them all, which is at Uffington, just 2½ miles outside the Wiltshire boundary and within that of Berkshire. * * * The one mediæval document in which the White Horse is mentioned is a cartulary of the Abbey of Abingdon, which must have been written either in the reign of Henry II or soon after, and which runs as follows: "It was then customary amongst the English that any monks who wished might receive money or landed estates and both use and devolve them according to their pleasure. Hence two monks of the monastery at Abingdon, named Leofric and Godric Cild, appear to have obtained by inheritance manors situated upon the banks of the Thames; one of them, Godric, becoming possessed of Spersholt, near the place commonly known as the White Horse Hill, and the other that of Whitchurch, during the time that Aldhelm was abbot of this place."

This Aldhelm appears to have been abbot from 1072 to 1084, and from the terms in which the White Horse Hill is mentioned the name was evidently an old one at that time.

Now it was only two hundred years before this time, viz, in 871, that a very famous victory had been gained by King Alfred over the Danes close to this very spot. "Four days after the battle of Reading," says Asser, "King Æthelred, and Alfred, his brother, fought against the whole army of the pagans at Ashdown. * * * And the flower of the pagan youths were there slain, so that neither before nor since was ever such destruction known since the Saxons first gained Britain by their arms." And it was in memory of this victory that, we are informed by local tradition, Alfred caused his men, the day after the battle, to cut out the White Horse, the standard of Hengist, on the hillside just under the castle. The name Hengist, or Hengst, itself means *Stone Horse* in the ancient language of the Saxons, and Bishop Nicholson, in his "English Atlas," goes so far as to suppose the names of Hengist and Horsa to have been not proper at all, but simply emblematical.

The Uffington horse measures 355 feet from the nose to the tail and 120 feet from the ear to the hoof. It faces to sinister, as do also those depicted upon all British coins. The slope of the portion of the hill upon which it is cut is 39°, but the declivity is very considerably greater beneath the figures. The exposure is southwest.

The author then describes the White Horse on Bratton Hill, near Westbury, Wilts, now obliterated, the dimensions of which were, extreme length, 100 feet; height, nearly the same; from toe to chest, 54 feet, and gives accounts of several other White Horses, the antiquity of which is not so well established. He then (*c*) treats of the Red Horse in the lordship of Tysoe, in Warwickshire, as follows:

This is traditionally reported to have been cut in 1461, in memory of the exploits of Richard, Earl of Warwick, who was for many years one of the most prominent figures in the Wars of the Roses. The earl had in the early part of the year found himself, with a force of forty thousand men, opposed to Queen Margaret, with sixty thousand, at a place called Towton, near Tadcaster. Overborne by numbers, the battle was going against him, when, dismounting from his horse, he plunged his sword up to the hilt in the animal's side, crying aloud that he would henceforth fight shoulder to shoulder with his men. Thereupon the soldiers, animated by their leader's example, rushed forward with such impetuosity that the enemy gave way and flew precipitately. No less than twenty-eight thousand Lancastrians are said to have fallen in this battle and in the pursuit which followed, for the commands of Prince Edward were to give no quarter. It was to this victory that the latter owed his elevation to the throne, which took place immediately afterwards.

The Red Horse used to be scoured every year, upon Palm Sunday, at the expense of certain neighboring landowners who held their land by that tenure, and the scouring is said to have been as largely attended and to have been the occasion of as great festivity as that of the older horse in the adjoining county of Berks. The figure is about 54 feet in extreme length by about 31 in extreme height.

The best known of Turf-Monuments other than horses is the Giant, on Trendle Hill, near Cerne Abbas, in Dorsetshire. This the same author (*d*) describes as follows:

This is a figure roughly representing a man, undraped, and with a club in his right hand; the height is 180 feet, and the outlines are marked out by a trench 2 feet wide and of about the same depth. It covers nearly an acre of ground. Hutchin imagines this figure to represent the Saxon god, Heil, and places its date as anterior to A. D. 600. * * * Britton, on the other hand, tells us that "vulgar tradition makes this figure commemorate the destruction of a giant who, having feasted on some sheep in Blackmoor and laid himself to sleep on this hill, was pinioned down like another Gulliver and killed by the enraged peasants, who immediately traced his dimensions for the information of posterity." There were formerly discernible some markings between the legs of the figure rather above the level of the ankles, which the country folk took for the numerals 748, and imagined to indicate the date. We need, perhaps, scarcely remark that Arabic numerals were unknown in Europe until at least six centuries later than this period.

SWEDEN.

Mr. Paul B. Du Chaillu (*a*) gives the following (condensed) account describing, among many more "rock tracings," as he calls them, those reproduced as Figs. 137 and 138:

There are found in Sweden large pictures engraved on the rocks which are of great antiquity, long before the Roman period.

These are of different kinds and sizes, the most numerous being the drawings of ships or boats, canoe-shaped and alike at both ends (with figures of men and animals), and of fleets fighting against each other or making an attack upon the shore. The hero of the fight, or the champion, is generally depicted as much larger than the other combatants, who probably were of one people, though of different tribes, for their arms are similar and all seem without clothing, though in some cases they are represented as wearing a helmet or shield.

On some rocks are representations of cattle, horses, reindeer, turtles, ostriches, and camels, the latter showing that in earlier times these people were acquainted with more southern climes. The greatest number and the largest and most complicated in detail of the tracings occur, especially in the present Sweden, in Bohuslän, "the ancient Viken of the Sagas," on the coast of the peninsula washed by the Cattegat. They are also found in Norway, especially in Smaalenene, a province contiguous to that of Bohuslän, but become more scarce in the north, though found on the Trondhjem fjord.

Fig. 137 is a copy of a petroglyph in Tanum parish, Bohuslän, Sweden. The large figure is doubtless a champion or commander, the exaggerated size of which is to be noted in connection with that of the

FIG. 137.—Petroglyph in Bohuslän, Sweden.

Zulu chiefs in Fig. 142, infra, from South Africa, and Fig. 1024, infra, from North America. There are numerous small holes and footprints between the chief and the attacking force. Height, 20 feet; width, 15 feet.

In Bohuslän the tracings are cut in the quartz, which is the geological formation of the coast. They are mostly upon slightly inclined rocks, which are generally 200 or 300 feet or more above the present level of the sea, and which have been polished by the action of the ice. The width of the lines in the same representation varies from 1 to 2 inches and even more, and their depth is often only a third or fourth of an inch, and at times so shallow as to be barely perceptible. Those tracings, which have for hundreds, perhaps for thousands, of years been laid bare to the ravages of the northern climate, are now most difficult to decipher, while those which have been protected by earth are as fresh as if they had been cut to-day. Many seem to

have been cut near the middle or base of the hills, which were covered with vegetation, and were in the course of time concealed by the detritus from above.

Fig. 138 is from the same author (*b*) and locality. Height, 29 feet;
width, 17 feet. The large birds and footprints and a chief designated
by his size will be noticed, and also a character in the middle of the
extreme upper part of the illustration which may be compared with
the largest human form in Fig. 983, infra, from Tule valley, California.

Fɪɢ. 138.—Petroglyph in Bohuslän, Sweden.

FRANCE.

Perrier du Carne (*a*), gives the following account (translated and condensed) of signs carved on the dolmen of Trou-aux-Anglais, in Épone:

This dolmen, situated in the commune of Épone, in a place called Le Bois de la
Garenne, was constructed beneath the ground; it was concealed from view and it is
to this circumstance, no doubt, that its preservation is due. Nothing indicates that
it has been surmounted by a tumulus; in any case this tumulus had long since dis-

appeared, and the ground was entirely leveled when the digging was commenced some years ago. * * *

The characters (Fig. 139) are carved in intaglio on the farthest stone of the entrance, on the left side. The whole of the inscription measures 1^m, 10 in height and 82 centimeters in width, and may be divided into two groups, an upper and a lower one.

The upper character represents a rectangular figure divided into three transverse sections; in the third section and almost in the center is a cupule.

The lower character is more complicated and more difficult to describe. The first, or left-hand portion, represents a stone hatchet with a shaft; there is no doubt as to this, in my mind, as the outlines are perfectly clear, the design of the hatchet being very distinct. This hatchet measures 0^m, 108 in length and 38$^{m.m}$ in width to the edge of the blade. These are precisely the most common dimensions of the hatchets of our country. As to the remainder of the character, I think an interpretation of it difficult and premature.

On the whole, the result of an examination of these inscriptions leaves the impression that the author did not seek to cover a stone with ornamentation, for these outlines have nothing whatever of the ornamental, but that he wished to represent to his people, by intelligible symbols, some particular idea.

FIG. 139.—Petroglyph in Épone, France.

É. Cartailhac (*a*) begins an account of petroglyphs in the Department of Morbihan, in the old province of Brittany, translated and condensed as follows:

It is hardly possible to give a description of the designs in the covered way of Gavr' inis. They are various linear combinations, the lines being straight, curved, undulating, isolated, or parallel, ramified like a fern, segments of concentric circles, limited or not, and decorating certain compartments with close winding spirals, recalling vividly the figures produced by the lines on the skin in the hollow of the hand and on the tips of the fingers.

In the midst of accumulated and very oddly grouped lines, which no doubt are merely decorative, there are found signs which must have had a meaning, and some figures easy to determine.

The hatchet, the stone hatchet and no other, the large hatchet of Tumiac, of Mané-er-Hroèg, and of Mont Saint Michel, is represented in intaglio or in relief, real size. A single pillar of Gavr' inis bears eighteen of them. Less numerous groups are seen on some other blocks of the same covered way.

On a little block placed under the ceiling in order to wedge up one of the covering slabs, is seen the image of a hatchet with handle, conformable to a type found in the marsh of Ehenside in Cumberland, England. On many other monuments the presence of the same figures of hatchets, with handles or without, has been observed. The most curious slab is certainly that of Mané-er-Hroèg. It had been broken, and its three pieces had been thrown in disorder before the threshold of the crypt. One of its faces, very well smoothed off, bears a cartouche in the form of a stirrup, filled with enigmatic signs and surrounded above and below by a dozen hatchets with handles, all engraved.

One other sign, the imprint of the naked foot, is to be noted, found only once on this slab. Two human footprints are traced on one of the pillars of the crypt of the of the Petit-Mont in Arzon. They are said to be divided off, by a slight relief, from the rest of the granite frame on which they are sculptured, and which contains other drawings. Similar figures, engraved on rock or on tombstones, are cited from abroad, in lands far apart. In Sweden, the prints of naked or sandaled feet are common among the rock sculptures of the age of bronze which represent the curious scenes of the life of the people of that period. It is proper to note that these Scandinavian and Morbihan sculptures are not synchronous; the idea of an immediate influence of one people on the other can not be entertained. One might, however, maintain the identity of origin.

The other inscriptions of Brittany are enigmatic in every respect. But they probably had a conventional value, a determined meaning. There is first of all a sort of complicated cartouche, plainly defined, having the appearance of a buckler or heraldic shield. Among the isolated signs it is proper to note a figure of the shape of the letter U with the ends spread wide apart and curved in opposite directions. It recalls, with some aid from the imagination, the character which on the Scandinavian rocks represents more plainly ships and barks.

The sculpturing of hands and feet is to be remarked in connection with similar characters on the rocks in America, many illustrations of which appear in the present work.

B. Souché (a) in 1879 described and illustrated curious characters on the walls of the crypt of the tumulus of Lisières (Deux-Sèvres), France, some of which in execution markedly resemble several found in the United States and figured in this work.

SPAIN.

Mr. T. Jagor (a) communicated a brochure in reference to the Cueva de Altamira, transmitted to him by Prof. Vilanova in Madrid: "Short notes on some prehistoric objects of the province of Santander," in which Don Marcelino de Sautuola describes the wall pictures and other finds in the cave discovered by him at Altamira. Mr. Jagor remarks as follows on the subject:

The reproductions of the large wall pictures discovered in that cave displayed, in part, so excellent technique that the question arose how much of this excellence is to be attributed to the prehistoric artist, and how much to his modern copyist. Mr. Vilanova, who visited the cave soon after its discovery, and who regards the wall pictures as prehistoric, being about equal in age to the Danish Kjökken-möddings, states that the pictures given are pretty faithful imitations of the originals. The published drawings are all found on the ceiling of the first cave; on the walls of the subsequent caves are seen sketches of those pictures, which the artist afterwards completed. The outlines of all the drawings have been cut in the wall with coarse instruments, and nearly all the bone implements found in the cave show scratches, which render it probable that they were used for this purpose. The colors used consist merely of various kinds of ocher found in the province, without further preparation. Finally Mr. Vilanova reports that in the cave farthest back there was found, in his presence, an almost perfect specimen of *Ursus spelæus.*

Don Manuel de Góngora y Martinez (a) gives the account translated as follows:

The inscriptions of Fuencaliente are of great interest and importance. About one league east of the town, on a spur of the Sierra de Quintana, at the site of the Piedra Escritá, there is an almost inaccessible place, the home of wild beasts and mountain goats. Beyond the river de los Batanes and the river de las Piedras, looking toward sunset and toward the town, the artisans of a remote age cut skillfully and symmetrically with the point of the pickax into the flank of the rock and of the mountain, which is of fine flint, leaving a façade or frontispiece 6 yards in height and twice as wide, and excavating there two contiguous caves, which are wide at the mouth and end in a point, making two triangular niches polished on their four faces. On the two outer fronts to the left and right appear more than 60 symbols or hieroglyphs, written in a simple and rustic way with the index finger of a rude hand, and with a reddish bituminous pigment. The niches, about a yard and a half in height, 1 yard deep, and half a yard at the mouth, are covered by the exceedingly hard and immense rock of the mountain. There is formed, as it were, a vestibule or esplanade before the monument, and it is defended by a rampart made of the rocks torn from the niches, strengthened with juniper, oaks, and cork trees. The half-moon, the sun, an ax, a bow and arrows, an ear of corn, a heart, a tree, two human figures, and a head with a crown stand out among those signs, the foreshadowings of primitive writing.

The inscription on the first triangular face of the second cave is reproduced here as the left-hand group of the upper part of Fig. 1108, infra, and that "on the outer plane to the right, which already turns pyramidally to the north," is reproduced as the right-hand group of the same figure. They are inserted at that place for convenient comparison with other characters on the figure mentioned and with those in Figs. 1097 and 1107.

ITALY.

Mr. Moggridge (in Jour. Anthrop. Inst. Gr. Br. and I., VIII, p. 65) observes that one of the designs, q, reported by Dr. Von Haast from New Zealand (see Fig. 133), was the same as one which had been seen on rocks 6,900 feet above the sea in the northwest corner of Italy. He adds:

The inscriptions are not in colors, as are those given in Dr. Von Haast's paper, but are made by the repeated dots of a sharp pointed instrument. It is probable that if we knew how to read them they might convey important information, since the same signs occur in different combinations, just as the letters of our alphabet recur in different combinations to form words. Without the whole of these figures we can not say whether the same probability applies to them.

SECTION 4.

AFRICA.

The following examples are selected from the large number of petroglyphs known to have been discovered in Africa apart from those in Egypt, which are more immediately connected with the first use of syllabaries and alphabets, with symbolism and with gesture signs, under which headings some examples of the Egyptian hieroglyphics appear in this work.

ALGERIA.

In the Revue Géographique Internationale (a) is a communication upon the rock inscriptions at Tyout (Fig. 140) and Moghar (Fig. 141) translated, with some condensation, as follows:

On the last military expedition made in the Sahara Gen. Colonieu made a careful restoration of the inscriptions on the rocks, whose existence was discovered at Tyout and Moghar. At Tyout these inscriptions are engraved on red or Vosgian sandstone, and at Moghar on a hard compact calcareous stone. At Moghar the designs are more complicated than those at Tyout. An attempt has been made to render ideas by more learned processes; to the simplicity of the line, the artlessness of the poses which are seen at Tyout, there are added at Moghar academic attitudes difficult to render, and which must be intended to represent some custom or ceremony in use among the peoples who then inhabited this country. The costume at Moghar is also more complicated. The ornaments of the head recall those of Indians, and the woman's dress is composed of a waist and a short skirt fastened by a girdle with flowing ends. All this is very decent and elegant for the period. The infant at the side is swaddled. The large crouching figure is the face view of a man who seems to be bearing his wife on his shoulders. At the right of this group is a giraffe or large antelope. In the composition above may be distinguished a solitary individual in a crouching attitude, seen in front, the arms crossed in the attitude of prayer or astonishment. The animals which figure in the designs at Moghar are cattle and partridges. The little quadruped seated on its haunches may be a gerboise (kind of rat), very common in these parts.

In the inscriptions at Tyout we easily recognize the elephant, long since extinct in these regions, but neither horse nor camel is seen, probably not having been yet imported into the Sahara country.

Fig. 140.—Petroglyphs at Tyout, Algeria.

EGYPT.

While the picture-writings of Egypt are too voluminous for present discussion and fortunately are thoroughly presented in accessible publications, it seems necessary to mention the work of the late Mrs. A. B. Edwards (a). She gives a good account of the petroglyphs on the rocks bounding the ancient river bed of the Nile below Philæ, which show their employment in a manner similar to that in parts of North America:

These inscriptions, together with others found in the adjacent quarries, range over a period of between three and four thousand years, beginning with the early reigns of the ancient empire and ending with the Ptolemies and Cæsars. Some are mere autographs. Others run to a considerable length. Many are headed with figures of gods and worshippers. These, however, are for the most part mere graffiti, ill drawn and carelessly sculptured. The records they illustrate are chiefly votive. The passer-by adores the gods of the cataract, implores their protection, registers his name, and states the object of his journey. The votaries are of various ranks, periods, and nationalities; but the formula in most instances is pretty much the same. Now it is a citizen of Thebes performing the pilgrimage to Philæ, or a general at the head of his troops returning from a foray in Ethiopia, or a tributary prince doing homage to Rameses the Great and associating his suzerain with the divinities of the place.

SOUTH AFRICA.

Dr. Richard Andree, in Zeichen bei den Naturvölkern (*a*), presents well-considered remarks, thus translated:

The Hottentots and the Bantu peoples of South Africa produce no drawings, though the latter accomplish something in indifferent sculptures. The draftsmen

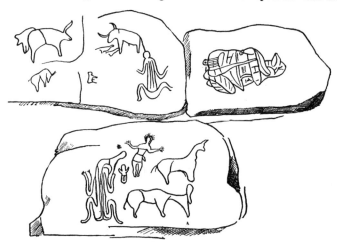

FIG. 141.—Petroglyphs at Moghar, Algeria.

and painters of South Africa are the Bushmen, who in this way, as well as by many other striking ethnic traits, testify to their independent ethnic position. The extraordinary multitude of figures of men and animals drawn by this people within its whole area, now greatly reduced, from the cape at the south to the lands and deserts north of the Orange river, and which they still draw at this day in gaudy colors, testify to an uncommonly firm hand, a keenly observing eye, and a very effective characterization. The Bushman artist mostly selects the surfaces of the countless rock bowlders, the walls of caves, or rock walls protected by overhanging crags, to serve as the canvas whereon to practice his art. He either painted his figures with colors or chiseled them with a hard sharp stone on the rock wall, so that they appear in intaglio. The number of these figures may be judged from the fact that Fritsch at Hopetown found "thousands" of them, often twenty or more on one block; Hubner, at "Gestoppte Fontein," in Transvaal, saw two hundred to three hundred together, carved in a soft slate. The earth colors employed are red, ochre, white, black, mixed with fat or also with blood. What instrument (brush?) is employed in applying the colors has not yet been ascertained, since, so far as I know, no Bushman artist has yet been observed at his work. As regards the paintings themselves, various classes may be distinguished, but in all cases the subjects are representations of figures; ornaments and plants are excluded. First of all, there are fights and hunting scenes, in which white men (boers) play a part, demonstrating the modern origin of these paintings. Next there are representations of animals, both of domestic animals (cattle, dogs) and of game, especially the various antelope species, giraffes, ostriches, elephants, rhinoceroses, monkeys, etc. A special class consists of representations of obscene nature, and, by way of exception, there has been drawn in one instance a ship or a palm tree.

Dr. Emil Holub (a) says:

The Bushmen, who are regarded as the lowest type of Africans, in one thing excel all the other South African tribes whose acquaintance I made between the south coast and 10° south latitude. They draw heads of gazelles, elephants, and hippopotami astonishingly well. They sketch them in their caves and paint them with ochre or chisel them out in rocks with stone implements, and on the tops of mountains we may see representations of all the animals which have lived in those parts in former times. In many spots where hippopotami are now unknown I found beautiful sketches of these animals, and in some cases fights between other native races and Bushmen are represented.

G. Weitzecker (a) gives a report of a large painting, in a cave at Thaba Phatsoua district of Léribé, here presented as Fig. 142, containing eighteen characters, with the addition of eight boys' heads. It represents the flight of Bushman women before some Zulu Kaffirs (Matebele). The description, translated, is as follows:

As usual, the Bushmen are represented as dwarfs and painted in bright color as contrasted with the Kaffirs, who are painted large and of dark color. The scene is full of life, a true artistic conception, and in the details there are many important things to be noted. For this reason I add a sketch of it, with the figures numbered, in order to be able to send you some brief annotations.

I will premise that as far as the women are concerned, in the small figures, no mistaken notion should be entertained in regard to the anterior appendages which catch, or rather strike, the eye in some of them. There is question simply of the pudendal coverings of the Bushman women, consisting of a strip of skin, and flapping in the wind.

a seems to represent a woman in an advanced interesting condition, who in her headlong flight has lost even her mantle. She holds in her hand a mogope (disproportionate); that is to say, a gourd dipper, such as are found, I believe, among all the south African tribes.

b. This figure, besides the mogope which she holds in her left hand, carries away in her flight, steadying it on her head with her right hand, a nkho (sesuto), a baked earthenware vessel, in which drinks are kept, and of which the ethnographic museum now contains some specimens. This woman, too, has lost all her clothing except the pudendal covering, and she looks pregnant. The attitudes of flight, while maintaining equilibrium, I deem very fine.

c, f, g, h, l, m, and perhaps *j.* Women carrying their babies on their backs, as is the practice of the natives, in the so-called thari; that is, a sheepskin so prepared that they can fasten it to their bodies and hold it secure, even while bent to the ground or running.

l and *m.* Women with twins. It may be worthy of note that the painter has placed them last, hampered as they are with a double weight.

c. Apparently a woman who has fallen in her flight. Figures *e* and *i* represent men, who by their stature might be thought to be Bushmen, as also by their color, which, so far as I remember, is not the same as that of the men coming up after them, being rather similar to that of the women. In that case *e* would stoop to raise the woman *c* who has fallen, and *i* would point the way to the others. Otherwise, if there is question of Matebeles, which is rendered plausible by the fact that *n* (which evidently represents an enemy) is not larger in stature than those two, then *e* would stoop to snatch the baby of the fallen woman, and *i* would strive to catch up with the two women *g* and *h*, who flee before it.

j. I can not explain this unless as a diffusion of color, which has transformed into something unrecognizable the figure of the child carried by its mother, who has fallen, like *b*.

k seems to be a woman resigned to her fate, who touches her neck with the left hand, unless, indeed, the line which I take to be the arm is the sketch of the thari with the baby.

l. A woman who runs toward the looker-on.

m represents a woman who has sat down, perhaps in order to place her twins better in the thari, while behind her *n* arrives, preparing to spear her. With *n* the band of enemies begins plainly, *o* seeming to be the leader, who, standing still, gives the signal. But this figure must have been altered by the water, which by diluting the color of the body has made it appear as a garment.

p and *q.* These admirable portraits of impetuosity and menace are a pictorial translation of the saying "having long legs so as to run fast."

r. A fine type of an attitude in the poise of running.

The author's discussion respecting the difference in size between the male human figures mentioned as indicating their respective tribes would have been needless had he considered the frequent expedient of representing chiefs or prominent warriors by figures of much larger stature than that of common soldiers or subjects. This device is common in the Egyptian glyphs, and examples of it also appear in the present work. (See Figs. 138, 139, and 1024.)

FIG. 142.—Petroglyph in Léribé, South Africa.

The same author, loc. cit., gives a brief account of two petroglyphs found by him near Leribo, in Basutoland, South Africa. They were on a large hollow rock overlooking a plain where the bushmen might spy game. The rock was all covered with pictures to a man's height. Many of them were entirely or almost entirely spoiled, both by the hands of herdsmen and by water running down the walls in time of rain. Some of them, however, are still very well preserved. They are shown on Fig. 143.

The left hand character represents a man milking an animal; the latter, judging by the back part, especially by the legs, was at first taken for an elephant; but the fore parts, especially the fore legs, evidently are those of a bovine creature or of an elk (eland). The enormous proportions of the back part are probably due to diffusion of colors, through the action of water running down the rock. The right hand character represents the sketch of an elk (eland), on which and under which are depicted four monkeys, admirable for fidelity of expression. The legs, with one exception, are not finished.

FIG. 143.—Petroglyphs in Basutoland, South Africa.

CANARY ISLANDS.

These islands are considered in connection with the continent of Africa.

S. Berthelot (a) gives an account, referring to Figs. 144 and 145, from which the following is extracted and translated:

A site very little frequented, designated by the name of Los Letreros, appears to have been inhabited in very ancient times by one of the aboriginal tribes estab-

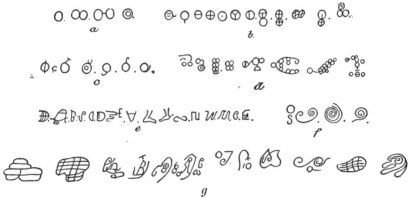

FIG. 144.—Petroglyphs in the Canary islands.

lished on the Island of Fer, one of the Canary islands. At a distance of about three-quarters of a league from the coast all the land sloping and broken by volcanic mounds extends in undulations to the edge of the cliffs which flank the coast. It is on this desert site, called Los Letreros, that inscriptions are found engraved on an ancient flow of basaltic lava, with a smooth surface, over an extent of more than 400 meters. On all this surface, at various distances and without any relation to each other, but placed where the lava presents the smoothest spots, rendered shining and glassy by the light varnish left by the volcanic matter in cooling, are the various groups of characters.

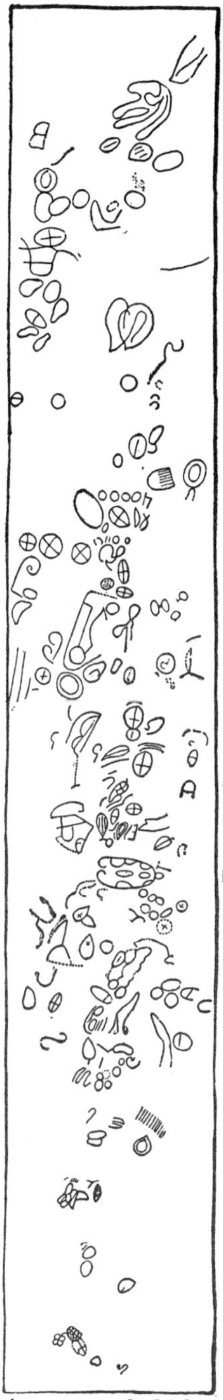

When we examine closely these different signs or characters so deeply engraved [pecked] on the rock, doubtless by means of some hard stone (obsidian or basalt), the first thing observed is that several identical signs are reproduced several times in the same group. These are, first, round and oval characters, more or less perfect, sometimes simple and isolated, again agglomerated in one group. These characters so often reproduced are again seen in juxtaposition or united, sometimes to others which are similar, sometimes to different ones, and even inclosed in others similar to them; for example, a in Fig. 144.

Round or more or less oval characters reappear several times in b.

Others, which are not met with more than once or twice among the groups of signs, also present notable variations; examples in c.

Of these are formed composite groups d, which belong, however, to the system of round signs.

Other analogous but not identical signs appear to assume rather the ovoid form than the round, and seem to have been so traced as not to be confounded with the round symbols. Some of them resemble leaves or fruit.

Another system of simple characters is the straight line, which can be represented by a stroke of the pen, isolated or repeated as if in numeration, and sometimes accompanied by other signs.

Other peculiar signs shown in e, which are not repeated, figure in the different groups of characters which the author has reproduced.

We notice further, in f, a small number of signs which bear a certain analogy to each other, and several of which are accompanied by other and more simple characters.

Several others still more complicated are in eccentric shapes which it is attempted to present in g.

Including the common oval characters often repeated and those consisting of a simple stroke similar to the strokes made by school children, all the various engraved characters scarcely exceed 400.

Fig. 145 gives a view of a series of different groups of signs in the length of the whole lava flow. The copyist has expressed by dots those symbols which were confused, partly defaced by the weather, or destroyed by fissures in the rock.

The same author (b) gives an account of several strange characters found engraved on a rock of the grotto of Belmaco, in the island of La Palma, one of the Canaries. He says:

These drawings, presented that they may be compared with those of Fer Island (Los Letreros), show some fifteen signs, some of which are repeated several times and others partly effaced by weather, or at least feebly traced. But what seems most remarkable is that six or seven

FIG. 145.—Petroglyphs in Canary Islands.

signs are recognized as exactly similar to those of Letreros, of the island of Fer, and almost all the others are analogous, for we recognize at once in comparing them the same style of bizarre writing, formed of hieroglyphic characters, mainly rude arabesques.

SECTION 5.

ASIA.

A considerable number of petroglyphs found in Asia are described and illustrated under other headings of this work. The following are presented here for geographic grouping:

CHINA.

Prof. Terrien de Lacouperie (c) says:

It is apparently to the art of the aboriginal non-Chinese that the following inscription [not copied] belongs, should it be proved to be primitive; and it is the only precise mention I have ever found of the kind in my researches.

Outside of Li-tch'eng (in N. Shangtaug), at some 500 li on the west towards the north, is a stone cliff mountain, on the upper parts of which may be seen marks and lines representing animals and horses. They are numerous and well drawn, like a picture.

JAPAN.

Prof. Edward S. Morse (a) kindly furnishes the illustration, reduced from a drawing made by a Japanese gentleman, Mr. Morishima, which is here reproduced ($\frac{1}{30}$ original size) as Fig. 145 a:

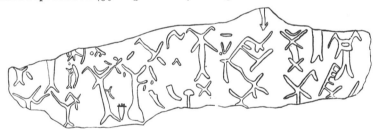

FIG. 145 a.—Petroglyph in Yezo, Japan.

Prof. Morse in a letter gives further information as follows:
"The inscriptions are cut in a rough way on the side of the cliff on the northwestern side of the bay of Otaru. Otaru is a little town on the western coast of Yezo. The cliffs are of soft, white tufa about 100 feet high, and the inscriptions were cut possibly with stone axes, and were 1 inch in width and from $\frac{1}{4}$ to $\frac{1}{2}$ of an inch in depth. They are about 4 feet from the ground."

Prof. John Milne (a) remarks upon the same petroglyph, of which he gives a rude copy, as follows:

So far as I could learn the Japanese are quite unable to recognize any of the characters, and they regard them as being the work of the Ainos.

I may remark that several of the characters are like the runic m. It has been suggested that they have a resemblance to old Chinese. A second suggestion was that they might be drawings of the insignia of rank carried by certain priests; a third idea was that they were phallic; a fourth that they were rough representations of men and animals, the runic *m* being a bird; and a fifth that they were the handicraft of some gentleman desirous of imposing upon the credulity of wandering archæologists.

I myself am inclined to think that they were the work of the peoples who have left so many traces of themselves in the shape of kitchen middens and various implements in this locality. In this case they may be Aino.

Another illustration from Japan is presented in Pl. LII.

INDIA.

Mr. Rivett-Carnac, in Archæologic Notes on Ancient Sculpturings on Rocks in Kumaon, India (*a*), gives a description of the glyphs copied in Fig. 146:

At a point about two miles and a half south of Dwara-Hath, and twelve miles north of the military station of Ranikhet in Kumaon, the bridle-road leading from the plains through Naini Tal and Ranikhet to Baijnath, and thence on to the celebrated shrine of Bidranath, is carried through a narrow gorge at the mouth of which is a temple sacred to Mahadeo, * * * which is locally known by the name of Chandeshwar.

About two hundred yards south of the temple, toward the middle of the defile, rises a rock at an angle of forty-five degrees presenting a surface upon which, in a space measuring fourteen feet in height by twelve in breadth, more than two hundred cups are sculptured. They vary from an inch and a half to six inches in diameter and from half an inch to an inch in depth, and are arranged in groups composed of approximately parallel rows.

The cups are mostly of the simple types and only exceptionally surrounded by single rings or connected by grooves.

SIBERIA.

N. S. Shtukin (*a*) referring to certain picture-writings on the cliffs of the Yenisei river, in the Quarterly Isvestia of the Imperial Geographical Society for 1882, says: "These are figured, but are not particularly remarkable, except as being the work of invaders from the far south, perhaps Persians. Camels and pheasants are among the animals represented."

Philip John von Strahlenberg, in An Historico-Geographical Description of the North and Eastern Parts of Europe and Asia, etc., reported inscriptions relating to the chase, on the banks of the river Yenesei. He says of one: "It takes its characteristic features from the natural history of the region; and we may suppose it to embrace rude representations of the Siberian hare, the cabarda or musk deer and other known quadrupeds."

He also furnishes a transcript of inscriptions found by him on a precipitous rock on the river Irtish. This rock, which is 36 feet high, is isolated. It has four sides, one of which faces the water and has a number of tombs or sepulchral caves beneath. All of the four faces

have rude representations of the human form, and other unintelligible
characters are drawn in red colors in a durable kind of pigment, which

Fig. 146.—Petroglyphs at Chandeshwar, India

is found to be almost indestructible and is much used for rock inscriptions.

Prof. Terrien de Lacouperie, op. cit., makes the following remarks:

Symbolical marks, incised or drawn graffitti, not properly speaking inscriptions, have been found in Siberia, but they are not the expected primitive remains of ancient writings. Some are purely Tartar, being written in Mongolian and Kalmuck; others, obviously the work of common people, may be Arabic, while some others found on the left bank of the Jenissei river are much more interesting. They seem to me to be badly written in Syriac, from right to left horizontally, before the time of the adaptation of this writing to the Uigur and Mongol. The characters are still separated one from the other. On one of these graffitti found at the same place several Chinese characters, as written by common people, are recognizable.

Some hieroglyphical graffitti have been discovered on rocks above Tomsk, on the right bank of the Tom river, in Siberia. They are incised at a height of more than 20 feet. They are very rude, and somewhat like the famous Livre de Sauvages of merry fame in palæography. Quadrupeds, men, heads, all roughly drawn, and some indistinct lines, are all that can be seen. It looks more like the pictorial figures which can be used as a means of notation by ignorant people at any moment than like an historical beginning of some writing. There is not the slightest appearance of any sort of regularity or conventional arrangement in them.

The last we have to speak of are quite peculiar and altogether different from the others. The signs are painted in red. They are made of straight lines, disposed like drawings of lattices and window shades, and also like the tree characters of the Arabs and like the runes. They are met with near the Irtisch river, on a rock over the stream Smolank.

Figs. 513, 721, 722, and 733, infra, have relation to this geographic region.

It is to be remarked that some of the Siberian and Tartar characters, especially those reproduced by Schoolcraft, I, Pls. 65 and 66, have a strong resemblance to the drawings of the Ojibwa, some of which are figured and described in the present work, and this coincidence is more suggestive from the reason that the totem or dodaim, which often is the subject of those drawings, is a designation which is used by both the Ojibwa and the Tartar with substantially the same sound and significance.

CHAPTER V.

CUP SCULPTURES

The simplest form of rock inscription is almost ubiquitous. In Europe, Asia, Africa, America, and Oceanica, shallow, round, cup-like depressions are found, sometimes in rows, sometimes singly, sometimes surrounded by a ring or rings, but often quite plain. The cup-markers often arranged their sculpturings in regularly spaced rows, not infrequently surrounding them with one or more clearly cut rings; sometimes, again, they associated them with concentric circles or spirals. Occasionally the sculptors demonstrated the artificial character of their work by carving it in spots beyond the reach of atmospheric influences, such as the interiors of stone cists or of dwellings. It must, however, be noted that, although there is thus established a distinction between those markings which are natural and those which are artificial, it is possible that there may have been some distant connection between the two, and that the depressions worn by wind and rain may have suggested the idea of the devices, now called cup-markings, to those who first sculptured them.

Vast numbers of these cup stones are found in the British islands, often connected with other petroglyphs. In the county of Northumberland alone there are 53 stones charged with 350 sculptures, among which are many cup depressions. So also in Germany, France, Denmark, and indeed everywhere in Europe, but these forms took their greatest development in India.

The leading work relating to this kind of sculpture is that of Prof. J. Y. Simpson (a), afterward known as Sir James Simpson, who reduces the forms of the cup sculptures to seven elementary types, here reproduced in Fig. 147. His classification is as follows:

First type. *Single cups.*—They are the simplest type of these ancient stone-cuttings. Their diameter varies from 1 inch to 3 inches and more, while they are often only half an inch deep, but rarely deeper than an inch or an inch and a half. They commonly appear in different sizes on the same stone or rock, and although they sometimes form the only sculptures on a surface they are more frequently associated with figures of a different character. They are in general scattered without order over the surface, but occasionally four or five or more of them are placed in more or less regular groups, exhibiting a constellation-like arrangement.

Second type. *Cups surrounded by a single ring.*—The incised rings are usually much shallower than the cups and mostly surround cups of comparatively large size. The ring is either complete or broken, and in the latter case it is often traversed by a radial groove which runs from the central cup through and even beyond the ring.

189

Third type. *Cups surrounded by a series of concentric complete rings.*—In this complete annular form the central cup is generally more deeply cut than the surrounding rings, but not always.

Fourth type. *Cups surrounded by a series of concentric, but incomplete rings having a straight radial groove.*—This type constitutes perhaps the most common form of the

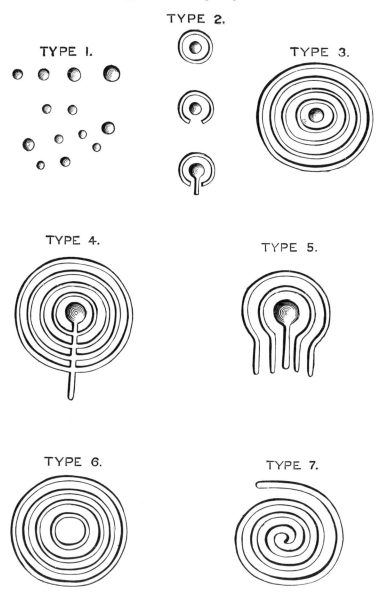

FIG. 147.—Types of cup sculptures.

circular carvings. The rings generally touch the radial line at both extremities, but sometimes they terminate on each side of it without touching it. The radial groove occasionally extends considerably beyond the outer circle, and in most cases it runs in a more or less downward direction on the stone or rock. Sometimes it runs on and unites into a common line with other ducts or grooves coming from other circles, till thus several series of concentric rings are conjoined into a larger or smaller cluster, united together by the extension of their radial branch-like grooves.

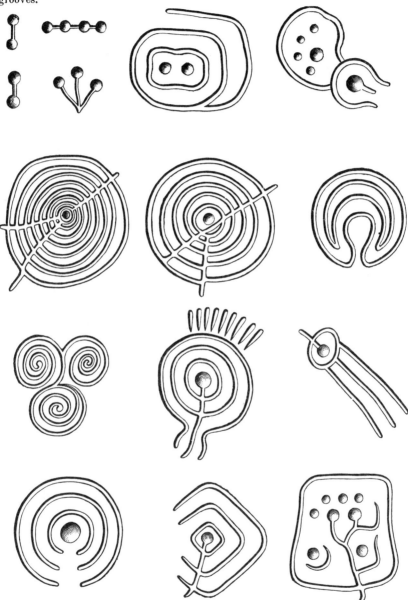

FIG. 148.—Variants of cup sculptures.

Fifth type. *Cups surrounded by concentric rings and flexed lines.*—The number of inclosing or concentric rings is generally fewer in this type than in the two last preceding types, and seldom exceeds two or three in number.

Sixth type. *Concentric rings without a central cup.*—In many cases the concentric rings of the types already described appear without a central cup or depression, which is most frequently wanting in the complete concentric circles of the third type.

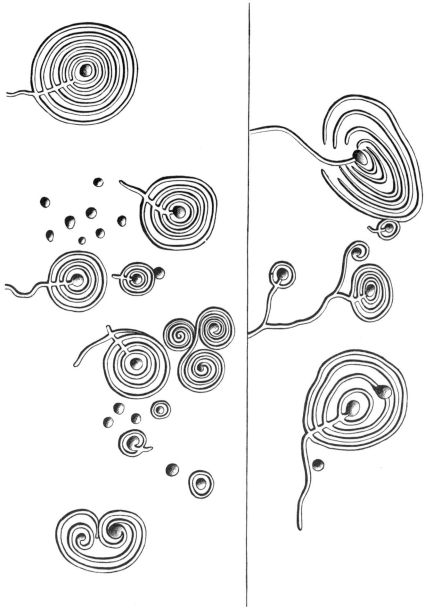

Fig. 149.—Cup sculptures at Auchnabreach, Scotland.

Seventh type. *Concentric circular lines of the form of a spiral or volute.*—The central beginning of the spiral line is usually, but not always, marked by a cup-like excavation.

It often occurs that two, three, or more of these various types are found on the same stone or rock, a fact indicating that they are intimately allied to each other.

Prof. Simpson presents what he calls "the chief deviations from the principal types" reproduced here as Fig. 148.

The first four designs represent cups connected by grooves, which is a noticeable and frequently occurring feature. In Fig. 149 views of sculptured rock surfaces at Auchnabreach, Argyleshire, Scotland, are given.

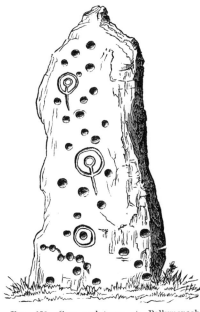

FIG. 150.—Cup sculptures at Ballymenach, Scotland.

Simple cups, cups surrounded by one ring or by concentric rings, with radial grooves and spirals, appear here promiscuously mingled. Fig. 150 exhibits isolated as well as connected cups, a cup surrounded by a ring, and concentric rings with radial grooves, on a standing stone (menhir), belonging to a group of seven at Ballymenach, in the parish of Kilmichael-Glassary, in Argyleshire, Scotland.

Dr. Berthold Seeman remarks concerning the characters in Fig. 105, supra, copied from a rock in Chiriqui, Panama, that he discovers in it a great resemblance to those of Northumberland, Scotland, and other parts of Great Britain. He says, as quoted by Dr. Rau (d):

It is singular that, thousands of miles away, in a remote corner of tropical America, we should find the concentric rings and several other characters typically identical with those engraved on the British rocks.

The characters in Chiriqui are, like those of Great Britain, incised on large stones, the surface of which has not previously undergone any smoothing process. The incised stones occur in a district of Veraguas (Chiriqui or Alanje), which is now thinly inhabited, but which, judging from the numerous tombs, was once densely peopled.

From information received during my two visits to Chiriqui and from what has been published since I first drew attention to this subject, I am led to believe that there are a great many inscribed rocks in that district. But I myself have seen only one, the now famous *piedra pintal* (i. e., painted stone), which is found on a plain at Caldera, a few leagues from the town of David. It is 15 feet high, nearly 50 feet in circumference, and rather flat on the top. Every part, especially the eastern side, is covered with incised characters about an inch or half an inch deep. The first figure on the left hand side represents a radiant sun, followed by a series of heads or what appear to be heads, all with some variation. It is these heads, particularly the appendages (perhaps intended for hair?), which show a certain resemblance to one of the most curious characters found on the British rocks, and calling to mind the so-called "Ogham characters." These "heads" are succeeded by scorpion-like or branched and other fantastic figures. The top of the stone and the other sides are covered with a great number of concentric rings and ovals, crossed by lines. It is especially these which bear so striking a resemblance to the Northumbrian characters.

Fig. 151 presents five selected characters from the rock mentioned: *a* attached to the respective numbers always refers to the Chiriqui and

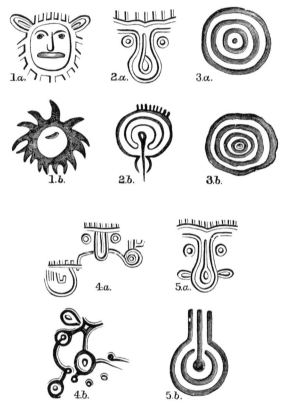

FIG. 151.—Cup sculptures in Chiriqui.

b to the British type of the several designs; 1*a* and 1*b* represent radiant suns; 2*a* and 2*b* show several grooves, radiating from an outer arch, resembling, as Dr. Seeman thinks, the Ogham characters; 3*a* and 3*b* show the completely closed concentric circles; 4*a* and 4*b* show how the various characters are connected by lines; 5*a* and 5*b* exhibit the groove or outlet of the circle.

Mr. G. H. Kinahan, in Journal of the Anthropological Institute of Great Britain and Ireland, 1889, p. 171, gives an account of Barnes's Inscribed Dallâus, County Donegal, Ireland. One of his figures bears four cups joined together by lines forming a cross. The remainder of the illustrations consist of concentric rings and cups resembling others already figured in this paper.

Marcano (*c*) describes Fig. 152 as follows:

The chain of Cuchivero, situated in Venezuela between the Orinoco and the Caura, shows on its flanks small plateaus on which are numerous stones which seem to have been aligned. This chain is separated by a deep valley from that of Tiramuto, from which were copied the petroglyphs here presented. The one represents a single sun,

FIG. 152.—Cup sculptures in Venezuela.

the other two suns joined together. The rays of the former run from one circumference to the other. The other two are joined together by a central stroke, and the rays all start from the outer circumference.

The same author (loc. cit.) thus describes Fig. 153:

These designs, taken on the little hills of the high Cuchivero, differ altogether from the preceding. *a* is a very regular horizontal grouping. It begins by a spiral

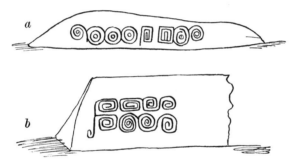

FIG. 153.—Cup sculptures in Venezuela.

joined to three figures similar among themselves, and similar also to the eyes of jaguars which we have often met with. There follows a sort of isolated fret; at its right is another, larger and joined to a circle different from the preceding; it has a central point, and the second circumference is interrupted. The figure terminates in a spiral like the one at the beginning of the line, and which, being turned in the opposite direction, serves at its pendant.

b is formed of two horizontal rows one above the other. We there find first of all two frets united by a vertical stroke ending in a hook. The characters which follow, resembling those of *a*, are distinct in each row, but on closer inspection they are seen to have a peculiar correspondence.

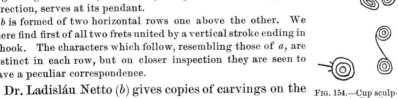

FIG. 154.—Cup sculptures in Brazil.

Dr. Ladisláu Netto (*b*) gives copies of carvings on the rocks in Brazil on the banks of the Rio Negro, from Moura to the city of Manaus, and remarks upon the characters reproduced here as Fig. 154, that they represent the figure of the multiple concentric circles joined together two by two, as were found on several other rocks in the same region, and as they appear in many inscriptions of Central America and at various points of North America.

Senhor Araripe (b) gives the following account:

In Banabuiu, Brazil, about three-quarters of a league from the plantation of Caza-nova, on the road to Castelo, is a stone resting upon another, at the height of a man, which the inhabitants call Pedra-furada (pierced stone) having on its western face the inscription in Fig. 155.

The characters have been much effaced by the rubbing of cattle against them; the stone has also cracked. Some fragments lying at the foot of it bear on their upper faces round holes made by a sharp tool, and resembling those shown in this figure.

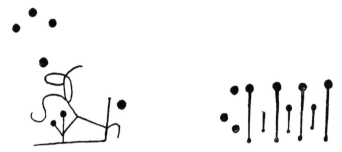

FIG. 155.—Cup sculptures in Brazil.

Cup stones, called by the French *pierres à ecuelles* and *pierres à cupules* and by the Germans *Schalensteine,* are found throughout Hindustan, on the banks of the Indus, at the foot of the Himalayas, in the valley of Cashmere, and on the many cromlechs around Nagpoor. At this very day one may see the Hindu women carrying the water of the Ganges all the way to the mountains of the Punjab, to pour into the cupules and thus obtain from the divinity the boon of motherhood earnestly desired.

The cup sculptures often become imposing by their number and combination. In the Kamaon mountains there are numerous blocks that support small basins. One of them is mentioned as being 13 feet in length by 9 in breadth and 7 in height, and showing five rows of cupules. At Chandeswar (see Fig. 146) the rocks themselves are covered with these signs. They present two different types. One of the most frequent groups shows a simple round cavity; in the others, the cupels are encircled by a sort of ring carved in intaglio and encircling figures. One of these figures recalls the swastika, the sacred sign of the Aryans. The present Hindus are absolutely ignorant of the origin of these sculptures; they are fain to attribute them to the Goalas, a mysterious race of shepherd kings who preceded the great invasions which imprinted an indelible stamp on the Indies as well as on Europe. These cupels are correlated with the worship of Mahadeo, one of the many names given to Siva, the third god of the Hindu triad, whose emblem is the serpent. Chandeswar is reached through a narrow gorge; at the entrance is found a temple sacred to Mahadeo. The columns and slabs bear cupules similar to those seen on the rocks.

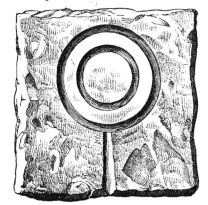

Some of the Mahadeo designs engraved on stone slabs in this temple (see Rivett-Carnac, loc. cit.) are represented in Fig. 156, showing a marked resemblance to and approaching identity with this class of cuttings on bowlders, rocks, and megalithic monuments in Europe.

A large number of stones with typical cup markings have been found in the United States of America. Some of those illustrated in this paper are presented in Pl. v, and Figs. 19 and 48.

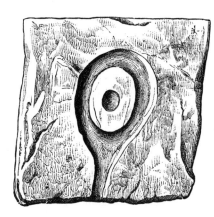

Among the many attempts, all hitherto unsatisfactory, to explain the significance of the cup stones as distributed over nearly all parts of the earth, one statement of Mr. Rivett-Carnac (b) is of value as furnishing the meaning now attached to them in India. He says:

Having seen sketches and notes on rock sculptures in India which closely resemble unexplained rock carvings in Scotland, and having myself found one of the Scotch forms cut on a bowlder in Kángrá, * * * being at Ayodhyá with a Hindu who speaks good English, I got a fakir and drew on the sand of the Gogra the figure ⊚ . I asked what that meant. The fakir at once answered,

"Mahadeo." I then drew ⊚ and got the same answer. At Delhi my old acquaintance, Mr. Shaw, told me that these two signs are chalked on stones in Kángrá by people marching in marriage processions. The meaning given to these two symbols now in India is familiarly known to the people.

FIG. 156.—Cup sculptures in India.

Mahadeo, more accurately Mahadiva, is the god of generation. He is worshiped by the Sawas, one of the numerous Hindu sects, under the

form of a phallus, often represented by a simple column, which sometimes is placed on the yoni or female organ. It is suggested that in a
common form of the sculptures the inner circle represents the Mahadeo
or lingam, and the outer or containing circle the yoni. No idea of
obscenity occurs from this representation to the Hindus, who adore
under this form the generative power in nature.

Prof. Douglas, in the Saturday Review, November 24, 1883, furnishes
some remarks on the topic now considered:

In Palestine and the country beyond Jordan some of the marks found are so large
that it has been supposed that they may have been used as small presses of wine, or
as mortars for pounding the gleanings of wheat. But there is an objection to these
theories as accounting for the marks generally, which is fatal to them. To serve
these purposes the rocks on which the marks occur should be in a horizontal position, whereas in a majority of cases all over the world the "cups" are found either
on shelving rocks or on the sides of perpendicular stones. This renders worthless
also the ideas which have at different times been put forward that they may have
been used for some sort of gambling game, or as sun-dials. A Swiss archæologist
who has lately devoted himself to the question believes that he has recognized, in
the sculpturings under his observation, maps of the surrounding districts, the
"cups" indicating the mountain peaks. In the same way others have thought that
similar markings may have been intended as maps or plans pointing out the direction and character of old circular camps and cities in their neighborhood. But if
any such resemblances have been discovered they can hardly be other than fortuitous,
since it is difficult to understand how rows of cup marks, arranged at regular
intervals and in large numbers, could have served as representatives either of the
natural features of a country or of camps and cities. But a closer resemblance may
be found in them as maps if we suppose that they were intended to represent things
in the heavens rather than on earth. The round cup-like marks are reasonably suggestive of the sun, moon, and stars, and if only an occasional figure could be found
representing a constellation, some color might be held to be given to the idea; but
unfortunately this is not the case. Nevertheless the shape of the marks has led
many to believe that they are relics of the ancient sun worship of Phœnicia, and
that their existence in Europe is due to the desire of the Phœnician colonists to con-
vert our forefathers to their faith. But there are many reasons for regarding this
theory, though supported by the authority of Prof. Nilsson, as untenable. The
observations of late years have brought to light cup marks and megalithic circles in
parts of Europe on which a Phœnician foot never trod; and it is a curious circumstance that in those portions of the British Isles most frequented by these indefatiga-
ble traders there are fewer traces of these monuments than in the northern and
inland districts, which were comparatively inaccessible to them.

The Swiss archæologist mentioned above by Prof. Douglas is Fritz
Roediger (a), of whose theory the following is a translated abstract:

What renders the deciphering of these sign stones exceedingly difficult (I pur-
posely avoid the words "map stones" because not all are such) is their great variety in
size, position, material, workmanship, and meaning. I will here speak of the latter
only, inasmuch as there are stones which in their smallest and their largest form
are yet frequently nothing else than boundary stones, whose origin can often not be
definitely established as prehistoric, while on the other hand again we discover
well-marked boundary stones, which at the same time show the outline of the piece
of ground which they guard. Similarly we find prehistoric (Gallic) "Leuk" stones,
differing from the meter-high communal and state boundary stones of modern times
in nothing but this, that they have some indistinct grooves and one or two hooks,

while on the other hand we meet "Leuk" stones, which on their restricted heads, often also on the side walls, indicate their environs for (Leuk) miles around, up, down, and sidewise, while a third class of this form merely adorn crossroads, and indicate deviations by means of lines and points (waranden). Thus we find quite extensive slabs or structures that signify only some hectares, often only one, while we meet very small ones, or, at any rate, of moderate size, which one man can move, that represent very large districts, some presenting only lines and grooves, others with shells of various sizes, a third kind with both kinds of ornaments and samples of ornaments, and again others with no sign at all, but yet respected as stones of special meaning by the population, and called "hot stone," "pointed stone," "heath stone," "child's stone," etc. Other stones have basin-like or platter-like depressions, and finally there are outcropping rocks with marks of one kind or another, holes, rents, clefts, etc. A further great difficulty hampering the deciphering of these wonderful stones is the lack of opportunities for comparison and experience. I have been markedly favored in this respect by my sojourn and wanderings in valley, mountain and alp. Western Switzerland is a very paradise for investigations of this kind, especially the lake country and the upper part of the canton of Solothurn (Soleure). A third difficulty, often insuperable, lies in the nonexistence of appropriate good maps for comparison. In this respect too we are well off in Switzerland.

According to my observations in this field, now continued nearly 12 years, prehistoric man had: (1) His land or province survey; (2) his circle, district, and communal surveys, in reference to which (3) the Alpine surveys deserve special mention, in cantons which down to the present day know nothing of such surveys; (4) private and special surveys. Thus it seems that my observations lend full confirmation to the oldest historic or traditional statements concerning the tenure of land of the Kelto-Germans or Germano-Kelts.

Among the Ojibwa concentric circles, according to Schoolcraft (*d*), constituted the symbol of time. It would be dangerous to explain the many markings of this character by the suggested symbolism, which also recalls that of Egypt in relation to the circle-figure. Inquiries have often been made whether the North American Indians have any superstitious or religious practices connected with the markings under consideration, e. g., in relation to the desire for offspring, which undoubtedly is connected with the sculpturing of cup depressions and furrows in the eastern hemisphere. No evidence is yet produced of any such correspondence of practice or tradition relating to it. In the absence of any extrinsic explanation the prosaic and disappointing suggestion intrudes that circular concentric rings are easy to draw and that the act of drawing them suggests the accentuation of depressions or hollows within their curves. Much stress is laid upon the fact that the characters are found in so many parts of the earth, with the implication that all the sculptors used them with the same significance, thus affording ground for the hypothesis that anciently one race of people penetrated all the regions designated. But in such an implication the history of the character formed by two intersecting straight lines is forgotten. The cross is as common as the cup-stone, and has, or anciently had, a different signification among the different people who used it, beginning as a mark and ending as a symbol. Therefore, it may readily be imagined that the rings in question, which are drawn nearly as easily as the cross, were at one time favorite but probably meaningless designs, perhaps, in popular expression, "instinctive" commencements of the artistic practice, as was the earliest delineation of the cross-figure. Afterward the rings, if employed as symbols or emblems, would naturally have a different meaning applied to them in each region where they now appear.

It must, however, be noted that the figures under discussion can be and often are the result of conventionalization. A striking remark is made by Mr. John Murdoch (a), of the Smithsonian Institution, that south of Bering strait the design of the "circle and dot," which may be regarded as the root of the cup sculpture, is the conventionalized representation of a flower, and is very frequently seen as an ornamental device.

An elucidation of some of the most common forms of cup sculptures is given, without qualification and also without authority, but with the serene consciousness of certainty, by the Rev. Charles Rogers, "D. D., LL. D., F. S. A., Scot., etc.," as follows:

The sculptures are sacred books, which the awe-inspired worshipper was required to revere and, probably, to salute with reverence. A single circle represented the sun, two circles in union the sun and moon—Baal and Ashtaroth. The wavy groove passing across the circle pointed to the course of water from the clouds, as discharged upon the earth. Groups of pit marks pointed to the stars or, more probably, to the oaks of the primeval temples.

CHAPTER VI.

PICTOGRAPHS GENERALLY.

In leaving the geographic distribution of petroglyphs to examine the comprehensive theme of pictographs in general, the first and correct impression is that the mist of the archaic and unknown is also left and that the glow of current significance is reached. The pictographs of the American Indians are seldom if ever cryptographs, though very often conventional and sometimes, for special reasons, preconcerted, as are their signals. They are intended to be understood without a key, and nearly all of those illustrated below in the present work are accompanied by an interpretation. As the art is in actual daily use it is free from the superstition pending from remote antiquity.

It will be noticed that a large proportion of the pictographs to be now presented, which are not petroglyphs, are Micmac, Abnaki, Dakota, and Ojibwa, although it is admitted that as many more could be obtained from other tribes, such as the Zuñi and the Navajo. The reason for the omission of details regarding the latter is that they are already published, or are in the course of publication, by Mrs. Stevenson, Dr. Matthews, Mr. Cushing, Mr. Fewkes, and other writers, who have specially devoted themselves to the peoples mentioned and the region occupied by them.

The present writer obtained a valuable collection of birch-bark pictographs immemorially and still made by the Passamaquoddy and Penobscot tribes of Abnaki in Maine, showing a similarity in the use of picture-writing between the members of the widespread Algonquian stock in the regions west of the great lakes and those on the northeastern seaboard. He also learned that the same art was common to the less known Montagnais and Nascapees in the wooded regions north of the St. Lawrence. This correlation of the pictographic practice, in manner and extent, was before inferentially asserted, but no satisfactory evidence of it had been furnished until the researches of the Bureau of Ethnology, in 1887 and 1888, made by the writer, brought into direct comparison the pictography of the Ojibwa with that of the Micmacs and the Abnaki. Many of the Indians of the last-named tribes still use marks and devices on birch bark in the ordinary affairs of life, especially as notices of departure and direction and for warning and guidance. The religious use of original drawings among them, which is still prominent among the Ojibwa, has almost ceased, but traces of it remain.

The most interesting of all the accounts regarding the pictographs of the North American Indians published before the last decade was contained in the works of Henry R. Schoolcraft, issued in 1853 and subsequent years, and the most frequently quoted part of his contributions on this subject describes the pictographs of the Ojibwa. He had special facilities for obtaining accurate information with regard to all matters relating to that tribe on account of his marriage to one of its women, a granddaughter of a celebrated chief, Waub-o-jeeg and daughter of a European named Johnson. She was educated in Ireland and had sufficient intelligence to understand and describe to her husband the points of interest relating to her tribe.

The accounts given by Mr. Schoolcraft, with numerous illustrations, convey the impression that the Ojibwa were nearly as far advanced in hieroglyphic writing as the Egyptians before their pictorial representations had become syllabic. The general character of his voluminous publications has not been such as to assure modern critics of his accuracy, and the wonderful combination of minuteness and comprehensiveness attributed by him to the Ojibwa "hieroglyphs" has of late been generally regarded with suspicion. It was considered in the Bureau of Ethnology an important duty to ascertain how much of truth existed in these remarkable accounts, and for that purpose the writer, with Dr. Hoffman as assistant, examined the most favorable points in the present habitat of the tribe, namely, the northern regions of Minnesota and Wisconsin, to ascertain how much was yet to be discovered.

The general results of the comparison of Schoolcraft's statements with what is now found show that he told the truth in substance, but with much exaggeration and coloring. The word "coloring" is particularly appropriate, because in his copious illustrations various colors were used freely and with apparent significance, whereas, in fact, the general rule in regard to the birch-bark rolls was that they were never colored at all; indeed, the bark was not adapted to coloration. The metaphorical coloring was also flourished by him in a manner which seems absurd to any thorough student of the Indian philosophy and religions. Metaphysical concepts are attached by him to some of the devices which he calls "symbols," which could never have been entertained by a people in the stage of culture of the Ojibwa. While some symbolism, in the wide sense of the term, may be perceived, iconography and ideography are more apparent.

The largest part of the bark rolls and other pictographs of the Ojibwa obtained by the Bureau, relates to the ceremonies of the Midē′ and of the shamanistic orders; another division refers to the Jessakid performances, which can be classed under the head of jugglery; and a third part embraces the more current and practical uses. Examples of all of these are given, infra.

The difficulties sometimes attending the pursuit of ceremonial pictographs were exemplified to the writer at Odanah, Wisconsin. Very few of the Ojibwa in that neighborhood, who are generally civilized and in easy circumstances, had any more than a vague knowledge that such things as inscribed bark rolls had ever existed. Three, however, were traced and one was shown. The owner, an uncompromising heathen, was called Kitche-sha-bads. "Kitche" means big, "sha" is an attempt at the French form of John, and "bads" is a bad shot at Baptiste, the whole translation, therefore, being "Big John the Baptist." This old fellow, though by no means as enterprising or successful as some of the younger generation, had a snug house and farm and $300 in the savings bank at Ashland. One thing, however, he needed, viz, whisky. The strictest regulations prevailed on the reservation, really prohibitory to the introduction of spirits, and, indeed, there was at the nearest town, Ashland, a severe penalty for selling any form of liquor to an Indian. To obtain whisky, therefore, was the only consideration which would tempt him to allow a copy of the roll to be taken or by which he could be induced to recite or rather to chant it in the manner prescribed. He was undoubtedly accomplished in the knowledge of the Midē′ rites, and the roll, which was shown in his hands, but not out of them, is substantially the same as one of those copied in the present work, which was discovered several hundred miles farther northwest among a different division of the same tribe. The shaman began rather mildly to plead that he was an old man and could not remember well unless his spirit was made good by a little whisky. This difficulty might have been obviated by a traveler's pocket flask, but his demands increased with great rapidity. He said that the roll could only be sung at night, that he must have another old man to help him, and the old man must have whisky; then that there must be a number of young men, who would join in the chorus, and all the young men must have whisky too. These demands made it evident that he was intending to have a drunken orgy, which resulted in a cloture of the debate. And yet the idea of the old shaman was in its way correct. The ceremonial chants could be advantageously pronounced only under inspiration, which was of old obtained by a tedious form of intoxication, now expedited by alcohol.

The fact that this work shows a large proportion of pictographs from the Siouan linguistic family, and especially from the Dakota division of that family, may be explained partly by the greater familiarity of the present writer with it than with most other Indian divisions. Yet probably more distinctive examples of evolution in ideography and in other details of picture-writing are found still extant among the Dakota than among any other North American tribe. The degree of advance made by the Dakota was well expressed by the Rev. S. D. Hinman, who was born, lived, married, and died in their midst, and, though unfortunately he committed to writing but little of his knowledge, was more thoroughly informed about that people than any other man of European descent.

To express his views clearly he gave to this writer in a manuscript communication his own classification of pictography (which is not in all respects approved) as follows:

I. Picturing.—[This is the method called by Prof. Brinton (*b*) iconographic writing.] This shows a simple representation of a thing or event in picture, as of a bear, a man's hand, a battle.

II. Ideography.—This arbitrarily, though significantly, recalls an idea or abstract quality, as love or goodness.

III. Picture-writing.—This will, in picture and character, arbitrarily or otherwise, recite a connected story, there being a picture or character for every word, even for conjunctions and prepositions.

IV. Phonetic writing.—This gives phonetic value to every picture and spells out the words by sound, almost as in later alphabets, as if a lion should stand for the "l" sound, a bear for the "b" sound, etc., and from this last by modification came alphabets. [This is the familiar theory, which is accurate so far as it is applicable, of the initial sound, but other elements are disregarded, such as the "rebus," for which special class Prof. Brinton, loc. cit., has invented the title of the Iconomatic method.]

Accepting this chronologic if not evolutionary arrangement, Mr. Hinman decided that the Dakota picture-writing had passed through stage I and was already entering upon stage II when it was first observed by the European explorers. Of III and IV he found no examples in Dakota pictography, though in sign language the Dakota had progressed further and had entered upon III.

As a summary of the topic it seems that pictographs other than petroglyphs which presumably are more modern than most of the latter, can be studied, not by geographic distribution, but by their ascertainable intent and use. Unless the classification of the remaining part of this work under its various headings has been defective, further discussion in this chapter is unnecessary.

CHAPTER VII.

SUBSTANCES ON WHICH PICTOGRAPHS ARE MADE.

Substances on which pictographs are made may be divided into—
  I. The human body.
  II. Natural objects other than the human body.
  III. Artificial objects.

SECTION 1.

THE HUMAN BODY.

Markings on human bodies are—(1) Those expressed by painting or such coloration as is not permanent. It has been found convenient to treat this topic under the heading of "Significance of Colors," Chap. XVIII, Sec. 3. (2) Those of intended permanence upon the skin, generally called tattoo, but including scarification. This enormous and involved topic is discussed, so far as space allows, under the heading of "Totems, Titles, and Names," Chapter XIII, Sec. 3, where it seems to be most convenient in the general arrangement of this work. Though logically it might have been divided among several of the headings, that course would have involved much repetition or cross reference.

SECTION 2.

NATURAL OBJECTS OTHER THAN THE HUMAN BODY.

Other natural objects may be divided into—(1) Stone; (2) bone; (3) skins; (4) feathers and quills; (5) gourds; (6) shells; (7) earth and sand; (8) copper; (9) wood.

STONE.

This caption comprises the pictographs upon stone surfaces or tablets which are not of the dimensions or in the position to be included under the heading of petroglyphs, as elsewhere defined. Accounts, with and without illustrations, have been published of several engraved tablets, regarding which there has been much discussion, and some examples appear, infra, under the appropriate heading. (See Chapter XXII, Sec. 1.) Other examples, in which the genuine aboriginal character of the work is undisputed, appear in the present work, and a large number of other engraved and incised stone objects could be referred to, some of which are in the possession of the Bureau of Ethnology, unpublished, others being figured in its several reports.   It is sufficient now for illustration of this subject to refer to the account accompanying Pl. LI, infra, describing and copying the Thruston tablet, which is, perhaps, the most interesting of any pictograph on stone yet discovered, the genuineness of which as Indian work has not been called in question.

BONE.

For instances of the use of bone, several Alaskan and Eskimo carvings figured in this work may be referred to, e. g., Figs. 334, 459–462, 534, 703, 704, 742, 771, 844, and 1228.

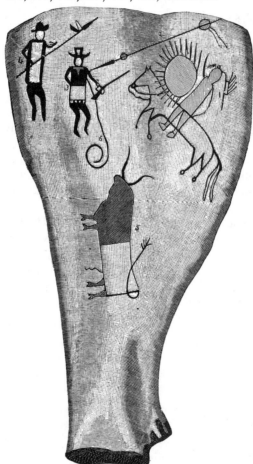

Fig. 157, copied from Schoolcraft (*e*), is taken from the shoulder-blade of a buffalo found on the plains in the Comanche country of Texas.   He says:

It is a symbol showing the strife for the buffalo existing between the Indian and white races. The Indian (1) presented on horseback, protected by his ornamented shield and armed with a lance, (2) kills a Spaniard (3) after a circuitous chase (6), the latter being armed with a gun. His companion (4), armed with a lance, shares the same fate.

It may be questioned whether Mr. Schoolcraft was not too active in the search for symbols in his explanation of (6) as a circuitous chase.   The device is either a lasso or a lariat, and relates to the possession or attempt to take possession of the buffalo.   The design (5), however, well expresses ideographically the fact that the buffalo at the time was in contention,

FIG. 157.—Comanche drawing on shoulder-blade.

and therefore was the property half of the Indians and half of the whites.

SKINS.

A large number of pictographs upon the hides of animals are mentioned in the present paper.   Pl. XX, with its description in the Dakota

Winter Counts, infra, Chap. x, Sec. 2, is one instance. Rawhide drumheads are also used to paint upon, as by the shamans of the Ojibwa.

The use of robes made of the hides of buffalo and other large animals, painted with biographic, shamanistic, and other devices, is also mentioned in various parts of this work. A description of very early observation is now introduced, taken from John Ribault in Hakluyt (*a*).

The king gaue our Captaine at his departure a plume or fanne of Hernshawes feathers died in red, and a basket made of Palmeboughes after the Indian fashion, and wrought very artificially and a great skinne painted and drawen throughout with the pictures of diuers wilde beasts so liuely drawen and pourtrayed, that nothing lacked but life.

With the American use of pictographic robes may be compared the following account of the same use by Australian natives by Dr. Richard Andree (*b*).

The inner side of the opossum skins worn by the blacks is also often ornamented with figures. They scratch lines into the skin, which afterward are rubbed over with fat and charcoal.

FEATHERS AND QUILLS.

Edward M. Kern, in Schoolcraft (*f*), reports that the Sacramento tribes of California were very expert in weaving blankets of feathers, many of them having beautiful figures worked upon them.

The feather work in Mexico, Central America, and the Hawaiian Islands is well known, often having designs properly to be considered among pictographs, though in modern times not often passing beyond ornamentation.

Worsnop (op. cit.) mentions that on grand occasions of the "Mindarie" (i. e., peace festival) the Australian natives decorate the bodies, face, legs, and feet with the down of wild fowl, stuck on with their own blood. The ceremony of taking the blood is very painful, yet they stand it without a murmur. It takes five or six men four to five hours to decorate one man. The blood is put on the body wet and the down stuck on the blood, showing, when finished, outlines of man's head, face, feet, snakes, emu, fish, trees, birds, and other outlines representing the moon, stars, sun, and Aurora Australis, the whole meaning that they are at peace with the world.

Mr. David Boyle (*a*) gives an account of a piece of porcupine quill work, with an illustration, a part of which is copied in Fig. 158.

Among the lost or almost lost arts of the Canadian Indians is that of employing porcupine quills as in the illustration. Partly on account of scarcity of material, but chiefly, it is likely, from change of habits and of taste, there are comparatively few Indian women now living who attempt to produce any fabric of this kind. * * *

The central figure is meant to represent the eagle or great thunder-bird, the belief in which is, or was, widely spread among the Indians over the northern part of this continent. * * *

This beautiful piece of quill work was produced from Ek-wah-satch, who resides at Baptiste lake. He informed me that it had belonged to his grandfather, who resided near Georgian bay.

See also Fig. 683 for another illustration of pictographic work by colored porcupine quills.

GOURDS.

After gourds have dried the contents are removed and small pebbles or bones placed in the empty vessel. Handles are sometimes attached. They serve as rattles in dances and in religious and shamanistic rites.

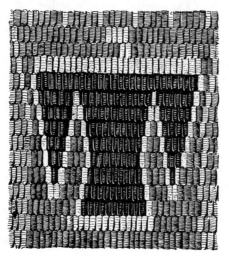

The representations of natural or mythical objects, connected with the ceremonies, for which the owner may have special reverence are often depicted upon their outer surfaces. This custom prevails among the Pueblos generally, and also among many other tribes, notably those of the Siouan linguistic stock.

Fig. 159 is a drawing of the Sci-Manzi or "Mescal Woman" of the Kiowa as it appears on a sacred gourd rattle in the mescal ceremony of that tribe, and was procured with full explanations in the winter

FIG. 158.—Quill pictograph.

of 1890–'91 by Mr. James Mooney of the Bureau of Ethnology.

It shows the rude semblance of a woman, with divergent rays about her head, a fan in her left hand, and a star under her feet.

The peculiarity of the drawing is its hermeneutic character, which is rarely ascertained by actual evidence as existing among the North

American Indians. It has a double meaning, and while apparently only a fantastic figure of a woman, it conveys also to the minds of the initiated a symbolic representation of the interior of the sacred mescal lodge. Turning the rattle with the handle toward the east, the lines forming the halo about the head of the figure represent the circle of devotees within the lodge. The head itself, with the spots for eyes and mouth, represents the large consecrated mescal which is placed upon a crescent-shaped mound of earth in the center of the lodge, this mound being represented in the figure

FIG. 159.—Pictograph on gourd.

by a broad, curving line, painted yellow, forming the curve of the shoulders. Below this is a smaller crescent curve, the original surface of the gourd, which symbolizes the smaller crescent mound of ashes built up within the crescent of earth as the ceremony progresses. The horns of both crescents point toward the door of the lodge on the east side which, in the figure, is toward the feet. In the chest of the body is a round globule painted red, emblematic of the fire within the horns of the crescent in the lodge. The lower part of the body is green, symbolic of the eastern ocean beyond which dwells the mescal woman who is the ruling spirit or divinity to whom prayers are addressed in the ceremony, and the star under her feet is the morning star which heralds her approach. In her left hand is a device representing the fan of eagle feathers used to shield the eyes from the glare of the fire during the ceremony.

SHELLS.

The admirable and well illustrated paper, Art in Shell of the Ancient Americans, by Mr. W. H. Holmes, in the Second Annual Report of the Bureau of Ethnology, and a similar paper, Burial Mounds of the Northern Section of the United States, by Prof. Cyrus Thomas, in the Fifth Annual Report of the same Bureau, render unnecessary present extended discussion under this head.

One example, however, which is unique in character and of established authenticity, is presented here as Pl. xv.

Dr. Edward B. Tylor (a) gives a description of the mantle copied upon that plate, which is condensed as follows:

Among specimens illustrative of native North American arts, as yet untouched by European influence, is the deerskin mantle ornamented with shellwork, recorded to have belonged to the Virginian chief, Powhatan. Of the group of Virginian mantles in Tradescant's collection there only now remains this shell embroidered one. It is entered as follows in the MS. catalogue of the Ashmoleon Museum, in the handwriting of the keeper, Dr. Plot, the well-known antiquary, about 1685: "205 Basilica Powhatan Regis Virginiani vestis, duabus cervorum cutibus consuta, et nummis indicis vulgo cori's dictis splendidè exornata." He had at first written "Roanoke," but struck his pen through this word, and wrote "cori's" (i. e. cowries) above, thus by no means improving the accuracy of his description.

The mantle measures about 2.2^m in length by 1.6^m in width. The two deerskins forming it are joined down the middle; no hair remains. The ornamental design consists of an upright human figure in the middle, divided by the seam; a pair of animals; 32 spirally-formed rounds (2 in the lowest line have lost their shells) and the remains of some work in the right lower corner. The marks where shellwork has come away plainly show the hind legs and tapering tails of both animals. It is uncertain whether the two quadrupeds represent in the conventional manner of picture-writing some real animal of the region, or some mythical composite creature such as other Algonquin tribes are apt to figure. The decorative shellwork is of a kind well known in North America. The shells used are *Marginella;* so far as Mr. Edgar A. Smith is able to identify them in their present weathered state, *M. nivosa.* They have been prepared for fastening on, in two different ways, which may be distinguished in the plate. In the animals and rounds, the shells have been perforated by grinding on one side, so that a sinew thread can be passed through the hole thus made and the mouth. In the man, the shells are ground away and rounded off at both ends into beads looking roughly ball-like at a distance.

The artistic skill of the North American Indians was not, as a rule, directed to represent the forms of animals with such accuracy as to allow of their identification as portraitures. Instead of attempting such accuracy they generally selected some prominent feature such as the claws of the bear, which were drawn with exaggeration, or the tail of the mountain lion which was portrayed of abnormal length over the animal's back. Those animals were, therefore, recognized by those selected features in much the same manner as if there had been a written legend—"this is a bear" or "a mountain lion," the want of iconographic accuracy being admitted. In the animals represented on the mantle no such indicating feature is obvious, and the general resemblance to the marten is the only guide to identification.

The habitat of the marten does not include Virginia as a whole, but the animal is found in the elevated regions of that state. This local infrequency is not, however, of much significance. If regarded as a clan totem, as is probable, it may well be that the clan of Powhatan was connected with the clans of the more northern Algonquian tribes among whom the marten frequently appears as a clan totem. What is generally termed the Powhatan confederacy was a union, not apparently ancient, of a large number of tribal divisions or villages, and it is not known to which clan (probably extending through many of these tribal divisions) the head chief Powhatan belonged. There is almost nothing on record of the clan system of those Virginian Indians, but it is supposed to be similar to that of the northern and eastern members of the same linguistic family, among whom the marten clan was and still is found.

The topic of wampum which, considered as to its material, belongs to the division of shellwork, is with regard to the purposes of the present paper, discussed under the head of "Mnemonic," Chap. IX, Sec. 3.

EARTH AND SAND.

The highly important work, The Mountain Chant, a Navajo Ceremony, in the Fifth Annual Report of the Bureau of Ethnology, by Dr. Washington Matthews, U. S. Army, and that of Mr. James Stevenson, Ceremonial of Hasjelti Dailjis and Mythical Sand Painting of the Navajo Indians, in the Eighth Annual Report of that Bureau, give accounts of most interesting sand paintings by the Navajo Indians, which were before unknown. These paintings were made upon the surface of the earth by means of sand, ashes, and powdered vegetable and mineral matter of various colors. They were highly elaborate, and were fashioned with care and ceremony immediately preceding the observance of specific rites, at the close of which they were obliterated with great nicety. The subject is further discussed by Dr. W. H. Corbusier, U. S. Army, in the present paper (see Chap. XIV, Sec. 5).

Mr. Frank Hamilton Cushing, of the Bureau of Ethnology, kindly contributes the following remarks with special reference to the Zuñi:

A study of characteristic features in these so-called sand pictures of the Navajos would seem to indicate a Pueblo origin of the art, this notwithstanding the fact that it is to-day more highly developed or at least more extensively practiced amongst the Navajos than now, or perhaps ever, amongst the Pueblos. When, during my first

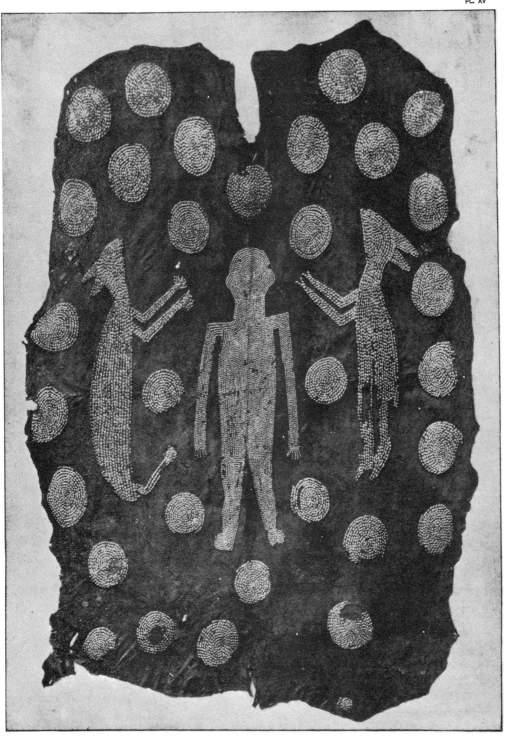

POWHATAN'S MANTLE.

sojourn with the Zuñi, I found this art practice in vogue among the tribal priest magicians and members of cult societies, I named it dry or powder painting. I could see at a glance that this custom of powder painting had resulted from the effort to transfer from a vertical, smooth, and stable surface, which could be painted on, to a horizontal and unstable surface, unsuited to like treatment, such symbolic and sacramental pictographs as are painted on the walls of the kivas, temporarily, as appurtenances to the dramaturgic ceremonials of the cult societies, and as supposed aids to the magical incantations and formulæ of all the monthly, semiannual, and quadrennial observances and fasts of the tribal priests; sometimes, also, in the curative or "Betterment" ceremonials of these priests. It is noteworthy that, with the exception of the invariable "Earth terrace," "Pathway of (earth) life," and a few other conventional symbols of mortal or earthly things (nearly always made of scattered prayer meal), powder painting is resorted to amongst the Zuñi only in ceremonials pertaining to *all* the regions or inclusive of the *lower* region. In such cases paintings typical of the North, West, South, and East are made on the four corresponding walls of the kiva, whilst the lower region is represented by appropriately powder or paint colored sand on the floor, and the upper region either by paintings on the walls near the ceiling or on stretched skins suspended from the latter. Thus the origin of the practice of floor powder painting may be seen to have resulted from the effort to represent with more dramatic appropriateness or exactness the lower as well as the other sacramental regions, and to have been incident to the growth from the quaternary of the sextenary or septenary system of world division so characteristic of Pueblo culture. Hence it is that I attribute the art of powder or sand painting to the Pueblos, and believe that it was introduced both by imitation and by the adoption of Pueblo men amongst the Navajos. Its greater prevalence amongst them to-day is simply due to the fact that having, as a rule, no suitable vertical or wall surfaces for pictorial treatment, all their larger ceremonial paintings have to be made on the ground, and can only or best be made, of course, by this means alone.

It is proper to add, as having a not inconsiderable bearing on the absence generally of screen or skin painting among the Navajos, that, with the Pueblos at least, these pictures are—must be—only temporary; for they are supposed to be spiritually shadowed, so to say, or breathed upon by the gods or god animals they represent, during the appealing incantations or calls of the rites; hence the paint substance of which they are composed is in a way incarnate, and at the end of the ceremonial must be killed and disposed of as dead if evil, eaten as medicine if good.

Further light is thrown on this practice of the Zuñi in making use of these suppositively vivified paintings by their kindred practice of painting not only fetiches of stone, etc., and sometimes of larger idols, then of washing the paint off for use as above described, but also of *powder painting in relief;* that is, of modeling effigies in sand, sometimes huge in size, of hero or animal gods, sacramental mountains, etc., powder painting them in common with the rest of the pictures, and afterwards removing the paint for medicinal or further ceremonial use.

The construction of the effigies in high relief last above mentioned should be compared with the effigy mounds mentioned below in this section.

In connection with the ceremonial use, for temporary dry painting on the ground, of colored earth and sand and also that of sacred corn meal, a remarkable parallel is found in India. Mr. Edward Carpenter (a) mentions that the Devadásis, who are popularly called Nautch girls, as a part of their duty, ornament the floor of the Hindu temples with quaint figures drawn in rice flour.

The well known mounds or tumuli more or less distinctly representing animal forms and sometimes called effigy mounds, found chiefly in Wisconsin and Illinois, come in this category, but it is not possible to properly discuss them and also give space to the many other topics in this paper, the facts and authorities upon which are less known or less accessible. A large amount of information is published by Rev. S. D. Peet (a). Other articles are by Mr. T. H. Lewis in Science, September 7, 1888, and No. 318, 1889. One upon the Serpent mound of Ohio, by Prof. F. W. Putnam (a), is of special interest. It may be suggested as a summation that there is not sufficient evidence of the erection of this class of effigy mounds merely for burial purposes. They seldom exceeded 6 feet in height and varied in expanse from 30 to 300 feet. The animals most frequently recognizable in the constructions are lizards, birds, and several more or less distinct quadrupeds; serpents and turtles also are identified. The species of fauna represented are those now or lately found in the same region. There is a strong probability that the forms of the mounds in question were determined by totemic superstitions or tribal habitudes.

In England the pictographs styled "turf monuments" are sometimes made by cutting the natural turf and filling with chalk the part of the surface thus laid bare. Sometimes the color depends wholly upon the limestone, granite, or other rock exposed by removing the turf. Rev. W. C. Plenderleath (a) gives a full account of this variety of pictograph.

COPPER.

This is the only metal on which it is probable that the North American Indians made designs. To present comparisons of pictures by other peoples on that or other metals or alloys would be to enter into a field, the most interesting part of which is classed as numismatic, and which would be a departure from the present heading. That virgin copper was used for diverse purposes, generally ornamental, by the North American Indians, is now established, and there is a presentation of the subject in Prof. Cyrus Thomas's (a) Burial Mounds. The most distinct and at the same time surprising account of a true pictographic record on copper is given by W. W. Warren (a), an excellent authority, and is condensed as follows:

The Ojibwa of the Crane family hold in their possession a circular plate of virgin copper, on which are rudely marked indentations and hieroglyphics denoting the number of generations of the family who have passed away since they first pitched their lodges at Shang-a-waum-ik-ong and took possession of the adjacent country, including the island of La Pointe.

When I witnessed this curious family register in 1842 it was exhibited to my father. The old chief kept it carefully buried in the ground and seldom displayed it. On this occasion he brought it to view only at the entreaty of my mother whose maternal uncle he was.

On this plate of copper were marked eight deep indentations, denoting the number of his ancestors who had passed away since they first lighted their fire at Shang-a-waum-ik-ong. They had all lived to a good old age.

By the rude figure of a man with a hat on its head, placed opposite one of these indentations, was denoted the period when the white race first made its appearance among them. This mark occurred in the third generation, leaving five generations which had passed away since that important era in their history.

Mr. I. W. Powell (a), Indian superintendent, in the report of the deputy superintendent-general of Indian affairs of Canada for 1879, gives an account of some tribes of the northwest coast, especially the Indians called in the report Newittees, a tribe now known as the Naqómqilis of the Wakashan family, who treasure pieces of copper peculiarly shaped and marked. The shape is that of one face of a truncated pyramid with the base upward. In the broad end appear marks resembling the holes for eyes and mouth, which are common in masks of the human face. The narrower end has a rough resemblance to an ornamental collar. These copper articles were made by the Indians originally from the native copper, and in 1879 a few were held by the chiefs who used them for presentation at the potlaches or donation feasts. The value which is attached to these small pieces of copper, which are intrinsically worthless, is astounding. For one of them 1,200 blankets were paid, which would at the time and place represent $1,800. Sometimes a chief in presenting one of them, in order to show his utter disregard of wealth, would break it into three or four pieces and give them away, each fragment being perhaps repurchased at an exorbitant sum. This competition in extravagance for display, under the guise of charity and humility, has had parallels in the silver-brick and flour-barrel auctions in parts of the United States, when the actors were white citizens. Apart from such public exhibitions, the copper tokens seem to partake of the natures both of fiat money and of talismans.

WOOD.

This division comprises:

(1) *The living tree*, of the use of which for pictographic purposes there are many descriptions and illustrations in this paper. In addition to them may be noted the remark made by Bishop De Schweinitz (a) in the Life and Times of Zeisberger, that in 1750 there were numerous tree carvings at a place on the eastern shore of Cayuga lake, the meaning of which was known to and interpreted by the Cayuga Indians.

This mode of record or notice is so readily suggested that it is found throughout the world, e. g., the "hieroglyph" in New Guinea, described by D'Albertis (a), being a drawing in black on a white tree.

(2) *Bark.*—The Abnaki and Ojibwa have been and yet continue to be in the habit of incising pictographic characters and mnemonic marks upon birch bark. Many descriptions and illustrations of this style are given in this paper, and admirable colored illustrations of it also appear in Pl. XIX of the Seventh Ann. Rept. Bureau of Ethnology. The lines appear sometimes to have been traced on the inner surface of young bark with a sharply pointed instrument, probably bone, but in other examples the drawings are made by simple puncturing. The

strips of bark, varying from an inch to several feet in length, roll up after drying, and are by heating straightened out for examination.

Another mode of drawing on birch bark which appears to be peculiar to the Abnaki is by scratching the exterior surface, thus displaying a difference in color between the outermost and the second layer of the rind, which difference forms the figure. The lower character in Pl. XVI shows this mode of picturing. It is an exact copy of part of an old bark record made by the Abnaki of Maine.

They also use the mode of incision, many examples of which appear in the present work, but their mode of scratching produced a much more picturesque effect, as is shown also in Fig. 659, than the mere linear drawing.

(3) *Manufactured wood.*—The Indians of the northwest coast generally employ wood as the material on which their pictographs are to be made. Totem posts, boats, boat paddles, the boards constituting the front wall of a house, and wooden masks, are among the objects used.

Many drawings among the Indians of the interior parts of the United States are also found upon pipestems made of wood, usually ash. Among the Arikara boat paddles are used upon which marks of personal distinction are reproduced, as shown in Fig. 578.

Mortuary records are also drawn upon slabs of wood. (See Figs. 728 and 729). Mnemonic devices, notices of departure, distress, etc., are also drawn upon slips of wood.

The examples of the use of wood for pictographs which are illustrated and described in this paper are too numerous for recapitulation; to them, however, may be added the following from Wilkes's (*a*) Exploring Expedition, referring to Fig. 160.

Near an encampment on Chickeeles river, near Puget Sound, Washington, were found some rudely carved painted planks, of which Mr. Eld made a drawing. These planks were placed upright and nothing could be learned of their origin. The colors were exceedingly bright, of a kind of red pigment.

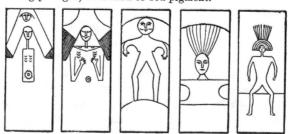

FIG. 160.—Pictographs on wood, Washington.

Mr. James O. Pattie (*a*) gives an account of a wooden passport given to him in 1824 by a Pawnee chief. He describes it, without illustration, as a small piece of wood curiously painted with characters something like "hieroglyphics." The chief told Mr. Pattie's party if they saw any of his warriors to give them the stick, in which case they would be kindly treated, which promise was fulfilled a few days later when the party met a large band of the same tribe on the warpath.

SECTION 3.

ARTIFICIAL OBJECTS.

Artificial objects may be classified, so far as is important for the present work, into, I, fictile fabrics and, II, textile fabrics.

FICTILE FABRICS.

A large number of articles of pottery bearing pictographs are figured in the illustrated collections by Mr. James Stevenson in the Second Annual Report, and by Mr. Stevenson and Mr. William H. Holmes in the Third Annual Report of the Bureau of Ethnology. Pipes on which totemic designs and property marks appear are also common.

The art of pottery was at first limited to vessel-making. In the earlier stages of culture, vases were confined to simple use as receptacles, but as culture ripened they were advanced to ceremonial and religious offices and received devices and representations in color and in relief connected with the cult to which they were devoted. Among some tribes large burial vases were fashioned to contain or cover the dead. An infinite variety of objects, such as pipes, whistles, rattles, toys, beads, trowels, calendars, masks, and figurines, were made of pottery. Clays of varying degrees of purity were used, and sometimes these were tempered with powdered quartz, shell, or like materials. The vessels were frequently built by coiling. The surface was smoothed by the hands or the modeling implement or was polished with a stone or other smoothing tool. Much attention was given to surface embellishment. The finger nails and various pointed tools were used to scarify and indent, and elaborate figures and designs were incised. Stamps with systematically worked designs were sometimes applied to the soft clay. Cords and woven fabrics were also employed to give diversity to the surface. With the more advanced tribes, though these simple processes were still resorted to, engraving, modeling in relief and in the round, and painting in colors were employed.

TEXTILE FABRICS.

Textile fabrics include those products of art in which the elements of their construction are filamental and mainly combined by using their flexibility. The processes employed are called wattling, interlacing, plaiting, netting, weaving, sewing, and embroidery. The materials generally used by primitive people were pliable vegetal growths, such as twigs, leaves, roots, canes, rushes, and grasses, and the hair, quills, feathers, and tendons of animals.

Unlike works in stone and clay, textile articles are seldom long preserved. Still, from historic accounts and a study of the many beautiful articles produced by existing Indian tribes, a fair knowledge of the range and general character of native fabrics may be obtained. In many cases buried articles of that character have been preserved by the impregnation of the engirding earths with preservative salts, and also some fabrics which had been wrapped about buried utensils, or ornaments of copper remained without serious decay. Charring has also been a means of preserving cloth, and much has been learned of the weaving done by ancient workers through impressions upon pottery which had been made by applying the texture while the clay was still soft. The weaving appliances were simple, but the results in plain and figured fabrics, in tapestry, in lace-like embroideries, and in feather-work are admirable.

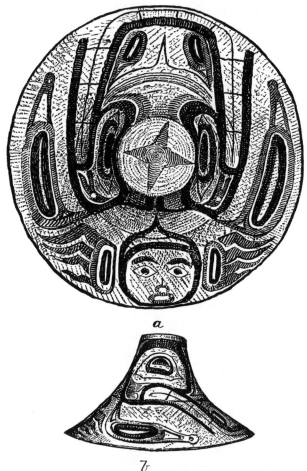

FIG. 161.—Haida basketry hat.

This subject is discussed by Mr. W. H. Holmes in his paper, A Study of the Textile Art, etc., in the Sixth Annual Report of the Bureau of Ethnology, in a manner so comprehensive as to embrace the field of pictography in its relation to woven articles.

Several examples of this application also appear in the present work. See Figs. 821, 976 and 1167. In addition the following are now presented.

Some of the California tribes are expert workers in grass and roots in the manufacture of baskets, upon which designs other than for mere ornamentation are frequently worked. The Yokuts, at Tule river Agency, in the southeastern part of the State, sometimes incorporate various human forms in which the arms are suspended at the sides of the body with the hands directed outward to either side. Above the head is a heavy horizontal line.

The following is extracted from Prof. O. T. Mason's (*a*) paper on basket work, describing Fig. 161:

a is a rain hat of twined basketry in spruce root from Haida Indians. This figure is the upper view and shows the ornamentation in red and black paint. The device in this instance is the epitomized form of a bird, perhaps a duck. Omitting the red cross on the top the beak, jaws, and nostrils are shown; the eyes at the sides near the top, and just behind them the ears. The wings, feet, and tail, inclosing a human face, are shown on the margin. The Haida, as well as other coast Indians from Cape Flattery to Mount Saint Elias, cover everything of use with totemic devices in painting and carving.

b shows the conical shape of *a*. The painted ornamentation on these hats is laid on in black and red in the conventional manner of ornamentation in vogue among the Haidas and used in the reproduction of their various totems on all of their houses, wood and slate carvings, and implements.

Mr. Niblack (*b*) says, describing Fig. 162:

The Chilkat and cedar-bark blankets are important factors in all ceremonial dances and functions. Other forms of ceremonial blankets or mantles are made from Hudson Bay Company blankets, with totemic figures worked on them in a variety of ways. The usual method is to cut out the totemic figure in red cloth and sew it on to the garment (ornamenting it with borders of beads and buttons) by the method known as appliqué work; another method is to sew pieces of bright abalone or pearl shell or pearl buttons on to the garment in the totemic patterns. The illustration is a drawing of a vestment which hangs down the back, representing the totem or crest of the wearer.

This specimen is mentioned as the workmanship of the Tsimshian Indians, at Point Simpson, British Columbia, and represents the halibut.

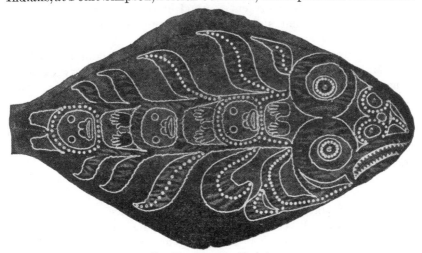

Fig. 162.—Tsimshian blanket.

CHAPTER VIII.

INSTRUMENTS AND MATERIALS BY WHICH PICTOGRAPHS ARE MADE.

So far as appears on ancient pictographic works the kind of instruments and materials with which they were made can be inferred only from its aspect, though microscopic examination and chemical analysis have sometimes been successfully applied. A few examples relating to the topic are given as follows, though other descriptions appear elsewhere in this treatise.

SECTION 1.

INSTRUMENTS FOR CARVING.

This title, as here used, is intended to include cutting, pecking, scratching, and rubbing. The Hidatsa, when scratching upon stone or rocks, as well as upon pieces of wood, employ a sharply pointed piece of hard stone, usually a fragment of quartz. The present writer successfully imitated the Micmac scratchings at Kejimkoojik lake, Nova Scotia, by using a stone arrow point upon the slate rocks.

The bow-drill was largely used by the Innuit of Alaska in carving bone and ivory. Their present method of cutting figures and other characters is by a small steel blade, thick, though sharply pointed, resembling a graver.

Many petroglyphs, e. g., those at Conowingo, Maryland, at Machiasport, Maine, and in Owens valley, California, present every evidence of having been deepened if not altogether fashioned by rubbing, either with a piece of wood and sand or with pointed stone.

To incise or indent lines upon birch bark the Ojibwa, Ottawa, and other Algonquian tribes used a sharply pointed piece of bone, though they now prefer an iron nail. Examples of scratching upon the outer surface of bark are mentioned elsewhere.

Several examples of producing characters on stone by pecking with another stone are mentioned in this paper, and Mr. J. D. McGuire (a), of Ellicott City, Maryland, has been remarkably successful in forming petroglyphs with the ordinary Indian stone hammer. Some of the results established by him are published in The American Anthropologist.

218

SECTION 2.

INSTRUMENTS FOR DRAWING.

Drawings upon small slabs of wood, found among the Ojibwa, were made with a piece of red-hot wire or thin iron rod hammered to a point. Such figures are blackened by being burned in.

When in haste or when better materials are not at hand, the Hidatsa sometimes drew upon a piece of wood or the shoulder-blade of a buffalo with a piece of charcoal from the fire or with a piece of red chalk or red ocher, with which nearly every warrior is at all times supplied.

Mr. A. W. Howitt, in Manuscript Notes on Australian Pictographs, says:

Not having any process such as is used by some of the savage tribes to soften skins, the harshness of these rugs is remedied by marking upon them lines and patterns, which being partly cut through the skin give to it a certain amount of suppleness. In former times, before the white man enabled the black fellow to supplement his meager stock of implements with those of civilization, a Kumai made use of the sharp edge of a mussel shell (unio) to cut these patterns. At the present time the sharpened edge of the bowl of a metal spoon is used, partly because it forms a convenient instrument, partly, perhaps, because its bowl bears a resemblance in shape to the familiar ancestral tool.

SECTION 3.

COLORING MATTER AND ITS APPLICATION.

Painting upon robes or skins is executed by means of thin strips of wood or sometimes of bone. Tufts of antelope hair are also used, by tying them to sticks to make a brush, but this is evidently a modern innovation. Pieces of wood, one end of which is chewed so as to produce a loose fibrous brush, are also used at times, as has been specially observed among the Teton Dakota.

The Hidatsa and other Northwest Indians usually employ a piece of buffalo rib or a piece of hard wood having an elliptical form. This is dipped in a solution of glue, with or without color, and a tracing is made, which is subsequently filled up and deepened by a repetition of the process with the same or a stronger solution of the color.

Of late years in the United States colors of civilized manufacture are readily obtained by the Indians for painting and decoration. Frequently, however, when the colors of commerce can not be obtained, the aboriginal colors are still prepared and used. The ferruginous clays of various shades of brown, red, and yellow occur in nature so widely distributed that these are the most common and leading tints. Black is generally prepared by grinding fragments of charcoal into a very fine powder. Among some tribes, as has also been found in some of the "ancient" pottery from the Arizona ruins, clay had evidently been mixed with charcoal to give better body. The black color made by some of the Innuit tribes is made with blood and charcoal intimately mixed, which is afterwards applied to incisions in ivory, bone, and wood.

Among the Dakota, colors for dyeing porcupine quills were obtained chiefly from plants. The vegetable colors, being soluble, penetrate the substance of the quills more evenly and beautifully than the mineral colors of eastern manufacture.

The black color of some of the Pueblo pottery is obtained by a special burning with pulverized manure, into which the vessel is placed as it is cooling after the first baking. The coloring matter—soot produced by smoke—is absorbed into the pores of the vessel, and does not wear off as readily as when colors are applied to the surface by brushes.

In decorating skins or robes the Arikara Indians boil the tail of the beaver, thus obtaining a viscous fluid which is thin glue. The figures are first drawn in outline with a piece of beef-rib, or some other flat bone, the edge only being used after having been dipped into the liquor. The various pigments to be employed in the drawing are then mixed with some of the same liquid, in separate vessels, when the various colors are applied to the objects by means of a sharpened piece of wood or bone. The colored mixture adheres firmly to the original tracing in glue.

When similar colors are to be applied to wood, the surface is frequently pecked or slightly incised to receive the color more readily.

Jacques Cartier, in Hakluyt (b), reports the Indian women of the Bay of Chaleur as smearing the face with coal dust and grease.

A small pouch, discovered on the Yellowstone river in 1873, which had been dropped by some fleeing hostile Sioux, contained several fragments of black micaceous iron. The latter had almost the appearance and consistence of graphite, so soft and black was the result upon rubbing with it. It had evidently been used for decorating the face as war-paint.

Mr. Wm. H. Dall (a), treating of the remains found in the mammalian layers in the Amakuak cave, Unalaska, remarks:

In the remains of a woman's work-basket, found in the uppermost layer in a cave, were bits of this resin [from the bark of pine or spruce driftwood], evidently carefully treasured, with a little birch-bark case (the bark also derived from drift logs) containing pieces of soft hematite, graphite, and blue carbonate of copper, with which the ancient seamstress ornamented her handiwork.

The same author reports (f):

The coloration of wooden articles with native pigments is of ancient origin, but all the more elaborate instances that have come to my knowledge bore marks of comparatively recent origin. The pigments used were blue carbonates of iron and copper; the green fungus, or peziza, found in decayed birch and alder wood; hematite and red chalk; white infusorial or chalky earth; black charcoal, graphite, and micaceous ore of iron. A species of red was sometimes derived from pine bark or the cambium of the ground willow.

Stephen Powers (a) states that the Shastika women "smear their faces all over daily with choke-cherry juice, which gives them a bloody, corsair aspect"

Mr. A. S. Gatschet, of the Bureau of Ethnology, reports that the Klamaths of southwestern Oregon employ a black color, lgú, made of burnt plum seeds and bulrushes, which is applied to the cheeks in the form of small round spots. This is used during dances. Red paint, for the face and body, is prepared from a resin exuding from the spruce tree, pánam. A yellow mineral paint is also employed, consisting probably of ocher or ferruginous clay. He also says that the Klamath spál, yellow mineral paint, is of light yellow color, but turns red when burned, after which it is applied in making small round dots upon the face. The white infusorial clay is applied in the form of stripes or streaks over the body. The Klamaths use charcoal, lgúm, in tattooing.

Mud and white clay were used by the Winnebago for the decoration of the human body and of horses. Some of the California Indians in the vicinity of Tulare river used a white coloring matter, consisting of infusorial earth, obtained there. The tribes at and near the geysers north of San Francisco bay procured vermilion from croppings of cinnabar. The same report is made with probability of truth concerning the Indians at the present site of the New Almaden mines, where tribes of the Mutsun formerly lived. Some of the black coloring matter of pictographs in Santa Barbara, California, proved on analysis to be a hydrous oxide of manganese. The Mojave pigments are ocher, clay, and charcoal mingled with oil.

Rev. J. Owen Dorsey, of the Bureau of Ethnology, reports regarding the Osage that one of their modes of obtaining black color for the face was by burning a quantity of small willows. When these were charred they were broken in small pieces and placed in pans, with a little water in each. The hands were then dipped into the pan and rubbed together and finally rubbed over the parts to be colored.

Dr. Hoffman reports that among the Hualpai, living on the western border of the Colorado plateau, Arizona, some persons appeared as if they had been tattooed in vertical bands from the forehead to the waist, but upon closer examination it was found that dark and light bands of the natural skin were produced in the following manner: When a deer or an antelope had been killed the blood was rubbed over the face and breast, after which the spread and curved fingers were scratched downward from the forehead over the face and breast, thus removing some of the blood; that remaining soon dried and gave the appearance of black stripes. The exposed portion of the skin retained the natural dark-tanned color, while that under the coating of coagulated blood became paler by being protected against the light and air. These persons did not wash off the marks and after a while the blood began to drop off by desquamation, leaving lighter spots and lines which for a week or two appear like tattoo marks. Similar streaks of blood have been held to have originated tattoo designs in several parts of the world to record success in hunting or in war, but such evolution does not appear to have resulted from the transient decoration in the case mentioned.

It is well known that the meal of maize called kunque is yet commonly used by the Zuñi for ceremonial coloration of their own persons and of objects used in their religious rites. Hoddentin is less familiarly known. It is the pollen of the tule, which is a variety of cat-tail rush growing in all the ponds of the southwestern parts of the United States. It is a yellow powder with which small buckskin bags are filled and those bags then attached to the belts of Apache warriors. They are also worn as amulets by members of the tribe. In dances for the cure of sickness the shaman applied the powder to the forehead of the patient, then to his breast in the figure of a cross; next he sprinkles it in a circle around his couch, then on the heads of the chanters and the assembled friends of the patient, and lastly upon his own head and into his own mouth.

Everard F. im Thurn (c) gives the following details concerning British Guiana:

The dyes used by the Indians to paint their own bodies, and occasionally to draw patterns on their implements, are red faroah, purple caraweera, blue-black lana, white felspathic clay and, though very rarely, a yellow vegetable dye of unknown origin.

Faroah is the deep red pulp around the seed of a shrub (*Bixa orellana*) which grows wild on the banks of some of the rivers, and is cultivated by the Indians in their clearings. It is mixed with a large quantity of oil. When it is to be used either a mass of it is taken in the palm of the hand and rubbed over the skin or other surface to be painted, or a pattern of fine lines is drawn with it by means of a stick used as a pencil.

Caraweera is a somewhat similar dye, of a more purplish red, and by no means so commonly used. It is prepared from the leaves of a yellow-flowered bignonia (*B. chicka*) together with some other unimportant ingredients. The dried leaves are boiled. The pot is then taken from the fire and the contents being poured into bowls are allowed to subside. The clear water left at the top is poured away and the sediment is of a beautiful purple color.

Lana is the juice of the fruit of a small tree (*Genipa americana*) with which without further preparation, blue-black lines are drawn in patterns, or large surfaces are stained on the skin. The dye thus applied is for about a week indelible.

Paul Marcoy (a), in Travels in South America, says the Passés, Yuris, Barrés and Chumanas of Brazil, employ a decoction of indigo or genipa in tattooing.

F. S. Moreat, M. D., in Jour. Roy. Geog. Soc., XXXII, 1862, p. 125, says that the Andaman Islanders rubbed earth on the top of the head, probably for the purpose of ornamentation.

Dr. Richard Andree (b) says:

Long before Europeans came to Australia, the Australian blacks knew a kind of pictorial representation, exhibiting scenes from their life, illustrating it with great fidelity to nature. An interesting specimen of that kind was found on a piece of bark that had served as cover of a hut on Lake Tyrrell. The black who produced this picture had had intercourse with white people, but had had no instruction whatever in drawing. The bark was blackened by smoke on the inside, and on this blackened surface the native drew the figures with his thumb nail.

CHAPTER IX.

MNEMONIC.

This is the most obvious and probably was the earliest use to which picture-writing was applied. The contrivance of drawing the representations of objects, to fix in the memory either the objects themselves or the concepts, facts, or other matters connected with them, is practiced early by human individuals and is found among peoples the most ancient historically or in the horizons of culture. After the adoption of the characters for purely mnemonic purposes, those at first intended to be iconographic often became converted into ideographic, emblematic, or symbolic designs, and perhaps in time so greatly conventionalized that the images of the things designed could no longer be perceived by the imagination alone.

It is believed, however, that this form and use of picturing were preceded by the use of material objects which afterwards were reproduced graphically in paintings, cuttings, and carvings. In the present paper many examples appear of objects known to have been so used, the graphic representations of which, made with the same purpose, are explained by knowledge of the fact. Other instances are mentioned as connected with the evolution of pictographs, and they possibly may interpret some forms of the latter which are not yet understood.

This chapter is divided into (1) knotted cords and objects tied; (2) notched or marked sticks; (3) wampum; (4) order of songs; (5) traditions; (6) treaties; (7) appointment; (8) numeration; (9) accounting.

SECTION 1.

KNOTTED CORDS AND OBJECTS TIED.

Dr. Hoffman reports a device among the Indians formerly inhabiting the mountain valleys north of Los Angeles, California, who brought or sent to the settlements blankets, skins, and robes for sale. The man trusted to transport and sell those articles was provided with a number of strings made of some flexible vegetable fiber, one string for each class of goods, which were attached to his belt. Every one confiding an article to the agent fixed the price, and when he disposed of it a single knot was tied to the proper cord for each real received, or a double knot for each peso. Thus any particular string indicated the kind of goods sold, as well as the whole sum realized for them, which was distributed according to the account among the former owners of the goods.

Mr. George Turner (*a*) says that among the South Sea Islanders tying a number of knots in a piece of cord was a common way of noting and remembering things in the absence of a written language.

A peculiar and ingenious mode of expressing thoughts without pronouncing or writing them in language is still met with among the Indian shepherds in the Peruvian Cordilleras, though it is practiced merely in the accounts of the flocks. This system consists of a peculiar intertwining of various strings into a net-like braidwork, and the diverse modes of tying these strings form the record, the knots and loops signifying definite ideas and their combination the connection of these ideas. This system of mnemonic device, which was practiced by the ancient Peruvians, was called quipu, and, though a similar knot-writing is found in China, Tartary, eastern Asia, on many islands of the Pacific, and even in some parts of Africa, yet in Peru, at the time of the Incas, it was so elaborately developed as to permit its employment for official statistics of the government. Of course, as this writing gave no picture of a word and did not suggest sounds, but, like the notched stick, merely recalled ideas already existing, the writing could be understood by those only who possessed the key to it; but it is noteworthy that when the Jesuit missions began their work in Peru they were able to use the quipus for the purpose of making the Indians learn Latin prayers by heart.

A more detailed account of the ancient quipu is extracted from Dr. von Tschudi's Travels in Peru (*a*) with condensation as follows:

This method consisted in the dexterous intertwining of knots on strings, so as to render them auxiliaries to the memory. The instrument was composed of one thick head or top string, to which, at certain distances, thinner ones were fastened. The top string was much thicker than these pendent strings and consisted of two doubly twisted threads, over which two single threads were wound. The branches, or pendent strings, were fastened to the top ones by a single loop; the knots were made in the pendent strings and were either single or manifold. The length of the strings was various. The transverse or top string often measures several yards, and sometimes only a foot; the branches are seldom more than 2 feet long, and in general they are much shorter.

The strings were often of different colors, each having its own particular signification. The color for soldiers was red; for gold, yellow; for silver, white; for corn, green, etc. The quipu was especially employed for numerical and statistical tables; each single knot representing ten; each double knot stood for one hundred; each triple knot for one thousand, etc.; two single knots standing together made twenty; and two double knots, two hundred.

In this manner the ancient Peruvians kept the accounts of their army. On one string were numbered the soldiers armed with slings; on another the spearmen; on a third, those who carried clubs, etc. In the same manner the military reports were prepared. In every town some expert men were appointed to tie the knots of the quipu and to explain them. These men were called *quipucamayocuna* (literally, officers of the knots.) The appointed officers required great dexterity in unriddling the meaning of the knots. It, however, seldom happened that they had to read a quipu without some verbal commentary. Something was always required to be added if the quipu came from a distant province, to explain whether it related to the numbering of the population, to tributes, or to war, etc. This method of calculation is still practiced by the shepherds of Puna. On the first branch or string they usually place the number of the bulls; on the second, that of the cows, the latter being classed into those which were milked and those which were not milked; on the next string were numbered the calves according to their ages and sizes. Then came the sheep, in several subdivisions. Next followed the number of foxes killed, the quantity of salt consumed, and, finally, the cattle that had been slaughtered. Other quipus showed the produce of the herds in milk, cheese, wool, etc. Each list was distinguished by a particular color or by some peculiarity in the twisting of the string.

Other accounts tell that the descendants of the Quiches still use the quipu, perhaps as modified by themselves, for numeration. They pierce beans and hang them by different colored strings, each of which represents one of the column places used in decimal arithmetic. A green string signifies 1,000; a red one, 100; a yellow, 10, and a white refers to the 9 smaller digits. Thus if 7 beans are on a green, 2 on a red, 8 on a yellow, and 6 on a white string, and the whole tied together, the bundle expresses the number 7,286.

Before the time of their acquaintance with the quipus, the Peruvians used in the same way pebbles or maize-beans of various colors. The same practice was known in Europe in the prehistoric period. The habit of many persons in civilized countries to tie a knot in the handkerchief to recall an idea or fact to mind is a familiar example to show how naturally the action would suggest itself for the purpose, and perhaps indicates the inheritance of the practice.

Dr. Andree (b) gives an illustration of a quipu (here reproduced as part of Pl. XVI), which he represents as taken from Perez, and states that the drawing was made soon after the exhuming of the object from an ancient Peruvian grave.

Capt. Bourke (a) gives descriptions and illustrations of varieties of the izze-kloth or medicine cord of the Apache. A condensed extract of his remarks is as follows:

These cords, in their perfection, are decorated with beads and shells strung along at intervals, with pieces of the sacred green chalchihuitl, which has had such a mysterious ascendancy over the minds of the American Indians—Aztec, Peruvian, Quiche, as well as the more savage tribes like the Apache and Navajo; with petrified wood, rock crystal, eagle down, claws of the hawk or eaglet, claws of the bear, rattle of the rattlesnake, buckskin bags of hoddentin, circles of buckskin in which are inclosed pieces of twigs and branches of trees which have been struck by lightning, small fragments of the abalone shell from the Pacific coast, and much other sacred paraphernalia of a similar kind.

That the use of these cords was reserved for the most sacred and important occasions I soon learned. They were not to be seen on occasions of no moment, but the dances for war, medicine, and summoning the spirits at once brought them out, and every medicine man of any consequence would appear with one hanging from his right shoulder over his left hip.

These cords will protect a man while on the warpath, and many of the Apache believe firmly that a bullet will have no effect upon the warrior wearing one of them. This is not their only virtue by any means; the wearer can tell who has stolen ponies or other property from him or from his friends, can help the crops, and cure the sick. If the circle attached to one of these cords is placed upon the head it will at once relieve any ache, while the cross attached to another prevents the wearer from going astray, no matter where he may be; in other words, it has some connection with cross-trails and the four cardinal points, to which the Apache pay the strictest attention.

I was at first inclined to associate these cords with the quipus of the Peruvians and also with the wampum of the aborigines of the Atlantic coast, and investigation only confirms this first suspicion.

The praying beads of the Buddhists and of many Oriental peoples, who have used them from high antiquity, are closely allied to the quipu. They are more familiar now in the shape of the rosaries of Roman Catholics. In the absence of manufactured articles, arranged on wires, the necessary materials were easily procured. Berries, nuts, pease, or beans strung in any manner answered the purpose. The abacus of the Chinese and Greeks was connected in origin with the same device.

E. F. im Thurn (d) says of the Nikari-Karu Indians of Guiana:

At last, after four days' stay, we got off. The two or three people from Euwari-manakuroo who came with us gave their wives knotted strings of quippus, each knot representing one of the days they expected to be away, and the whole string thus forming a calendar to be used by the wives until the return of their husbands.

That the general idea or invention for mnemonic purposes appearing in the quipu was actually used pictorially is indicated in the illustrations of the sculptures of Santa Lucia Cosumalhuapa in Guatemala given by Dr. S. Habel (b). Upon these he remarks:

It has been frequently affirmed that the aborigines of America had nowhere arisen high enough in civilization to have characters for writing and numeral signs, but the sculptures of Santa Lucia exhibit signs which indicate a kind of cipher-writing higher in form than mere hieroglyphics. From the mouth of most of the human beings, living or dead, emanates a staff, variously bent, to the sides of which nodes are attached. These nodes are of different sizes and shapes, and variously distributed on the sides of the staff, either singly or in twos and threes, the last named either separated or in shape of a trefoil. This manner of writing not only indicates that the person is speaking or praying, but also indicates the very words, the contents of the speech or prayer. It is quite certain that each staff, as bent and ornamented, stood for a well-known petition, which the priest could read as easily as those acquainted with a cipher dispatch can know its purport. Further, one may be allowed to conjecture that the various curves of the staves served the purpose of strength and rhythm, just as the poet chooses his various meters for the same purpose.

The following notices of the ancient mnemonic use of knotted cords and of its survival in various parts of the world are extracted from the essay of Prof. Terrien de Lacouperie (d):

The Yang tung, south of Khoten, and consequently north of Tibet, who first communicated with China in A. D. 641, had no written characters. They only cut notches in sticks and tied knots in strings for records.

The Bratyki and Buriats of Siberia are credited with the use of knotted cords.

The Japanese are also reputed to have employed knots on strings or bind-weeds for records.

The Li of Hainan, being unacquainted with writing, use knotted cords or notched sticks in place of bonds or agreements.

In the first half of the present century cord records were still generally used in the Indian archipelago and Polynesia proper. The tax-gatherers in the island of Hawaii by this means kept accounts of all the articles collected by them from the inhabitants. A rope 400 fathoms long was used as a revenue book. It was divided

Plate XVI.

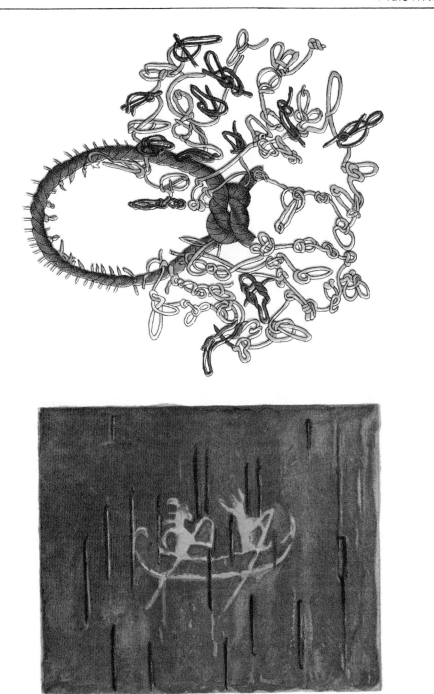

PERUVIAN QUIPU AND BIRCH BARK DRAWING.

into numerous portions corresponding to the various districts of the island; the portions were under the care of the tax-gatherers, who, with the aid of loops, knots, and tufts of different shapes, colors, and sizes, were enabled to keep an accurate account of the hogs, pigs, and pieces of sandal wood, etc., at which each person was taxed.

In Timor island, according to the Chinese records in 1618, the people had no writing. When they wanted to record something they did it with flat stones, and a thousand stones were represented by a string.

Knotted cords were originally used in Tibet, but we have no information about their system of using them. The bare statement comes from the Chinese annals.

The following statement regarding the same use by the Chinese is made by Ernest Faber (a). He says: "In the highest antiquity, government was carried on successfully by the use of knotted cords to preserve the memory of things. In subsequent ages, the sages substituted for these written characters. By means of these the doings of all the officers could be regulated and the affairs of all the people accurately examined."

SECTION 2.

NOTCHED OR MARKED STICKS.

The use of notches for mere numeration was frequent, but there are also instances of their special significance.

The Dakotas, Hidatsa, and Shoshoni have been observed to note the number of days during which they journeyed from one place to another by cutting lines or notches upon a stick.

The coup sticks carried by Dakota warriors often bear a number of small notches, which refer to the number of the victims hit with the stick after they had been wounded or killed.

The young men and boys of the several tribes at Fort Berthold, Dakota, frequently carry a stick, upon which they cut a notch for every bird killed during a single expedition.

In Seaver's (a) life of Mary Jemison it is set forth that the war chief in each tribe of Iroquois keeps a war-post, in order to commemorate great events and preserve the chronology of them. This post is a peeled stick of timber 10 or 12 feet high, and is erected in the village. For a campaign they make, or rather the chief makes, a perpendicular red mark about 3 inches long and half an inch wide. On the opposite side from this, for a scalp taken, they make a red cross, thus

On another side, for a prisoner taken alive, they make a red cross in this manner $\times$ with a head or dot, and by placing these significant signs in so conspicuous a situation they are enabled to ascertain with great certainty the time and circumstances of past events.

It is suggested that the device first mentioned represents the scalp severed and lifted from the head, and that the second refers to the

Fig. 163.—Wampum strings.

manner in which the prisoners were secured at night, pegged and tied in the style called spread-eagle.

Rev. Richard Taylor (a) notes that the Maori had neither the quipus nor wampum, but only a board shaped like a saw, which was called "he rakau wakapa-paranga," or genealogical board. It was, in fact, a tally, having a notch for each name, and a blank space to denote where the male line failed and was succeeded by that of the female; youths were taught their genealogies by repeating the names of each ancestor to whom the notches referred.

It is supposed that the use by bakers of notched sticks or tallies, as they are called, still exists in some civilized regions, and there is an interesting history connected with the same wooden tallies, which until lately were used in the accounts of the exchequer of Great Britain. They also appear more recently and in a different use as the Khe-mou circulated by Tartar chiefs to designate the number of men and horses required to be furnished by each camp.

SECTION 3.

WAMPUM.

Prof. Robert E. C. Stearns (a) says that wampum consisted of beads of two principal colors having a cylindrical form, a quarter of an inch, more or less, in length, the diameter or thickness being usually about half the length. The color of the wampum determined its value. The term wampum, wampon, or wampom, and wampum-peege was apparently applied to these beads when strung or otherwise connected, fastened, or woven together. The illustration given by him is now reproduced as Fig. 163.

In the Jesuit Relations, 1656, p. 3, the first present of an Iroquois chief to Jesuit missionaries at a council is described. This was a great figure of the sun, made of 6,000 beads of wampum, which explained to them that the darkness shall not influence them in the councils and the sun shall enlighten them even in the depth of night.

Among the Iroquoian and Algonquian tribes wampum belts were generally used to record treaties. Mr. John Long (a) describes one of them:

The wampum belts given to Sir William Johnson, of immortal Indian memory, were in several rows, black on each side and white in the middle; the white being placed in the center was to express peace and that the path between them was fair and open. In the center of the belt was a figure of a diamond made of white wampum, which the Indians call the council fire.

In the Jesuit Relations, 1642, p. 53, it is said that among the northern Algonquins a present to deliver a prisoner consisted of three strings of wampum to break the three bonds by which he was supposed to be tied, one around the legs, one around the arms, and the third around the middle.

In the same Relations, 1653, p. 19, is a good example of messages attached to separate presents of wampum, etc. This was at a council in 1653 at the Huron town, 2 leagues from Quebec:

The first was given to dry the tears which are usually shed at the news of brave warriors massacred in combat.

The second served as an agreeable drink, as an antidote to whatever bitterness might remain in the heart of the French on account of the death of their people.

The third was to furnish a piece of bark or a covering for the dead, lest the sight of them should renew the old strife.

The fourth was to inter them and to tread well the earth upon their graves, in order that nothing should ever come forth from their tombs which could grieve their friends and cause the spirit of revenge to arise in their minds.

The fifth was to serve as a wrapping to pack up the arms which were henceforth not to be touched.

The sixth was to cleanse the river, soiled with so much blood.

The last, to exhort the Hurons to agree to what Onontio, the great captain of the French, should decide upon touching the peace.

As a rule there was no intrinsic significance in a wampum belt, or collar, as the French sometimes called it. It was not understood except by the memory of those to whom and by whom it was delivered. This is well expressed in a dialogue reported by Capt. de Lamothe Cadillac (a) in 1703:

[Council of Hurons at Fort Ponchartrain, June 3, 1703.]

QUARANTE-SOLS. I come on my way to tell you what I propose to do at Montreal. Here is a collar which has been sent to us by the Iroquois, and which the Ottawas have brought to us; we do not know what it signifies.

M. de LAMOTHE. How have you received this collar without knowing the purpose for which it was sent you?

QUARANTE-SOLS. It has already been long since we received it. I was not there, and our old men have forgotten what it said.

M. de LAMOTHE. Your old men are not regarded as children to have such a short memory.

QUARANTE-SOLS. We do not accept this collar; but we are going to take it to Sonnontouan [the Seneca town] to find out what it means; because it is a serious matter not to respond to a collar; it is the custom among us. The Ottawas can tell you what it is, because our people have forgotten it.

M. de LAMOTHE. The Ottawas will reply that having received it you should remember it, but since this collar is dumb and has lost its speech I am obliged to be silent myself.

In the Diary of the Siege of Detroit (a) it is narrated that after receiving a belt of wampum from the commanding officer the Pottawatomi chief called it the officer's "mouth," and said that those to whom it was sent would believe it when "they saw his mouth."

But wampum designs, besides being mere credentials, and thus like the Australian message sticks, and also mnemonic, became, to some

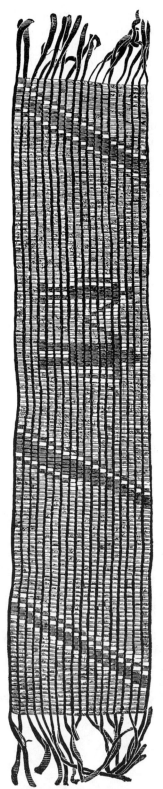

FIG. 164.—Penn wampum belt.

extent, conventional. The predominance of white beads indicated peace, and purple or violet meant war.

On the authority of Sir Daniel Wilson (a) a string of black wampum sent round the settlement is still among the Indians of the Six Nations the notice of the death of a chief.

The Iroquois belts had an arrangement of wampum to signify the lakes, rivers, mountains, valleys, portages, and falls along the path of trail between them and the Algonkins, who were parties to their treaty in 1653.

On the authority of a manuscript letter from St. Ange to D'Abbadie, September 9, 1764, quoted by Parkman (a), Pontiac's great wampum belt was 6 feet long, 4 inches wide, and was wrought from end to end with the symbols of tribes and villages, 47 in number, which were leagued with him.

In addition to becoming conventional the designs in wampum, perhaps from expertness in their workmanship, exhibited ideographs in their later development, of which the following description, taken from Rev. Peter Jones's (a), "History of the Ojebway Indians" is an instance:

Johnson then explained the emblems contained in the wampum belt brought by Yellowhead, which, he said, they acknowledged to be the acts of their fathers. Firstly, the council fire at the Sault Ste. Marie has no emblem, because then the council was held. Secondly, the council fire at Mamtoulni has the emblem of a beautiful white fish; this signifies purity, or a clean white heart—that all our hearts ought to be white toward each other. Thirdly, the emblem of a beaver, placed at an island on Penetanguishew bay, denotes wisdom—that all the acts of our fathers were done in wisdom. Fourthly, the emblem of a white deer, placed at Lake Simcoe, signified superiority; the dish and ladles at the same place indicated abundance of game and food. Fifthly, the eagle perched on a tall pine tree at the Credit denotes watching, and swiftness in conveying messages. The eagle was to watch all the council fires between the Six Nations and the Ojebways, and being far-sighted, he might, in the event of anything happening, communicate the tidings to the distant tribes. Sixthly, the sun was hung up in the center of the belt to show that their acts were done in the face of the sun, by whom they swore that they would forever after observe the treaties made between the two parties.

In the same work, p. 119, is a description of a wampum belt that recorded the first treaty between the Ojibwa and the Six Nations of the Iroquois confederacy. It has the figure of a dish or bowl at its middle to represent that the Ojibwa and the Six Nations were all to eat out of the same dish, meaning, ideographically, that all the game in the region should be for their common use.

Mr. W. H. Holmes (c) gives an illustration of the well-known Penn wampum belt, reproduced here as Fig. 164, with remarks condensed as follows:

It is believed to be the original belt delivered by the Leni-Lenape sachems to William Penn at the celebrated treaty under the elm tree at Schackamaxon in 1682. Up to the year 1857 this belt remained in the keeping of the Penn family. In March, 1857, it was presented to the Pennsylvania Historical Society by Granville John Penn, a great-grandson of William Penn. Mr. Penn, in his speech on this occasion, states that there can be no doubt that this is the identical belt used at the treaty, and presents his views in the following language:

"In the first place, its dimensions are greater than of those used on more ordinary occasions, of which we have one still in our possession—this belt being composed of 18 strings of wampum, which is a proof that it was the record of some very important negotiation. In the next place, in the center of the belt, which is of white wampum, are delineated in dark-colored beads, in a rude, but graphic style, two figures—that of an Indian grasping with the hand of friendship the hand of a man evidently intended to be represented in the European costume wearing a hat, which can only be interpreted as having reference to the treaty of peace and friendship which was then concluded between William Penn and the Indians, and recorded by them in their own simple but descriptive mode of expressing their meaning by the employment of hieroglyphics."

SECTION 4.

ORDER OF SONGS.

The Indian songs or, more accurately, chants, with which pictography is connected, have been preserved in their integrity by the use of pictured characters. They are in general connected with religious ceremonies, and are chiefly used in the initiation of neophytes to secret religious orders. Some of them, however, are used in social meetings or ceremonies of cult societies, though the distinction between social or any other general associations and those to be classified as religious is not easily defined. Religion was the real life of the tribes, permeating all their activities and institutions.

The words of these songs are invariable, even to the extent that by their use for generations many of them have become archaic and form no part of the colloquial language. Indeed, they are not always understood by the best of the shaman songsters, which fact recalls the oriental memorization of the Veda ritual through generations by the priests, who thus, without intent, preserved a language. The sounds were memorized, although the characters designating or, more correctly, recalling them, were not representations of sound, but of idea.

Practically, the words—or sounds, understood or not, which passed for words—as well as the notes, were memorized by the singers, and their memory, or that of the shaman, who acted as leader or conductor or precentor, was assisted by the charts. Exoteric interpretation of any ideographic and not merely conventional or purely arbitrary characters in the chart, which may be compared for indistinctness with the translated libretto of operas, may suggest the general subject-matter, perhaps the general course, of the chant, but can not indicate the exact words, or, indeed, any words, of the language chanted.

A simple mode of explaining the amount of symbolism necessarily contained in the charts of the order of songs is by likening them to the illustrated songs and ballads lately published in popular magazines, where every stanza has at least one appropriate illustration. Let it be supposed that the text was obliterated forever, indeed, the art of reading lost, the illustrations remaining, as also the memory to some persons of the words of the ballad. The illustrations, kept in their original order, would always supply the order of the stanzas and also the particular subject-matter of each particular stanza, and that subject-matter would be a reminder of the words. This is what the rolls of birchbark supply to the initiated Ojibwa. Schoolcraft pretended that there is intrinsic symbolism in the characters employed, which might imply that the words of the chants were rather interpretations of those characters than that the latter were reminders of the words. But only after the vocables of the actual songs and chants have been learned can the mnemonic characters be clearly understood. Doubtless the more ideographic and the less arbitrary the characters the more readily can they be learned and retained in the memory, and during the long period of the practical use of the mnemonic devices many exhibiting ideography and symbolism have been invented or selected.

The ceremonial songs represented pictorially in Pl. xvii, A, B, C, and D, were obtained from Ojibwa shamans at White Earth, Minnesota, by Dr. Hoffman, and pertain to the ceremony of initiating new members into the Midē' wiwin or Grand Medicine Society. The language, now omitted, differs to some extent from that now spoken. The songs and ritual are transmitted from generation to generation, and although an Indian who now receives admission into the society may compose his own songs for use in connection with his profession, he will not adopt the modern Ojibwa words, but employs the archaic whenever practicable. To change the ancient forms would cause loss of power in the charms which such songs are alleged to possess.

The translation of the songs was given by the Ojibwa singers, while the remarks in smaller type further elucidate the meaning of the phrases, as afterwards explained by the shaman.

The characters were all drawn upon birch bark, as is usual with the "medicine songs" of the Ojibwa, and the words suggested by the incisions were chanted. The incompleteness of some of the phrases was accounted for by the shaman by the fact that they are gradually

ORDER OF SONGS—OJIBWA.

being forgotten. The ceremonies are now of infrequent occurrence, which tends to substantiate this assertion.

One song, as presented on a single piece of birch bark, really consists of as many songs as there are mnemonic characters. Each phrase, corresponding to a character, is repeated a number of times; the greater the number of repetitions the greater will be the power of inspiration in the singer. One song or phrase may, therefore, extend over a period of from two to ten or more minutes.

The song covers much more time when dancing accompanies it, as is the case with the first one presented below. The dancing generally commences after a pause, designated by a single vertical bar.

The following characters are taken from A, Pl. XVII, and are here reproduced separately to facilitate explanation:

The earth, spirit that I am, I take medicine out of the earth.

The upper figure represents the arm reaching down toward the earth, searching for hidden remedies.

(Because of) a spirit that I am, my son.

The headless human figure emerging from the circle is a mysterious being, representing the power possessed by the speaker. He addresses a younger and less experienced Midē′ or shaman.

Bar or rest.

The vertical line denotes a slight pause in the song, after which the chant is renewed, accompanied by dancing.

They have pity on me, that is why they call us to the Grand Medicine.

The inner circle represents the speaker's heart; the outer circle, the gathering place for shamans, while the short lines indicate the directions from which the shamans come together.

I want to see you, medicine man.

The figure of a head is represented with lines running downward (and forward) from the eyes, donating sight. The speaker is looking for the shaman, spoken to, to make his appearance within the sacred structure where the Midē′ ceremonies are to take place.

My body is a spirit.

The character is intended to represent the body of a bear, with a line across the body, signifying one of the most powerful of the sacred Man′idōs or spirits, of the Midē′ wiwin or "Grand Medicine Society."

You would [know] it, it being a spirit.

The figure of a head is shown with lines extending both upward and downward from the ears, denoting a knowledge of things in realm of the Man′idōs above, and of the secrets of the earth beneath.

As I am dressed, I am.

The otter is emerging from the sacred Midē′ inclosure; the otter typifies the sacred Man′idō who received instruction for the people from Mi′nabō′zho, the intermediary between the "Great Spirit" and the Ânishinâbeg.

That is what ails me, I fear my Midē′ brothers.

The arm reaching into a circle denotes the power of obtaining mysterious influence from Kítschi Man′idō, but the relation between the pictograph and the phrase is obscure; unless the speaker fears such power as possessed by others.

The following is the order of another Midē′ song. The general style of the original resembles the specific class of songs which are used when digging medicines, i. e., plants or roots. The song is shown in Pl. XVII, B as the character appears on the bark.

As I arise from [slumber].

The speaker is shown as emerging from a double circle, his sleeping place.

What have I unearthed?

The speaker has discovered a bear Man′idō, as shown by the two hands grasping that animal by the back.

Down is the bear.

The bear is said to have his legs cut off, by the outline of the Midē′ structure, signifying he has become helpless because he is under the influence of the shamans.

Big, I am big.

The speaker is great in his own estimation; his power of obtaining gifts from superior beings is shown by the arm reaching for an object received from above; he has furthermore overcome the bear Man′idō and can employ it to advantage.

You encourage me.

Two arms are shown extended toward a circle containing spots of mī′gis, or sacred shells. The arms represent the assistance of friends of the speaker encouraging him with their assistance.

I can alight in the medicine pole.

The eagle or thunder-bird is perched upon the medicine pole erected near the shamans' sacred structure. The speaker professes to have the power of flight equal to the thunder-bird, that he may transport himself to any desired locality.

The following is another example of a pictured Midē' song, and is represented in Pl. XVII, C.

I know you are a spirit.

The figure is represented as having waving lines extending from the eyes downward toward the earth, and indicating search for secrets hidden beneath the surface of the earth. The hands extending upward indicate the person claims supernatural powers by which he is recognized as "equal to a spirit."

I lied to my son.

The signification of the phrase could not be explained by the informant, especially its relation to the character, which is an arm, reaching beyond the sky for power from Ki'tshi Man'idō. The waving line upon the arm denotes mysterious power.

Spirit I am, the wolf.

The speaker terms himself a wolf spirit, possessing peculiar power. The animal as drawn has a line across the body signifying its spirit character.

At last I become a spirit.

The circle denotes the spot occupied by the speaker; his hands extended are directed toward the source of his powers.

I give you the mī'gis.

The upper character represents the arm reaching down giving a sacred shell, the mī'gis, the sacred emblem of the "Grand Medicine Society." The "giving of the mī'gis" signifies its "being shot" into the body of a new member of the society to give him life and the power of communing with spirits, or Man'idōs.

You are speaking to me.

An arm is extended toward a circle containing a smaller one, the latter representing the spot occupied by Midē friends.

The characters next explained are taken from the last line, D, of the series given in Pl. XVII. The speaker appears to have great faith in his own powers as a Midē′.

Spirit I am, I enter.

The otter, which Man′idō, the speaker, professes to represent, is entering the sacred structure of Midē′ lodge.

Midē′ friends, do you hear me?

The circles denote the locality where the Midē′ are supposed to be congregated. The waving lines signify hearing, when, as in this case, attached to the ears.

The first time I heard you.

The speaker asserts that he heard the voices of the Man′idōs When he went through his first initiation into the society. He is Still represented as the otter.

The spirit, he does hear (?)

The interpretation is vague, but could not be otherwise explained. The lines from the ears denote hearing.

They, the Midē′ friends, have paid enough.

The arm in the attitude of giving, to Ki′tshi Man′idō, signifies that the Midē′ have made presents of sufficient value to be enabled to possess the secrets, which they received in return.

They have pity on me, the chief Midē′.

The arms of Ki′tshi Man′idō are extended to the Midē′ lodge, giving assistance as besought.

The song mnemonically represented in Pl. XVIII A (reproduced from Pl. X A. of the Seventh Ann. Rep. Bur. of Ethn.) is sung by the Ojibwa preceptor who has been instructing the candidate for initiation. It praises the preceptor's efforts and the character of the knowledge he has imparted. Its delivery is made to extend over as much time as possible.

The mnemonic characters were drawn by Sikas′sigĕ, and are a copy of an old birchbark scroll, which has for many years been in his posses-

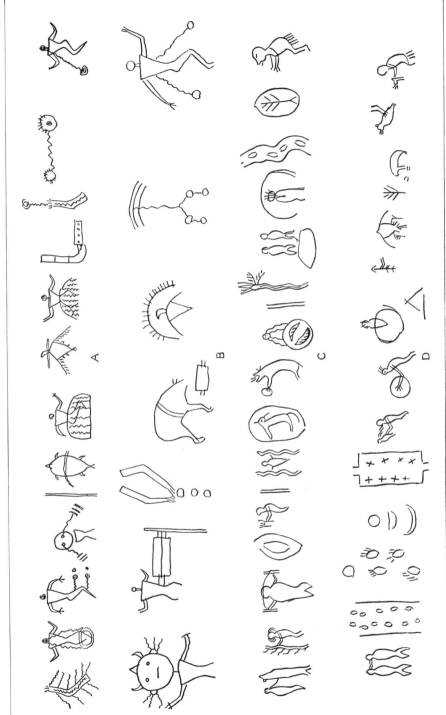

MNEMONIC SONGS—OJIBWA.

sion, and which was a transcript of one in the possession of his father Baiédzĭk, one of the leading Midē′ at Mille Lacs, Minnesota.

My arm is almost pulled out with digging medicine. It is full of medicine.

The short zigzag lines signifying magic influence, erroneously designated "medicine."

Almost crying because the medicine is lost.

The lines extending downward from the eye signify weeping; the circle beneath the figure, the place where the "medicine" is supposed to exist. The idea of "lost" signifies that some information has been forgotten through death of those who possessed it.

Yes, there is much medicine you may cry for.

Refers to that which is yet to be taught.

Yes, I see there is plenty of it.

The Midē′ has knowledge of more than he has imparted, but reserves that knowledge for a future time. The lines of "sight" run to various medicines which he perceives or knows of.

Rest.

When I come out the sky becomes clear.

When the otter-skin Midē′ sack is produced the sky becomes clear, so that the ceremonies may proceed.

The spirit has given me power to see.

The Midē′ sits on a mountain the better to commune with the good Man′idō.

I brought the medicine to bring life.

The Midē′ Manidō′, the Thunderer, after bringing some of the plants—by causing the rains to fall—returns to the sky. The short line represents part of the circular line usually employed to designate the imaginary vault of the sky.

I too, see how much there is.

His power elevates the Midē′ to the rank of a Man′idō, from whose position he perceives many secrets hidden in the earth.

I am going to the medicine lodge.

The vertical, left-hand figure denotes a leg going toward the Midē′wigân.

I take life from the sky.

The Midē′ is enabled to reach into the sky and to obtain from Ki′tshi Man′idō′ the means of prolonging life. The circle at the top denotes the sacred migis or shell.

Let us talk to one another.

The circles denote the places of the speaker (Midē′) and the hearer (Ki′tshi Man′idō), the short lines signifying magic influences, the Midē′ occupying the left hand and smaller seat.

The spirit is in my body, my friend.

The mī′gis, given by Ki′tshi Man′idō, is in contact with the Midē′′s body, and he is possessed of life and power.

In the order of song, Pl. XVIII, B, reproduced from Pl. IX, C, of the Seventh Ann. Rep. of the Bureau of Ethnology, the preceptor appears to feel satisfied that the candidate is prepared to receive the initiation, and therefore tells him that the Midē′ Man′idō announces to him the assurance. The preceptor therefore encourages his pupil with promises of the fulfillment of his highest desires:

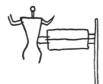

I hear the spirit speaking to us.

The Midē′-singer is of superior power, as designated by the horns and pointer upon his head. The lines from the ears indicate hearing.

I am going into the medicine lodge.

The Midē′wigân is shown with a line through it, to signify that the preceptor is going through it in imagination, as in the initiation.

I am taking (gathering) medicine to make me live.

The disks indicate the sacred objects sought for, which are successively obtained by the speaker, who represents the officiating shaman.

I give you medicine, and a lodge, also.

The Midē′, as the personator of Makwá Man′idō, is empowered
to offer this privilege to the candidate.

I am flying into my lodge.

Represents the thunder-bird, a deity flying into the arch of
the sky, the abode of spirits or Man′idōs. The short lines cutting the curve are spirit lines.

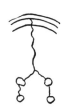

The spirit has dropped medicine from the sky where
we can get it.

The line from the sky, diverging to various points, indicates
that the sacred objects fall in scattered places.

I have the medicine in my heart.

The singer's heart is filled with knowledge relating to sacred
objects from the earth.

The song depicted in Pl. XVIII C, was drawn by "Little Frenchman,"
an Ojibwa Midē′ of the first degree, who reproduced it from a bark
record belonging to his preceptor. "Little Frenchman" had not yet
received instruction in these characters, and consequently could not
sing the songs, but from his familiarity with mnemonic delineations of
the order of the Grand Medicine of ideas he was able to give an outline
of the signification of the figures and the phraseology which they suggested to his mind. In the following description the first line pertaining to a character is the objective description, the second being the
explanation.

It is furthermore to be remarked that in this chart and the one following the interpretation of characters begins at the right hand instead
of the left, contrary to rule. The song is reproduced from Pl. XXII, A,
of the Seventh Annual Report of the Bureau of Ethnology:

From the place where I sit.

A man, seated and talking or singing.

The big tree in the middle of the earth.

Tree; inclosure represents the world as visible from a given spot of observation—horizon.

I will float down the fast running stream.

Stream of water; the spots indicate progress of traveler, and may be rude indications of canoes or equally rude foot tracks, the usual pictograph for traveling.

The place that is feared I inhabit; the swift running stream.

A spirit surrounded by a line indicating the shore.

You who speak to me.

Two spirits communing.

I have long horns.

Horned water monster.

Rest; dancing begins with next character.

I, observing, follow your example.

Man listening to water monster (spirit).

You are my body; you see anybody; you see my nails are worn off in grasping the stone (from which medicine is taken).

Bear, with claws, scratching; depression shown by line under claws, where scratching has been done.

You (i. e., the spirits who are there), to whom I am speaking.

Spirit panther.

I am floating down smoothly.

Spirit otter, swimming; outer lines are river banks.

Rest.

I have finished my drum.

Spirit holding drum; sound ascending.

My body is like unto you.

This is the mī′gis shell—the special symbol of the Midē′ wiwin.

Hear me, thou, who art talking to me.

Listening, and wanting others (spirits) to hear.

See what I am taking.

Spirit (Midē′) taking "medicine root."

See me whose head is out of the water.

Otters, two spirits, the left-hand one being the "speaker."

The Midē′ song, Pl. XVIII, D, was also copied by "Little Frenchman" upon birchbark, from one in the possession of his preceptor, but upon which he had not yet received careful instruction; hence the incompleteness of some of his interpretations. It is reproduced from Pl. XXII, B, of the Seventh Ann. Rep. Bureau of Ethnology.

I am sitting down with my pipe.

Man sitting, holding a pipe. He has been called upon to "make medicine." The short lines beneath the body represent that he is seated. He holds a filled pipe which he is not yet smoking.

I, me the spirit, the spirit of the owl.

Owl, held by Midē′; arm above bird. This character appears upon the Grand Medicine chart from Red Lake, as passing from the midē′ lodge to the ghost lodge.

It stands, that which I am going after.

Tree; showing tracks made by bear spirit. The speaker terms himself equal with this spirit and represents himself seeking remedies.

I, who fly.

Medicine bag, flying. The figure is that of the thunder bird (eagle) whose skin was used for a bag. The trees beneath show the bird to have ascended beyond their tops.

Kibinan is what I use—the magic arrow.

An arrow, held by hand.

I am coming to the earth.

Otter spirit. Circle denotes the surrounding sky in which is the spirit. The earth is shown by the horizontal line above which is the Indian hut. The speaker likens himself to the otter spirit who first received the rites of the Midē′ initiation.

I am feeling for it.

Man (spirit) seeking for hidden medicine. The circle represents a hole in the earth.

I am talking to it.

Medicine bag made of an owl skin is held by shaman; latter is talking to the magic elements contained therein.

They are sitting in a circle ("around in a row").

Midē′ lodge; Midē′ sitting around. The crosses represent the persons present.

You who are newly hung, and you who have reached half, and you who are now full.

Full moon, one half, and quarter moon.

I am going for my dish.

Footprints leading to dish (ghost society dish). The circular objects here each denotes a "feast," usually represented by a "dish."

I go through the medicine lodge.

Grand medicine lodge; tracks leading through it. The speaker, after having prepared a feast, is entitled to enter for initiation.

Let us commune with one another.

Two men conversing; two Midē'.

The mnemonic order of song, Pl. XIX a, is another example from Red Lake, prepared by the Ojibwa last mentioned:

"Carved images."

Carved images. These represent the speaker to say that he prepares fetishes for hunting, love, etc.

I am holding my grand medicine sack.

Man holding "medicine bag."

"Wants a woman." [No interpretation was ventured by "Little Frenchman."]

Hear me, great spirit.

Lines from the ears, to denote hearing.

I am about to climb.

Medicine tree at grand lodge. The marks on either side are bear tracks, the footprints of the bear spirit—the speaker representing him.

I am entering the grand medicine lodge.

The Midē'wigân, showing footprints of the bear Man'idō which are simulated by the boastful shaman.

I am making my tracks on the road.

Footprints on the path.

I am resting at my home.

Human figure, with "voice" issuing—singing.

Pl. XIX b is a similar song, also made by "Little Frenchman," and relates to magic remedies and his powers of incantation:

The stars.

Stars, preceded by a mark of rest or beginning. It may be noticed that one star has eight and the other six rays, showing that their number is not significant.

The wolf that runs.

Wolf; the banded tail distinguishes it from the otter.

See me what I have; what I have (goods given in the midē′ wigwân).

Man holding bow.

See what I am about to do.

Arm, holding a gun.

The house of the beaver.

Beaver, in his house.

I, who make a noise.

A frog, croaking, shown by "voice" lines.

My white hair.

Head with hair. The signification of white hair is great age, though there is no way to ascertain this without oral statement by the singer.

The house of the otter.

Otter in his burrow.

Hear me, you, to whom I am talking.

Mī′gis, spoken to by man, lines showing hearing. The sacred emblem of the Midē′wiwin is implored for aid in carrying out a desired scheme.

I stoop as I walk.

An old man. Age is denoted by the act of walking with a staff.

I stand by the tree.

Standing near medicine tree. The speaker knows of valued remedies which he desires to dispose of for payment.

I am raising a rock.

Man with stone for Midē′ lodge. Carrying stone to Midē′ lodge, against which to place a patient.

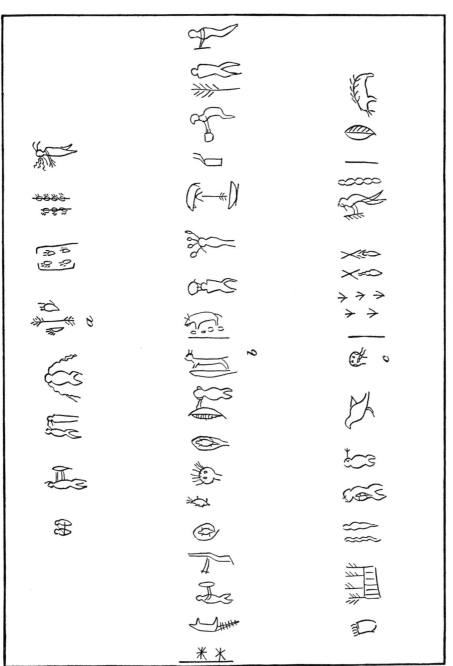

MNEMONIC SONGS—OJIBWA.

I am holding my pail.

Vessel of medicine; arm reaching down to it.

My arrow point is of iron, and about to kill a male bear.

Bear, above arrow. Bow—lower character.

I am about to speak to the sky.

Speaking to the "sky." Power of communing with the Great Spirit, Ki'tshi Man'idō'.

I am about to depart; I will liken myself to a bear.

Bear, tracks and path.

I am walking on the hard sand beach.

Body of water, and lynx. The ellipse denotes a lake.

Another song of a similar character, reproduced from birchbark on Pl. XIX c, is explained below. It was also made by "Little Frenchman," and relates to the searching for and preparation of objects used in sorcery.

It is fiery, that which I give you.

Vessel, with flames on top. Contains strong water wi-bĭn', a magical decoction.

It is growing, the tree.

Mīdē'wigân, with trees growing around it at four corners.

I cover the earth with my length.

Snakes; guardians of the first degree.

The bear is contained within me.

Bear spirit within the man—i. e., the speaker. This indicates that he possesses the power of the Bear Man'idō, one of the most powerful of the guardians of the Midē' society.

He has Man'idō (spirit) in his mouth.

Possessing the power of curing by "sucking" bad spirits from patient's body. This is the practice of the lower shamans, known as Jēs'sakkīd'.

The hawk genus et sp.

Ki-ni-en', the hawk from which "medicine" is obtained.

I, who am about to talk.

Head of man; lines from mouth denote speech.

The interpretation now again proceeds from right to left.

I am about to walk.

Bear spirit, talking. The lines upon the back indicate his spirit character.

I am crawling away.

Mi'gis shell. The sacred emblem of the Midē' society.

Rest.

From this, I wish to be able to walk.

Taking "medicine" trail (behind man). The speaker is addressing a Man'idō which he holds.

I am being called to go there.

Sacred lodges, with spirits within.

I am going.

Footprints, leading toward a wigwam.

Rest.

The Ojibwa chart, used in the "Song for the Metai, or for Medicine Hunting," is taken from Tanner's (*a*) Narrative and reproduced in Fig. 165. It should be noted that the Metai of Tanner's intepretation, which follows, is the same as the Midē' in the foregoing interpretations:

a. Now I hear it, my friends of the Metai, who are sitting about me. This and the three following are sung by the principal chief of the

Metai, to the beat of his bwoin ah-keek, or drum. The line from the sides of the head of the figure indicate hearing.

b. Who makes this river flow? The Spirit, he makes this river flow.

The second figure is intended to represent a river, and a beaver swimming down it.

c. Look at me well, my friends; examine me, and let us understand that we are all companions.

This translation is by no means literal. The words express the boastful claims of a man who sets himself up for the best and most skillful in the fraternity.

d. Who maketh to walk about, the social people? A bird maketh to walk about the social people.

By the bird the medicine man means himself; he says that his voice

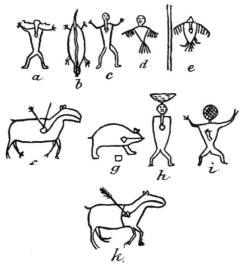

Fig. 165—Song for Medicine Hunting.

has called the people together. Weej-huh nish-a-nauba, or weeja-nish-a-nau-ba seems to have the first syllable from the verb which means to accompany. The two lines drawn across, between this figure and the next, indicate that here the dancing is to commence.

e. I fly about and if anywhere I see an animal, I can shoot him.

This figure of a bird (probably an eagle or hawk) seems intended to indicate the wakefulness of the senses and the activity required to insure success in hunting. The figure of the moose which immediately follows, reminding the singer of the cunning and extreme shyness of that animal, the most difficult of all to kill.

f. I shoot your heart; I hit your heart, oh, animal—your heart—I hit your heart.

This apostrophe is mere boasting and is sung with much gesticulation and grimace.

g. I make myself look like fire.

This is a medicine man disguised in the skin of a bear. The small parallelogram under the bear signifies fire, and the shamans, by some composition of gunpowder, or other means, contrive to give the appearance of fire to the mouth and eyes of the bear skin, in which they go about the village late at night, bent on deeds of mischief, oftentimes of blood. We learn how mischievous are these superstitions when we are informed that they are the principal men of the Metai, who thus wander about the villages in the disguise of a bear, to wreak their hatred on a sleeping rival or their malice on an unsuspecting adversary. But the customs of the Indians require of anyone who may see a medicine man on one of these excursions to take his life immediately, and whoever does so is accounted guiltless.

h. I am able to call water from above, from beneath, and from around.

Here the medicine man boasts of his power over the elements, and his ability to do injury or benefit. The segment of a circle with dots in it represents water and the two short lines touching the head of the figure indicate that he can draw it to him.

i. I cause to look like the dead, a man I did.

I cause to look like the dead, a woman I did.

I cause to look like the dead, a child I did.

The lines drawn across the face of this figure indicate poverty, distress, and sickness; the person is supposed to have suffered from the displeasure of the medicine man. Such is the religion of the Indians. Its boast is to put into the hands of the devout supernatural means by which he may wreak vengeance on his enemies whether weak or powerful, whether they be found among the foes of his tribe or the people of his own village. This Metai, so much valued and revered by them, seems to be only the instrument in the hands of the crafty for keeping in subjection the weak and the credulous, which may readily be supposed to be the greater part of the people.

k. I am such, I am such, my friends; any animal, any animal, my friends, I hit him right, my friends.

This boast of certain success in hunting is another method by which he hopes to elevate himself in the estimation of his hearers. Having told them he has the power to put them all to death, he goes on to speak of his infallible success in hunting, which will always enable him to be a valuable friend to such as are careful to secure his good will.

The following chart for the "Song for beaver hunting and the Metai," is taken from the same author, loc. cit., and reproduced in Fig. 166, with interpretations as follows:

a. I sit down in the lodge of the Metai, the lodge of the Spirit.

This figure is intended to represent the area of the Metai-we-gaun, or medicine lodge, which is called also the lodge of the Man'idō, and two men have taken their seats in it. The matter of the song seems to be merely introductory.

b. Two days must you sit fast, my friend; four days must you sit fast, my friend.

The two perpendicular lines on the breast of this figure are read ne-o-gone (two days), but are understood to mean two years; so of the four lines drawn obliquely across the legs, these are four years. The heart must be given to this business for two years, and the constrained attitude of the legs indicates the rigid attention and serious consideration which the subject requires.

c. Throw off, woman, thy garments, throw off.

The power of their medicines and the incantations of the Metai are not confined in their effect to animals of the chase, to the lives and

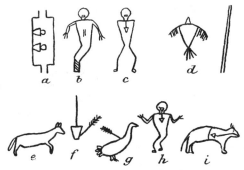

Fig. 166.—Song for beaver hunting.

health of men; they control also the minds of all and overcome the modesty as well as the antipathies of women. The Indians firmly believe that many a woman who has been unsuccessfully solicited by a man is not only by the power of the Metai made to yield, but even in a state of madness to tear off her garments and pursue after the man she before despised. These charms have greater power than those in the times of superstition among the English, ascribed to the fairies, and they need not, like the plant used by Puck, be applied to the person of the unfortunate being who is to be transformed; they operate at a distance through the medium of the Miz-zin-ne-neens.

d. Who makes the people walk about? It is I that calls you.

This is in praise of the virtue of hospitality, that man being most esteemed among them who most frequently calls his neighbors to his feast.

e. Anything I can shoot with it (this medicine) even a dog, I can kill with it.

f. I shoot thy heart, man, thy heart.

He means, perhaps, a buck moose by the word e-nah-ne-wah, or man.

g. I can kill a white loon, I can kill.

The white loon (rara avis nigroque similimo cygno) is certainly a rare and most difficult bird to kill; so we may infer that this boaster can kill anything, which is the amount of the meaning intended in that part of his song recorded by the five last figures. Success in hunting they look upon as a virtue of a higher character, if we may judge from this song, than the patience under suffering or the rakishness among women, or even the hospitality recommended in the former part.

h. My friends——

There seems to be an attempt to delineate a man sitting with his hands raised to address his friends; but the remainder of his speech is not remembered. This is sufficient to show that the meaning of the characters in this kind of picture writing is not well settled and re- quires a traditional interpretation to render it intelligible.

i. I open my wolf skin and the death struggle must follow.

This is a wolf skin used as a medicine bag and he boasts that when- ever he opens it something must die in consequence.

Tanner's Narrative (*b*) says of musical notation drawn on bark by Ojibwas:

Many of these songs are noted down by a method probably peculiar to the Indians, on birch bark, or small flat pieces of wood: the ideas being conveyed by emblematic figures, somewhat like those   *   *   *   used in communicating ordinary information.

Rev. P. J. De Smet (*a*) gives an account of the mnemonic order of songs among the Kickapoo and Pottawatomi. He describes a stick $1\frac{1}{2}$ inches broad and 8 or 10 long, upon which are arbitrary characters which they follow with the finger in singing the prayers, etc. There are five classes of these characters. The first represents the heart, the second heart and flesh (chair), the third life, the fourth their names, and the fifth their families.

A. W. Howitt (*b*) says:

The makers of the Australian songs, or of the combined songs and dances are the poets or bards of the tribe and are held in great esteem. Their names are known to the neighboring peoples, and their songs are carried from tribe to tribe until the very meaning of the words is lost as well as the original source of the song.

Such an instance is a song which was accompanied by a carved stick painted red, which was held by the chief singer. This traveled down the Murray river from some unknown source. The same song, accompanied by such a stick, also came into Gippsland many years ago from Melbourne and may even have been the above men- tioned one on its return.

SECTION 5.

TRADITIONS.

Even since the Columbian discovery some tribes have employed devices yet ruder than the rudest pictorial attempt as markers for the memory. An account of one of these is given in E. Winslow's Relation (A. D. 1624), Col. Mass. Hist. Soc., 2d series, IX, 1822, p. 99, as follows:

Instead of records and chronicles they take this course: Where any remarkable act is done, in memory of it, either in the place or by some pathway near adjoining, they make a round hole in the ground about a foot deep and as much over, which, when others passing by behold, they inquire the cause and occasion of the same, which, being once known, they are careful to acquaint all men as occasion serveth therewith. And lest such holes should be filled or grown over by any accident, as men pass by they will often renew the same, by which means many things of great antiquity are fresh in memory. So that as a man traveleth, if he can understand his guide, his journey will be the less tedious by reason of the many historical discourses which will be related unto him.

In connection with this section students may usefully consult Dr. Brinton's (*f*) Lenâpé and their Legends.

As an example of a chart used in the exact repetition of traditions, Fig. 167 is presented with the following explanation by Rev. J. Owen Dorsey:

The chart accompanies a tradition chanted by members of a secret society of the Osage tribe. It was drawn by an Osage, Red Corn.

The tree at the top represents the tree of life. By this flows a river. The tree

and the river are described later in the degrees. When a woman is initiated she is required by the head of her gens to take four sips of water (symbolizing the river), then he rubs cedar on the palms of his hands, with which he rubs her from head to foot. If she belongs to a gens on the left side of a tribal circle, her chief begins on the left side of her head, making three passes, and pronouncing the sacred name three times. Then he repeats the process from her forehead down; then on the right side of her head; then at the back of her head; four times three times, or twelve passes in all.

Beneath the river are the following objects: The Watse ʇuŋa, male slaying animal (?), or morning star, which is a red star. 2. Six stars called the "Elm rod" by the white people in the Indian territory. 3. The evening star. 4. The little star. Beneath these are the moon, seven stars, and sun. Under the seven stars are the peace pipe and war hatchet; the latter is close to the sun, and the former and the moon are on the same side of the chart. Four parallel lines extending across the chart, represent four heavens or upper worlds through which the ancestors of the Tsiou people passed before they came to this earth. The lowest heaven rests on an oak tree; the ends of the others appear to be supported by pillars or ladders. The tradition begins below the lowest heaven, on the left side of the chart, under the peace pipe. Each space on the pillar corresponds with a line of the chant; and each stanza (at the opening of the tradition) contains four lines. The first stanza precedes the arrival of the first heaven, pointing to a time when the children of the "former end" of the race were without human bodies as well as human

FIG. 167.—Osage chart.

souls. The bird hovering over the arch denotes an advance in the condition of the people; then they had human souls in the bodies of birds. Then followed the progress from the fourth to the first heaven, followed by the descent to earth. The ascent to four heavens and the descent to three, makes up the number seven.

When they alighted, it was on a beautiful day when the earth was covered with luxuriant vegetation. From that time the paths of the Osages separated; some marched on the right, being the war gentes, while those on the left were peace gentes, including the Tsiou, whose chart this is.

Then the Tsiou met the black bear, called in the tradition Káxe-wáhü-sa^{n'} (Crow-bone-white), in the distance. He offered to become their messenger, so they sent him to the different stars for aid. According to the chart he went to them in the following order: Morning star, sun, moon, seven stars, evening star, little star.

Then the black bear went to the Waɔiñɥa-ɔüɥse, a female red bird sitting on her nest. This grandmother granted his request. She gave them human bodies, making them out of her own body.

The earth lodge at the end of the chart denotes the village of the Hañɥa utaȼaⁿɥsi, who were a very warlike people. Buffalo skulls were on the tops of the lodges, and the bones of the animals on which they subsisted whitened on the ground. The very air was rendered offensive by the decaying bodies and offal.

The whole of the chart was used mnemonically. Parts of it, such as the four heavens and ladders, were tattooed on the throat and chest of the old men belonging to the order.

The tradition relating to Minabō'zho and the sacred objects received from Kítshi Man'idō is illustrated in Fig. 168, which represents a copy (one-third original size) of the record preserved at White Earth. This record is read from left to right and is, briefly, as follows:

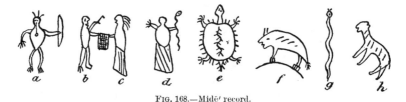

FIG. 168.—Midē' record.

a represents Minabō'zho, who says of the adjoining characters representing the members of the Midéwin: "They are the ones, they are the ones who put into my heart the life." Minabō'zho holds in his left hand the sacred medicine bag.

b and *c* represent the drummers; at the sound of the drum everybody rises and becomes inspired, because the Great Spirit is then present in the lodge.

d denotes that women also have the privilege of becoming members of the Midéwin. This figure holds a snake-skin "medicine bag" in her left hand.

e represents the tortoise, the good spirit, who was the giver of some of the sacred objects used in the rite.

f the bear, also a benevolent spirit, but not held in so great veneration as the tortoise. His tracks are visible in the lodge.

g the sacred medicine bag, Biñ-ji-gú-sân, which contains life and can be used by the Midē' to prolong the life of a sick person.

h represents a dog given by the spirits to Minabō'zho as a companion.

Fig. 169 gives copies, one-third actual size, of two records in possession of different Midē' at Red lake. The characters are almost identical, and one record appears to have been copied from the other. The lower figure, however, contains an additional character. The following is an

incomplete interpretation of the characters, the letters applying equally
to both:

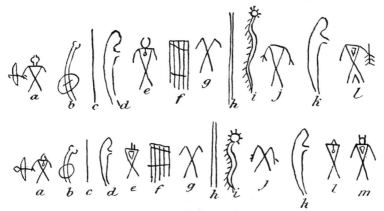

FIG. 169.—Midē′ records.

a, Esh′gibŏ′ga, the great uncle of the Unish′-in-ab′-aig, the receiver
of the Midéwin.

b, the drum and drumsticks.

c, a bar or rest, observed while chanting the words pertaining to the
records.

d, the bin′-ji-gu′-sân, or sacred medicine bag. It consists of an otter
skin, and is the mī′gis, or sacred symbol of the midē′wigân′ or grand
medicine lodge.

e, a Midē′ shaman, the one who holds the mī′gis while chanting the
Midē′ song in the grand medicine lodge, *f*. He is inspired, as indicated
by the line extending from the heart to the mouth.

f, representation of the grand medicine lodge. This character, with
slight addition, is usually employed by the southern division of the
Ojibwa to denote the lodge of a jĕssakkī′d, and is ordinarily termed a
"jugglery."

g, a woman, and signifies that women may also be admitted to the
midē′wigân′, shown in the preceding character.

h, a pause or rest in the chant.

i, the sacred snake-skin bag, having the power of giving life through
its skin. This power is indicated by the lines radiating from the head
and the back of the snake.

j represents a woman.

k, another illustration of the mī′gis, represented by the sacred otter.

l denotes a woman who is inspired, as shown by the line extending
from the heart to the mouth in the lower chart, and simply showing the
heart in the upper. In the latter she is also empowered to cure with
magic plants.

m represents a Midē′ shaman, but no explanation was obtained of the
special character delineated.

In Fig. 170 is presented a variant of the characters shown in *a* of Fig. 169. The fact that this denotes the power to cure by the use of plants would appear to indicate an older and more appropriate form than the delineation of the bow and arrow, as well as being more in keeping with the general rendering of the tradition.

FIG. 170.—Minabozho.

Fig. 171, two-thirds real size, is a reproduction, introduced here for comparison and explanation, of a record illustrating the alleged power of a Midē'.

FIG. 171.—Midē' practicing incantation.

a, the author, is the Midē', who was called upon to take a man's life at a distant camp. The line extending from the Midē' to *i*, explained below, signifies that his power extended to at least that distance.

b, an assistant Midē'.

c, d, e, and *f* represent the four degrees of the Midéwin, of which both shamans are members. The degrees are also indicated by the vertical lines above each lodge character.

g is the drum used in the ceremony.

h is an outline of the victim. A human figure is drawn upon a piece of birchbark, over which the incantations are made, and, to insure the death of the subject, a small spot of red paint is rubbed upon the breast and a sharp instrument thrust into it.

i, the outer line represents a lake, while the inner one is an island, upon which the victim resides.

The ceremony indicated in the above description actually occurred at White Earth during the autumn of 1884, and, by a coincidence, the Indian "conjured" died the following spring of pneumonia resulting from cold contracted during the winter. This was considered as the result of the Midē''s power, and naturally secured for him many new adherents and believers.

Fig. 172 represents a jĕssakkī'-ki, named Ne-wik'-ki, curing a sick

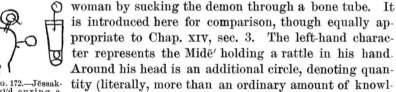

woman by sucking the demon through a bone tube. It is introduced here for comparison, though equally appropriate to Chap. XIV, sec. 3. The left-hand character represents the Midē' holding a rattle in his hand. Around his head is an additional circle, denoting quantity (literally, more than an ordinary amount of knowledge), the short line projecting to the right therefrom indicating the tube used. The right-hand character is the patient operated upon.

FIG. 172.—Jĕssakkī'd curing a woman.

The juggling trick of removing disease by sucking it through tubes is performed by the Midē′ after fasting and is accompanied with many ceremonies.

THE ORIGIN OF THE INDIANS.

Sikas′sigé, one of the officiating priests of the Midē′ society of the Ojibwa at White Earth, Minnesota, gives the following explanation of Fig. 173, which is a reduced copy of a pictorial representation of a tradition explaining the origin of the Indians:

In the beginning, Ki′tshi Man′idō—Dzhe Man′idō, a—made the Midē′ Man′idōs. He first created two men, b and c, and two women, d and e, but they had no power of thought or reason. Then Dzhe Man′idō made them reasoning beings. He then took them in his hands so that they should multiply; he paired them, and from this sprung the Indians. Then, when there were people, he placed them upon the earth; but he soon observed that they were subject to sickness, misery, and death, and that unless he provided them with the sacred medicine they would soon become extinct.

Between the position occupied by Dzhe Man′idō and the earth were four lesser spirits, f, g, h, and i, with whom Dzhe Man′idō decided to commune, and to impart the mysteries by which the Indians could be benefited; so he first spoke to a spirit at f, and told him all he had to say, who in turn communicated the same information to g, and he in turn to h, who also communed with i. Then they all met in council and determined to call in the four wind gods at j, k, l, and m. After consulting as to what would be best for the comfort and welfare of the Indians, these spirits agreed to ask Dzhe Man′idō to communicate the mystery of the sacred medicine to the people.

Dzhe Man′idō then went to the Sun Spirit (o) and asked him to go to the earth and instruct the people as had been decided upon by the council. The Sun Spirit, in the form of a little boy, went to the earth and lived with a woman (p) who had a little boy of her own.

This family went away in the autumn to hunt, and during the winter this woman's son died. The parents were so much distressed that they decided to return to the village and bury the body there; so they made preparations to return, and as they traveled along they would each evening erect several poles upon which the body was placed to prevent the wild beasts from devouring it. When the dead boy was thus hanging upon the poles the adopted child—who was the Sun Spirit—would play about the camp and amuse himself, and finally told his adopted father he pitied him, and his mother, for their sorrow. The adopted son said he could bring his dead brother to life, whereupon the parents expressed great surprise and desired to know how that could be accomplished.

The adopted boy then had the party hasten to the village, when he said, "Get the women to make a wig′iwam of bark (q), put the dead boy in a covering of birch bark and place the body on the ground in the middle of the wig′iwam." On the next morning, when this had been done, the family and friends went into this lodge and seated themselves around the corpse.

After they had all been sitting quietly for some time they saw, through the doorway, the approach of a bear (r), which gradually came toward the wig′iwam, entered it, and placed itself before the dead body, and said hŭ′, hŭ′, hŭ′, hŭ′, when he passed around it toward the left side, with a trembling motion, and as he did so the body began quivering, which increased as the bear continued, until he had passed around four times, when the body came to life and stood up. Then the bear called to the father, who was sitting in the distant right-hand corner of the wig′iwam, and addressed to him the following words:

Nōs Ka-wi′-na ni′-shi-nâ′-bi wis′-si a-ya′wi-an′ man′-i-do nin-gi′-sis.
My father   is not   an Indian   not   you are   a spirit   son.

Be-mai′-a-mi′-nik ni′-dzhi man′-i-do mi′-a-zhi′-gwa tshi-gi′-a-we-an′.
Insomuch   my fellow   spirit   now   as you are.

Nōs a-zhi′-gwa a-se′-ma tshi-a′-to-yek′. Â′-mi-kun′-dem mi-e′-ta
My father   now   tobacco   you shall put.   He speaks of   only

a-wi-dink′ dzhi-gŏsh′-kwi-tōt′ wen′-dzhi-bĭ-mâ′-di-zid′-o-ma′ a-ga′-wa
once   to be able to do it   why he shall live here   now

bi-mâ′-di-zid′-mi-o-ma′; ni′-dzhi man′-i-do mi′-a-zhi′-gwa tshi-gi′-we-an′.
that he scarcely lives;   my fellow   spirit   now I shall go   home.

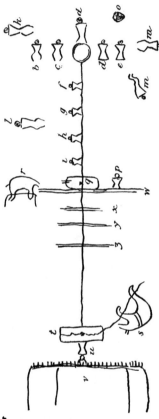

FIG. 173.—Origin of the Indians.

The little bear boy (r) was the one who did this. He then remained among the Indians (s) and taught them the mysteries of the Grand Medicine (t), and after he had finished he told his adopted father that as his mission had been fulfilled, that he was to return to his kindred spirits, the Indians would have no need to fear sickness, as they now possessed the Grand Medicine which would assist them to live. He also said that his spirit could bring a body to life but once, and he would now return to the sun from which they would feel his influence.

This is called Kwi′-wi-sĕns′ wed-di′-shi-tshi′ ge′-wi-nĭp′—"Little boy, his work."

From subsequent information it was learned that the line (w) denotes the earth, and that, being considered as one step in the course of initiation into the Midē′wiwin, three others must be taken before a candidate can be admitted. These steps, or rests, as they are denominated, are typified by four distinct gifts of goods, which must be remitted to the Midē′ priests before the ceremony can take place.

The characters s and t are repetitions of the figures alluded to in the tradition (q and r) to signify that the candidate must personate the Makwa′ Man′idō—bear spirit—when entering the Midē′wiwin (t); t is the Midē′ Man′idō, as Ki′tshi Man′idō is termed by the Midē′ priests. The device of horns, attached to the head, is a common symbol of superior power, found in connection with the figures of human and divine forms in many Midē′ songs and other mnemonic records; v represents the earth's surface, similar to that designated as w. w, x, y, and z represent the four degrees of the grand medicine.

SECTION 6.

TREATIES.

FIG. 174 is copy of a birchbark record which was made to commemorate a treaty of peace between the Ojibwa and Assinaboin Indians. The drawing on bark was made by an Ojibwa chief at White Earth, Minnesota.

The figure on the left, holding a flag, represents the Ojibwa chief, while that on the right denotes the chief acting on the part of the Assinaboins. The latter holds in his left hand the pipe which was used in the prelimi naries, and smoke is seen issuing from the mouth of the Assinaboin. He also holds in his right hand the drum used used as an ac companiment to the songs.

The Ojibwa holds a flag used as an emblem of peace.

FIG. 174.—Record of treaty.

A considerable number of pictographic records of treaties are pre sented in different parts of the present work (see under the headings of Wampum, Chap. ix, Sec. 3; Notices, Chap. xi; History, Chap. xvi; Winter Counts, Chap. x, Sec. 2.

SECTION 7.

APPOINTMENT.

Le Page Du Pratz (b) says in describing the council of conspiracy which resulted in the Natchez war of 1729:

An aged councillor advised that after all the nations had been informed of the necessity of taking this violent action, each one should receive a bundle of sticks, all containing an equal number, and which were to mark the number of days to pass before that on which they were all to strike at once; that in order to guard against any mistake it would be necessary to take care to extract one stick every day and to break it and throw it away; a man of wisdom should be charged with this duty. All the old men approved of his advice and it was adopted.

Père Nicholas Perrot (a) says:

Celui qui, chez les Hurons, prenait la parole en cette circonstance, recevait un petit faisceau de pailles d'pied de long qui luy servoient comme de jetons, pour sup puter les nombres et pour ayder la mémoire des assistans, les distribuant en divers lots, suyvant la diversité des choses. Dans l'Amérique du Sud, les Galibis de la rivière d'Amacourou et de l'Orénoque usaient du même procédé mnémotechnique, mais perfectionné. Le capitaine [Galibis] et moy, écrit le P. la Pierre (Voyage en terre ferme et à la coste de Paria, p. 15 du Ms. orig.), eusmes un grand discours . . . luy ayant demandé ce qu'il alloit faire à Barime, il me respondit qu'il alloit avertir tous les capitaines des aultres rivières, du jour qu'il en faudroit sortir pour aller donner l'attaque à leurs ennemis. Et, pour me faire comprendre la façon dont il s'y prenoit il me montra vingt petites buches liées ensemble qui se plient à la façon d'un rouleau. Les six premières estoient d'une couleur particulière; elles signifioent que, les six premiers jours, il falloit préparer du magnot [manioc] pour faire vivres. Les quatre suivantes estoient d'une aultre couleur pour marque qu'il falloit avertir les hommes. Les six d'aultre couleur et ainsi du reste, marquant par leur petites buches, faites en façon de paille, l'ordre que chaque capitaine doit faire observer à ses gens pour estre prest tous en mesme temps. La sortie devroit se faire dans vingt jours; car il n'y avoit que cest [vingt] petites buches.

Im Thurn (e) tells of the Indians of Guiana as follows:

When a paiwari feast is to be held, invitations are sent to the people of all neigh boring settlements inhabited by Indians of the same tribe as the givers of the feast.

The latter prepare a number of strings, each of which is knotted as many times as there are days before the feast day. One of these strings is kept by the headman of the settlement where the feast is to be held; the others are distributed, one to the headman of each of the settlements from which guests are expected. Every day one of the knots, on each of the strings, is untied, and when the last has been untied guests and hosts know that the feast day has come.

Sometimes, instead of knots on a string, notches on a piece of wood are used. This system of knot-tying, the quippoo system of the Peruvians, which occurs in nearly identical form in all parts of the world, is not only used as in the above instance for calendar-keeping, but also to record items of any sort; for instance, if one Indian owes another a certain number of balls of cotton or other articles, debtor and creditor each has a corresponding string or stick, with knots or notches to the number of the owed article, and one or more of these is obliterated each time a payment is made until the debt is wiped out.

Darius (Herodot. IV, 98) did something of the kind when he took a thong and, tying sixty knots in it, gave it to the Ionian chiefs, that they might untie a knot every day and go back to their own land if he had not returned when all the knots were undone.

Champlain (*a*) describes a mode of preparation for battle among the Canadian Algonquins which partook of the nature of a military drill as well as of an appointment of rank and order. It is in its essentials mnemonic. He describes it as follows:

Les chefs prennent des bâtons de la longueur d'un pied autant en nombre qu'ils sont et signalent par d'autres un peu plus grands, leurs chefs; puis vont dans le bois et esplanadent une place de cinq ou six pieds en quarré où le chef comme Sergent Major, met par ordre tous ces bâtons comme bon luy semble; puis appelle tous ses compagnons, qui viennent tous armez, et leur monstre le rang et ordre qu'ils deuvont tenir lors qu'ils se battront avec leurs ennemis.

The author adds detail with regard to alignment, breaking ranks, and resumption of array.

SECTION 8.

NUMERATION.

D. W. Eakins, in Schoolcraft I, p. 273, describes the mnemonic numeration marks of the Muskoki thus:

Each perpendicular stroke stood for one, and each additional stroke marked an additional number. The ages of deceased persons or number of scalps taken by them, or war-parties which they have headed, are recorded on their grave-posts by this system of strokes. The sign of the cross represents ten. The dot and comma never stood as a sign for a day, or a moon, or a month, or a year. The chronological marks that were and are in present use are a small number of sticks made generally of cane. Another plan sometimes in use was to make small holes in a board, in which a peg was inserted to keep the days of the week.

Capt. Bourke (*b*) gives the following account of an attempt at compromise between the aboriginal method of numbering days, weeks, and months, and that of the civilized intruders to whose system the Indians found it necessary to conform.

The Apache scouts kept records of the time of their absence on campaign. There were several methods in vogue, the best being that of colored beads which were strung on a string, six white ones to represent the days of the week, and one black, or other color, to stand for Sundays. This method gave rise to some confusion, because the Indians had been told that there were four weeks, or Sundays ("Domingos"), in each "Luna," or moon, and yet they soon found that their own method of determining time by the appearance of the crescent moon was much the more satisfactory. Among the Zuñi I have seen little tally sticks with the marks for the days and months incised on the narrow edges, and among the Apache another method of indicating the flight of time by marking on a piece of paper along a horizontal line a number of circles or of straight lines across the horizontal datum line to represent the full days which had passed, a heavy straight line for each Sunday, and a small crescent for the beginning of each month.

It is not necessary to discuss the obvious method of repeating strokes, dots, knots, human heads or forms, weapons, and totemic designs, to designate the number of persons or articles referred to in the pictographs where they appear.

SECTION 9.

ACCOUNTING.

The Abnaki, in especial the Passamaquoddy division of the tribe in Maine, during late years have been engaged in civilized industries in which they have found it necessary to keep accounts. These are interesting as exhibiting the aboriginal use of ideographic devices which are only partially supplemented by the imitation of the symbols peculiar to European civilization. Several of these devices were procured by the present writer in 1888, and are illustrated and explained as follows:

FIG. 175.—Shop account.

A deer hunter brings 3 deerskins, for which he is allowed $2 each, making $6; 30 pounds of venison, at 10 cents per pound, making $3. In payment thereof he purchases 3 pounds of powder, at 40 cents per pound; 5 pounds of pork, at 10 cents per pound; and 2 gallons of molasses, at 50 cents per gallon. The debit foots $3.30, according to the

Indian account, but it seems on calculation to be 30 cents in excess, an overcharge, showing the advance in civilization of the Passamaquoddy trader.

The following explanation will serve to make intelligible the characters employed, which are reproduced in Fig. 175. The hunter is shown as the first character in line *a*, and that he is a deer-hunter is furthermore indicated by his having a skin-stretcher upon his back, as well as the figure of a deer at which he is shooting. The three skins referred to are shown stretched upon frames in line *b*, the total number being also indicated by the three vertical strokes, between which and the drying frames are two circles, each with a line across it, to denote dollars, the total sum of $6 being the last group of dollar marks on line *b*.

The 30 pounds of venison are represented in line *c*, the three crosses signifying 30, the T-shaped character designating a balance scale, synonymous with pound, while the venison is indicated by the drawing of the hind quarter or ham. The price is given by uniting the X, or numeral, and the T, or pound mark, making a total of $3 as completing the line *c*.

FIG. 176.—Shop account.

The line *d* refers to the purchase of 3 pounds of powder, as expressed by the three strokes, the T, or scale for pound, and the powder horn, the price of which is four Xs or 40 cents per pound, or T; and 3 pounds of powder, the next three vertical strokes succeeded by a number of spots to indicate grains of powder, which is noted as being 10 cents per pound, indicated by the cross and T, respectively. The next item, shown on line *e*, charges for 5 pounds of pork, the latter being indicated by the outline of a pig, the price being indicated by the X cr 10, and T, scale or pound; then two short lines preceding one small oblong square or quart measure, indicates that 2 quarts of molasses, shown by the black spot, cost 5 crosses, or 50 cents per measure, the sum of the whole of the purchase being indicated by three rings with stems and three crosses, equivalent to $3.30.

Another Indian, whose occupation was to furnish basket wood, brought some to the trader for which he received credit to the amount of $1.15, taking in exchange therefor pork sufficient to equal the above amount.

In Fig. 176 the Indian is shown with a bundle of basket wood, the value of which is given in the next characters, consisting of a ring with a line across to denote $1, a cross to represent 10 cents, and the five short vertical lines for an additional 5 cents, making a total of $1.15. The pork received from the trader is indicated by the outline of a pig, while the crossed lines to the right denotes that the "account" is canceled.

Another customer, as shown in Fig. 177, was an old woman, the descendent of an ancient name—one known before the coming of white people. She was therefore called the "Owl," and is represented in the "account" given below. She had bought on credit 1 plug of smoking tobacco, designated by one vertical stroke for the quantity and an oblong square figure corresponding to the shape of the package, which was to be used for smoking, as indicated by the spiral lines to denote smoke. She had also purchased 2 quarts of kerosene oil, the quantity designated by the two strokes preceding the small squares to represent quart measures, and the liquid is indicated by the rude outline of a kerosene lamp. This is followed by two crosses, representing 20 cents, as the value of the amount of her purchases. This account was settled by giving one basket, as shown in the device nearly beneath the owl, half of which is marked with crossed lines, connected by a line of dots or dashes with the cancellation mark at the extreme right of the record.

FIG. 177.—Shop account.

Another Passamaquoddy Indian, unable to read or write, carries on business and keeps his books according to a method of his own invention. One account is reproduced in Fig. 178. It is with a very slim Indian, as will be observed from the drawing, who carries on "trucking" and owns a horse, that animal being represented in outline and connected by lines with its owner. For services he was paid $5.45, which sum is shown in the lower line of characters by five dollar-marks—i. e., rings with strokes across them—4 crosses or numerals signifying 10 cents each, and five short vertical lines for 5 cents. The date is shown in the upper line of characters, the 4 short lines in front of the horse signifying 4, the oval figure next, to the right and intended for a circle, denoting the moon—i. e., the fourth moon, or April—while the 10 short strokes signify the tenth day of the month—i. e., he was paid $5.45 in full for services to April 10.

Another account was with a young woman noted as very slim, and is shown in Fig. 179. The girl brought a basket to the store, for which she was allowed 20 cents. She received credit for 10 cents on account of a plug of tobacco bought some time previously.

In the illustration the decidedly slim form of the girl is portrayed, her hands holding out the basket which she had made. The unattached cross signifies 10 cents, which she probably received in cash, while the other cross is connected by a dotted line with the piece of plug tobacco

FIG. 178.—Book account.

for which she had owed 10 cents. The attachment of the plug to the unpaid dime is amusingly ideographic.

Another Indian, descended from the prehistoric Indians, was called "Lox," the evil or tricksy deity, appearing as an animal having a long body and tail and short legs, which is probably a wolverine, under which form Lox is generally depicted by the Passamaquoddy. His account with the trader is given in Fig. 180, and shows that he brought 1 dozen ax handles, for which he received $1.50.

Beneath the figure of Lox are 2 axes, the 12 short lines denoting the number of handles delivered, while

FIG. 179.—Book account. the dotted line to the right connects them with the amount received, which is designated by 1 one dollar mark and 5 crosses or dime marks.

Dr. Hoffman found in Los Angeles, California, a number of notched sticks, which had been invented and used by the Indians at the Mission of San Gabriel. They had chief herders, who had under their charge overseers of the several classes of laborers, herders, etc. The chief herder was supplied with a stick of hard wood, measuring about 1 inch in breadth and thickness and from 20 to 24 inches long.

FIG. 180.—Book account.

The corners were beveled at the handle. The general form of the stick is given in the upper character of Fig. 181, with the exception that the illustration is intentionally shortened so as to show both ends.

Upon each of the beveled surfaces on the handle are marks to indicate the kind of horned cattle referred to. The cross indicates that the corner of the stick upon which it is incised relates to heifers, each notch designating one head, the long transverse cut denoting ten, with an additional three cuts signifying that the herder has in charge thirteen heifers. Upon the next beveled edge appears an arrow-pointed mark, to denote in like manner which edge of the stick is to be notched for indicating the oxen. Upon the third beveled surface is one transverse cut for the record of the number of bulls in the herd, while upon the fourth bevel of the handle are two notches to note the number of cows.

The stick is notched at the end opposite the handle to signify that it refers only to horned cattle. That used to designate horses is sharpened from two sides only, so that the end is wedge-shaped, or exactly

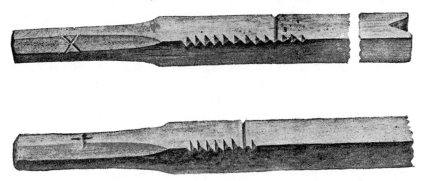

FIG. 181.—Notched sticks.

the reverse of the one first mentioned. The marks upon the handle would be the same, however, with this exception—that one cut would mean a stallion, two cuts a mare, the cross a gelding, and the arrow-shaped figure a colt. Sticks were also marked to denote the several kinds of stock and to record those which had been branded.

Another class of sticks were also used by the overseers, copies of which were likewise preserved by the laborers and herders, to keep an account of the number of days on which labor was performed, and to record the sums of money received by the workman.

The lower character of Fig. 181 represents a stick, upon the beveled edge of the handle of which is a cross to denote work. The short notches upon the corner of the stick denote days, each seventh day or week being designated by a cut extending across the stick.

Upon the opposite side of the handle is a circle or a circle with a cross within it to denote the number of reals paid, each real being indicated upon the edge of the stick by a notch, while each ten reals or peso is noted by making the cut all the way across that face of the stick.

Mr. Dall (*a*) says that the Innuit frequently keep accounts by tying knots in a string or notching a stick.   Capt. Bourke (*c*) reports:

In the Mexican state of Sonora I was shown, some twenty years ago, a piece of buckskin, upon which certain Opata or Yaqui Indians—I forget exactly which tribe, but it matters very little, as they are both industrious and honest—had kept account of the days of their labor.   There was a horizontal datum line as before, with complete circles to indicate full days and half circles to indicate half days, a long heavy black line for Sundays and holidays, and a crescent moon for each new month. These accounts had to be drawn up by the overseer or superintendent of the rancho at which the Indians were employed before the latter left for home each night.

Terrien de Lacouperie (*e*) says of the Southals of Bengal:

Their accounts are either notches on a stick, like those formerly used by the rustics for keeping scores at cricket matches in country villages in England, or knots on a piece of grass string, or a number of bits of straw tied together.   I well remember my astonishment while trying my first case between a grasping Mahajun and a Sonthal when I ordered them to produce their accounts.   * * *   The Sonthal produced from his back hair, where it had been kept, I suppose, for ornament, a dirty bit of knotted grass string and threw it on the table, requesting the court to count that, as it had got too long for him.   Each knot represented a rupee, a longer space between two knots represented the lapse of a year.

Many modes of accounting in a pictorial manner are noted in Europe and America among people classed as civilized.   Some of these are very curious, but want of space prevents their recital here.   A valuable description of the survival of the system in Brittany is given by M. Armand Landrin (*a*), translated and condensed as follows:

In the department of Finisterre the farmers, in keeping accounts, made bags of their old socks and coat sleeves, of different colors, each color representing one of the divisions of farm outlay or receipt, as cows, butter, milk, and corn.   Each amount received was placed in coin in the appropriate bag.   When any coins were taken out the same number of small stones or of peas or beans was put in to replace the coins.   Other farmers substituted for the bags small sticks of different length and thickness in which they made cuts representing the receipts.

In the accounts with the laborers and farm hands the women were designated by the triangle, intended to represent the Breton head dress *á grandes barbes*.   The kind of work performed was expressed by the tool connected with it, *e. g.*, a horseshoe denoted the blacksmith, a scythe the mower, an ax the carpenter, a saddle the harness-maker, and a tub the cooper.   The bill of a veterinary surgeon was rendered by drawing the figures of the several animals treated united in one group by a line.

Until quite recently the important accounts of the British exchequer were kept by wooden tallies, and some bakers in the United States yet persevere in keeping their accounts with their customers by duplicate tallies, one of which is rendered as a bill and is verified by the other.

CHAPTER X.

CHRONOLOGY.

It is not within the scope of the present work to examine the several systems of chronology of the American Indians, but only those pictorially exhibited. The Mexican system, much more scientific and more elaborate than that employed by the northern tribes, resembled it in the graphic record or detail of exhibit, and is highly interesting as compared with the Dakota Winter Counts. Although the principle of designating the years was wholly different, the mode of that designation was often similar, as is shown by collating the Codex Vaticanus and the Codex Telleriano Remensis with the Winter Counts of Lone Dog and Battiste Good, infra. It is also desirable to note the remarks of Prof. Brinton (e) with regard to the Chilan Balam. At the close of each of the Maya larger divisions of time (the so-called "Katum"), a "chilan" or inspired diviner uttered a prediction of the character of the year or epoch which was about to begin. This prophetic designation of the year was like a Zadkiel's almanac, while the Dakotan method was a selection of the most important events of the past.

SECTION 1.

TIME.

Dr. William H. Corbusier, surgeon, U. S. Army, gives the following information:

The Dakotas make use of the circle as the symbol of a cycle of time; a small one for a year and a large one for a longer period of time, as a life time. one old man.

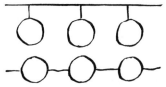

Fig. 182.—Device denoting succession of time. Dakota.

Also a round of lodges or a cycle of seventy years, as in Battiste Good's Winter Count. The continuance of time is sometimes indicated by a line extending in a direction from right to left across the page when on paper, and the annual circles are suspended from the line at regular intervals by short lines, as in Fig. 182, upper character, and the ideograph for the year is placed beneath each one. At other times the line is not continuous, but is interrupted at regular intervals by the yearly circle, as in the lower character of Fig. 182.

Under other headings in this paper are presented graphic expressions for divisions of time—month, day, night, morning, noon, and evening. See, for some of them, Chap. xx, Sec. 2.

WINTER COUNTS.

In the preliminary paper on "Pictographs of the North American Indians," published in the Fourth Annual Report of the Bureau of Ethnology, 58 pages of text and 46 full-page plates were devoted to the winter counts of the Dakota Indians. The minute detail of explanation, the systematic comparison, and the synoptic presentation which seemed to be necessary need not now be repeated to establish the genuine character of the invention. This consisted in the use of events, which were in some degree historical, to form a system of chronology. The record of the events was only the device by which was accomplished the continuous designation of years, in the form of charts corresponding in part with the orderly arrangement of divisions of time termed calendars. It was first made public by the present writer in a paper entitled "A Calendar of the Dakota Nation," which was issued in April, 1877, in Bulletin III, No. I, of the United States Geological and Geographical Survey. The title is now changed to that adopted by the Dakotas themselves, viz, Winter Counts—in the original, wan'iyetu wo'wapi.

The lithographed chart published with that paper, substantially the same as Pl. xx, Lone-Dog's Winter Count, now much better presented than ever before, is the winter count used by, or at least known to, a large portion of the Dakota people, extending over the seventy-one years commencing with the winter of A. D. 1800–'01.

The copy from which the lithograph was taken is traced on a strip of cotton cloth, in size 1 yard square, which the characters almost entirely fill, and is painted in two colors, black and red, used in the original, of which it is a facsimile. The plate is a representation of the chart as it would appear on the buffalo robe. It was photographed from the copy on linen cloth, and not directly from the buffalo robe. It was painted on the robe by Lone-Dog, an Indian belonging to the Yanktonais tribe of the Dakotas, who in the autumn of 1876 was near Fort Peck, Montana. His Dakota name is given in the ordinary English literation as Shunka-ishnala, which words correspond nearly with the vocables in Riggs's lexicon for dog-lone. Lone-Dog claimed that, with the counsel of the old men of his tribe, he decided upon some event or circumstance which should distinguish each year as it passed, and marked what was considered to be its appropriate symbol or device upon a buffalo robe kept for the purpose. The robe was at convenient times exhibited to other Indians of the tribe, who were thus taught the meaning and use of the signs as designating the several years.

It is not, however, supposed that Lone-Dog was of sufficient age in the year 1800 to enter upon the work. Either there was a predecessor from whom he received the earlier records or, when he had reached man-

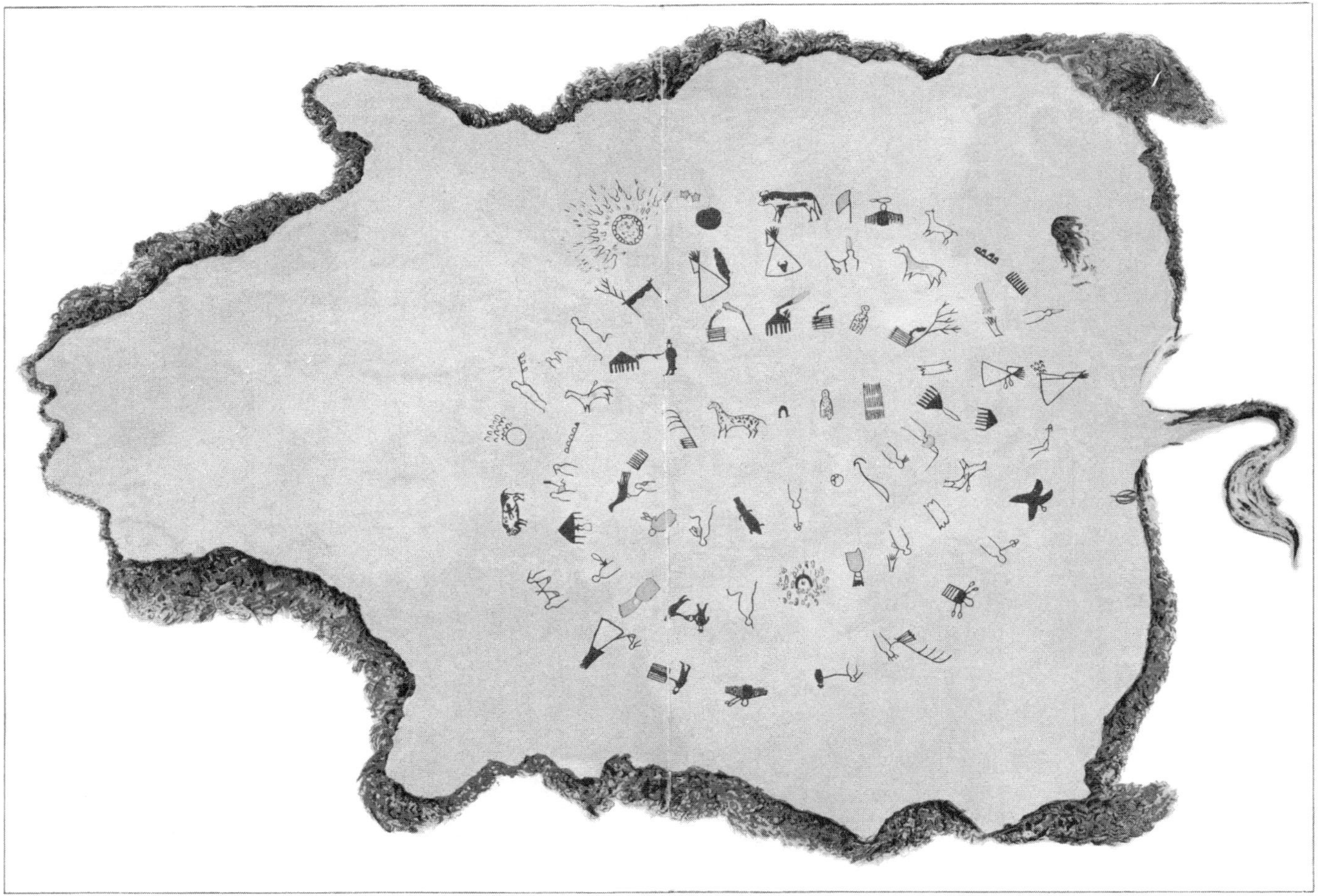

Plate XX

LONE DOG'S WINTER COUNT.

hood, he gathered the traditions from his elders and worked back, the object either then or before being to establish some system of chronology for the use of the tribe or more probably in the first instance for the use of his own band.

Present knowledge of the winter-count systems shows that Lone-Dog was not their originator. They were started, at the latest, before the present generation, and have been kept up by a number of independent recorders. The idea was one specially appropriate to the Indian genius, yet the peculiar mode of record was an invention, and it is not probably a very old invention, as it has not been used beyond a definite district and people. If an invention of that character had been of great antiquity it would probably have spread by intertribal channels beyond the bands or tribes of the Dakota, where alone the copies of such charts have been found and are understood.

The fact that Lone-Dog's Winter Count, the only one known at the time of its first publication, begins at a date nearly coinciding with the first year of the present century, as it is called in the arbitrary computation that prevails among most of the civilized peoples, awakened a suspicion that it might be due to civilized intercourse and was not a mere coincidence. If the influence of missionaries or traders started any plan of chronology, it is remarkable that they did not suggest one in some manner resembling the system so long and widely used, and the only one they knew, of counting the numbers from an era, such as the birth of Christ, the Hegira, the Ab Urbe Conditâ, or the first Olympiad. But the chart shows nothing of this nature. The earliest character merely represents the killing of a small number of Dakotas by their enemies, an event neither so important nor interesting as many others of the seventy-one shown in the chart, more than one of which, indeed, might well have been selected as a notable fixed point before and after which simple arithmetical notation could have been used to mark the years. Instead of any plan that civilized advisers would naturally have introduced, the one actually adopted was to individualize each year by a specific recorded symbol. The ideographic record, being preserved and understood by many, could be used and referred to with ease and accuracy. Definite signs for the first appearance of the smallpox and for the first capture of wild horses were dates as satisfactory to the Dakota as the corresponding expressions A. D. 1802 and 1813 are to the Christian world, and far more certain than the chronology expressed in terms of A. M. and B. C. The arrangement of separate characters in an outward spiral starting from a central point is a clever expedient to dispense with the use of numbers for noting the years, yet allowing every date to be determined by counting backward or forward from any other known. The whole conception seems one strongly characteristic of the Indians, who in other instances have shown such expertness in ideography. The discovery of several other charts, which differ in their times of commencement and ending from that of Lone-Dog and from each other, removed any inference arising from the above-mentioned coincidence in beginning with the present century. The following copies of charts, substantially the same as that of Lone-Dog, are now or have been in the possession of the present writer:

1. A chart made and kept by Bo-i'-de, The-Flame, a Dakota, who, in 1877, lived near Fort Sully, Dakota.

The facsimile copy is on a cotton cloth about a yard square and in black and red, thus far similar to the copy of Lone-Dog's chart, but the arrangement is different. The character for the first year mentioned appears in the lower left-hand corner, and the record proceeds toward the right to the extremity of the cloth, then crossing toward the left and again toward the right at the edge of the cloth, and so throughout, in the style called boustrophedon. It thus answers the same purpose of orderly arrangement, allowing constant additions, like the more circular spiral of Lone-Dog. This record is for the years 1786–'87 to 1876–'77, thus commencing earlier and ending later than that of Lone-Dog.

2. A Minneconjou chief, The-Swan, kept another record on the dressed skin of an antelope or deer, claiming that it had been preserved in his family for seventy years.

The characters are arranged in a spiral similar to those in Lone-Dog's chart, but more oblong in form. The course of the spiral is from left to right, not from right to left.

3. Another chart was kindly loaned to the writer by Bvt. Maj. Joseph Bush, captain Twenty-second U. S. Infantry. It was procured by him in 1870 at the Cheyenne Agency. This copy is one yard by three-fourths of a yard, spiral, beginning in the center, from right to left. The figures are substantially the same as those in Lone-Dog's chart, with which it coincides in time, except that it ends at 1869–'70, but the interpretation differs from that accompanying the latter in a few particulars.

4. The chart of Mato Sapa, Black-Bear. He was a Minneconjou warrior, residing in 1868 and 1869 on the Cheyenne Agency reservation, on the Missouri river, near the mouth of the Cheyenne river.

This copy is on a smaller scale than that of Lone-Dog, being a flat and elongated spiral, 2 feet 6 inches by 1 foot 6 inches. The spiral reads from right to left. This chart, which begins like that of Lone-Dog, ends with the years 1868–'69.

5. A most important and interesting Winter Count is that made by Battiste Good, a Brulé Dakota, which was kindly contributed by Dr. Wi,liam H. Corbusier, surgeon U. S. Army. It begins with peculiar cyclic devices from the year A. D. 900, and in thirteen figures embraces the time to A. D. 1700, all these devices being connected with myths, and some of them showing European influence. From 1700–'01 to 1879–'80 a separate character is given for each year, with its interpre-

tation, in much the same style as shown in the other charts mentioned. Several Indians and half-breeds said that this count formerly embraced about the same number of years as the others, but that Battiste Good gathered the names of many years from the old people and placed them in chronological order as far back as he was able to learn them.

Another Winter Count, communicated by Dr. Corbusier, is that in the possession of American-Horse, an Oglala Dakota, at the Pine Ridge agency in 1879, who asserted that his grandfather began it, and that it is the production of his grandfather, his father, and himself.

A third Winter Count is communicated by Dr. Corbusier as kept by Cloud-Shield. He was also an Oglala Dakota, at the Pine Ridge agency, but of a different band from American-Horse. The last two counts embrace nearly the same number of years, viz, from A. D. 1775 to 1878. Two dates belong to each figure, as a Dakota year covers a portion of two of the calendar years common to civilization.

Dr. Corbusier also saw copies of a fourth Winter Count, which was kept by White-Cow-Killer, at the Pine Ridge agency. He did not obtain a copy of it, but learned most of the names given to the winters.

With reference to all the Winter Counts and to the above remarks that a Dakota year covers a portion of two calendar years, the following explanation may be necessary: The Dakota count their years by winters (which is quite natural, that season in their high levels and latitudes practically lasting more than six months), and say a man is so many snows old, or that so many snow seasons have passed since an occurrence. They have no division of time into weeks, and their months are absolutely lunar, only twelve, however, being designated, which receive their names upon the recurrence of some prominent physical phenomenon. For example, the period partly embraced by February is called the "raccoon moon;" March, the "sore-eye moon;" and April, that "in which the geese lay eggs." As the appearance of raccoons after hibernation, the causes inducing inflamed eyes, and oviposition by geese vary with the meteorological character of each year, and as the twelve lunations reckoned do not bring back the point in the season when counting commenced, there is often dispute in the Dakota tipis toward the end of winter as to the correct current date. In careful examination of the several counts it often is left in doubt whether the event occurred in the winter months or was selected in the months immediately before or in those immediately after the winter. No regularity or accuracy is noticed in these particulars.

In considering the extent to which Lone-Dog's chart is understood and used, it may be mentioned that every intelligent Dakota of full years to whom the writer has shown it has known what it meant, and many of them knew a large part of the years portrayed. When there was less knowledge, there was the amount that may be likened to that of an uneducated person or a child who is examined about a map of the United States, which had been shown to him before, with some explanation only partially apprehended or remembered. He would tell that it was a map of the United States; would probably be able to point out with some accuracy the state or city where he lived; perhaps the capital of the country; probably the names of the states of peculiar position or shape, such as Maine, Delaware, or Florida. So the Indian examined would often point out in Lone-Dog's chart the year in which he was born, or that in which his father died, or in which there was some occurrence that had strongly impressed him, but which had no relation whatever to the significance of the character for the year in question. It had been pointed out to him before, and he had remembered it, while forgetting the remainder of the chart.

On comparing all the Winter Counts it is found that they often correspond, but sometimes differ. In a few instances the differences are in the succession of events, but they are usually due to an omission or to the selection of another event. When a year has the same name in all of them, the bands were probably encamped together, or else the event fixed upon was of general interest; and when the name is different the bands were scattered, or nothing of general interest occurred. Many of the recent events are fresh in the memory of the people, as the warriors who strive to make their exploits a part of the tribal traditions proclaim them on all occasions of ceremony, count their coups, as the performance is called. Declarations of this kind partake of the nature of affirmations made in the invoked presence of a supposed divinity. War shirts, on which scores of the enemies killed are kept, and which are carefully transmitted from generation to generation, help to refresh their memories in regard to some of the events.

The study of all the charts renders plain some points remaining in doubt while the Lone-Dog chart was the only example known. It became clear that there was no fixed or uniform mode of exhibiting the order of continuity of the year-characters. They were arranged spirally or lineally, or in serpentine curves, by boustrophedon or direct, starting backward from the last year shown or proceeding uniformly forward from the first year selected or remembered. Any mode that would accomplish the object of continuity with the means of regular addition seemed equally acceptable. So a theory advanced that there was some symbolism in the right-to-left circling of Lone-Dog's chart was abandoned, especially when an obvious reproduction of that very chart was made by an Indian with the spiral reversed. It was also obvious that when copies were made, some of them probably from memory, there was no attempt at Chinese accuracy. It was enough to give the graphic or ideographic character, and frequently the character is better defined on one of the charts than on the others for the corresponding year. One interpretation would often throw light on the others. It also appeared that, while different events were selected by the recorders of the different systems, there was sometimes a selection of the same event for the same year and sometimes for the next, such as would be natural in the progress of a famine or epidemic, or as an event gradually became known over a vast territory.

A test of the mode of selecting events for designating the Winter Counts may be found in a suggestion made by the present writer in his account of Lone-Dog's chart, published in 1877, as follows:

The year 1876 has furnished good store of events for the recorder's choice, and it will be interesting to learn whether he has selected as the distinguishing event the victory over Custer, or, as of still greater interest, the general seizure of ponies, whereat the tribes, imitating Rachel, weep and will not be comforted, because they are not.

It now appears that two of the Counts made for 1876 and observed by the writer several years later have selected the event of the seizure of the ponies, and that none of them make any allusion to the defeat of Custer.

After examination of all the charts it is obvious that the design is not narrative, that the noting of events is being subordinated to the marking of the years by them, and that the pictographic serial arrangements of sometimes trivial though generally notorious incidents having been selected with special adaptation for use as a calendar. That in a few instances small personal events, such as the birth of the recorder or the death of members of his family, are set forth, may be regarded as interpolations in or unauthorized additions to the charts. If they had exhibited a complete national or tribal history for the years embraced in them, their discovery would have been in some respects more valuable, but they are interesting to anthropologists because they show an attempt before unsuspected among the northern tribes of American Indians to form a system of chronology.

While, as before mentioned, it is not now necessary to recapitulate the large amount of matter before published concerning the Winter Counts of the Dakota, it has been decided to present in an abbreviated form the characters and interpretations of the Lone-Dog chart as being the system which was first discovered, and the publication of which occasioned the discovery of all the other charts mentioned. The Winter Count of Battiste Good has not hitherto been published, and it possesses special importance and interest apart from its chronology, for which reason it is inserted in the present paper, see infra.

The several charts of The-Flame, The-Swan, American-Horse, and Cloud-Shield, published in the Fourth Annual Report of the Bureau of Ethnology, are omitted, but selections from all of them are presented under the headings of Ideography, Tribal and Personal Designations, Religion, Customs, History, Biography, Conventionalizing, Comparison, and in short are interspersed through the present paper where they appropriately belong.

The reader of the Lone-Dog and Battiste Good charts may find it convenient to note the following brief account of the tribal names frequently mentioned:

The great linguistic stock or family which embraces not only the Sioux or Dakota proper, but the Missouri, Omaha, Ponka, Osage, Kansa, Oto, Assinaboin, Gros Ventre or Minnitari, Crow, Iowa, Mandan, and some others, has been frequently styled the Dakota family. Maj. J. W. Powell, the Director of the Bureau of Ethnology, from consideration of priority, has lately adopted the name Siouan for the family, and for the grand division of it popularly called Sioux has used the term Dakota, which the people claim for themselves.

The word "Dakota" is translated in Riggs's dictionary of that language as "leagued" or "allied." The title Sioux, which is indignantly repudiated by the people, is either the last syllable or the last two syllables, according to pronunciation, of "Nadowesioux," which is the French plural of the Algonkin name for the Dakotas "Nadowessi," "hated foe." The Ojibwa called the Dakota "Nadowessi," which is their word meaning rattlesnake, or, as others translate, adder, with a contemptuous or diminutive termination; the plural is Nadowessiwak or Nadawessyak. The French gave the name their own form of the plural and the voyagers and trappers cut it down to "Sioux."

The more important of the tribes and organized bands into which the Dakotas are now divided, being the dislocated remains of the "Seven Great Council Fires," are as follows:

Yankton and Yanktonai or Ihankto^{n}wa^n, both derived from a root meaning "at the end," alluding to the former locality of their villages.

Sihasapa, or Blackfeet.

Oheno^{n}pa, or Two-Kettles.

Itaziptco, Without Bow. The French equivalent Sans Arc is more commonly used.

Minneconjou, translated "Those who plant by the water," the physical features of their old home.

Sitca^{n}gu, Burnt Hip or Brulé.

Santee, subdivided into Wahpeton, Men among Leaves, i. e., among forests, and Sisseton, Men of Prairie Marsh. Two other bands, now practically extinct, formerly belonged to the Santee, or as it is more correctly spelled, Isanti tribes, from the root "Issan," knife. Their former territory furnished the material for stone knives, from the manufacture of which they were called the "knife people."

Uncpapa, once the most warlike and probably the most powerful of all the bands, though not the largest.

Oglala. The meaning and derivation of this name and of Uncpapa have been the subjects of controversy.

Hale, Gallatin, and Riggs designate a "Titon tribe" as located west of the Missouri, and as much the largest division of the Dakotas, the latter authority subdividing into the Sicha^{n}gu, Itazipcho, Sihasapa, Minneconjou, Ohenonpa, Oglala, and Huncpapa, seven of the tribes specified above, which he calls bands. "Titon," (from the word ti^{n}tan, meaning "at or on land without trees or prairie,") was the name of a tribal division, but it has become only an expression for all those tribes whose ranges are on the prairie, and thus it is a territorial and accidental, not a tribular distinction. One of the Dakotas at Fort Rice spoke to the present writer of the "hostiles" as "Titons," with obviously the same idea of locality, "away on the prairie," it being well known that they were a conglomeration from several tribes.

LONE-DOG'S WINTER COUNT.

Fig. 183, 1800–'01.—Thirty Dakotas were killed by Crow Indians. The device consists of thirty parallel black lines in three columns, the outer lines being united. In this chart, such black lines always signify the death of Dakotas killed by their enemies.

The Absaroka or Crow tribe, although belonging to the Siouan family, has nearly always been at war with the Dakotas proper since the whites have had any knowledge of either. They are noted for the extraordinary length of their hair, which frequently distinguishes them in pictographs.

FIG. 183.

Fig. 184, 1811–'02.—Many died of smallpox. The smallpox broke out in the tribe. The device is the head and body of a man covered with red blotches. In this, as in all other cases where colors in this chart are mentioned, they will be found to correspond with Pl. xx, but not in that respect with the text figures, which have no coloration.

FIG. 184.

Fig. 185, 1802–'03.—A Dakota stole horses with shoes on, i. e., stole them either directly from the whites or from some other Indians who had before obtained them from whites, as the Indians never shoe their horses. The device is a horseshoe.

FIG. 185.

Fig. 186, 1803–'04.—They stole some "curly horses" from the Crows. Some of these horses are still on the plains, the hair growing in closely curling tufts. The device is a horse with black marks for the tufts. The Crows are known to have been early in the possession of horses.

FIG. 186.

Fig. 187, 1804–'05.—The Dakota had a calumet dance and then went to war. The device is a long pipestem, ornamented with feathers and streamers. The feathers are white, with black tips, evidently the tail feathers of the adult golden eagle (Aquila chrysaëtos), highly prized by the Plains Indians. The streamers anciently were colored strips of skin or flexible bark; now gayly colored strips of cloth are used. The word calumet is a corruption of the French chalumeau. Capt. Carver (c) in his Three Years' Travels Through the Interior Parts of North America, after puzzling over the etymology of "calumet," describes the pipe as "about 4 feet long, bowl of red marble, stem of

FIG. 187.

a light wood curiously painted with hieroglyphics in various colors and adorned with feathers. Every nation has a different method of decorating these pipes and can tell at once to what band it belongs. It is used as an introduction to all treaties, also as a flag of truce is among Europeans." Among the Indian tribes generally the pipe, when presented or offered to a stranger or enemy, was the symbol of peace, yet when used ceremonially by members of the same tribe among themselves was virtually a token of impending war. For further remarks on this point see the year 1842–'43 of this Winter Count.

Fig. 188, 1805–'06.—The Crows killed eight Dakotas. Again the short parallel black lines, this time eight in number, united by a long stroke. The interpreter, Fielder, says that this character with black strokes is only used for grave marks.

FIG. 188.

Fig. 189, 1806–'07.—A Dakota killed an Arikara (Ree) as he was about to shoot an eagle. The sign gives the head and shoulders of a man with a red spot of blood on his neck, an arm being extended, with a line drawn to a golden eagle.

The drawing represents an Indian in the act of catching an eagle by the legs, as the Arikara were accustomed to catch eagles in their earth traps. These were holes to which the eagles were attracted by baits and in which the Indians were concealed. They rarely or never shot war eagles. The Arikara was shot in his trap just as he put his hand up to grasp the bird.

FIG. 189.

Fig. 190, 1807–'08.—Red-Coat, a chief, was killed. The figure shows the red coat pierced by two arrows, with blood dropping from the wounds.

FIG. 190.

Fig. 191, 1808–'09.—The Dakota who had killed the Ree shown in this record for 1806–'07 was himself killed by the Rees. He is represented running, and shot with two arrows, blood dripping. These two figures, taking in connection, afford a good illustration of the method pursued in the chart, which was not intended to be a continuous history, or even to record the most important event of each year, but to exhibit some one of special peculiarity. There was some incident about the one Ree who was shot when, in fancied security, he was bringing down an eagle, and whose death was avenged by his brethren the second year afterward. It would, indeed, have been impossible to have graphically distingushed the many battles, treaties, horse-stealings, big hunts, etc., so most of them were omitted and other events of greater individuality and better adapted for portrayal were taken for the year count, the criterion being not that they were of historic moment, but

FIG. 191.

that they were of general notoriety, or perhaps of special interest to the recorders.

Fig. 192, 1809–'10.—A chief, Little-Beaver, set fire to a trading store, and was killed. The character simply designates his name-totem. The other interpretations say that he was a white trapper, but probably he had gained a new name among the Indians.

FIG. 192.

Fig. 193, 1810–'11.—Black-Stone made medicine. The expression medicine is too common to be successfully eliminated, though it is altogether misleading. The "medicine men" have no connection with therapeutics, feel no pulses, and administer no drugs, or, if sometimes they direct the internal or external use of some secret preparation, it is as a part of superstitious ceremonies, and with main reliance upon those ceremonies. Their incantations are not only to drive away disease, but for many other purposes, such as to obtain success in war, avert calamity, and were very frequently used to bring within reach the buffalo, on which the Dakotas depended for food. The rites are those known as shamanism, noticeable in the ethnic periods of savagery and FIG. 193. barbarism. In the ceremonial of "making medicine," a buffalo head, and especially the head of an albino buffalo, held a prominent place among the plains tribes. Many references to this are to be found in the Prince of Wied's Travels in the Interior of North America. Also see infra, Chap. XIV. The device in the chart is the man figure, with the head of an albino buffalo held over his own.

Fig. 194, 1811–'12.—The Dakota fought a battle with the Gros Ventres and killed a great many. Device, a circle inclosing three round objects with flat bases, resembling heads severed from trunks, which are too minute in this device for decision of FIG 194. objects represented; but they appear more distinct in the record for 1864–'65 as the heads of enemies slain in battle. In the sign language of the plains, the Dakota are denoted by drawing a hand across the throat, signifying that they cut the throats of their enemies. The Dakota count by the fingers, as is common to most peoples, but with a peculiarity of their own. When they have gone over the fingers and thumbs of both hands, one finger is temporarily turned down for *one ten.* At the end of the next ten another finger is turned, and so on to a hundred. *Opawinge* (*Opawi^{n}xe*), one hundred, is derived from pawinga (pawi^{n}xa), to go round in circles, to make gyrations, and contains the idea that the round of all the fingers has again been made for their respective tens. So the circle is never used for less than one hundred, but sometimes signifies an indefinite number greater than a hundred. The circle, in this instance, therefore, was at first believed to express the killing in battle of many enemies. But the other interpretations removed all symbolic character, leaving the circle simply as the rude drawing of a dirt lodge to which the Gros Ventres were driven. The present writer, by no means devoted to symbolism, had supposed a legitimate symbol to be indicated, which supposition further information on the subject showed to be incorrect.

Fig. 195, 1812–'13.—Wild horses were first run and caught by the Dakotas. The device is a lasso. The date is of value, as showing when the herds of prairie horses, descended from those animals introduced by the Spaniards in Mexico, or those deposited by them on the shores of Texas and at other points, had multiplied so as to extend into the far northern regions. The Dakotas undoubtedly learned the use of the horse and perhaps also that of the lasso from southern tribes, with whom they were in contact; and it is noteworthy that notwithstanding the tenacity with which they generally adhere to ancient customs, in only two generations since they became familiar with the horse they had been so revolutionized in their habits as to be utterly helpless, both in war and the chase, when deprived of that animal.

FIG. 195.

FIG. 196.

FIG. 197.

FIG. 198.

Fig. 196, 1813–'14.—The whooping-cough was very prevalent and fatal. The sign is suggestive of a blast of air coughed out by the man-figure.

The interruption in the cough peculiar to the disease is more clearly delineated in the Winter Count of The-Flame for the same year, Fig. 197, and still better in The-Swan's Winter Count, Fig. 198.

FIG. 199.

Fig. 199, 1814–'15.—A Dakota killed an Arapaho in his lodge. The device represents a tomahawk or battle-ax, the red being blood from the cleft skull.

Fig. 200, 1815–'16.—The Sans Arcs made the first attempt at a dirt lodge. This was at Peoria Bottom, Dakota. Crow Feather was their chief, which fact, in the absence of the other charts, seemed to explain the fairly drawn feather of that bird protruding from the lodge top, but the figure must now be admitted to be a badly drawn bow, in allusion to the tribe Sans Arc, without, however, any sign of negation. As the interpreter explained the figure to be a crow feather and as Crow-

FIG. 200.

Feather actually was the chief, Lone-Dog's chart with its interpretation may be independently correct.

Fig. 201, 1816–'17.—"Buffalo belly was plenty." The device rudely portrays a side of buffalo.

FIG. 201.

Fig. 202, 1817–'18.—La Framboise, a Canadian, built a trading store with dry timber. The dryness is shown by the dead tree. La Framboise was an old trader among the Dakota, who once established himself in the Minnesota valley. His name is mentioned by various travelers.

FIG. 202.

Fig. 203, 1818–'19.—The measles broke out and many died. The device in the copy is the same as that for 1801–'02, relating to the small-pox, except a very slight difference in the red blotches; and, though Lone-Dog's artistic skill might not have been sufficient to distinctly vary the appearance of the two patients, both diseases being eruptive, still it is one of the few serious defects in the chart that the sign for the two years is so nearly identical that, separated from the continuous record, there would be confusion between them. Treating the document as a mere aide-de-mémoire no inconvenience would arise, it probably being well known

FIG. 203.

that the smallpox epidemic preceded that of the measles; but care is generally taken to make some, however minute, distinction between the characters. It is also to be noticed that the Indian diagnosis makes little distinction between smallpox and measles, so that no important pictographic variation could be expected. The head of this figure is clearly distinguished from that in 1801–'02.

Fig. 204, 1819–'20.—Another trading store was built, this time by Louis La Conte, at Fort Pierre, Dakota. His timber, as one of the Indians consulted especially mentioned, was rotten.

FIG. 204.

Fig. 205, 1820–'21.—The trader, La Conte, gave Two-Arrow a war dress for his bravery. So translated an interpreter, and the sign shows the two arrows as the warrior's name-totem; likewise the gable of a house, which brings in the trader; also a long strip of black tipped with red streaming from the roof, which possibly may be the piece of parti-colored material out of which the dress was fashioned. This strip is not intended for sparks and

FIG. 205.

smoke, which at first sight was suggested, as in that case the red would have been nearest the roof instead of farthest from it.

Fig. 206, 1821–'22.—The character represents the falling to earth of a very brilliant meteor.

FIG. 206.

Fig. 207, 1822–'23.—Another trading house was built, which was by a white man called Big-Leggings, and was at the mouth of the Little Missouri or Bad river. The drawing is distinguishable from that for 1819–'20.

FIG. 207.

Fig. 208, 1823–'24.—White soldiers made their first appearance in the region. So said the interpreter, Clement, but from the unanimous

interpretation of others the event portrayed is the attack of the United States forces accompanied by Dakotas upon the Arikara villages, the historic account of which is given in some detail in Chap. XVI, infra.

FIG. 208.

The device represents an Arickara palisaded village and attacking soldiers. Not only the remarkable character and triumphant result of this expedition, but the connection that the Dakotas themselves had with it, made it a natural subject for the year's totem.

All the winter counts refer to this expedition.

Fig. 209, 1824–'25.—Swan, chief of the Two-Kettle tribe, had all of his horses killed. Device, a horse pierced by a lance, blood flowing from the wound.

FIG. 209.

Fig. 210, 1825–'26.—There was a remarkable flood in the Missouri river and a number of Indians were drowned. With some exercise of fancy the symbol may suggest heads appearing above a line of water, and this is more distinct in some of the other charts.

FIG. 210.

Fig. 211, 1826–'27.—"An Indian died of the dropsy." So Basil Clement said. It was at first suggested that this circumstance was noted because the disease was so unusual in 1826 as to excite remark. Baron de La Hontan (c), a good authority concerning the Northwestern Indians before they had been greatly affected by intercourse with whites, specially mentions dropsy as one of the diseases unknown to them. Carver, op. cit., also states that this malady was extremely rare. The interpretations of other charts ex-

FIG. 211.

plained, however, that some Dakotas on the warpath had nearly perished with hunger when they found and ate the rotting carcass of an old buffalo on which the wolves had been feeding. They were seized soon after with pains in the stomach, their abdomens swelled, and gas poured from the mouth. This disease is termed tympanites, the external appearance occasioned by it much resembling that of dropsy.

Fig. 212, 1827–'28.—Dead-Arm was stabbed with a knife or dirk by a Mandan. The illustration is quite graphic, showing the long-handled dirk in the bloody wound and withered arm.

FIG. 212.

Fig. 213, 1828–'29.—A white man named Shadran, who lately, as reported in 1877, was still living in the same neighborhood, built a dirt lodge. The hatted head appears under the roof. This name should probably be spelled Chadron, with whom Catlin hunted in 1832, in the region mentioned.

FIG. 213.

Fig. 214, 1829–'30.—A Yanktonai Dakota was killed by Bad-Arrow Indians.

The Bad-Arrow Indians is a translation of the Dakota name for a certain band of Blackfeet Indians.

FIG. 214.

Fig. 215, 1830–'31.—Bloody battle with the Crows, of whom it is said twenty-three were killed. Nothing in the sign denotes number, it being only a man figure with red or bloody body and red war bonnet.

FIG. 215.

Fig. 216, 1831–'32.—Le Beau, a white man, killed another named Kermel. Le Beau was still alive at Little Bend, 30 miles above Fort Sully, in 1877.

FIG. 216.

Fig. 217, 1832–'33.—Lone-Horn had his leg "killed," as the interpretation gave it. The single horn is on the figure, and a leg is drawn up as if fractured or distorted, though not unlike the leg in the character for 1808–'09, where running is depicted.

FIG. 217.

Fig. 218, 1833–'34.—"The stars fell," as the Indians all agreed. This was the great meteoric shower observed all over the United States on the night of November 12 of that year. In this chart the moon is black and the stars are red.

FIG. 218.

Fig. 219, 1834–'35.—The chief Medicine-Hide was killed. The device shows the body as bloody, but not the war bonnet, by which it is distinguished from the character for 1830–'31.

FIG. 219.

Fig. 220, 1835–'36.—Lame-Deer shot a Crow Indian with an arrow; drew it out and shot him again with the same arrow. The hand is drawing the arrow from the first wound. This is another instance of the principle on which events were selected. Many fights occurred of greater moment, but with no incident precisely like this. Lame-Deer was a distinguished chief among the hostiles in 1876. His camp of five hundred and ten lodges was surprised and destroyed by Gen. Miles, and four hundred and fifty horses, mules, and ponies were captured.

FIG. 220.

Fig. 221, 1836–'37.—Band's-Father, chief of the Two Kettles, died. The device is nearly the same as that for 1816–'17, denoting plenty of buffalo belly.

Interpreter Fielder throws light on the subject by saying that this character was used to designate the year when The-Breast, father of The-Band, a Minneconjou, died. The-Band himself died in 1875, on Powder river. His name was O-ye-a-pee. The character was, therefore, the Buffalo-Breast, a personal name.

FIG. 221.

Fig. 222, 1837–'38.—Commemorates a remarkably successful hunt, in which it is said 100 elk were killed. The drawing of the elk is good enough to distinguish it from the other quadrupeds in this chart.

FIG. 222.

Fig. 223, 1838–'39.—A dirt lodge was built for Iron-Horn. The other dirt lodge (1815–'16) has a mark of ownership, which this has not. A chief of the Minneconjous is mentioned in Gen. Harney's report in 1856 under the name of The-One-Iron-Horn. The word translated "iron" in this case and appearing thus several times in the charts does not always mean the metal of that name. According to Rev. J. Owen Dorsey it has a mystic significance, in some manner connected with water and with water spirits. In pictographs objects called iron are painted blue when that color can be obtained.

FIG. 223.

FIG. 224.

Fig. 224, 1839–'40.—The Dakotas killed an entire village of Snake or Shoshoni Indians. The character is the ordinary tipi pierced by arrows.

FIG. 225.

Fig. 225, 1840–'41.—The Dakotas made peace with the Cheyennes. The symbol of peace is the common one of the approaching hands of two persons. The different coloration of the two hands and arms shows that they belonged to two different persons, and in fact to different tribes. The mere unceremonial hand grasp or "shake" of friendship was not used by the Indians before it was introduced by Europeans.

FIG. 226.

Fig. 226, 1841–'42.—Feather-in-the-Ear stole 30 spotted ponies. The spots are shown red, distinguishing them from those of the curly horse in the character for 1803–'04.

A successful theft of horses, demanding skill, patience, and daring, is generally considered by the Plains Indians to be of equal merit with the taking of scalps. Indeed, the successful horse thief is more popular than a mere warrior, on account of the riches gained by the tribe, wealth until lately being generally estimated in ponies as the unit of value.

FIG. 227.

Fig. 227, 1842–'43.—One-Feather raised a large war party against the Crows. This chief is designated by his long solitary red eagle feather, and holds a pipe with black stem and red bowl, alluding to the usual ceremonies before starting on the warpath. For further information on this subject see Chap. XV. The Red-War-Eagle-Feather was at this time a chief of the Sans Arcs.

FIG. 228.

Fig. 228, 1843–'44.—Th Sans Arcs made medicine to bring the buffalo. The medicine tent is denoted by a buffalo's head drawn on it, which in this instance is not the head of an albino buffalo.

FIG. 229.

Fig. 229, 1844–'45.—The Minneconjous built a pine fort. Device, a pine tree connected with a tipi. Another account explains that they went to the woods and erected their tipis there as affording some protection from the unusually deep snow. This would account for the pine tree.

FIG. 230.

Fig. 230, 1845–'46.—Plenty of buffalo meat, which is represented as hung upon poles and trees to dry. This device has become the conventional sign for plenty and frequently appears in the several charts.

FIG. 231.

Fig. 231, 1846–'47.—Broken-Leg died. Rev. Dr. Williamson says he knew him. He was a Brulé. There is enough difference between this device and those for 1808–'09 and 1832–'33 to distinguish each.

FIG. 232.

Fig. 232, 1847–'48.—Two-Man was killed. His totem is drawn, two small man figures side by side. Another interpretation explains the figure as indicating twins.

FIG. 233.

Fig. 233, 1848–'49.—Humpback was killed. An ornamented lance pierces the distorted back. Other records name him Broken-Back. He was a distinguished chief of the Minneconjous.

FIG. 234.

Fig. 234, 1849–'50.—The Crows stole a large drove of horses (it is said eight hundred) from the Brulés. The circle is a design for a camp or corral from which a number of horse-tracks are departing.

Fig. 235, 1850–'51.—The character is a distinct drawing of a buffalo containing a human figure. Clément translated that "a buffalo cow was killed in that year and an old woman found in her belly;" also that all the Indians believed this. Good-Wood, examined through another interpreter, could or would give no explanation except that it was "about their religion." The Dakotas have long believed in the appearance from time to time of a monstrous animal that swallows human beings. This superstition was perhaps suggested by the bones of mastodons, often found in the territory of those Indians; and, the buffalo being the largest living animal known to them, its name was given to the legendary monster, in which nomenclature they were not wholly wrong, as the horns of the fossil *Bison latifrons* are 10 feet in length.

FIG. 235.

Major Bush suggests that perhaps some old squaw left to die sought the carcass of a buffalo for shelter and then died. He has known this to occur.

Fig. 236, 1851–52.—Peace with the Crows. Two Indians, with differing arrangement of hair, showing
two tribes, are exchanging pipes for a peace smoke.

FIG. 236.

Fig. 237, 1852–'53.—The Nez Percés came to Lone-Horn's lodge at midnight. The device shows an Indian touching with
a pipe a tipi, the top of which is black or opaque, sig-
nifying night.

Touch-the-Clouds, a Minneconjou, son of Lone-
Horn, when this chart was shown to him by the present writer, designated this character as being particularly known to him from the fact of its being his
father's lodge. He remembered all about it from talk
in his family, and said it was the Nez Percés who came.

FIG. 237.

Fig. 238, 1853–'54.—Spanish blankets were first brought
to the country. A fair drawing of one of those striped
blankets is held out by a white trader.

FIG. 238.

Fig. 239, 1854–'55.—Brave-Bear was killed. His extended arms are ornamented with pendent stripes.

FIG. 239.

Fig. 240, 1855–'56.—Gen. Harney, called by the Dakota Putinska
("white beard" or "white mustache"), made peace
with a number of the tribes or bands of the Dakotas.
The figure shows an officer in uniform shaking hands
with an Indian.

FIG. 240.

Executive document No. 94, Thirty-fourth Congress,
first session, Senate, contains the "minutes of a council held at Fort Pierre, Nebraska, on the 1st day of March, 1856, by Brevet Brig. Gen. William S. Harney, U. S. Army, commanding the Sioux expedition, with the delegations from nine of the bands of the Sioux, viz, the Two Kettle band, Lower Yankton, Uncpapas, Blackfeet Sioux, Minneconjous, Sans Arcs, Yanctonnais (two bands), Brulés of the Platte."

Fig. 241, 1856–'57.—Four-Horn was made a calumet or medicine man.

FIG. 241.

A man with four horns holds out the same kind of ornamented pipestem shown in the character for 1804–'05, it being his badge of office. Four-Horn was one of the subchiefs of the Uncpapas, and was introduced to Gen. Harney at the council of 1856 by Bear-Rib, head chief of that tribe.

Interpreter Clément, in the spring of 1874, said that Four-Horn and Sitting-Bull were the same person, the name Sitting-Bull being given him after he was made a calumet man. No other authority tells this.

FIG. 242.

Fig. 242, 1857–'58.—The Dakotas killed a Crow squaw. She is pierced by four arrows, and the peace made with the Crows in 1851–'52 seems to have been short lived.

FIG. 243.

Fig. 243, 1858–'59.—Lone-Horn, whose solitary horn appears, made buffalo "medicine," doubtless on account of the scarcity of that animal. Again the head of an albino bison. One-Horn, probably the same individual, is recorded as the head chief of the Minneconjous at this date.

FIG. 244.

Fig. 244, 1859–'60.—Big-Crow, a Dakota chief, was killed by the Crows. He had received his name from killing a Crow Indian of unusual size.

Fig. 245, 1860–'61.—Device, the head and neck of an elk, similar to

FIG. 245.

that part of the animal for 1837–'38, with a line extending from its mouth, at the extremity of which is the albino buffalo head. "The elk made you understand the voice while he was walking." The interpreter persisted in this oracular rendering. This device and its interpretation were unintelligible to the writer until examination of Gen. Harney's report, above referred to, showed the name of a prominent chief of the Minneconjous set forth as "The Elk that Holloes Walking." It then became probable that the device simply meant that the aforesaid chief made buffalo medicine, which conjecture, published in 1877, was verified by the other records subsequently discovered.

Interpreter A. Lavary said, in 1867, that The-Elk-that-Holloes-Walking, then chief of the Minneconjous, was then at Spotted-Tail's camp. His father was Red-Fish. He was the elder brother of Lone-Horn. His name is given as A-hag-a-hoo-man-ie, translated The Elk's Voice Walking; compounded of he-ha-ka, elk, and omani, walk; this according to Lavary's literation. The correct literation of the Dakota word meaning elk is heqaka; voice, ho; and to walk, walking, mani.

Their compound would be heqaka-ho-mani, the translation being the same as above given.

Fig. 246, 1861–'62.—Buffalo were so plentiful that their tracks came close to the tipis. The cloven-hoof mark is cleverly distinguished from the tracks of horses in the character for 1849–'50.

FIG. 246.

Fig. 247, 1862–'63.—Red-Feather, a Minneconjou, was killed. His feather is shown entirely red, while the "one-feather" in 1842–'43 has a black tip.

It is to be noted that there is no allusion to the great Minnesota massacre, which commenced in August, 1862, and in which many of the Dakotas belonging to the tribes familiar with these charts were engaged. Little-Crow was the leader. He escaped to the British possessions, but was killed in July, 1863. Perhaps the reason of the omission of any character to designate the massacre was the terrible retribution that followed it.

FIG. 247.

Fig. 248, 1863–'64.—Eight Dakotas were killed. Again the short, parallel black lines united by a long stroke. In this year Sitting-Bull fought General Sully in the Black Hills.

FIG. 248.

Fig. 249, 1864–'65.—The Dakotas killed four Crows. Four of the same rounded objects, like severed heads, shown in 1825–'26, but these are bloody, thus distinguishing them from the cases of drowning.

FIG. 249.

Fig. 250, 1865–'66.—Many horses died for want of grass. The horse here drawn is sufficiently distinct from all others in the chart.

FIG. 250.

Fig. 251, 1866–'67.—Swan, father of Swan, chief of the Minneconjous in 1877, died. With the assistance of the name the object intended for his totem may be recognized as a swan swimming on the water.

FIG. 251.

Fig. 252, 1867–'68.—Many flags were given them by the Peace Commission. The flag refers to the visit of the Peace Commissioners, among whom were Generals Sherman, Terry, and other prominent military and civil officers. Their report appears in the Annual Report of the Commissioner of Indian Affairs for 1868. They met at Fort Leavenworth, August 13, 1867, and between August 30 and September 13 held councils with the various bands of the Dakota Indians at Forts Sully and Thompson, and also at

FIG. 252.

the Yankton, Ponka, and Santee reservations. These resulted in the Dakota treaty of 1868.

Fig. 253, 1868–'69.—Texas cattle were brought into the country. This was done by Mr. William A. Paxton, a well-known business man, resident in Dakota in 1877.

FIG. 253.

Fig. 254, 1869–'70.—An eclipse of the sun. This was the solar eclipse of August 7, 1869, which was central and total on a line drawn through the Dakota country. This device has been criticised because Indians generally believe an eclipse to be occasioned by a dragon or aerial monster swallowing the sun, and it is contended that they would so represent it. An answer is that the design is objectively good, the sun being painted

FIG. 254.

black, as concealed, while the stars come out red, i. e., bright, and graphic illustration prevails throughout the charts where it is possible to employ it.

Dr. Washington Matthews, surgeon, U. S. Army, communicated the fact that the Dakotas had opportunities all over their country of receiving information about the real character of the eclipse. He was at Fort Rice during the eclipse and remembers that long before it occurred the officers, men, and citizens around the post told the Indians of the coming event and discussed it with them so much that they were on the tip-toe of expectancy when the day came. Two-Bears and his band were then encamped at Fort Rice, and he and several of his leading men watched the eclipse along with the whites and through their smoked glass, and then and there the phenomenon was thoroughly explained to them over and over again. There is no doubt that similar explanations were made at all the numerous posts and agencies along the river that day. The path of the eclipse coincided nearly with the course of the Missouri for over a thousand miles. The duration of totality at Fort Rice was nearly two minutes (1′ 48″).

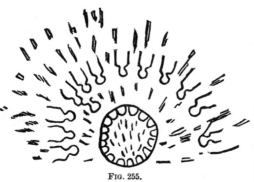

FIG. 255.

Fig. 255, 1870–'71.—The Uncpapas had a battle with the Crows, the former losing, it is said, 14, and killing 29 out of 30 of the latter, though nothing appears to show those numbers. The central object is not a circle denoting multitude, but an irregularly rounded object, perhaps intended for one of the wooden inclosures or forts frequently erected by the Indians, and especially the Crows. The Crow fort is shown as nearly surrounded, and bullets, not arrows or lances, are flying. This is the first instance in this chart in which any combat or killing is protrayed where guns explicitly appear to be used by Indians, though nothing in the chart is at variance with the fact that the Dakotas had for a number of years been familiar with firearms. The most recent indications of any weapon were those of the arrows piercing the Crow squaw in 1857–'58, and Brave-Bear in 1854–'55, while the last one before those was the lance used in 1848–'49, and those arms might well have been employed in all the cases selected, although rifles and muskets were common. There is an obvious practical difficulty in picturing, by a single character, killing with a bullet, not arising as to arrows, lances, dirks, and hatchets, all of which can be and are shown in the chart projecting from the wounds made by them. Other pictographs show battles in which bullets are denoted by continuous dotted lines, the spots at which they take effect being sometimes indicated, and the fact that they did hit the object aimed at is expressed by a specially invented symbol. It is, however, to be noted that the bloody wound on the Ree's shoulder (1806–'07) is without any protruding weapon, as if made by a bullet.

More distinct information regarding this fight, the record of which concludes the original Lone-Dog chart, has been kindly communicated by Mr. Luther S. Kelly, of Garfield County, Colorado.

The war party of Uncpapas mentioned charged upon a small trading post for the Crows on the Upper Missouri river, at the mouth of Musselshell river. Usually this post was garrisoned by a few frontiersmen, but on that particular day there happened to be a considerable force of freighters and hunters. The Indians were afoot and, being concealed by the sage brush, got within shooting distance of the fort before being discovered. They were easily driven off, and going a short distance took shelter from the rain in a circular washout, not having any idea of being followed by the whites. Meanwhile the whites organized and followed. The surprise was complete, the leading white man only being killed. The Indians sang their song and made several breaks to escape, but were shot down as fast as they rose above the bank. Twenty-nine were killed.

BATTISTE GOOD'S WINTER COUNT.

Dr. William H. Corbusier, surgeon, U. S. Army, while stationed in 1879 and 1880 at Camp Sheridan, Nebraska, near the Pine Ridge Indian Agency, Dakota, obtained a copy of this Winter Count from its recorder Baptiste, commonly called Battiste Good, a Brulé Dakota, whose Dakotan name is given as Wa-po-ctaⁿ-xi, translated Brown-Hat. He was then living at the Rose Bud Agency, Dakota, and explained the meaning of the pictographs to the Rev. Wm. J. Cleveland, of the last named agency, who translated them into English.

The copy made by Battiste Good from his original record, of which it is said to be a facsimile, is painted in five colors besides black, in which the outlines are generally drawn, but with the exception of red blood-marks these colors do not often appear to be significant. This copy, which was kindly contributed by Dr. Corbusier, is made in an ordinary paper drawing-book, the last page of which contains the first record. This is represented in Fig. 256, and pictures what is supposed to be an introduction in the nature of a revelation. The next page, reading backwards and corresponding with Pl. XXI, is a pretended record of a cycle comprising the years (presumed to be in the Christian chronology) from 901 to 930. Eleven similar pages and cycles bring the record down to 1700. These pages are only interesting from the mythology and tradition referred to and suggested by them, and which must be garnered from the chaff of uncomprehended missionary teaching. From 1700 to 1880, when the record closes, each year, or rather winter, is represented by a special character according to the Dakota system above explained.

Battiste Good, by his own statement in the present record, was born in the year 1821–'22. Any careful examination of the figures as worked over by his own hand shows that he has received about enough education in English and in writing to induce him to make unnecessary additions and presumptuous emendations on the pictographs as he found them and as perhaps he originally kept and drew the more recent of them. He has written English words and Arabic numerals over and connected with the Dakota devices, and has left some figures in a state of mixture including the methods of modern civilization and the aboriginal system. To prevent the confusion to the reader which might result from Battiste's meddlesome vanity, these interpolated marks are in general omitted from the plates and figures as now presented, but, as specimens of the kind and amount of interference referred to, the designs on the copy for the years 1700–'01, 1701–'02, and 1707–'08 are given below as furnished.

The facts stated to have occurred so long ago as the beginning of the last century can not often be verified, but those of later date given by Battiste are corroborated by other records in the strongest manner—that is, by independent devices which are not mere copies. Therefore, notwithstanding Battiste's mythic cycles and English writing, the body of his record, which constitutes the true Winter Counts, must be regarded as genuine. He is simply the bad editor of a good work. But whether or not the events occurred as represented, the pictography is of unique interest. It may be remarked that Battiste's record is better known among the Oglala and Brulé, and Lone-Dog's Winter Count among the Minneconjou.

It should be noted that when allusions are made to coloration in Fig. 256, and in any one of the other figures in the text which illustrate this Winter Count, they must be understood as applicable to the original. Pls. XXI, XXII, and XXIII are colored copies of those furnished by Battiste Good, reduced, however, in size.

Fig. 256 illustrates Battiste Good's introduction. He is supposed to be narrating his own experience as follows: "In the year 1856, I went to the Black Hills and cried, and cried, and cried, and suddenly I saw a bird above me, which said: 'Stop crying; I am a woman, but I will tell you something: My Great-Father, Father God, who made this place, gave it to me for a home and told me to watch over it. He put

FIG. 256.—Battiste Good's Revelation.

a blue sky over my head and gave me a blue flag to have with this beautiful green country. [Battiste has made the hill country, as well as the curve for sky and the flag, blue in his copy.] My Great-Father, Father God (or The Great-Father, God my Father) grew, and his flesh was part earth and part stone and part metal and part wood and part water; he took from them all and placed them here for me, and told me to watch over them. I am the Eagle-Woman who tell you this.

*Reproduced in black and white in the present edition.

The whites know that there are four black flags of God; that is, four divisions of the earth. He first made the earth soft by wetting it, then cut it into four parts, one of which, containing the Black Hills, he gave to the Dakotas, and, because I am a woman, I shall not consent to the pouring of blood on this chief house (or dwelling place), i. e., the Black Hills. The time will come that you will remember my words; for after many years you shall grow up one with the white people.' She then circled round and round and gradually passed out of my sight. I also saw prints of a man's hands and horse's hoofs on the rocks [here he brings in petroglyphs], and two thousand years, and one hundred millions of dollars ($100,000,000). I came away crying, as I had gone. I have told this to many Dakotas, and all agree that it meant that we were to seek and keep peace with the whites."

(NOTE BY DR. CORBUSIER.—The Oglálas and Brulés say that they, with the rest of the Dakota nation, formerly lived far on the other side of the Missouri River. After they had moved to the river, they lived at first on its eastern banks, only crossing it to hunt. Some of the hunting parties that crossed at length wandered far off from the rest and, remaining away, became the westernmost bands.)

Pl. XXI A. The record shown by this figure dates from the appearance of The-Woman-from-Heaven, 901 A. D.; but the Dakotas were a people long before this. The circle of lodges represents a cycle of thirty years, from the year 901 to 930, and incloses the "legend" by which this period is known. All the tribes of the Dakota nation were encamped together, as was then their custom, when all at once a beautiful woman appeared to two young men. One of them said to the other, "Let us catch her and have her for our wife." The other said, "No; she may be something waka^n" (supernatural or sacred). Then the woman said to them, "I came from Heaven to teach the Dakotas how to live and what their future shall be." She had what appeared to be snakes about her legs and waist, but which were really braids of grass. She said, "I give you this pipe; keep it always;" and with the pipe she gave them a small package, in which they found four grains of maize, one white, one black, one yellow, and one variegated. The pipe is above the buffalo. She said, "I am a buffalo, The White-Buffalo-Cow. I will spill my milk all over the earth, that the people may live." She meant by her milk maize, which is seen in the picture dropping from her udders. The colored patches on the four sides of the circle are the four quarters of the heavens (the cardinal points of the compass). In front of the cow are yellow and red. She pointed in this direction and said, "When you see a yellowish (or brownish) cloud toward the north, that is my breath; rejoice at the sight of it, for you shall soon see buffalo. Red is the blood of the buffalo, and by that you shall live. Pointing east [it will be noticed that Battiste has placed the east toward the top of the page], she said, "This pipe is related to the heavens, and you shall live with it." The line running from the

Plate XXI.

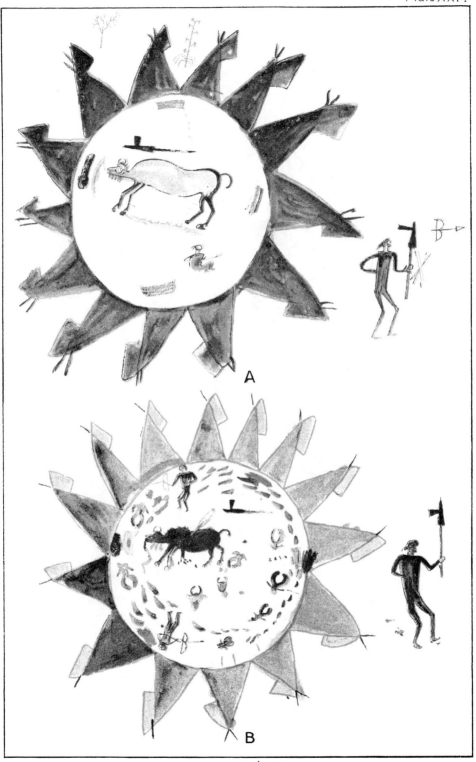

A

B

BATTISTE GOOD'S CYCLES.

A 901 – 930   B 931 – 1000.

Plate XXII.

BATTISTE GOOD'S CYCLES.

A 1141 – 1210. **B** 1211 – 1280.

Plate XXIII.

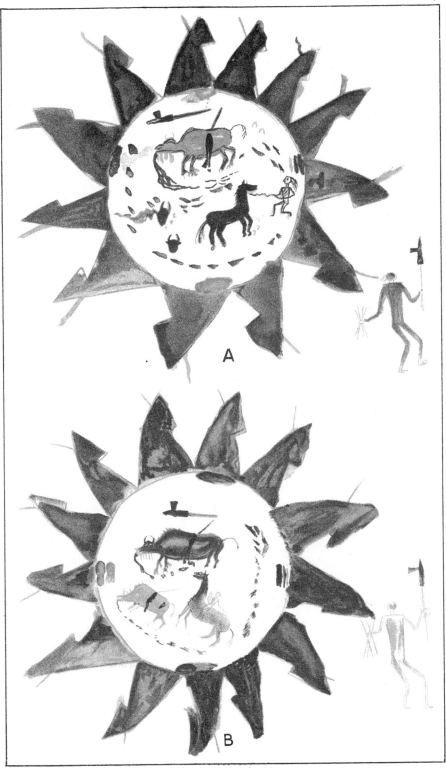

BATTISTE GOOD'S CYCLES.

A 1421 - 1490.   B 1631 - 1700.

pipe to the blue patch denotes the relation. The Dakotas have always supposed she meant by this that the blue smoke of the pipe was one with or nearly related to the blue sky; hence, on a clear day, before smoking, they often point the stem of the pipe upward, in remembrance of her words. Pointing south, she said, "Clouds of many colors may come up from the south, but look at the pipe and the blue sky and know that the clouds will soon pass away and all will become blue and clear again." Pointing west, i. e., to the lowest part of the circle, she said, "When it shall be blue in the west, know that it is closely related to you through the pipe and the blue heavens, and by that you shall grow rich." Then she stood up before them and said, "I am The White-Buffalo-Cow; my milk is of four kinds; I spill it on the earth that you may live by it. You shall call me Grandmother. If you young men will follow me over the hills you shall see my relatives." She said this four times, each time stepping back from them a few feet, and after the fourth time, while they stood gazing at her, she mysteriously disappeared. [It is well known that four is the favorite or magic number among Indian tribes generally, and has reference to the four cardinal points.] The young men went over the hills in the direction she took and there found a large herd of buffalo.

(NOTE BY DR. CORBUSIER.—Mr. Cleveland states that he has heard several different versions of this tradition.)

The man who first told the people of the appearance of the woman is represented both inside and outside the circle. He was thirty years old at the time, and said that she came as narrated above, in July of the year of his birth. Outside of the circle, he is standing with a pipe in his hand; inside, he is squatting, and has his hands in the position for the gesture-sign for pipe. The elm tree and yucca, or Spanish bayonet, both shown above the tipis, indicate that in those days the Dakota obtained fire by rapidly revolving the end of a dry stalk of the yucca in a hole made in a rotten root of the elm. The people used the bow and stone-pointed arrows, which are shown on the right. From time immemorial they have kept large numbers of sticks, shown by the side of the pipe, each one about as thick and as long as a lead-pencil (sic), for the purpose of counting and keeping record of numbers, and they cut notches in larger sticks for the same purpose.

(NOTE BY DR. CORBUSIER.—They commonly resort to their fingers in counting, and the V of the Roman system of notation is seen in the outline of the thumb and index, when one hand is held up to express five, and the X in the crossed thumbs, when both hands are held up together to express ten.)

The bundle of these sticks drawn in connection with the ceremonial pipe suggests the idea of an official recorder.

Pl. XXI B, 931–1000. From the time the man represented in Pl. XXI A was seventy years of age, i. e., from the year 931, time is counted by cycles of seventy years until 1700. This figure illustrates the manner of killing buffalo before and after the appearance of The-Woman. When the

Dakotas had found the buffalo, they moved to the herd and corralled it by spreading their camps around it. The Man-Who-Dreamed-of-a-Wolf, seen at the upper part of the circle, with bow and arrow in hand, then shot the chief bull of the herd with his medicine or sacred arrow; at this, the women all cried out with joy, " He has killed the chief bull!" On hearing them shout the man with bow and arrow on the opposite side, The-Man-Who-Dreamed-of-the-Thunder - and - received - an - arrow- from - the-Thunder-Bird (wakinyan, accurately translated " the flying one") shot a buffalo cow, and the women again shouted with joy. Then all the men began to shout, and they killed as many as they wished. The buffalo heads and the blood-stained tracks show what large numbers were killed. They cut off the head of the chief bull, and laid the pipe beside it until their work was done. They prayed to The-Woman to bless and help them as they were following her teachings. Having no iron or knives, they used sharp stones, and mussel shells, to skin and cut up the buffalo. They rubbed blood in the hides to soften and tan them. They had no horses, and had to pack everything on their own backs.

The cyclic characters that embrace the period from 1001 to 1140 illustrate nothing of interest not before presented. Slight distinction appears in the circles so that they can be identified, but without enough significance to merit reproduction.

Pl. XXII A, 1141–1210. Among a herd of buffalo, surrounded at one time during this period, were some horses. The people all cried out, "there are big dogs with them," having never seen horses before, hence the name for horse, sunka (dog) tanka (big), or sunka (dog) wakan (wonderful or mysterious). After killing all the buffalo they said " let us try and catch the big dogs;" so they cut a thong out of a hide with a sharp stone and with it caught eight, breaking the leg of one of them. All these years they used sharpened deer horn for awls, bone for needles, and made their lodges without the help of iron tools. [All other Dakota traditions yet reported in regard to the first capture of horses, place this important event at a much later period and long after horses were brought to America by the Spaniards. See this count for the year 1802–'03, and also Lone-Dog's Winter Count for the same year.]

Pl. XXII B, 1211–1280. At one time during this period a war party of enemies concealed themselves among a herd of buffalo, which the Dakotas surrounded and killed before they discovered the enemy. No one knows what people, or how many they were; but the Dakotas killed them all. The red and black lodges indicate war, and that the Dakotas were successful.

The pages of the copy which embrace the period from 1281 to 1420 are omitted as valueless.

Pl. XXIII A, 1421–1490. " Found horses among the buffalo again and caught six." Five of the horses are represented by the hoof prints. The lasso or possibly the lariat is shown in use. The bundle of sticks is now in the recorder's hands.

Battiste's pages which embrace the period from 1491 to 1630 are omitted for the same reason as before offered.

Pl. XXIII B, 1631–1700. This represents the first killing of buffalo on horseback. It was done in the year 1700, inside the circle of lodges pitched around the herd, by a man who was tied on a horse with thongs and who received the name of Hunts-inside-the-lodges. They had but one horse then, and they kept him a long time. Again the bundle of count-sticks is in the recorder's hands.

This is the end of the obviously mythic part of the record, in which Battiste has made some historic errors. From this time forth each year is distinguished by a name, the explanation of which is in the realm of fact.

It must be again noted that when colors are referred to in the description of the text figures, the language (translated) used by Battiste is retained for the purpose of showing the coloration of the original and his interpretation of the colors, which are to be imagined, as they can not be reproduced by the process used.

Fig. 257, 1700–'01.—"The-two-killed-on-going-back-to-the-hunting-ground winter (or year)." Two Dakotas returned to the hunting ground, after the hunt one day, and were killed by enemies, of what tribe is unknown. The blood-stained arrow in the man's side signifies killed; the numeral 2 over his head, the number killed; and, the buffalo heads, the carcass of a buffalo—which had been left behind because it was too poor to eat—together with the arrow pointing toward them, the hunting-ground. The dot under the figure 2, and many of the succeeding ones, signifies, That is it. This corresponds with some

FIG. 257.

gesture signs for the same concept of declaration, in which the index finger held straight is thrust forward with emphasis and repeatedly as if always hitting the same point.

With regard to the numeral 2 over the head of the man see remarks, page 288.

Fig. 258, 1701–'02.—"The-three-killed-who-went-fishing winter." The arrow pointing toward the 3, indicates that they were attacked; the arrow in the man's arm, and the blood stain, that they were killed; the pole, line, and fish which the man is holding, their occupation at the time.

FIG. 258.

Fig. 259, 1702–'03.—"Camped-cutting-the-ice-through winter." A long lake toward the east, near which the Dakotas were encamped, was frozen over, when they discovered about one thousand buffalo. They

FIG. 259.

secured them all by driving them on the ice, through which they broke, and in which they froze fast. Whenever the people wanted meat, they cut a buffalo out of the ice. In the figure, the wave lines represent the water of the lake; the straight lines, the shore; the blue lines outside the black ones, trees; the blue patches inside, the ice through which the heads of the buffalo are seen; the line across the middle, the direction in which they drove the buffalo. The supply of meat lasted one year. (NOTE by DR. CORBUSIER.—The Apache of Arizona, the Ojibwa, and the Ottawa also represent water by means of waved lines.)

Fig. 260, 1703–'04.—"The-burying winter," or "Many-hole winter."—They killed a great many buffalo during the summer, and, after drying the meat, stored it in pits for winter's use. It lasted them all winter, and they found it all in good condition. The ring surrounding the buffalo head, in front of the lodge, represents a pit. The forked stick, which is the symbol for meat, marks the pit. [Other authorities suggest that the object called by Battiste a pit, which is more generally called "cache," is a heap, and means many or much.]

FIG. 260.

Fig. 261, 1704–'05.—"Killed-fifteen-Pawnees-who-came-to-fight winter." The Dakotas discovered a party of Pawnees coming to attack them. They met them and killed fifteen. In this chart the Pawnee of the Upper Missouri (Arikara or Ree), the Pawnee of Nebraska, and the Omaha are all depicted with legs which look like ears of corn, but an ear of corn is symbol for the Rees only. The Pawnee of Nebraska may be distinguished by a lock of hair at the back of the head; the Omaha, by a cropped head or absence of the scalp-lock. The absence of all signs denotes Dakota. Dr. W. Matthews, in Ethnography and Philology of the Hidatsa Indians, states that the Arikara separated from the Pawnee of the Platte valley more than a century ago. [To avoid confusion the literation of the tribal divisions as given by the translator of Battiste Good are retained, though not considered to be accurate.]

FIG. 261.

FIG. 262.

Fig. 262, 1705–'06.—"They-came-and-killed-seven-Dakotas winter." It is not known what enemies killed them.

Fig. 263, 1706–'07.—"Killed-the-Gros-Ventre-with-snowshoes-on winter." A Gros-Ventre (Hidatsa), while hunting buffalo on snowshoes, was chased by the Dakotas. He accidentally dropped a snowshoe, and, being then unable to get through the snow fast enough, they gained on him, wounded him in the leg, and then killed him. The Gros-Ventres and the Crows are tribes of the same nation, and are therefore both represented with striped or spotted hair, which denotes the red clay they apply to it.

FIG. 263.

Fig. 264, 1707–'08.—"Many-kettle winter." A man—1 man—named Corn, killed (3) his wife, 1 woman, and ran off. He remained away for a year, and then came back, bringing three guns with him, and told the people that the English, who had given him these guns, which were the first known to the Dakotas, wanted him to bring his friends to see them. Fifteen of the people accordingly went with him, and when they returned brought home a lot of kettles or pots. These were the first they ever saw. Some numerical marks for reference and the written words in the above are retained as perhaps

FIG. 264.

the worst specimens of Battiste's mixture of civilized methods with the aboriginal system of pictography. See remarks above, page 288.

Fig. 265, 1708–'09.—"Brought-home-Omaha-horses winter." The cropped head over the horse denotes Omaha.

FIG. 265.

Fig. 266, 1709–'10.—"Brought-home-Assiniboin-horses winter." The Dakota sign for Assiniboin, or Hohe, which means the voice, or, as some say, the voice of the musk ox, is the outline of the vocal organs, as the Dakotas conceive them, and represents the upper lip and roof of the mouth, the tongue, the lower lip and chin, and the neck.

FIG. 266.

Fig. 267, 1710–'11.—"The-war-parties-met, or killed-three-on-each-side winter." A war party of Assiniboins met one of Dakotas, and in the fight which ensued three were killed on each side.

FIG. 267.

Fig. 268, 1711–'12.—"Four-lodges-drowned winter." When the thun-

FIG. 268.

ders returned in the summer the Dakotas were still in their winter camp, on the bottom lands of a large creek. Heavy rains fell, which caused the creek to rise suddenly; the bottoms were flooded, and the occupants of four lodges were swept away and drowned. Water is represented by waved lines, as before. The lower part of the lodge is submerged. The human figure in the doorway of the lodge indicates how unconscious the inmates were of their peril.

FIG. 269.

Fig. 269, 1712–'13.—"Killed-the-Pawnee-who-was eagle-hunting winter." A Pawnee (Ree) was crouching in his eagle-trap, a hole in the ground covered with sticks and grass, when he was surprised and killed by the Dakotas. This event is substantially repeated in this count for the year 1806–'07.

FIG. 270.

Fig. 270, 1713–'14.—"Came-and-shot-them-in-the-lodge winter." The Pawnee (Rees) came by night, and, drawing aside a tipi door, shot a sleeping man, and thus avenged the death of the eagle-hunter.

FIG. 271.

Fig. 271, 1714–'15.—"Came-to-attack-on-horseback-but-killed-nothing winter." The horseman has a pine lance in his hand. It is not known what tribe came. (NOTE BY DR. CORBUSIER.—It is probable that horses were not numerous among any of the Indians yet, and that this mounted attack was the first one experienced by the Brulé.)

FIG. 272.

Fig. 272, 1715–'16.—"Came-and-attacked-on-horseback-and-stabbed-a-boy-near-the-lodge winter." Eagle tail-feathers hang from the butt end of the lance.

Fig. 273, 1716–'17.—"Much-pemmican winter." A year of peace and

FIG. 273.

prosperity. Buffalo were plentiful all the fall and winter. Large quantities of pemmican (wasna) were made with dried meat and marrow. In front of the lodge is seen the backbone of a buffalo, the marrow of which is used in wasna; below this is the buffalo stomach, in which wasna is packed for preservation.

FIG. 274.

Fig. 274, 1717–'18.—"Brought-home-fifteen-Assiniboin-horses winter." The sign for Assiniboin is above the horse.

Fig. 275, 1718–'19.—"Brought - home - Pawnee-horses winter." The sign for Ree, i. e., an ear of corn, is in front of the horse.

FIG. 275.

Fig. 276, 1719–'20.—"Wore-snowshoes winter." The snow was very deep, and the people hunted buffalo on snowshoes with excellent success.

FIG. 276.

Fig. 277, 1720–'21.—"Three - lodges - starved - to-death winter." The bare ribs of the man denote starvation. [The gesture-sign for poor or lean indicates that the ribs are visible. In the Ojibwa and Ottawa pictographs lines across the chest denote starvation.]

FIG. 277.

Fig. 278, 1721–'22.—"Wore-snowshoes-and-dried-much-buffalo-meat winter." It was even a better year for buffalo than 1719–'20.

FIG. 278.

Fig. 279, 1722–'23.—"Deep - snow - and - tops - of-lodges-only-visible winter." The spots are intended for snow.

FIG. 279.

FIG. 280.

Fig. 280, 1723–'24.—"Many-drying-sticks-set-up winter." They set up more than the usual number of sticks for scaffolds, etc., as they dried the buffalo heads, hides, and entrails, as well as the meat. This figure is repeated with differentiation for the year 1745–'46 in this chart.

FIG. 281.

Fig. 281, 1724–'25.—"Blackens-himself-died winter." This man was in the habit of blacking his whole body with charcoal. He died of some kind of intestinal bend [sic] as is indicated by the stomach and intestines in front of him, which represent the bowels in violent commotion, or going round and round.

FIG. 282.

Fig. 282, 1725–'26.—"Brought-home-ten-Omaha-horses winter." The sign for Omaha is the head, as before.

FIG. 283.

Fig. 283, 1726–'27.—"Killed-two-Pawnees-among-the-lodges winter." The Pawnees (Rees) made an assault on the Dakota Village, and these two ran among the lodges without any arrows. The sign for Ree is, as usual, an ear of corn.

FIG. 284.

Fig. 284, 1727–'28.—"Killed-six-Assiniboins winter." Two signs are given here for Assiniboin. There is some uncertainty as to whether they were Assiniboins or Arikaras, so the signs for both are given.

FIG. 285.

Fig. 285, 1728–'29.—"Brought-home-Gros-Ventre-horses winter." A Gros Ventre head is shown in front of the horse.

Fig. 286, 1729–'30.—"Killed-the-Pawnees-camped-alone-with-their-wives winter." Two Pawnees and their wives, who were hunting buffalo by themselves, and living in one lodge, were surprised and killed by a war party of Dakotas.

FIG. 286.

Fig. 287, 1730–'31.—" Came-from-opposite-ways-and-camped-together winter." By a singular coincidence, two bands of Dakotas selected the same place for an encampment, and arrived there the same day. They had been separated a long time, and were wholly ignorant of each others movements. The caps of the tipis face one another.

FIG. 287.

Fig. 288, 1731–'32.—" Came-from-killing-one-Omaha-and-danced winter." This is the customary feast at the return of a successful war party. The erect arrow may stand for "one," and the Omaha is drawn at full length with his stiff short hair and painted cheeks.

FIG. 288.

Fig. 289, 1732–'33.—"Brought-home-Assiniboin-horses winter." The sign for Assiniboin is as before, over the horse.

FIG. 289.

Fig. 290, 1733–'34.—" Killed-three-Assiniboins winter." There is again uncertainty as to whether they were Assiniboins or Arikaras, and both signs are used.

FIG. 290.

FIG. 291.

Fig. 291, 1734–'35.—"Used-them-up-with-belly-ache winter." About fifty of the people died of an eruptive disease which was accompanied by pains in the bowels. The eruption is shown on the man in the figure. This was probably the first experience by the Dakotas of the smallpox, which has been so great a factor in the destruction of the Indians.

FIG. 292.

Fig. 292, 1735–'36.—"Followed-them-up-and-killed-five winter." A war party of Dakotas were chased by some enemies, who killed five of them. The arrows flying from behind at the man indicate pursuit, and the number of the arrows, each with a bloody mark as if hitting, is five.

FIG. 293.

Fig. 293, 1736–'37.—"Brought - home - Pawnee-horses winter." This date must be considered in connection with the figure in this record for 1802–'03. There is a distinction between the wild and the shod horses, but the difference in tribe is great. The ear of corn showing the husk is as common in this record for Pawnee as for Arikara.

FIG 294.

Fig. 294, 1737–'38.—"Killed-seven-Assiniboins-bringing - them - to - a - stand-under-a-bank winter." The daub, blue in the original, under the crouching figure, represents the bank.

FIG. 295.

Fig. 295, 1738–'39.—"The-four-who-went-on-the-war-path-starved-to-death winter." Starvation is indicated as before.

Fig. 296, 1739–'40.—"Found-many-horses winter." The horses had thongs around their necks,
and had evidently been lost by some other tribe.
Hoof prints are represented above and below the
horse, that is all around.

FIG. 296.

Fig. 297, 1740–'41.—"The-two-came-home-having-
killed-an-enemy winter." They took his entire
scalp, and carried it home at the end of a pole.
Only a part of the scalp is ordinarily taken, and
that from the crown of the head.

FIG. 297.

Fig. 298, 1741–'42.—"Attacked-them-while-gather-
ing-turnips winter." Some women, who were digging turnips (pomme blanche) near the camp, were
assaulted by a party of enemies, who, after knock-
ing them down, ran off without doing them any
further harm. A turnip, and the stick for digging
it, are seen in front of the horseman.

FIG. 298.

Fig. 299, 1742–'43.—"Killed-them-on-the-way-home-from-the-hunt
winter." The men were out hunting, and about
100 of their enemies came on horseback to attack
the camp, and had already surrounded it, when a
woman poked her head out of a lodge and said.
"They have all gone on the hunt. When I heard
you, I thought they had come back." She pointed
toward the hunting-ground, and the enemies going

FIG. 299.

in that direction, met the Dakotas, who killed many of them with their
spears, and put the rest to flight. Hoof-prints surround the circle of
lodges, and are on the trail to the hunting-ground.

Fig. 300, 1743–'44.—"The-Omahas-came-and-killed
them-in-the-night winter." They wounded many, but
killed only one. The Dakotas were all encamped together.

FIG. 300.

FIG. 301.

Fig. 301, 1744–'45.—"Brought-home-Omaha-horses winter.

FIG. 302.

Fig. 302, 1745–'46.—" Many-drying-scaffolds winter." It was even a better year for buffalo than 1723–'24.

FIG. 303.

Fig. 303, 1746–'47.—" Came-home-having-killed-one-Gros-Ventre winter.

FIG. 304.

Fig. 304, 1747–'48.—"Froze-to-death-at-the-hunt winter." The arrow pointing toward the buffalo head indicates they were hunting, and the crouching figure of the man, together with the snow above and below him, that he suffered severely from cold or froze to death.

FIG. 305.

Fig. 305, 1748–'49.—"Eat-frozen-fish winter." They discovered large numbers of fish frozen in the ice, and subsisted on them all winter.

FIG. 306.

Fig. 306, 1749–'50.—"Many-hole-camp-winter." The same explanation as for Fig. 260, for the year 1703–'04. The two figures are different in execution though the same in concept. There would, however, be little confusion in distinguishing two seasons of exceptional success in the hunt that were separated by forty-six years.

FIG. 307.

Fig. 307, 1750–'51.—" Killed-two-white-buffalo-cows winter." (Note by Dr. Corbusier: Two white buffalo are so rarely killed one season that the event is considered worthy of record. Most Indians regard the albinos among animals with the greatest reverance. The Ojibwas, who look upon a black loon as the most worthless of birds regard a white one as sacred.)

Fig. 308, 1751–'52.—" Omahas-came-and-killed-two-in-the-lodge winter." An Omaha war party surprised them in the night, shot into the lodge, wounding two, and then fled. The two shot died of their wounds.

FIG. 308.

Fig. 309, 1752–'53.—" Destroyed-three-lodges-of-Omahas winter." The Dakotas went to retaliate on the Omahas, and finding three lodges of them killed them. It will be noticed that in this figure the sign for Omaha is connected with the lodge, and in the preceding figure with the arrow.

FIG. 309.

Fig. 310, 1753–'54.—" Killed-two-Assiniboines-on-the-hunt winter."

FIG. 310.

Fig. 311, 1754–'55.—" Pawnees-shouted-over-the-people winter." The Pawnees (Rees) came at night, and standing on a bluff overlooking the Dakota village shot into it with arrows, killing one man, and alarmed the entire village by their shouts.

FIG. 311.

Fig. 312, 1755–'56.—" Killed-two-Pawnees-at-the-hunt winter." A war party of Dakotas surprised some Pawnee (Ree) hunters and killed two of them.

FIG. 312.

Fig. 313, 1756–'57.—" The-whole-people-were-pursued-and-two-killed winter." A tribe, name unknown, attacked and routed the whole band. The man in the figure is retreating, as is shown by his attitude; the arrow on his bow points backward at the enemy, from whom he is retreating. The two blood-stained arrows in his body mark the number killed.

FIG. 313.

FIG. 314.

Fig. 314, 1757–'58.—"Went-on-the-warpath-on-horseback-to-camp-of-enemy-but-killed-nothing winter." The lack of success may have been due to inexperience in mounted warfare as the Dakotas had probably for the first time secured a sufficient number of horses to mount a war party.

FIG. 315.

Fig. 315, 1758–'59.—"Killed-two-Omahas-who-came-to-the-camp-on-war-path winter."

FIG. 316.

Fig. 316, 1759–'60.—"War-parties-met-and-killed-a-few-on-both-sides winter." The attitude of the opposed figures of the Dakota and Gros Ventre and the footprints indicate that the parties met; the arrows in opposition, that they fought; and the blood-stained arrow in each man that some were killed on both sides.

FIG. 317.

Fig. 317, 1760–'61.—Assiniboins-came-and-attacked-the-camp-again winter;" or "Assiniboins-shot-arrows-through-the-camp winter."

FIG. 318.

Fig. 318, 1761–'62.—"Killed-six-Pawnees (Rees) winter." Besides the arrow sticking in the body another is flying near the head of the man figure, who has the tribal marks for Pawnee or Ree, as used in this record.

Fig. 319, 1762–'63.—"The-people-were-burnt winter." They were living somewhere east of their present country when a prairie fire de-

stroyed their entire village. Many of their children and a man and his
wife, who were on foot some distance away from the village,
were burned to death, as also were many of their horses.
All the people that could get to a long lake, which was
near by, saved themselves by jumping into it. Many of
these were badly burned about the thighs and legs, and
this circumstance gave rise to the name Sican-zhu, burnt
thigh (or simply burnt as translated Brulé by the French),

FIG. 319.

by which they have since been known, and also to the gesture sign, as
follows: "Rub the upper and outer part of the right thigh in a small
circle with the open right hand, fingers pointing downward."

Fig. 320, 1763–'64.—"Many-sticks-for-drying-beef winter. They dried so much meat that the village was crowded
with drying poles and scaffolds.

FIG. 320.

Fig. 321, 1764–'65.—"Stole-their-horses-while-they-
were-on-the-hunt winter." A Dakota war party
chanced to find a hunting party of Assiniboins asleep
and stole twenty of their horses. It was storming at
the time and horses had their packs on and were
tied. The marks which might appear to represent a
European saddle on the horse's back denote a pack
or load. Hunting is symbolized as before, by the
buffalo head struck by an arrow.

FIG. 321.

Fig. 322, 1765–'66.—"Killed-a-war-party-of-four-
Pawnees winter." The four Pawnees (Rees) made an
attack on the Dakota camp.

FIG. 322.

Fig. 323, 1766–'67.—"Brought-home-sixty-Assini-
boin-horses (one spotted) winter." They were all
the horses the Assiniboins had and were on an island
in the Missouri river, from which the Dakotas
cleverly stole them during a snowstorm.

FIG. 323.

FIG. 324.

Fig. 324, 1767–'68.—"Went-out-to-ease-themselves-with-their-bows-on winter." The Dakotas were in constant fear of an attack by enemies. When a man left his lodge after dark, even to answer the calls of nature, he carried his bows and arrows along with him and took good care not to go far away from the lodge. The squatting figure, etc., close to the lodge tells the story.

FIG. 325.

Fig. 325, 1768–'69.—"Two-horses-killed-something winter." A man who had gone over a hill just out of the village was run down by two mounted enemies who drove their spears into him and left him for dead, one of them leaving his spear sticking in the man's shoulder, as shown in the figure. He recovered, however. (Note by Dr. Corbusier: They frequently speak of persons who have been very ill and have recovered as dying and returning to life again, and have a gesture sign to express the idea.)

FIG. 326.

Fig. 326, 1769–'70.—"Attacked-the-camp-from-both-sides winter." A mounted war party—tribe unknown—attacked the village on two sides, and on each side killed a woman. The footprints of the enemies' horses and arrows on each side of the lodge, which represents the village, show the mode of attack.

FIG. 327.

Fig. 327, 1770–'71.—"Came-and-killed-the-lodges winter." The enemy came on horseback and assailed the Dakota lodges, which were pitched near together, spoiling some of them by cutting the hide coverings with their spears, but killing no one. They used spears only, but arrows are also depicted, as they symbolize attack. No blood is shown on the arrows, as only the lodges were "killed."

FIG. 328.

Fig. 328, 1771–'72.—"Swam-after-the-buffalo winter." In the spring the Dakotas secured a large supply of meat by swimming out and towing ashore buffalo that were floating past the village and which had fallen into the river on attempting to cross on the weak ice.

FIG. 329.

Fig. 329, 1772–'73.—"Killed-an-Assiniboin-and-his-wife winter."

FIG. 330.

Fig. 330, 1773–'74.—"Killed - two - Pawnee - boys-while-playing winter." A war party of Dakotas surprised two Pawnee (Ree) boys who were wrestling and killed them while they were on the ground.

FIG. 331.

Fig. 331, 1774–'75.—"Assiniboins-made-an-attack winter." They were cowardly, however, and soon retreated. Perhaps the two arrows of the Assiniboins compared with the one arrow of the attacked Dakotas suggests the cowardice.

FIG. 332.

Fig. 332, 1775–'76.—"Assiniboins-went-home-and-came-back-mad-to-make-a-fresh-attack winter." They were brave this time, being thoroughly aroused. They fought with bows and arrows only.

FIG. 333.

Fig. 333, 1776–'77.—"Killed - with - war - club-in-his-hand winter." A Dakota war club is in the man's hand and an enemy's arrow is entering his body.

FIG. 334.

Fig. 334, 1777–'78.—"Spent-the-winter - in - no - particular-place winter." They made no permanent camp, but wandered about from place to place.

Fig. 335, 1778–'79.—"Skinned-penis-used-in-the-game-of-haka winter." A Dakota named as mentioned was killed in
a fight with the Pawnees and his companions left
his body where they supposed it would not be found,
but the Pawnees found it and as it was frozen stiff
they dragged it into their camp and played haka with
it. The haka-stick which, in playing the game, they
cast after a ring, is represented on the right of the
man. This event marks 1777–'78 in the Winter Count
of American-Horse and 1779–'80 in that of Cloud-
Shield. The insult and disgrace made it remarkable.

FIG. 335.

FIG. 336.

Fig. 336, 1779–'80.—"Smallpox-used-them-up winter." The eruption and pains in the stomach and
bowels are shown as before.

FIG. 337.

Fig. 337, 1780–'81.—"Smallpox-used-them-up-again
winter." There is in this figure no sign for pain but
the spots alone are shown. An attempt to discrim-
inate and distinguish the year-devices is perceived.

FIG. 338.

Fig. 338, 1781–'82.—"Came-and-attacked-on-horse-
back-for-the-last-time winter." The name of the tribe
is not known, but it is the last time they ever attacked
the Dakotas.

FIG. 339.

Fig. 339, 1782–'83.—" Killed-the-man-with-the-scar-let-blanket-on winter." It is not known what tribe killed him.

FIG. 340.

Fig. 340, 1783–'84.—"Soldier-froze-to-death winter." The falling snow and the man's position with his legs drawn up to his abdomen, one hand in an armpit and the other in his mouth, are indicative of intense cold.

Fig. 341, 1784–'85.—"The-Oglala-took-the-cedar winter." During a great feast an Oglala declared he was wakan and could draw a cedar tree out of the ground. He had previously fastened the middle of a stick to the lower end of a cedar with a piece of the elastic ligament from the neck of the buffalo and then planted the tree with the stick crosswise beneath it. He went to this tree, dug away a little earth from around it and pulled it partly out of the ground and let it spring back again, saying "the cedar I drew from the earth has gone home again."

FIG. 341.

After he had gone some young men dug up the tree and exposed the shallow trick.

Fig. 342, 1785–'86.—"The-Cheyennes-killed-Shadow's-father winter." The umbrella signifies, shadow; the arrow which touches it, attacked; the three marks under the arrow (not shown in the copy), Cheyenne; the blood-stained arrow in the man's body, killed. Shadow's name and the umbrella in the figure intimate that he was the first Dakota to carry an umbrella. The advantages of the umbrella were soon recognized by them, and the first they obtained from the whites were highly prized. It is now considered an in-dispensable article in a Sioux outfit. They formerly wore a wreath of green leaves or carried green boughs, to shade them from the sun. The marks used for Chey-

FIG. 342

enne stand for the scars on their arms or stripes on their sleeves, which also gave rise to the gesture-sign for this tribe, see Fig. 495, infra.

FIG. 343

Fig. 343, 1786–'87. — "Iron-Head-Band-killed-on-war-path winter." They formerly carried burdens on their backs, hung from a band passed across the forehead. This man had a band of iron which is shown on his head. So said the interpreter, but probably the band was not of the metal iron. The word so translated has a double meaning and is connected with religious ideas of water, spirit, and the color blue.

Fig. 344, 1787–'88.—"Left-the-heyoka-man-behind winter." A certain

FIG. 344.

man was heyoka—that is, his mind was disordered and he went about the village bedecked with feathers singing to himself, and, while so, joined a war party. On sighting the enemy the party fled, and called to him to turn back also; as he was heyoka, he construed everything that was said to him as meaning the very opposite, and therefore, instead of turning back, he went forward and was killed. If they had only had sense enough to tell him to go on, he would then have run away, but the thoughtless people talked to him just as if he had been in an ordinary condition and of course were responsible for his death. The mental condition of this man and another device for the event are explained by other records (see Fig. 651).

FIG. 345.

Fig. 345, 1788–'89.—"Many-crows-died winter." Other records for the same year give as the explanation of the figure and the reason for its selection that the crows froze to death because of the intense cold.

FIG. 346.

Fig. 346, 1789–'90.—"Killed-two-Gros-Ventres-on-the-ice winter."

FIG. 347.

Fig. 347, 1790–'91.—"Carried-a-flag-about-with-them winter." They went to all the surrounding tribes with the flag, but for what purpose is unknown. So said the interpreter, but The-Flame's chart explains the figure by the statement: "The first United States flags in the country brought by United States troops."

Fig. 348, 1791–'92.—" Saw-a-white-woman winter." The dress of the woman indicates that she was not an Indian. This is obviously noted as being the first occasion when the Dakotas, or at least the bands which this record concerns, saw a white woman.

FIG. 348.

Fig. 349, 1792–'93.—" Camped-near-the-Gros-Ventres winter." They were engaged in a constant warfare during this time. A Gros Ventre dirt lodge, with the entrance in front, is depicted in the figure and on its roof is a Gros Ventre head.

FIG. 349.

Fig. 350, 1793–'94.—" Killed-a-long-haired-man-at-Rawhide-butte winter." The Dakotas attacked a village of 58 lodges and killed every soul in it. After the fight they found the body of a man whose hair was done up with deer-hide in large rolls, and, on cutting them open, found it was all real hair, very thick, and as long as a lodge-pole. [Mem. Catlin tells of a Crow called Long-Hair whose hair, by actual measurement, was 10 feet and 7 inches long.] The fight was at Rawhide butte (now so called by the whites), which the Dakotas named Buffalo-Hide butte, because they found so many buffalo hides in the lodges. According-

FIG. 350.

ing to Cloud-Shield, Long-Hair was killed in 1786–'87, and according to American-Horse, Long-Hair, a Cheyenne, was killed in 1796–'97.

Fig. 351, 1794–'95.—" Killed-the-little-faced-Pawnee winter." The Pawnee's face was long, flat, and narrow, like a man's hand, but he had the body of a large man.

White-Cow-Killer calls it: " Little-Face-killed winter."

FIG. 351.

FIG. 352.

Fig. 352, 1795–'96. — "The-Rees-stood-the-frozen-man-up-with-the-buffalo-stomach-in-his-hand winter." The body of a Dakota who had been killed in an encounter with the Rees (Pawnees), and had been left behind, frozen. The Rees dragged it into their village, propped it up with a stick, and hung a buffalo stomach filled with ice in one hand to make sport of it. The buffalo stomach was in common use at that time as a water-jug.

FIG. 353.

Fig. 353, 1796–'97.—"Wears-the-War-Bonnet-died winter." He did not die this winter, but received a wound in the abdomen from which the arrowhead could not be extracted, and he died of the "belly-ache" years after.

Fig. 354, 1897–'98.—"Took-the-God-Woman-captive winter." A Dakota war party captured a woman—tribe unknown—who, in order to

FIG. 354.

gain their respect, cried out, "I am a Wakan-Tanka," meaning that she belonged to God, where-upon they let her go unharmed. This is the origin of their name for God (Wakan Tanka, the Great Holy, or Supernatural One). They had never heard of a Supernatural Being before, but had offered their prayers to the sun, the earth, and many other objects, believing they were endowed with spirits. [Those are the remarks of Battiste Good, who is only half correct, being doubtless influenced by missionary teaching. The term is much older and signifies mystic or unknown.]

FIG. 355.

Fig. 355, 1798–'99.—"Many-women-died-in-child-birth winter." They died of bellyache. The convoluted sign for pain in the abdominal region has appeared before. Cloud-Shield's winter count for the same year records the same mortality among the women which was perhaps an epidemic of puerperal fever.

Fig. 356, 1799–1800.—"Don't-Eat-Buffalo Heart-made-a-commemoration-of-the-dead winter." A buffalo heart is represented above the man. Don't Eat is expressed by the gesture sign for negation, a part of which is indicated, and the line connecting the heart with his mouth. The red flag which is used in the ceremony is employed as its symbol. The name Don't Eat-Buffalo-Heart refers to the man for whom that viand is taboo, either by gentile rules or from personal visions. The religious ceremony of commemoration of the dead is mentioned elsewhere in this work, see Chapter XIV, section 6.

FIG. 356.

Fig. 357, 1800–'01.—"The-Good-White-Man-came winter." Seven white men came in the spring of the year to their village in a starving condition; after feeding them and treating them well, they allowed them to go on their way unmolested. The Dakotas [of the recorder's band] had heard of the whites, but had never seen any before. In the fall some more came, and with them, The-Good-White-Man, who is represented in the figure, and who was the first one to trade with them. They became very fond of him because of his fair dealings with them. The gesture made by his hands is similar to benediction, and suggests a part of the Indian gesture sign for "good."

FIG. 357.

Fig. 358, 1801–'02.—"Smallpox-used-them-up-again winter." The man figure is making a part of a common gesture sign for death, which consists substantially in changing the index from a perpendicular to a horizontal position and then pointing to the ground.

FIG. 358.

Fig. 359, 1802–'03.—"Brought-home-Pawnee-horses-with-iron-shoes-on winter." The Dakotas had not seen horseshoes before. This agrees with and explains Lone-Dog's Winter Count for the same year.

FIG. 359.

FIG. 360.

Fig. 360, 1803–'04.—"Brought-home-Pawnee-horses-with-their-hair-rough-and-curly winter." The curly hair is indicated by the curved marks. Lone-Dog's Winter Count for the same year records the same incident, but states that the curly horses were stolen from the Crows.

FIG. 361.

Fig. 361, 1804–'05.—" Sung-over-each-other-while-on-the-war-path winter." A war party while out made a large pipe and sang each other's praises. The use of an ornamented pipe in connection with the ceremonies of organizing a war party is mentioned in Chapter xv.

FIG. 362.

Fig. 362, 1805–'06.—"They-came-and-killed-eight winter." The enemy killed eight Dakotas, as shown by the arrow and the eight marks beneath it.

FIG. 363.

Fig. 363, 1806–'07.—"Killed-them-while-hunting-eagles winter." Some Dakota eagle-hunters were killed by enemies. See Lone-Dog's Winter Count for the same year.

Fig. 364, 1807–'08.—"Came-and-killed-man-with-red-shirt-on winter." Other records say that Red-Shirt killed in this year was an Uncpapa Dakota, and that he was killed by Arikaras.

FIG. 364.

Fig. 365, 1808–'09.—"Pawnees-(Rees)-killed-Blue-Blanket's-father winter." A blanket, which in the original record is blue, is represented above the arrow and across the man's body.

FIG. 365.

Fig. 366, 1809–'10.—"Little-Beaver's-house-burned winter." Little-Beaver was an English trader, and his trading house was a log one.

FIG. 366.

Fig. 367, 1810–'11.—"Brought-home-horse-with-his-tail-braided-with-eagle-feathers winter." They stole a band of horses beyond the South Platte. One of them was very fleet, and had his tail ornamented as described.

FIG. 367.

Fig. 368, 1811–'12.—"First-hunted-horses winter." The Dakotas caught wild horses in the Sand Hills with braided lariats.

FIG. 368.

FIG. 369.

Fig. 369, 1812–'13.—"Rees-killed-Big-in-the-Middle's-father winter." Other records call this warrior Big-Waist and Big-Belly.

FIG. 370.

Fig. 370, 1813–'14.—"Killed-six-Pawnees (Rees) winter." Six strokes are under the arrow, but are not shown in the copy.

FIG. 371.

Fig. 371, 1814–'15.—"Smashed-a-Kiowa's-head-in winter." The tomahawk with which it was done is sticking in the Kiowa's head.

FIG. 372.

Fig. 372, 1815–'16.—"The-Sans-Arcs-made-large-houses winter."

FIG. 373.

Fig. 373, 1816–'17.—"Lived-again-in-their-large-houses winter."

FIG. 374.

Fig. 374, 1817–'18.—"Chozé-built-a-house-of-dead-logs winter." The house was for trading purposes. The Frenchman's name is evidently a corruption.

Fig. 375, 1818–'19.—" Smallpox - used - them - up - again-winter." They at this time lived on the Little White river, about 20 miles above the Rosebud agency. The two fingers held up may mean the second time the fatal epidemic appeared in the par-ticular body of Indians concerned in the record.

Fig. 375.

Fig. 376, 1819–'20.—" Chozé - built-a-house-of-rot-ton-wood winter." Another trading house was built.

Fig. 376.

Fig. 377, 1820–'21.—"They-made-bands-of-strips-of-blanket-in-the-winter." These bands were of mixed colors and reached from the shoulders to the heels. They also made rattles of deer's hoofs by tying them to sticks with bead-covered strings. The man has a sash over his shoulders and a rattle in his hand.

Fig. 377.

Fig. 378, 1821–'22.—" Star-passed-by-with-loud-noise winter," "Much-whisky winter," and "Used-up-the-Omahas winter." In the figure the meteor, its pathway, and the cloud from which it came are shown. Whisky was fur-nished to them for the first time and without stint. It brought death to them in a new form, many since then having died from the excessive use of it, Red-Cloud's father among the number. Battiste Good, alias Wa-po 'stan-gi, more accurately Wa-po-cta^n-xi (Brown-Hat), historian and chief, was born. He says that Omaha bullets were whizzing through the

Fig. 378.

village and striking and piercing his mother's lodge as she brought him forth. Red-Cloud was also born. In the count of American-Horse for this year he makes no mention of the meteor, but strongly marks the whisky as the important figure for the winter.

Fig. 379, 1822–'23.—" Peeler-froze-his-leg winter." Peeler was a white trader, and his leg was frozen while he was on his way to or from the Missouri river. The name is explained by White Cow Killer's record as follows: "White-man-peels-the-stick-in-his-hand-broke-his-leg winter." He was probably a Yankee addicted to whittling.

Fig. 379.

FIG. 380.

Fig. 380, 1823–'24.—"General ——— -first-appeared-and - the-Dakotas-aided-in-an-attack-on-the-Rees winter." Also "Much-corn winter." The gun and the arrow in contact with the ear of corn show that both whites and Indians fought the Rees. This refers to Gen. Leavenworth's expedition against the Arikara in 1823, when several hundred Dakotas were his allies. This expedition is mentioned several times in this work.

FIG. 381.

Fig. 381, 1824–'25.—"Killed-two-picking-plums winter." A Dakota war party surprised and killed two Pawnees who were gathering plums.

Fig. 382, 1825–'26. — "Many - Yanktonais - drowned winter." The

FIG. 382.

river bottom on a bend of the Missouri river, where they were encamped, was suddenly submerged, when the ice broke and many women and children were drowned. All the Winter Counts refer to this flood.

Fig. 383, 1826–'27.—"Ate-a-whistle-and-died winter." Six Dakotas on the war path (shown by bow and arrow) had nearly perished with hunger, when they found and ate the rotting carcass of an old buffalo, on which the wolves had been feeding. They were seized soon after with pains in the stomach, the abdomen swelled, and gas poured from mouth and anus, and they died of a whistle or from eating a whistle. The sound of gas escaping from the mouth is illustrated in the figure.

FIG. 383.

FIG. 384.

Fig. 384, 1827–'28.—"Wore-snowshoes winter." The snow was very deep.

Fig. 385, 1828–'29.—"Killed-two-hundred-Gros Ventres (Hidatsas) winter."

FIG. 385.

Fig. 386, 1829–'30.—"Old-Speckled-Face-clung-to-his-son-in-law winter." The daughter of Speckled-Face, who was coming out second best in an altercation with her husband, called to her father for help. The latter ran and grabbed his son-in-law around the waist, and, crying "That is my daughter," stabbed him. The son-in-law fell and the old man fell on top of him, and, clinging to him, begged the lookers on to put an end to him also, as he wished to bear his beloved son-in-law com-

FIG. 386.

pany to the spirit land. No one, however, was in the humor to speed him on the journey, and he remained with the living.

Fig. 387, 1830–'31.—"Shot-many-white-buffalo-cows winter."

FIG. 387.

Fig. 388, 1831–'32.—"Killed-him-while-looking-about-on-the-hill winter." A Dakota, while watching for buffalo at Buffalo Gap, in the Black Hills, was shot by the Crows. The man is represented on a hill, which is dotted with pine trees and patches of grass. Battiste makes the grass blue. Blue and green are frequently confounded by other Indians than Battiste, and some tribes have but one name for the two colors.

FIG. 388.

Fig. 389, 1832–'33.—"Stiff-Leg-with-War-Bonnet-on-died winter." He was killed in an engagement with the Pawnees on the Platte river, in which the Brulés killed one hundred Pawnees.

FIG. 389.

FIG. 390.

Fig. 390, 1833–'34.—"Storm-of-stars winter." All the Winter Counts refer to this great meteoric display, which occurred on the night of November 12, 1833, and was seen over most of the United States.

FIG. 391.

Fig. 391, 1834–'35.—"Killed-the-Cheyenne-who-came-to-the-camp winter." A Cheyenne who stole into the village by night was detected and killed. The village was near what is now the Pine Ridge agency.

FIG. 392.

Fig. 392, 1835–'36.—"Killed-the-two-war-party leaders winter." A Dakota war party met one of Pawnees and killed two of their leaders, whereupon the rest ran.

FIG. 393.

Fig. 393, 1836–'37.—"Fight-on-the-ice winter." They fought with the Pawnees on the ice, on the Platte river, and killed seven of them. The two vertical marks, which are for the banks of the river, and the two opposed arrows, signify that the tribes were on opposite sides of the river.

FIG. 394.

Fig. 394, 1837–'38.—"Spread-out-killed winter." A Santee man, whose name is indicated by his spread hands, was killed by soldiers.

Fig. 395, 1838–'39.—"Came-and-killed-five-Oglálas winter." They were killed by Pawnees. The man in the figure has on a capote, the hood of which is drawn over his head. This garment is used here as a sign for war, as the Dakotas commonly wear it on their war expeditions.

FIG. 395.

Fig. 396, 1839–'40.—"Came-home-from-the-starve-to-death-war-path winter." All of the Dakota tribes united in an expedition against the Pawnees. They killed one hundred Pawnees, but nearly perished with hunger.

FIG. 396.

Fig. 397, 1840–'41.—"Came-and-killed-five-of-Little-Thunder's-brothers winter," and "Battiste-alone-returns winter." The five were killed in an encounter with the Pawnees. Battiste Good was the only one of the party to escape. The capote is shown again.

FIG. 397.

Fig. 398, 1841–'42.—"Pointer-made-a-commemoration-of-the-dead winter." Also "Deep-snow winter." The extended index denotes the man's name, the ring and spots deep snow.

FIG. 398.

Fig. 399, 1842–'43.—"Killed-four-lodges-of-Shoshoni-and-brought-home-many-horses winter."

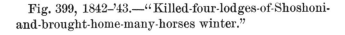

FIG. 399.

FIG. 400.

Fig. 400, 1843–'44.—"Brought-home-the-magic-arrow winter." This arrow originally belonged to the Cheyennes from whom the Pawnees stole it. The Dakotas captured it this winter from the Pawnees and the Cheyennes then redeemed it for one hundred horses.

FIG. 401.

Fig. 401, 1844–'45.—"The-Crows-came-and-killed-thirty-eight-Oglálas winter." The Oglálas were on the warpath, as indicated by the capote.

FIG. 402.

Fig. 402, 1845–'46.—"Broke-out-on-faces-had-sore-throats-and-camped-under-the-bluff winter." "Also-had-bellyache." The position of the camp is shown, also the suggestive attitude of the man.

FIG. 403.

Fig. 403, 1846–'47.—"Winter-camp-broke-his-neck winter." He was thrown from his horse while on a hunt. The red on his neck is the break.

FIG. 404.

Fig. 404, 1847–'48.—"The-Teal-broke-his-leg winter." His arm is lengthened to direct attention to his leg. The Chinese radical and phonetic character for the same concept, Fig. 1193, infra, may be compared, as also Fig. 231, supra.

Fig. 405, 1848–'49.—"Killed-the-hermaphrodite winter" and "Big-horse-stealing winter." They captured a Crow who pretended to be a woman, but who proved to be a man, and they killed him. It is probable that this was one of the men, not uncommon among the Indian tribes, who adopt the dress and occupation of women. This is sometimes compulsory from failure to pass an ordeal or from exhibition of cowardice. Eight hundred horses were stolen from the Dakotas, but seven hundred of them were recovered. The Crows killed one Dakota, as is indicated by the arrow in contact with the red spot in the hoof print.

FIG. 405.

Fig. 406, 1849–'50.—"Brought-the-Crows-to-a stand winter." This was done at Crow Butte, near Camp Robinson, Nebraska. It is said that a party of Crows, who were flying from the Dakotas, took refuge on the Butte about dark and that the Dakotas surrounded them, confident of capturing them the next morning, but the Crows escaped during the night, very much to the chagrin of the Dakotas. The Crow's head is just visible on the summit of the hill, as if the body had gone down.

FIG. 406.

Fig. 407, 1850–'51.—"The-big-smallpox winter."

FIG. 407.

Fig. 408, 1851–'52.—"First-issue-of-goods winter." The colored patches outside the circle are at the four cardinal points, the colored patches inside the circle are meant for blankets and the other articles issued, and the circle of strokes the people sitting. The Dakotas were told that fifty-five years after that issue they would have to cultivate the ground, and they understood that they would not be required to do it before.

FIG. 408.

Fig. 409, 1852–'53.—"Deep-snow-used-up-the-horses winter." The spots around the horses represent snow.

FIG. 409.

FIG. 410.

Fig. 410, 1853–'54.—"Cross-Bear-died-on-the-hunt winter." The travail means they moved; the buffalo, to hunt buffalo; the bear with mouth open and paw advanced, Cross-Bear; the stomach and intestines, took the bellyache and died. The gesture sign for bear is made as follows: Slightly crook the thumbs and little fingers, and nearly close the other fingers; then, with their backs upward, hold the hands a little in advance of the body or throw them several times quickly forward a few inches. The sign is sometimes made with one hand only.

For explanation of the word "travail," applied to the Indian sledge made of the joined tent poles, see Fig. 764 and accompanying remarks.

FIG. 411.

Fig. 411, 1854–'55.—"Killed-five-Assiniboins winter." The Dakotas are ashamed of the part they took in the following deplorable occurrence and it is not therefore noted in the record, although it really marks the year. In consequence of a misunderstanding in regard to an old foot-sore cow, which had been abandoned on the road by some emigrants and which the Dakotas had innocently appropriated, Lieut. Grattan, Sixth U. S. Infantry, killed Conquering Bear (Mato-way′uhi, Startling Bear properly) about ten miles east of Fort Laramie, August 19, 1854. The Dakotas then, in retaliation, massacred Lieut. Grattan and the thirty men of Company G, Sixth U. S. Infantry, he had with him.

The figure without the above statement tells the simple story about the killing of five Assiniboins who are denoted by the usual tribal sign, the number being designated by the five strokes below the arrow.

FIG. 412.

Fig. 412, 1855–'56.—"Little-Thunder-and-Battiste-Good-and-others-taken-prisoners-at-Ash-Hollow-on-the Blue-creek winter," and one hundred and thirty Dakotas were killed by the white soldiers. Also called "Many-sacrificial-flags winter." The last-mentioned name for the winter is explained by other records and by Executive Document No. 94, Thirty-fourth Congress, first session, Senate, to refer to a council held on March 18, 1856, by Brevet Brig. Gen. W. S. Harney, U. S. Army, with nine of the bands of the Dakotas.

FIG. 413.

Fig. 413, 1856–'57.—"Bad-Four-Bear-trades-with-Battiste-Good-for-furs-all winter." Bad-Four-Bear, a white trader, is represented sitting smoking a pipe in front of Battiste's tipi under a bluff at Fort Robinson, Nebraska.

FIG. 414.

Fig. 414, 1857–'58.—"Hunted-bulls-only winter." They found but few cows, the buffalo being composed principally of bulls. The travail is shown.

Fig. 415, 1858–'59.—"Many-Navajo-blankets winter."
A Navajo blanket is shown in the figure. Several of
the records agree in the explanation about the bringing of these blankets at that time.

Fig. 415.

Fig. 416, 1859–'60.—"Came-and-killed-Big-Crow winter." The two marks under the arrow indicate that
two were killed.

Fig. 416.

Fig. 417, 1860–'61.—"Broke-out-with-rash-and-died-
with-pains-in-the-stomach winter."

Fig. 417.

Fig. 418, 1861–'62.—"Killed-Spotted-Horse winter."
Spotted Horse and another Crow came and stole many
horses from the Dakotas, who followed them, killed
them, and recovered their horses.

Fig. 418.

Fig. 419, 1862–'63.—"Cut-up-the-boy-in-the-camp
winter." The Crows came to the lodges and cut up the
boy while the people were away. The knife above his
head shows that he was cut to pieces.

Fig. 419.

Fig. 420, 1863–'64.—"Crows-came-and-killed-eight
winter." Some of the eight were Cheyennes. The
marks below the arrow represent the killed.

Fig. 420.

Fig. 421, 1864–'65.—"Roaster-made-a-commemora-
tion-of-the-dead winter." A piece of roasted meat is
shown on the stick in the man's hand. The Dakotas
roast meat on a stick held in front of the fire.

Fig. 421.

FIG. 422.

Fig. 422, 1865–'66.—"Deep-snow-used-up-the-horses winter." The horse is obviously in a deplorable condition.

FIG. 423.

Fig. 423, 1866–'67.—"Beaver's-Ears-killed winter."

FIG. 424.

Fig. 424, 1867–'68.—"Battiste-Good-made-peace-with-General-Harney-for-the-people winter." This refers to the great Dakota treaty of 1868 in which other general officers besides Gen. Harney were active and other Indian chiefs much more important than Battiste took part. The assumption of his intercession is an exhibition of boasting.

FIG. 425.

Fig. 425, 1868–'69.—"Killed-Long-Fish winter" and "Killed-fifteen winter." The Crows killed fifteen Sans Arcs and Long-Fish also, a Lower Brulé. The long fish is shown attached by a line to the mouth of the man figure in the manner that personal names are frequently portrayed in this paper.

FIG. 426.

Fig. 426, 1869–'70.—"Trees-killed-them winter." A tree falling on a lodge killed a woman.

FIG. 427.

Fig. 427, 1870–'71.—"Came-and-killed-High-Back-Bone winter." He was a chief. The Crows and Shoshoni shot him at long range, and the pistol with which he was armed was of no service to him.

FIG. 428.

Fig. 428, 1871–'72.—"Gray-Bear-died winter." He died of the bellyache.

FIG. 429.

Fig. 429, 1872–'73.—"Issue-year winter." A blanket is shown near the tipi. A blanket is often used as the symbol for issue of goods by the United States Government.

FIG. 430.

Fig. 430, 1873–'74.—"Measles-and-sickness-used-up-the-people winter."

FIG. 431.

Fig. 431, 1874–'75.—"Utes-stole-horses winter." They stole five hundred horses. The Utes are called "black men," hence the man in the figure is represented as black. He is throwing his lariat in the direction of the hoof prints.

FIG. 432.

Fig. 432, 1875–'76.—"Bull-Head-made-a-commemoration-of-the-dead winter."

FIG. 433.

Fig. 433, 1876–'77.—"Female-Elk-Walks-Crying-died winter." For some explanation of this figure see Lone Dog's Winter Count for 1860–'61.

FIG. 434.

Fig. 434, 1877–'78. — "Crazy-Horse-came-to-make-peace-and-was-killed-with-his-hands-stretched-out winter." This refers to the well-known killing of the chief Crazy-Horse while a prisoner.

Fig. 435, 1878–'79.—"Brought-the-Cheyennes-back-and-killed-them-in-the-house winter." The Cheyennes are shown in prison surrounded by blood stains, and with guns pointing toward them. The Cheyennes referred to are those who left the Indian Territory in 1878 and made such a determined effort to reach their people in the north, and who, after committing many atrocities, were captured and taken to Fort Robinson, Nebraska. They broke from the house in which they were confined and attempted to escape January 9, 1879. Many of them were killed; it was reported at the time among the Dakotas that they were massacred in their prison by the troops.

FIG. 435.

FIG. 436.

Fig. 436, 1879–'80.—"Sent-the-boys-and-girls-to-school winter." A boy with a pen in his hand is represented in the picture.

CHAPTER XI.

NOTICES.

This is an important division of the purposes for which pictographs are used. The pictographs and the objective devices antecedent to them under this head may be grouped as follows: 1st. Notice of visit, departure, and direction. 2d. Direction by drawing topographic features. 3d. Notice of condition. 4th. Warning and guidance.

SECTION 1.

NOTICE OF VISIT, DEPARTURE, AND DIRECTION.

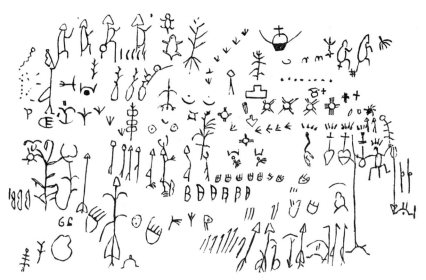

FIG. 437.—Petroglyphs at Oakley spring, Arizona.

Mr. G. K. Gilbert, of the U. S. Geological Survey, discovered drawings at Oakley spring, Yavapai County, Arizona, in 1878. He remarks that an Oraibi chief explained them to him and said that the "Mokis make excursions to a locality in the canyon of the Colorado Chiquito to get salt. On their return they stop at Oakley spring and each Indian makes a picture on the rock. Each Indian draws his crest or totem, the symbol of his gens (?). He draws it once, and once only, at each visit." Mr. Gilbert adds, further, that—

There are probably some exceptions to this, but the drawings show its general truth. There are a great many repetitions of the same sign and from two to ten will often appear in a row. In several instances I saw the end drawings of a row quite fresh while the others were not so. Much of the work seems to have been performed by pounding with a hard point, but a few pictures are scratched on. Many drawings are weather-worn beyond recognition, and others are so fresh that the dust left by the tool has not been washed away by rain. Oakley spring is at the base of the Vermilion cliff, and the etchings are on fallen blocks of sandstone, a homogeneous, massive, soft sandstone. Tubi, the Oraibi chief above referred to, says his totem is the rain cloud, but it will be made no more, as he is the last survivor of the gens.

A group from Oakley spring, of which Fig. 437 is a copy, furnished by Mr. Gilbert, measures 6 feet in length and 4 feet in height. Interpretations of several of the separated characters are given in Chapter XXI, infra.

Champlain (b) reports:

Quelque marque ou signal par où ayont passé leurs ennemis, ou leurs amis, ce qu'ils cognoissent par de certaines marques que les chefs se donnent d'une nation a l'autre, qui ne sont pas toujours semblables, s'advertisans de temps en temps quand ils en changent; et par ce moyen ils recognoissent si ce sont amis ou ennemis qui ont passé.

A notice of departure, direction, and purpose made in 1810 by Algonquins, of the St. Lawrence River, is described by John Merrick in the Collections of the Maine Historical Society (a), of which the following is an abstract:

It was drawn with charcoal on a chip cut from a spruce tree and wedged firmly into the top of a stake. It represented two male Indians paddling a canoe in an attitude of great exertion, and in the canoe were bundles of baggage and a squaw with a papoose; over all was a bird on the wing ascertained to be a loon. The whole was interpreted by an Indian pilot on the St. Lawrence, to be a Wickheegan or Awickheegan, and that it was left by a party of Indians for the information of their friends. The attitude of exertion showed that the party, consisting of two men, a woman, and a child, were going upstream. They intended to remain during the whole period allotted by Indians to the kind of hunting which was then in season, because they had all their furniture and family in the canoe. The loon expressed the intention to go without stopping anywhere before they arrived at the hunting ground, as the loon, from the shortness of its legs, walking with great difficulty, never alighted on its way.

The following account is from Doc. Hist. N. Y. (a).

When they go to war and wish to inform those of the party who may pass their path, they make a representation of the animal of their tribe, with a hatchet in his dexter paw; sometimes a saber or a club; and if there be a number of tribes together of the same party, each draws the animal of his tribe, and their number, all on a tree from which they remove the bark. The animal of the tribe which heads the expedition is always the foremost.

The three following figures show the actual use of the wikhegan by the Abnaki in the last generation. Wikhegan is a Passamaquoddy word which corresponds in meaning nearly to our missive, or letter, being intelligence conveyed to persons at a distance by marks on a piece of birch bark, which may be either sent to the person or party with whom it is desired to hold communication, or may be left in a conspicuous place for such persons to notice on their expected arrival. In the cases now figured the wikhegan was left as notice of departure and direction. They were made at different times by the brother, now dead, of Big Raven, baptized as Noel Joseph, who lived all alone on Long Lake, a few miles from Princeton, Maine. He would not have anything to do with civilization, and subsisted by hunting and fishing in the old fashion, nor would he learn a word of French or English. When he would go on any long expedition his custom was to tie to a stick conspicuously attached to his wigwam a small roll of birch bark, with the wikhegan on it for the information of his friends.

The upper device of Fig. 438 means, I am going across the lake to hunt deer.

The middle device means, I am going towards the lake and will turn off at the point where there is a pointer, before reaching the lake.

The lower device means, I am going hunting—will be gone all winter, the last information indicated by snowshoes and packed sledge.

FIG. 438.—Hunting notices.

The following description of a pictograph on the Pacific coast is extracted from Dr. Gibbs' (*a*) account, "Tribes of Western Washington," etc., Contrib. to N. A. Ethn. I, p. 222, of the Sound tribes.

A party of Snakes are going to hunt strayed horses. A figure of a man, with a long queue or scalp lock, reaching to his heels, denoted Shoshone; that tribe being in the habit of braiding horse or other hair into their own in that manner. A number of marks follow, signifying the strength of the party. A footprint, pointing in the direction they take, shows their course, and a hoof mark turned backward, that they expect to return with animals. If well armed, and expecting a possible attack, a little powder mixed with sand tells that they are ready, or a square dotted about the figures indicates that they have fortified. These pictographs are often an object of study to decipher the true meaning. The shrewder or more experienced old men consult over them. It is not everyone that is sufficiently versed in the subject to decide correctly.

Dr. W. J. Hoffman obtained the original of the accompanying drawing, Fig. 439, from Naumoff, an Alaskan, in San Francisco in 1882; also the interpretation.

The drawing was in imitation of similar ones made by the natives to inform their visitors or friends of their departure for a purpose designated. They are depicted upon strips of wood, which are placed in conspicuous places near the doors of the habitations.

FIG. 439.—Alaskan notice of hunt.

The following is the explanation of the characters: *a*, the speaker, with the right hand indicating himself and with the left pointing in the direction to be taken; *b*, holding a boat-paddle, going by boat; *c*, the right hand to the side of the head, to denote sleep, and the left elevated with one finger erect to signify one night; *d*, a circle with two marks in the middle, signifying an island with huts upon it; *e*, same as *a*; *f*, a circle to denote another island; *g*, same as *c*, with an additional finger elevated, signifying two nights; *h*, the speaker, with his harpoon, making the sign of a sea-lion with the left hand. The flat hand is held edgewise with the thumb elevated, then pushed outward from the body in a slightly downward curve. At *i* is represented a sea-lion; *j*, shooting with bow and arrow; *k*, the boat with two persons in it, the paddles projecting downward; *l*, the winter or permanent habitation of the speaker.

The following, Fig. 440, is of a similar nature to the preceding, and was obtained under similar circumstances.

FIG. 440.—Alaskan notice of departure.

The explanation of the above characters is as follows: ·

The letters *a, c, e, g*, represent the person spoken to.

b. Indicates the speaker with his right hand to the side or breast, indicating *self*, the left hand pointing in the direction in which he is going.

d. Both hands elevated, with fingers and thumbs signifies many, according to the informant. When the hands are thus held up, in sign-language, it signifies *ten*, but when they are brought toward and backward from one another, *many*.

f. The right hand is placed to the head to denote sleep—*many sleeps*, or, in other words, *many nights and days;* the left hand points downward, *at that place.*

h. The right hand is directed toward the starting point, while the left is brought upward toward the head—*to go home*, or *whence he came.*

The drawing presented in Fig. 441 was made by a native Alaskan, and represents information to the effect that the artist contemplates making a journey to hunt deer. The drawing is made upon a narrow strip of wood, and placed on or near the door of the house, where visitors will readily perceive it.

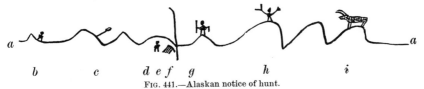

a b c d e f g h i a

FIG. 441.—Alaskan notice of hunt.

In this figure the curves a a represent the contour lines of the country and mountain peaks; b, native going away from home; c, stick placed on hilltop, with bunch of grass attached, pointing in the direction he has taken; d, native of another settlement, with whom the traveler remained over night; e, lodge; f, line representing the end of the first day, i. e., the time between two days; rest; g, traveler again on the way; h, making signal that on second day (right hand raised with two extended fingers) he saw game (deer, i,) on a hilltop, which he secured, so terminating his journey; i, deer.

Figs. 442, 443, and 444 were drawn by Naumoff and signify " Have gone home."

FIG. 442.—Alaskan notice of direction.

His explanation of this figure is as follows:

When one of a hunting party is about to return home and wishes to inform his companions that he has started, he ascends the hilltop nearest to which they became separated, where he ties a bunch of grass or other light-colored material to the top of a long stick or pole. The lower end of the stick is placed firmly in the ground, leaning in the direction taken. When another hill is ascended, another stick with similar attachment is erected, again leaning in the direction to be taken. These sticks are placed at proper intervals until the village is sighted. This device is employed by Southern Alaskan Indians.

He explained Fig. 443 as follows:

Seal hunters thus inform their comrades that they have returned to the settlement. The first to return to the regular landing place sometimes sticks a piece of wood into the ground, leaning toward the village, upon which is drawn or scratched the outline of a baidarka, or skin canoe, heading toward one or more outlines of lodges, signifying that the occupants of the boat have gone toward their homes.

FIG. 443.—Alaskan notice of direction.

This device is used by coast natives of Southern Alaska and Kadiak. He explained Fig. 444 as follows:

When hunters become separated, the one first returning to the forks of the trail puts a piece of wood in the ground, on the top of which he makes an incision, into which a short piece of wood is secured horizontally, so as to point in the direction taken.

Fig. 444.—Alaskan notice of direction.

Maj. Long—Keating's Long (*a*)—says:

When we stopped to dine, White Thunder (the Winnebago chief that accompanied me), suspecting that the rest of his party were in the neighborhood, requested a piece of paper, pen, and ink, to communicate to them the intelligence of his having come up with me. He then seated himself and drew three rude figures, which, at my request, he explained to me. The first represented my boat with a mast and flag, with three benches of oars and a helmsman. To show that we were Americans, our heads were represented by a rude cross, indicating that we wore hats. The representation of himself was a rude figure of a bear over a kind of cipher, representing a hunting ground. The second figure was designed to show that his wife was with him; the device was a boat with a squaw seated in it; over her head lines were drawn in a zigzag direction, indicating that she was the wife of White Thunder. The third was a boat with a bear sitting at the helm, showing that an Indian of that name [or of the bear gens] had been seen on his way up the river and had given intelligence where the party were. This paper he set up at the mouth of Kickapoo creek, up which the party had gone on a hunting trip.

An ingenious mode of giving intelligence is practiced at this day by the Abnaki, as reported by H. L. Masta, chief of that tribe, lately living at Pierreville, Quebec. When they are in the woods, to say "I am going to the east," a stick is stuck in the ground pointing in that direction, Fig. 445, *a*. "I am not gone far," another stick is stuck across the former, close to the ground, same figure, *b*. "Gone far" is the reverse, same figure, *c*. The number of days' journey of proposed absence is shown by the same number of sticks across the first; thus, same figure, *d*, signifies five days' journey.

Fig. 446, scratched on birch bark, was given to the present writer at Fredericton, New Brunswick, in August, 1888, by Gabriel Acquin, an Amalecite, then 66 years old, who spoke English quite well. The circumstances under which it was made and used are in the Amalecite's words, as follows:

"When I was about 18 years old I lived at a village 11 miles above Fredericton and went with canoe and gun. I canoed down to Washademoak lake, about 40 miles below Fredericton; then took river until it became too narrow for canoe; then 'carried' to Buctoos river; followed down to bay of Chaleur; went up the northwest Mirimachi, and

'carried' into the Nepisigiut.   There spent the summer.   On that river
met a friend of my time; we camped there.

"One time while I was away my friend had gone down the river by
himself and had not left any wikhe'gan for me.   I had planned to go off
and left for him this wikhe'gan, to tell where I would be and how long
gone.   The wigwam at the lower left-hand corner showed the one used
by us, with the river near it.   The six notches over the door of the
wigwam meant that I would be gone six days.   The canoe and man

FIG. 445.—Abnaki notice of direction.

nearest to the wigwam referred to my friend, who had gone in the opposite direction to that I intended to travel.   Next to it I was represented
in my own canoe, with rain falling, to show the day I started, which
was very rainy.   Then the canoe carried by me by a trail through woods
shows the 'carry' to Nictaux lake, beside which is a very big mountain.
I stayed at that lake for six days, counting the outgoing and returning.
As I had put the wikhe'gan in the wigwam before I started, my friend
on his return understood all about me, and, counting six from and in-

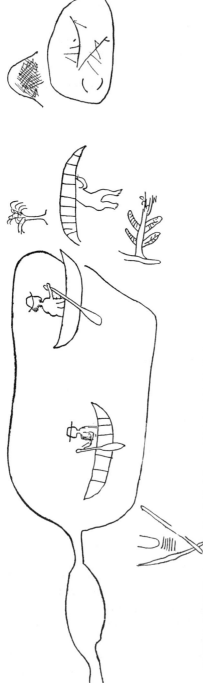

FIG. 446.—Amalecite notice of trip.

cluding the rainy day, knew just when I was coming back, and was waiting for me."

The chief point of interest in this notice is the ingenious mode of fixing the date of departure. The marks for rain are nearly obliterated, but it flows from the man's hair. The topograpyh is also delineated.

The following is extracted from James Long's Expedition (b):

On the bank of the Platte river was a semicircular row of sixteen bison skulls, with their noses pointing down the river. Near the center of the circle which this row would describe, if continued, was another skull marked with a number of red lines.

Our interpreter informed us that this arrangement of skulls and other marks here discovered were designed to communicate the following information, namely, that the camp had been occupied by a war party of the Skeeree or Pawnee Loup Indians, who had lately come from an excursion against the Cumancias, Ietans, or some of the western tribes. The number of red lines traced on the painted skull indicated the number of the party to have been thirty-six; the position in which the skulls were placed, that they were on their return to their own country. Two small rods stuck in the ground, with a few hairs tied in two parcels to the end of each, signified that four scalps had been taken.

When a hunting party of the Hidatsa arrived at any temporary camping ground from which some of them had left on a short reconnoitering expedition, the remainder, having occasion to move, erect a pole and cause it to lean in the direction taken. At the foot of this pole a buffalo shoulder blade or other flat bone is placed, upon which is depicted the reason of departure; e. g. should buffalo or antelope be seen, the animal is drawn with a piece of charred wood or red lead.

When a Hidatsa party has gone on the warpath, and a certain number is detailed ·to take another direction, the point of separation is taken as the rendezvous. After the return of the first party to the rendezvous, should the second not come up in a reasonable length of time, they will set sticks in the ground leaning in the direction to be taken, and notches are cut into the upper ends of the sticks to represent the number of nights spent there by the waiting party.

A party of Hidatsa who may be away from home for any purpose whatever often appoint a rendezvous, from which point they return to their respective lodges. Should one of the party return to the rendezvous before any others and wish to make a special trip, he will, for the information of the others, place a stick of about 3 or 4 feet in length in the ground, upon the upper end of which a notch is cut, or perhaps a split made for the reception of a thinner piece of twig or branch having a length of about a foot. This horizontal top piece is inserted at one end, so that the whole may point in the direction to be taken. Should he wish to say that the trail would turn at a right angle, to either side, at about half the distance of the whole journey in prospect, the horizontal branch is either bent in that direction or a naturally curved branch is selected having the turn at the middle of its entire length,

FIG. 447.—Ojibwa notice of direction.

thus corresponding to the turn in the trail. Any direction can be indicated by curves in the top branch.

No prescribed system of characters is used at the present time by the Ojibwa, in the indication of direction or travel. When anyone leaves camp or home for any particular hunting or berry ground, a concerted arrangement is made by which only those interested can, with any certainty, recognize "blaze" or trail marks.

Three characters cut upon the bark of large pine trees observed in the forest near Red Lake, Minnesota, are shown in Fig. 447. The Ojibwa using such a mark will continue on a trail leading from his home, until he leaves the trail, when a conspicuous tree, or in its absence a piece of wood or bark, is selected upon which a human figure is cut, with one arm elevated and pointing in the direction to be taken. These figures measure about 18 inches in height. Those represented on the two sides of the copy were cut into the bark of a "jack pine" without coloration, and the one in the middle had been rubbed with red chalk upon the wood of the trunk after the bark had been removed and the incision made. The middle figure indicates the direction by its bearings, although the pointers are differently arranged.

Plain sticks are sometimes used by the Ojibwa to indicate direction. These vary in length according to the fancy of the person and the requirements of the case. They are stuck into the ground, and lean in the direction to which notice is invited.

When a preconcerted arrangement is made, scrolls of birch bark are used, upon which important geographic features are delineated, so that the reader can, with little difficulty, learn the course taken by the traveler. For instance, a hunter upon leaving his home, deposits there a scroll bearing marks such as appear in Fig. 448:

FIG. 448.—Ojibwa notice of direction.

a is a stream to be followed to a lake *b*, where the hunter will erect his lodge *c*, during his stay. The do-dém (totem) is added, used between persons or parties communicating, to show who was the one that drew it. It is in the nature of a signature.

Fig. 449 shows a still existing use of the wikhegan between a Penobscot Indian and his nephew. It is copied from the original, incised on birch bark, by Nicholas Francis, a Penobscot, of Oldtown, Maine, which was obtained and kindly presented by Miss A. L. Alger of Boston.

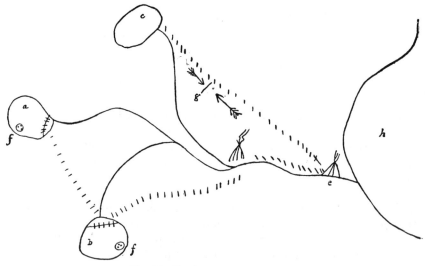

FIG. 449.—Penobscot notice of direction.

Pitalo (Roaring Lion), English name, Noel Lyon, and his old uncle, aged over 70 years, went trapping for beaver in 1885 and camped at *d*, near Moosehead Lake *h*, having their supply tent at *e*. They visited the ponds *a* and *b* and knew there were beaver there, and set traps for them, *f f*. The beaver dams are also shown extending across the outlets of the streams. Noel came back from pond *b* one day to the

camping tent and found this birch-bark wikhegan made by the old
uncle, who still used the pictographic method, as he does not know how
to write, and by this Noel knew his uncle had gone to pond *c* to see if
there were any beaver there and would be gone one night, the latter
expressed by one line *g* drawn between the two arrows pointing in opposite directions, showing the going and returning on the same trail.

The notable part of the above description is that the wikhegan consisted of the chart of the geographic features before traversed by the
two trappers, with the addition of new features of the country undoubtedly known to both of the Indians, but not before visited in the present
expedition. This addition exhibited the departure, its intent, direction,
and duration.

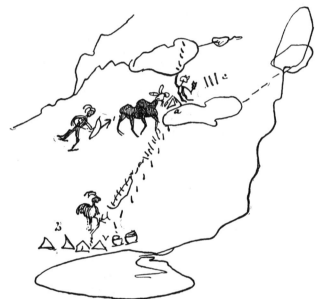

FIG. 450.—Passamaquoddy notice of direction.

Sapiel Selmo, a chief of the Passamaquoddy tribe, who gave to the
writer the wikhegan copied as Fig. 450, in 1887, was then a very aged
man and has since died. He lived at Pleasant point, 7 miles north of
Eastport, Maine. He was the son of a noted chief, Selmo Soctomah
(a corruption of St. Thomas), who, as shown by a certificate exhibited,
commanded 600 Passamaquoddy Indians in the Revolutionary war.
When a young man Sapiel, with his father, had a temporary camp, *a*,
at Machias Lake. He left his father and went to their permanent
home at Pleasant Point, *b*, to get meat, and then returned to the first
camp (route shown by double track) and found that his father had
gone, but that he had left in the temporary wigwam the wikhegan on
birch bark, showing that he had killed one moose, the meat of which
Sapiel found in the snow, and that the father was going to hunt moose

on the other lake (East Machias lake) and would camp there three days, shown by the same number of strokes at *c;* so he waited for him until he came back.

Josiah Gregg (*a*) says of the Plains tribes:

When traveling they will also pile heaps of stones upon mounds or conspicuous points so arranged as to be understood by their passing comrades; and sometimes they set up the bleached buffalo heads, which are everywhere scattered over those plains, to indicate the direction of their march, and many other facts which may be communicated by those simple signs.

Putnam (*a*) gives one example of this character:

A family of five persons were killed—a tall man, a short, fat woman, and three children—at some place to the north. Five sticks were cut of various lengths. The longest being forked or split indicated the man, the thick short one the woman, and three of smaller sizes and lengths the children. They were all scalped, as is shown by the peeling of the bark. There were thirteen Indians, as we are informed by the stick with stripes and thirteen notches; and they have fled south with two prisoners, as we judge from the pointer and little strips of bark seemingly tied together. Sometimes all the intimations would be on one stick or piece of bark. A spy finding, at places well known, some of these mysterious articles, would bring them to the station, where a consultation would be held and conclusion drawn as to the meaning. A spy or hunter would intimate to his friend his want of powder or lead or other want and the place at which he would look for supplies.

Hind (*a*) speaks of a special form of notice by the natives of the Labrador peninsula:

To indicate their speed and direction on a march, the Nasquapees of the Labrador peninsula thrust a stick in the ground, with a tuft of grass at the top, pointing toward their line of route, and they show the rate at which they are traveling by the greater or less inclination of the stick. This mode of communicating intelligence to those who may follow is universal among Indians; but the excellent and simple contrivance for describing the speed at which they travel is not generally employed as far as I am aware, by other nations.

Mr. Charles G. Leland, in a letter, tells that the English gypsies, at a crossroad, drew the ordinary Latin cross with the long arm pointing in the direction taken. Others pulled up three bunches of grass by the roots and laid the green points in the direction. Others again, at the present time, take a small stick and set it up inclining at an angle of 45 degrees in the line of travel.

Dr. George M. Dawson (*a*) reports of the Shuswap people of British Columbia—

A rag of clothing, particularly a small piece or pieces of colored or other easily recognizable material from a woman's dress, left in a forked twig, indicates that a person or party of persons has passed. If the stick stands upright, it means that the hour was noon, if inclined it may either point to the direction of the sun at the time or show the direction in which the person or party went. If it is desired to show both, a larger stick points to the position of the sun, a smaller to that of the route followed. If those for whose information the signs are left are likely to arrive after an interval of several days, a handful of fresh grass or a leafy branch may be left, from the condition of which an estimate of the time which has elapsed can be formed. Such signs are usually placed near the site of the camp fire.

The device to indicate the time of depositing the notice may be compared with that shown in Fig. 446.

SECTION 2.

DIRECTION BY DRAWING TOPOGRAPHIC FEATURES.

Fig. 451 is a notice by Micmac scouts, which tribe was then at war with the Passamaquoddy, erected on a tree, to warn the rest of the tribe that ten Passamaquoddy Indians have been observed in canoes on the lake going toward the outlet of the lake and probably down the river. The Passamaquoddy tribal pictograph is shown and the whole topography is correctly drawn.

Notes in literature relating to the skill of the North American Indians in delineating geographic features are very frequent. The following are selected for reference:

Champlain (c), in 1605, described how the natives on the coast drew with charcoal its bays, capes, and the mouths of rivers with such accuracy that Massachusetts bay and Merrimack river have been identified.

FIG. 451.—Micmac notice of direction.

Lafitau (d) says of the northeastern tribes of Indians—

Ils tracent grossierement sur des écorces, ou sur le sable, des Cartes exactes, et ausquelles il ne manque que la distinction des degrés. Ils conservent même de ces sortes de Cartes Geographiques dans leur Trésor public, pour les consulter dans le besoin.

Sir Alexander Mackenzie, (a) in 1793, spoke of the skilled manner of chart-making by an Athabascan tribe, in which the Columbia river was drawn.

An interesting facsimile of a map with which the treaty of Hopewell, in 1875, made by the Cherokees, is connected, appears in American State Papers, Indian Affairs, I, 40.

Hind (b) writes:

On lake Tash-ner-nus-kow, Labrador, was found a "letter" stuck in a cleft pole overhanging the bank. It was written on birchbark, and consisted of a small map of the country, with arrows showing the direction the writer had taken, some crosses indicating where he had camped, and a large cross to show where he intended to make his first winter quarters It was probably written by some Nasquapees as a guide to others who might be passing up the river or hunting in the country.

The Tegua Pueblos, of New Mexico, "traced upon the ground a sketch of their country, with the names and locations of the pueblos occupied in New Mexico," a copy of which, "somewhat improved," is given by Lieut. Whipple (c).

A Yuma map of the Colorado river, with the names and locations of tribes within its valley, is also figured in the last mentioned volume, page 19. The map was originally traced upon the ground.

A Piute map of the Colorado river, which was obtained by Lieut. Whipple, is also figured in the same connection.

Lean-Wolf, of the Hidatsa, who drew the picture of which Fig. 452 is a copy, made a trip on foot from Fort Berthold to Fort Buford, Dakota, to steal a horse from the Dakotas encamped there. The returning horse tracks show that he was successful and that he rode home. The following is his explanation of the characters:

Lean-Wolf is represented at *a* by the head only of a man to which is attached the outline of a wolf; *b*, Hidatsa earth lodges, circular in form, the spots representing the pillars supporting the roof—Indian village at Fort Berthold, Dakota; *c*, human footprints, the course taken by the recorder; *d*, the Government buildings at Fort Buford (square); *e*, several Hidatsa lodges (round), the occupants of which

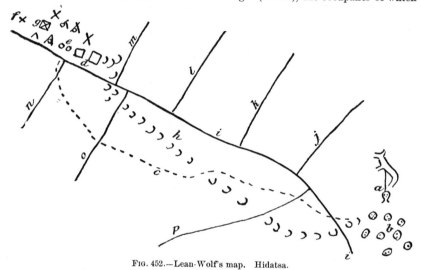

FIG. 452.—Lean-Wolf's map. Hidatsa.

had intermarried with the Dakotas; *f*, Dakota lodges; *g*, a small square—a white man's house—with a cross marked upon it to represent a Dakota lodge, which denotes that the owner, a white man, had married a Dakota woman, who dwelt there; *h*, horse tracks returning to Fort Berthold; *i*, the Missouri river; *j*, Tule creek; *k*, Little Knife river; *l*, White Earth river; *m*, Muddy creek; *n*, Yellowstone river; *o*, Little Missouri river; *p*, Dancing Beard creek.

The following illustration, Fig. 453, is the chart of the field of a battle between Ojibwas and Sioux with its description. The illustration, made by Ojibwa, the old Indian elsewhere mentioned, was drawn on birch bark, while the details of the description were oral. The locality referred to is above the mouth of Crow river, near Sauk rapids, Minnesota.

The chart refers to an episode of war in 1854, when 3 Ojibwa were pursued by 50 Dakota. Many of the lakes appear to be duplicated in name, simply because no special name for them was known.

Dr. Hoffman tells how at Grapevine springs, Nevada, in 1871, the Paiute living at that locality informed the party of the relative position of Las Vegas, the objective point. The Indian sat upon the sand and with his hands formed an oblong ridge to represent Spring mountain, and southeast of this ridge another gradual slope, terminating on the eastern side more abruptly; over the latter he passed his fingers to represent the side valleys running eastward. He then took a stick and

Fig. 453.—Chart of battle field.

In the description *a* is the Mississippi river; *b*, Crow river; *c*, branch of Crow river; *d, e, f,* Crow lakes; *g,* Rice lake; *h,* Clear Water lake; *i,* Clear Water river; *j,* Sauk river; *k,* Big Sauk lake; *l,* Big prairie lake; *m,* Osakis lake; *n,* Sauk rapids; *o* and *p,* canoe and deer-hunting and fishing grounds; *q,* 1 man and 2 women killed (Ojibwas); *r,* Sauk Center; *s,* copses of timber—known as timber islands—on the prairie.

showed the direction of the old Spanish trail running east and west over the lower portion of the last-named ridge. When this was completed, with a mixture of English, Spanish, Paiute, and gesture signs, he told that from where they were now they would have to go southward east of Spring mountain to the camp of Paiute Charlie, where they would have to sleep; then indicated a line southeastward to another spring (Stump's) to complete the second day; then he followed the line representing the Spanish trail to the east of the divide of the second ridge above named, where he left it, and passing northward to the first valley he thrust the short stick into the ground and said, 'Las Vegas."

Mr. W. von Streeruwitz, of the Geological Survey of Texas, contributes the copy of a map, evidently the work of Indians, which is received too late for reproduction. The map is roughly scratched into the flat surface of a large granite block, and is an approximately correct sketch of a pass and the nearest surrounding. The rock is situated in the pass above the so-called rattlesnake or mica tank, in a spur on the west side of the Van Horn mountains, El Paso county, Texas. An Indian trail passes near the very rough and weathered rear part of the rock, which on this side shows weak traces of some scratched-in drawings, which are nearly weathered off, made no doubt with the purpose to lead the attention of passing parties to the other side of the rock upon which the map is drawn. An old trail leads from the Rio Grande across the Eagle mountains to this pass and in the shortest line from the Green river valley to the northern main range of the Van Horn and from there east to the Davis mountains, formerly Apache mountains, and thence through the southern extension of the Guadeloupe mountains to this range and into New Mexico; also through the Sierra Carrizo to the Sierra Diablo; so that this trail must be regarded as one of the best warpaths for raids across the Rio Grande. An arrowhead at the upper end of the trail points out water (small or doubtful supply), as far as could be ascertained from drawings made by Apaches.

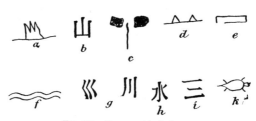

FIG. 454.—Topographic features.

Following are modes of exhibiting pictographically topograpic features, Fig. 454:

a, from Copway's Ojibway Nation, p. 136, represents "mountains."

b is the Chinese character for "mountain," from Edkins, p. 14. "A picture of the object. More anciently, two upright cones or triangles connected at their bases."

c is the representation by the Dakotas of a gap in the mountains, taken from Red-Cloud's census.

d, from Copway, p. 135, represents "islands."

e, from the same, p. 134, is a representation of the character for "sea" or "water," probably a large body of water, e. g., lake, such as the Ojibwa were familiar with.

f is from the same authority, p. 134. It shows the character for "river" or "stream."

g gives two Chinese characters for "river," "stream," from Edkins, p. 14. Three parallel lines drawn downward express "flowing" in all cases.

h is the Chinese character for "flowing water," from Edkins, p. 23.
"In the Chwen wen three strokes descending indicate the appearance
of flowing water as seen in a river. The two outside strokes are broken
in the middle."

The same authority, p. 155, gives another character, i, with the same

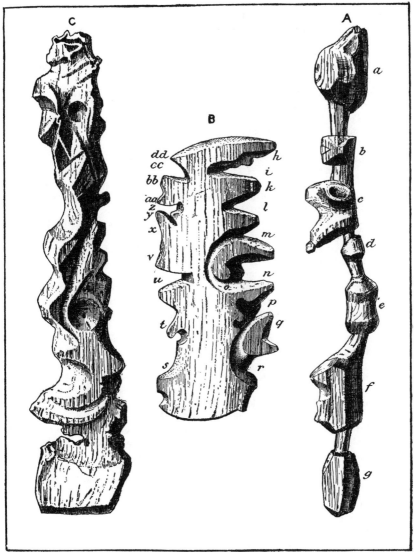

FIG. 455.—Greenland map.

meaning as the last. The author says: "It is supposed to be turned
on end. It is better to regard the old form with its three descending
lines as a picture of water flowing downward."

k, from Copway (a), represents the character for "land." It is a turtle, and refers to a common cosmologic myth concerning the recovery of land after the deluge.

G. Holm (a) gives the following account, translated and condensed, descriptive of Fig. 455, a wooden map made by the natives of the east coast of Greenland:

In reference to map making I will only remark that many are inclined to enlarge the scale as they approach the better known places, which in fact is quite natural, as they would not otherwise find room for all details. As a natural result, map drawing in the form of ground plat is something quite new to them. Their mode of representing their land is by carving it on wood. This has the advantage that not only the contour of the land, but also its appearance and rock forms, can in a certain degree be represented.

The block of wood brought back represents the tract between Kangerdluarsikajik, east of Sermiligak, and Sieralik, north of Kangerdlugsuatsiak. The mainland continues from one side of the wooden block to the other, while the islands are located on the accompanying block without regard to the distance between them in reference to the mainland. All places where there are old ruins of houses, and therefore good storage places, are marked on the wood map, which also shows the points where a kayak can be carried over the ground between two fiords when the sea ice blocks the headland outside. This kind of models serves to represent the route the person in question has followed, inasmuch as during his recital he moves the stick, so that the islands are shown in their relative positions. The other wooden map, which was prepared by request, represents the peninsula between Sermiligak and Kangerdluarsikajik.

A and B represent the tract between Kangerdluarsikajik (immediately east of Sermiligak) and Sieralik (slightly north of Kangerdlugsuatsiak). B represents the coast of the mainland, and is continuous from one side of the block to the other, while the outlying islands are represented by the wooden block of A, on which the connecting pieces between the various islands must be imagined as being left out. While the narrator explains the map he moves the stick to and fro, so as to get the islands into the right position in reference to the mainland.

Kunit explained the map to me. The names of the islands on A are: a, Sardlermiut, on the west side of which is the site of an old settlement; b, Nepinerkit (from napavok), having the shape of a pyramid; c, Ananak, having the site of an old settlement on the southwest point. (Note.—Others give the name Ananak to the cape on the mainland directly opposite, calling the island Kajartalik.) d, Aputitek; e, Itivdlersuak; f, Kujutilik; g, Sikivitik.

For B I obtained the following names, beginning at the north, as in the case of the islands: h, Itivdlek, where there are remains of a house; i, Sierak, a small fiord, in which salmon are found; k, Sarkarmiut, where there are remains of a house; l, Kangerdlugsuatsiak, a fiord of such length that a kayak can not even in a whole day row from the mouth to the head of the fiord and back again; m, Erserisek, a little fiord; n, Nutugat, a little fiord with a creek at the bottom; o, Merkeriak, kayak portage from Nutugkat to Erserisek along the bank of the creek, when the heavy ice blocks the headland between the two fiords; p, Ikerasakitek, a bay in which the land ice goes straight out to the sea; q, Kangerajikajik, a cape; r, Kavdlunak, a bay into which runs a creek; s, Apusinek, a long stretch where the land ice passes out into the sea; t, Tatorisik; u, Iliartalik, a fiord with a smaller creek; v, Nuerniakat; x, Kugpat; y, Igdluarsik; z, Sangmilek, a-little fiord with a creek; aa, Nutugkat; bb, Amagat; cc, Kangerdluarsikajik, a smaller fiord; dd, Kernertuarsik.

C represents the peninsula between the fiords Sermiligak and Kangerdluarsikajik.

NOTICE OF CONDITION.

In the curious manuscript of Gideon Lincecum, written with Roman characters in the Choctaw language about 1818, and referring to the ancient customs of that tribe, appears the following passage (p. 276):

They had a significant and very ingenious method of marking the stakes so that each iksa could know its place as soon as they saw the stake that had been set up for them. Every clan had a name, which was known to all the rest. It was a species of heraldry, each iksa having its coat of arms. The iksas all took the name of some animal—buffalo, panther, dog, terrapin, any race of animals—and a little picture of whatever it might be, sketched on a blazed tree or stake, indicated the clan to which it belonged. They could mark a tree when they were about to leave a camp, in their traveling or hunting excursions, with a set of hieroglyphs, that any other set of hunters or travelers who might pass that way could read, telling what iksa they belonged to, how long they had remained at that camp, how many there were in the company, if any were sick or dead, and if they had been successful or otherwise in the hunt. Thus, drawn very neatly on a peeled tree near the camp, a terrapin; five men marching in a row, with bows ready strung in their hands, large packs on their backs, and one man behind, no pack, bow unstrung; one circle, half circle, and six short marks in front of the half circle; below, a bear's head, a buffalo head, and the head of an antelope. The reading is, "Terrapin iksa, 6 men in company, one sick; successful hunt in killing bear, buffalo, and antelope; that they remained at the camp a moon and a half and six days, and that they have gone home."

Among the Abnaki of the Province of Quebec, as reported by Masta, their chief, cutting the bark off from a tree on one, two, three, or four sides near the butt means "Have had poor, poorer, poorest luck." Cutting it off all around the tree means "I am starving." Smoking a piece of birch bark and hanging it on a tree means "I am sick."

Tanner's Narrative (c) mentions regarding the Ojibwa that, in cases where the information to be communicated is that the party mentioned is starving, the figure of a man is sometimes drawn, and his mouth is painted white, or white paint may be smeared about the mouth of the animal, if it happens to be one, which is his totem.

Fig. 456 is a copy of a drawing incised on birch bark by the old Passamaquoddy chief, Sapiel Selmo, who made comments upon it as follows: Two hunters followed the river a until it branches off b, c. Indian d takes one river and its lakes and small branches, and the other hunter (not figured in the chart) follows the other branch and also claims its small streams and lakes. Sometimes during the winter they visit one another. If it happen that the other hunter was away from his wigwam e and if the visiting hunter wishes to leave word with his friend and wishes to inform him of his luck, he makes a picture on a piece of birch bark and describes such animals he has killed with the number of animals as seen in f and g (figure of moose's head) which, with two crosses to each, means 20 moose. He killed in each hunt altogether 40. h is a whole moose, also with two crosses, and means 20, and also the figure of a caribou i with one cross means 10 caribou, and also a figure of a bear with four crosses *j* means 40 bears, and *k* shows a figure of bear with one cross which means 10 bears, and also a sable *l* with five crosses means 50 sables.   If he wish to inform him he is in poor luck and hungry, he marked a figure of an Indian with a pot on one hand, the pot upside down; this means hunger.   A figure of an Indian in lying position means sickness.

Fig. 457 was also incised on birch bark by Sapiel Selmo and described by him.

Two Indian hunters follow the river to hunt.   They go together as far as the river's forks and then separate.   One went to the river *c*. The other follows river *e* and kills a moose.   They both build their winter wigwams.

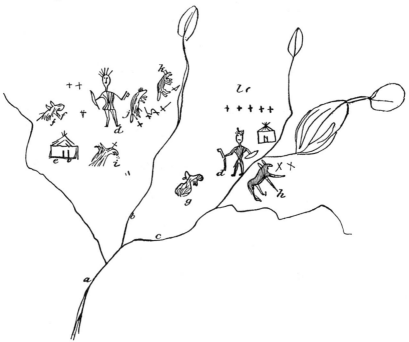

FIG. 456.—Passamaquoddy wikhegan.

Indian *b* went to hunt and found a bear's den under the foot of a big tree.   He attempted to stab the bear, but missed the vital part.   The bear got hold of him, bit him severely, and mortally wounded him.   He went to his wigwam *h* and thinks he is going to die, so he makes his mark or wikhegan on a birch-bark.   He makes notches *j* on the bark to mean his tracks and also marks a tree as in *f* and also a bear as in *g*. His friend *d* came to visit him and found him lying dead in his wigwam, and also found the marks on the piece of birch-bark, which he read and knew at once his partner was killed by the bear, and he followed his bear tracks, and he also found the bear dead.

a. Main river.   *b*. One of the Indians who goes up *c*, branch of river.

d. The other Indian who goes on *e,* another branch of river. *f.* Tree above the bear's den. *g.* Bear. *h.* Wigwam of Indian *b.* *i.* Moose which Indian *d* killed. *j.* Tracks of Indian *b.* *k.* Bear's den under the tree. *l.* Indian *d*'s wigwam.

Fig. 458 originally scraped on birch bark tells its own story, but was described by Sapiel Selmo, who drew it, thus:

Two Indian hunters, *b* and *c,* went to hunt and follow river, *a.* They continued together as far as *d,* where the river branches off. Indian *c* follows the east branch *e.* He went as far as lake *f,* where he built

FIG. 457.—Passamaquoddy wikhegan.

his wigwam *g.* Indian *c* is very unlucky; he doesn't kill any bears or moose, so he became very hungry. Indian *b,* who had followed the north branch and built his wigwam, *l,* near lake *k,* went to visit Indian *c,* who was away at the time, but *b* found mark on the birch bark, a pot upside down, *h;* this means hunger. He also makes his own mark, *i,* a moose's head, showing success. He appoints lake *j,* where he killed moose, and wants him, *c,* to come to his, *b*'s, wigwam *l.*

o, lower lake, not connected with the story, but doubtless drawn to complete the topography. The two trails, *m* and *n*, are designated by notches showing foot-path or snow-shoe tracks. The Abnaki have footpaths or snow-shoe tracks where the line of kelhign sisel, or sable dead falls, extends from one hunting camp to another, between two lakes or rivers.

The Ottawa and the Pottawatomi Indians indicate hunger and starvation by drawing a black line across the breast or stomach of the figure of a man. (See Fig. 1046.) This drawing is either incised upon a piece

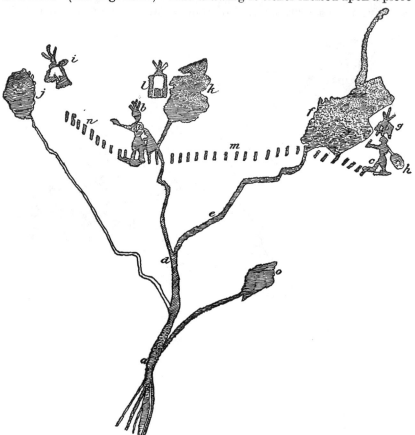

FIG. 458.—Passamaquoddy wikhegan.

of wood, or drawn on it with a mixture of powdered charcoal and glue water, or red ocher. The piece of wood is then attached to a tree or fastened to a pole, and erected near the lodge on a trail, where it will be observed by passers by, who are thus besought to come to the rescue of the sufferer who erected the notice.

Fig. 459 illustrates information with regard to distress in another village, which occasioned the departure of the party giving the notification. The drawing was made in 1882 by the Alaskan, Naumoff, in imitation of drawings used at his home. The designs are traced upon a strip of wood, which is then stuck upon the roof of the house belonging to the draftsman.

a, the summer habitation, showing a stick leaning in the direction to be taken; b, the baidarka, containing the residents of the house; the first person is observed pointing forward, indicating that they "go by boat to the other settlement"; c, a grave stick, indicating a death in the settlement; d, e, summer and winter habitations, denoting a village.

FIG. 459.—Alaskan notice of distress.

The drawing, Fig. 460, also made in 1882, by a native Alaskan, in imitation of originals familiar to him in Alaska, is intended to be placed in a conspicious portion of a settlement which has been attacked by a hostile force and finally deserted. The last one to leave prepares the drawing upon a strip of wood to inform friends of the resort of the survivors.

a represents three hills or ranges, signifying that the course taken

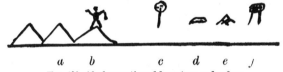

FIG. 460. Alaskan notice of departure and refuge.

would carry them beyond that number of hills or mountains; b, the draftsman, indicating the direction, with the left hand pointing to the ground, *one* hill, and the right hand indicating the number *two*, the number still to be crossed; c, a circular piece of wood or leather, with the representation of a face, placed upon a pole and facing the direction to be taken from the settlement; in this instance the drawing of the character denotes a hostile attack upon the town, for which misfortune such devices are sometimes erected; d, e, winter and summer habita-

FIG. 461.—Notice of departure to relieve distress. Alaska.

tions; f, storehouse, erected upon upright poles. The latter device is used by Alaskan coast natives generally.

The design shown in Fig. 461 is in imitation of drawings made by natives of Southern Alaska to convey to the observer the information that the draftsman had gone away to another settlement, the inhabitants of which were in distress. The drawings were made on a strip of wood which was placed at the door of the house, where it might be seen by visitors or inquirers.

Naumoff gave the following explanation: *a*, a native making the gesture of indicating *self* with the right hand and with the left indicating direction of *going*; *b*, the native's habitation; *c*, scaffold used for drying fish; upon the top of a pole is placed a piece of wood tied so that the longest end points in the direction to be taken by the relief party; *d*, the baidarka conveying it; *e*, a native of the settlement to be visited; *f*, summer habitation; *g*, "shaman stick," or grave stick, erected to the memory of a recently deceased person, the cause which has necessitated the journey; *h*, winter habitation. This, together with *f*, indicates a settlement.

Fig. 462, also drawn by Naumoff, means "ammunition wanted."

When a hunter is tracking game and exhausts his ammunition, he returns to the nearest and most conspicuous part of the trail and sticks his ihúⁿŭk in the ground, the top leaning in the direction taken. The ihúⁿŭk is the pair of sticks arranged like the letter

FIG. 462.—Ammunition wanted. Alaska.

A, used as a gun-rest. This method of transmitting the request to the first passer is resorted to by the coast people of Southern Alaska.

Fig. 463, also drawn by Naumoff, means "discovery of bear; assistance wanted."

When a hunter discovers a bear and requires assistance, he ties together a bunch of grass, or other fibrous matter, in the form of the animal and places it upon a long stick or pole which is erected at a conspicuous point. The head of the effigy is directed toward the locality where the animal was last seen.

FIG. 463.—Assistance wanted in hunt. Alaska.

This device is used by most of the Alaskan Indians.

Fig. 464 was also drawn by Naumoff, and signifies "starving hunters."

Hunters who have been unfortunate, and are suffering from hunger, scratch or draw on a piece of wood characters similar to those figured, and place the lower end of the stick in the ground on the trail where there is the greatest chance of its discovery. The stick is inclined

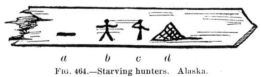

FIG. 464.—Starving hunters. Alaska.

toward their shelter. The following are the details of the information contained in the drawing:

a, A horizontal line denoting a canoe, showing the persons to be fishermen; *b*, a man with both arms extended signifying *nothing*, corresponding with the gesture for negation; *c*, a person with the right hand to the mouth, signifying *to eat*, the left hand pointing to the house occupied by the hunters; *d*, the shelter.

The whole signifies that there is *nothing to eat* in the *house*. This is used by natives of Southern Alaska.

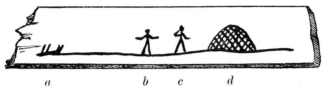

FIG. 465.—Starving hunters. Alaska.

Fig. 465, with the same signification and from the same hand, is similar to the preceding in general design. This is placed in the ground near the landing place of the canoemen, so that the top points toward the lodge. The following is the explanation of the characters:

a, Baidarka, showing double projections at bow, as well as the two men, owners, in the boat; *b*, a man making the gesture for *nothing* (see in this connection Fig. 983); *c*, gesture drawn, denoting *to eat*, with the right hand, while the left points to the lodge; *d*, a winter habitation.

This is used by the Alaskan coast natives.

SECTION 4.

WARNING AND GUIDANCE.

The following description of an Ojibwa notice of a murderer's being at large is extracted from Tanner's Narrative: (*d*).

As I was one morning passing one of our usual encamping places I saw on shore a little stick standing in the bank and attached to the top of it a piece of birchbark. On examination I found the mark of a rattlesnake with a knife, the handle touching the snake and the point sticking into a bear, the head of the latter being down. Near the rattlesnake was the mark of a beaver, one of its dugs, it being a female, touching the snake. This was left for my information, and I learned from it that Wa-me-gon-a-biew, whose totem was She-she-gwah, the rattlesnake, had killed a man whose totem was Muk-kwah, the bear. The murderer could be no other than Wa-me-gon-a-biew, as it was specified that he was the son of a woman whose totem was the beaver, and this I knew could be no other than Net-no-kwa.

An amusing instance of the notice or warning, "No thoroughfare," is presented in Fig. 466. It was taken in 1880 from a rock drawing in Canyon de Chelly, New Mexico, by Mr. J. K. Hillers, photographer of the U. S. Geological Survey.

The design on the left is undoubtedly a notice in the nature of warning, that, although a goat can climb up the rocky trail, a horse would tumble down.

During his connection with the geographic surveys west of the one hundredth meridian, Dr. Hoffman observed a practice among the Tivátikai Shoshoni, of Nevada, of erecting heaps of stones along or near trails to indicate the direction to be taken and followed to reach springs of water.   Upon slight elevations of ground, or at points where a trail branched into two or more directions, or at the intersection of two trails, a heap of stones would be placed varying in height according to the elevation requisite to attract attention.   Upon the top of this would be fixed an elongated piece of rock so placed that the most conspicuous point projected and pointed in the course to be followed.   This was

FIG. 466.—No thoroughfare.

continued sometimes at intervals of several miles unless indistinct portions of a trail or intersections demanded a repetition at shorter distances.   A knowledge of this custom proved very beneficial to the early prospectors and pioneers.

Fig. 467 is a copy, one-sixteenth actual size, of colored petroglyphs found by Dr. Hoffman in 1884 on the North fork of the San Gabriel river, also known as the Azuza canyon, Los Angeles county, California.

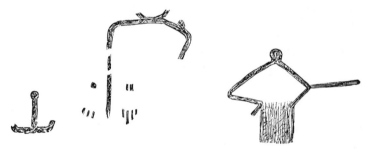

FIG. 467.—Rock painting, Azuza canyon, California.

The bowlder upon which the paintings occur measures 8 feet long, about 4 feet high, and the same in width.   The figures are on the eastern side of the rock, so that the left arm of the human figure on the right points toward the north.

Fig. 468 is a map drawn on a scale of 1,000 yards to the inch, showing the topography of the immediate vicinity and the relative positions of the rocks bearing the paintings.

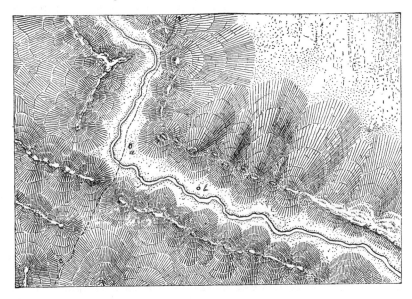

FIG. 468.—Site of paintings in Azuza canyon, California.

The stream is hemmed in by precipitous mountains, with the exception of two points marked *c c*, over which the old Indian trail passed in going from the Mojave desert on the north to the San Gabriel valley below, this course being the nearest for reaching the mission settlements at San Gabriel and Los Angeles. In attempting to follow the water course the distance would be greatly increased and a rougher

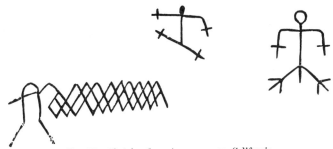

FIG. 469.—Sketches from Azuza canyon, California.

trail encountered. Fig. 467, painted on the rock marked *b* on the map, shows characters in pale yellow upon a bowlder of almost white granite partly obliterated by weathering and annual floods, though still enough remains to indicate that the right-hand figure is directing the observer to the northeast, although upon taking that course it would be necessary to round the point a short distance to the west. It may have been placed as a notification of direction to those Indians who might have come up the canyon instead of on the regular trail. Farther west, at the spot marked *a* on the map, is a granite bowlder bearing a large number of paintings, part of which have become almost obliterated. These were drawn with red ocher (ferric oxide). A selection of these is shown in Fig. 469.

This is on the almost vertical western face of the rock. These characters also appear to refer to the course of the trail, which might readily be lost on account of the numerous mountain ridges and spurs. The left-hand human figure appears to place its hand upon a series of ridges, as if showing pantomimically the rough and ridged country over the mountains.

The middle figure is making a gesture which in its present connection may indicate direction of the trail, i. e., toward the left, or northward in an uphill course, as indicated by the arm and leg, and southward, or downward, as suggested by the lower inclination of the leg and lower forearm and hand on the right of the painting.

These illustrations, as well as other pictographs on the same rock, not now represented, exhibit remarkable resemblance to the general type of Shoshonean drawing, and from such evidence as is now attainable it is probable that they are of Chemehuevi origin, as that tribe at one time ranged far to the west, though north of the mountains, and also visited the valley and settlements at Los Angeles to trade. It is also known that the Mojaves came at stated periods to Los Angeles as late as 1845, and the trail indicated at point *a* of the map would appear to have been their most practicable and convenient route. There is strong evidence that the Moki sometimes visited the Pacific coast and might readily have taken this same course, marking the important portions of the route by drawings in the nature of guideboards.

The following curious account is taken from The Redman, Carlisle, October, 1888:

A ranchman visiting a deserted camp of Piegans found the following notice:

We called at this ranch at dinner time. They treated us badly, giving us no dinner and sending us away. There is a head man who has two dogs, one of which has no tail. There are two larger men who are laborers. They have two pairs of large horses and two large colts, also another smaller pair of horses and two ponies which have two colts.

The notice was composed thus: A circle of round stones represented the horses and ponies, the latter being smaller stones; the stones outside of the circle meant there were so many colts. Near the center was a long narrow stone, upon the end of which was a small one. This denoted the head man or owner, whose two dogs were shown by two pieces of bark, one with a square end while the other had a twig stuck in for a tail. Two other long narrow stones, larger than the first, stood for the laborers; these had no small stones on them. Some sticks of wood, upon which was a small pile of buffalo chips, meant that dinner was ready; and empty shells turned upside down told they got nothing to eat, but were sent away.

Mr. Charles W. Cunningham, formerly of Phœnix, Arizona, reports the finding of petroglyphs in Rowe canyon, one-half mile from the base of Bradshaw mountain, Arizona. The characters are pecked upon its vertical wall of hard porphyry, covering a space between 12 or 15 feet in length and about 30 feet above the surface of the earth. They consist of human figures with outstretched arms, apparently driving animals resembling sheep or goats, while at the head of the procession appears the figure of a bear. The explanation given seems to be a notification to Indian herders that in going through the canyon they should be careful to guard against bears or possibly other dangerous animals, as the trail or canyon leads down to some water tanks where the herders may habitually have driven the stock.

D'Albertis (b) mentions of the Papuans that a warning not to enter a dwelling is made by erecting outside of it a stick, on the top of which is a piece of bark or a cocoanut, and in Yule island these warnings or taboo sticks are furnished with stone heads.

When a Tartar shaman wished to be undisturbed he placed a dried goat's-head, with its prominent horns, over a wooden peg outside of his tent and then dropped the curtain. No one would dare to venture in.

The following is quoted from Franz Keller (b):

In the immense primeval forests, extending between the Ivahy and the Parana-panama, the Paraná and the Tibagy, the rich hunting grounds of numerous Coroado hordes, one frequently encounters, chiefly near forsaken palm sheds, a strange collection of objects hung up between the trees on thin cords or cipós, such as little pieces of wood, feathers, bones, and the claws and jaws of different animals.

In the opinion of those well versed in Indian lore these hieroglyphs are designed as epistles to other members of the tribe regarding the produce of the chase, the number and stay of the huntsmen, domestic intelligence, and the like; but this strange kind of composition, reminding one of the quippus (knotted cords), of the old Peruvians, has not yet been quite unraveled, though it is desirable that it should be, for the naïve son of the woods also uses it sometimes in his intercourse with the white man.

Settlers in this country, on going in the morning to look after their very primitive mills near their cottages, have frequently discovered them going bravely, but bruising pebbles instead of the maize grains, while on the floor of the open shed names and purposes of the unwelcome nocturnal visitors have been legibly written in the sand. Among the well-drawn zigzag lines were inserted the magnificent long tail feathers of the red and blue macaw, which are generally used by the Coroados for their arrows; and, as these are the symbols of war and night attacks, the whole was probably meant for a warning and admonition ad hominem: "Take up your bundle and go or beware of our arrows."

CHAPTER XII.

COMMUNICATIONS.

Under this heading notes and illustrations are grouped of transmitted drawings, which were employed as letters and missives now are by people who possess the art of writing. To the drawings are added some descriptions of objects sent for the same purposes. These are sometimes obviously ideographic, but often appear to be conventional or arbitrary. It is probable that the transmittal or exchange of such objects anteceded the pictorial attempt at correspondence, so that the former should be considered in connection with the latter. The topic is conveniently divided by the purposes of the communications, viz, (1) declaration of war, (2) profession of peace and friendship, (3) challenge, (4) social and religious missives, (5) claim or demand.

SECTION 1.

DECLARATION OF WAR.

Le Page du Pratz (*a*), in 1718, reported the following:

The Natchez make a declaration of war by leaving a hieroglyphic picture against a tree in the enemy's country, and in front of the picture they place, saltierwise, two red arrows. At the upper part of the picture at the right is the hieroglyphic sign which designates the nation that declares war; next, a naked man, easy to recognize, who has a casse-tête in his hand. Following is an arrow, drawn so as in its flight to pierce a woman, who flees with her hair spread out and flowing in the air. Immediately in front of this woman is a sign belonging to the nation against which war is declared; all this is on the same line. That which is below is not so clear or so much relied upon in the interpretation. This line begins with the sign of a moon (*i. e.*, month) which will follow in a short time. The days that come afterward are indicated by straight strokes and the moon by a face without rays. There is also a man who has in front of him many arrows which seem directed to hit a woman who is in flight. All that announces that when the moon will be so many days old they will come in great numbers to attack the designated nation.

Lahontan (*a*) writes:

The way of declaring war by the Canadian Algonquian Indians is this: They send back to the nation that they have a mind to quarrel with a slave of the same country, with orders to carry to the village of his own nation an axe, the handle of which is painted red and black.

The Huron-Iroquois of Canada sent a belt of black wampum as a declaration of war.

Material objects were often employed in declaration of war, some of which may assist in the interpretation of pictographs. A few instances are mentioned:

358

Capt. Laudonnière (a) says: "Arrows, to which long hairs are attached, were stuck up along the trail or road by the Florida Indians, in 1565, to signify a declaration of war."

Dr. Georg. Schweinfurth (a) gives the following:

I may here allude to the remarkable symbolism by which war was declared against us on the frontiers of Wando's territory. * * * Close on the path, and in full view of every passenger, three objects were supended from the branch of a tree, viz, an ear of maize, the feather of a fowl, and an arrow. * * * Our guides readily comprehended and as readily explained the meaning of the emblems, which were designed to signify that whoever touched an ear of maize or laid his grasp upon a single fowl would assuredly be the victim of the arrow.

In the Notes on Eastern Equatorial Africa, by MM. V. Jacques (a) and É. Storms, it is stated that when a chief wishes to delare war he sends to the chief against whom he has a complaint an ambassador bearing a leaden bullet and a hoe. If the latter chooses the bullet, war ensues; if the hoe, it means that he consents to enter into negotiations to maintain peace.

Terrien de Lacouperie, op. cit., pp. 420, 421, reports:

The following instance in Tibeto-China is of a mixed character. The use of material objects is combined with that of notched sticks. When the Li-su are minded to rebel they send to the Moso chief (who rules them on behalf of the Chinese Government) what the Chinese call a muhki and the Tibetans a shing-tchram. It is a stick with knife-cut notches. Some symbols are fastened to it, such, for instance, as a feather, calcined wood, a little fish, etc. The bearer must explain the meaning of the notches and symbols. The notches may indicate the number of hundreds or thousands of soldiers who are coming; the feather shows that they arrive with the swiftness of a bird; the burnt wood, that they will set fire to everything on their way; the fish, that they will throw everybody into the water, etc. This custom is largely used among all the savage tribes of the region. It is also the usual manner in which chiefs transmit their orders.

SECTION 2.

PROFESSION OF PEACE AND FRIENDSHIP.

The following account of pictorial correspondence leading to peace was written by Governor Lewis Cass, while on one of his numerous missions to the Western tribes, before 1820:

Some years before, mutually weary of hostilities, the chiefs of the Ojibwas and the Dakotas met and agreed upon a truce. But the Sioux, disregarding the solemn contract which they had formed, and actuated by some sudden impulse, attacked the Ojibwas and murdered a number of them.

On our arrival at Sandy lake I proposed to the Ojibwa chiefs that a deputation should accompany us to the mouth of the St. Peters, with a view to establish a permanent peace between them and the Sioux. The Ojibwas readily acceded to this, and ten of their principal men descended the Mississippi with us. The computed distance from Sandy lake to the St. Peters is 600 miles. As we neared this part of the country we found our Ojibway friends cautious and observing.

The Ojibwa landed occasionally to examine whether any of the Sioux had recently visited that quarter. In one of these excursions an Ojibwa found in a conspicuous place a piece of birch bark, made flat by fastening between two sticks at each end, and about 18 inches long by 2 broad.

This bark contained the answer of the Sioux nation. So sanguinary had been the contest between these two tribes that no personal communication could take place. Neither the sanctity of office nor the importance of the message could protect the ambassador of either party from the vengeance of the other.

Some time preceding, the Ojibwas, anxious for peace, had sent a number of their young men into these plains with a similar piece of bark, upon which they represented their desire. This bark had been left hanging to a tree, in an exposed situation, and had been found and taken away by a party of Sioux.

The proposition had been examined and discussed in the Sioux villages, and the bark contained their answer. The Ojibwa explained to us with great facility the intention of the Sioux.

The junction of the St. Peters with the Mississippi, where the principal part of the Sioux reside, was represented, and also the American fort, with a sentinel on duty, and a flag flying.

The principal Sioux chief was named The-Six, alluding, I believe, to the band of villages under his influence. To show that he was not present at the deliberation upon the subject of peace, he was represented on a smaller piece of bark, which was attached to the other. To identify him, he was drawn with six heads and a large medal. Another Sioux chief stood in the foreground, holding a pipe in his right hand and his weapons in his left. Even we could not misunderstand that; like our own eagle with the olive branch and arrows, he was desirous for peace, but prepared for war.

The Sioux party contained fifty-nine warriors, indicated by fifty-nine guns, drawn upon one corner of the bark.

The encampment of our troops had been removed from the low grounds upon the St. Peters to a high hill upon the Mississippi. Two forts were therefore drawn upon the bark, and the solution was not discovered until our arrival at St. Peters.

The effect of the discovery of the bark upon the minds of the Ojibwas was visible and immediate.

The Ojibwa bark was drawn in the same general manner, and Sandy lake, the principal place of their residence, was represented with much accuracy. To remove any doubts respecting it, a view was given of the old northwestern establishment, situated upon the shore, and now in the possession of the American Fur Company.

No proportion was preserved in their attempt at delineation. One mile of the Mississippi, including the mouth of the St. Peters, occupied as much space as the whole distance to Sandy Lake, nor was there anything to show that one part was nearer to the spectator than another.

The above pictorially professed attitude of being ready for either peace or war may be compared with the account in Champlain—Voyages (d)—of the chief whose name was Mariston, but he assumed that of Mahigan Atticq, translated as Wolf Deer. He thereby proclaimed that when at peace he was mild as a deer, but when at war was savage as a wolf.

In Davis' Conquest of New Mexico (a) it is stated that Vargas' Expedition in 1694 was met by the Utes, who hoisted a deerskin in token of peace.

The following "speech of an Ojibwa chief in negotiating a peace with the Sioux, 1806," from Maj. Pike's (a) Expeditions, etc., shows the pictographic use of the pipe as a profession of peace:

My father, tell the Sioux on the upper part of the river St. Peters that they mark trees with the figure of a calumet; that we of Red lake who may go that way should we see them, that we may make peace with them, being assured of their pacific disposition when we shall see the calumet marked on the trees.

D'Iberville, in 1699, as printed in Margry, IV, 153, said that the Indians met by him near the mouth of the Mississippi river indicated their peaceful and friendly purposes by holding up in the air a small stick of whitened wood. The same authority, in the same volume, p. 175, tells that the Oumas bore a white cross as a similar declaration; and another journal, in the same volume, p. 239, describes a stick also so borne as being fashioned like a pipe. The actual use of the pipe in profession of peace and friendship is mentioned in several parts of the present paper. See, also, the passport mentioned on p. 214 and wampum, p. 225.

Lieut. Col. Woodthorpe, in Jour. Anthr. Inst. Gr. Br. and I., XI, p. 211, says of the wild tribes of the Naga Hills, on the northeastern frontier of India:

On the road to Niao we saw on the ground a curious mud figure of a man in slight relief presenting a gong in the direction of Senua. This was supposed to show that the Niao men were willing to come to terms with Senua, then at war with Niao. Another mode of evincing a desire to turn away the wrath of an approaching enemy and induce him to open negotiations is to tie up in his path a couple of goats, sometimes also a gong, with the universal symbol of peace, a palm leaf planted in the ground hard by.

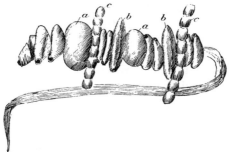

Fig. 470.—West African message.

G. W. Bloxam (*a*) gives the following description of Fig. 470:

It represents a message of peace and good news from the King of Jebu to the King of Lagos, after his restoration to the throne on the 28th of December, 1851. It appears complicated, but the interpretation is simple enough. First we find eight cowries arranged in pairs, and signifying the people in the four corners of the world, and it will be observed that, while three of the pairs are arranged with their faces upwards, the fourth and uppermost, i. e., the pair in the most important position, are facing one another, thus signifying that the correspondents, or the people of Jebu and Lagos, are animated by friendly feeling towards each other; so, too, there are two each of all the other objects, meaning, "you and I," "we two." The two large seeds or warres, *a, a,* express a wish that "you and I" should play together as intimate friends do, at the game of "warre," in which these seeds are used and which is the common game of the country, holding very much the same position as chess or draughts with us; the two flat seeds, *b, b,* are seeds of a sweet fruit called "osan," the name of which is derived from the verb, "san," to please [Mem. Notice the rebus] they, therefore, indicate a desire on the part of a sender of the message to please and to be pleased; lastly, the two pieces of spice, *c, c,* signify mutual trust. The following is the full meaning of the hieroglyphic:

Of all the people by which the four corners of the world are inhabited, the Lagos and Jebu people are the nearest.

As "warre" is the common play of the country, so the Jebus and Lagos should always play and be friendly with each other.

Mutual pleasantness is my desire; as it is pleasant with me so may it be pleasant with you.

Deceive me not, because the spice would yield nothing else but a sweet and genuine odor unto god. I shall never deal doubly with you.

SECTION 3.

CHALLENGE.

H. H. Bancroft (a), in Native Races, says that the Shumeias challenged the Pomos (in central California) by placing three little sticks notched in the middle and at both ends, on a mound which marked the boundary between the two tribes. If the Pomos accept they tie a string round the middle notch. Heralds then meet and arrange time and place and the battle comes off as appointed.

The sending of material objects was the earliest and most natural mode for low cultured tribes to communicate when out of sight and hearing. Such was the system in use among the Scythians at the time of the invasion of their land by Darius. The version of the story in Herodotus is that commonly cited, but there is another by Pherecydes of Heros, who relates that Idanthuras, the Scythian king, when Darius had crossed the Ister, threatened him with war, sending him not a letter, but a composite symbol, which consisted of a mouse, a frog, a bird, an arrow, and a plow. When there was much discussion concerning the meaning of this message, Orontopagas, the chiliarch, maintained that it was a surrender; for he conjectured the mouse to mean their dwelling, the frog their waters, the bird their air, the arrow their arms, and the plow their country. But Xiphodres offered a contrary interpretation, thus: "Unless like birds we fly aloft, or like mice burrow under the ground, or like frogs take ourselves to the water, we shall never escape their weapons, for we are not masters of their country."

SECTION 4.

SOCIAL AND RELIGIOUS MISSIVES.

Fig. 471 is a letter, one-half actual size, written by an Ojibwa girl, the daughter of a Midē', to a favored lover, requesting him to call at her lodge. This girl had taken no Midē' degrees, but had simply acquired her pictographic skill from observation in her home.

The explanation of the figure is as follows:

a. The writer of the letter, a girl of the Bear totem, as indicated by that animal, *b*.

e and *f*. The companions of *a*, the crosses signifying that the three girls are Christians.

c and *g*. The lodges occupied by the girls. The lodges are near a large lake, *j*, a trail leading from *g* to *h*, which is a well-traveled road.

The letter was written to a man of the Mud Puppy totem, as indicated in *d*.

i. The road leading to the lodge occupied by the recipient of the letter.

k and *l*. Lakes near which the lodges are built.

In examining *c*, the writer's hand is seen protruding from an opening to denote beckoning and to indicate which lodge to visit. The clear indications of the locality serve as well as if in a city a young woman had sent an invitation to her young man to call at a certain street and number.

Fig. 472 is a letter sent by mail from a Southern Cheyenne, named Turtle-following-his-Wife, at the Cheyenne and Arapaho Agency, Indian Territory, to his son Little-Man, at the Pine Ridge Agency, Dakota. It was drawn on a half-sheet of ordinary writing paper, without a word

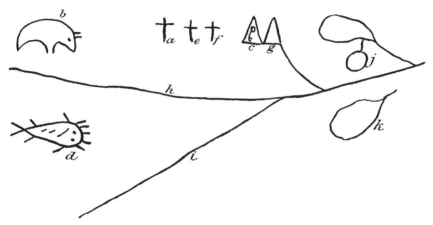

FIG. 471.—Ojibwa love letter.

written, and was inclosed in an envelope, which was addressed to " Little-Man, Cheyenne, Pine Ridge Agency," in the ordinary manner, written by some one at the first named agency. The letter was evidently understood by Little-Man, as he immediately called upon Dr. V. T. McGillycuddy, Indian agent at Pine Ridge Agency, and was aware that the sum of $53 had been placed to his credit for the purpose of enabling him to pay his expenses in going the long journey to his father's home in Indian Territory. Dr. McGillycuddy had, by the same mail, received a letter from Agent Dyer, inclosing $53, and explaining the reason for its being sent, which enabled him also to understand the pictographic letter. With the above explanation it very clearly shows, over the head of the figure to the left, the turtle following the turtle's wife united with the head of the figure by a line, and over the head of the other figure, also united by a line to it, is a little man. Also over the right arm of the last-mentioned figure is another little man in the act of springing or advancing toward Turtle-following-his-Wife, from whose mouth proceed two lines, curved or hooked at the end, as if drawing the little figure toward him. It is suggested that the last mentioned part of the pictograph is the substance of the communication, i. e., "come to me," the larger figures with their name totems being the persons addressed and addressing. Between and above the two large figures are fifty-three round objects intended for dollars. Both the Indian figures have on breechcloths, corresponding with the information given concerning them, which is that they are Cheyennes who are not all civilized or educated.

Sagard (a) tells of the Algonkins of the Ottawa river, that when a feast was to be given, the host sent to each person whose presence was

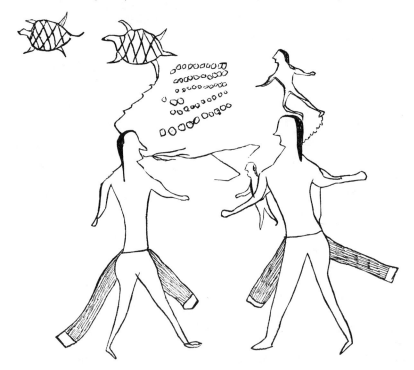

FIG. 472.—Cheyenne letter.

desired a little stick of wood, peculiar to them (i. e., probably marked or colored) of the length and thickness of the little finger, which he was obliged to show on entering the lodge, as might be done with a card of invitation and admission. The precaution was seemingly necessary both for the host's larder and the satisfaction of the guests, as on an occasion mentioned by the good brother, each of the guests was provided with a big piece of sturgeon and plenty of "sagamite huylée." There was probably some principle of selection connected with totems or religious societies on such occasions, not told by the narrator, as the ordinary custom among Indians is to keep open house to all comers, who generally were the aboriginal "tramps," with the result of waste and subsequent famine.

The Rev. Peter Jones (b), an educated Ojibwa missionary, in speaking of the eastern bands of the Ojibwa says:

Their method of imploring the favor or appeasing the anger of their deities is by offering sacrifices to them in the following order: When an Indian meets with ill-luck in hunting, or when afflictions come across his path, he fancies that by the neglect of some duty he has incurred the displeasure of his munedoo, for which he is angry with him; and in order to appease his wrath, he devotes the first game he takes to making a religious feast, to which he invites a number of the principal men and women from the other wigwams. A young man is generally sent as a messenger to invite the guests, who carries with him a bunch of colored quills or sticks, about 4 inches long. On entering the wigwam he shouts out "Keweekomegoo;" that is, "You are bidden to a feast." He then distributes the quills to such as are invited; these answer to the white people's invitation cards. When the guests arrive at the feast-maker's wigwam the quills are returned to him; they are of three colors, red, green, and white; the red for the aged, or those versed in the wahbuhnoo order; the green for the media order, and the white for the common people.

Mr. David Boyle (b) refers to the above custom, and quotes Rev. Peter Jones, also giving as illustrations copies of the quills and sticks pre-

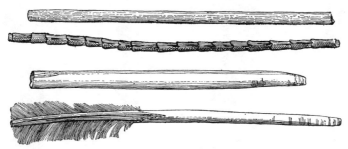

Fig. 473.—Ojibwa invitations.

sented by Dr. P. E. Jones which had been brought by his father, the author above mentioned, from the Northwest fifty years ago. These are reproduced in Fig. 473.

When the ceremony of the Grand Medicine Society of the Ojibwa is to be performed, the chief midē' priest sends out a courier to deliver to each member an invitation to attend. These invitations consist of sticks of cedar, or other wood when that can not be found, measuring from 4 to 6 inches in length and of the thickness of an ordinary lead pencil. They may be plain, though the former custom of having one end painted red or green is sometimes continued. The colored band is about the width of one-fifth of the length of the stick. It is stated that in old times these invitation sticks were ornamented with colored porcupine quills, or strands of beads, instead of with paint.

The courier detailed to deliver invitations is also obliged to state the day, and locality of the place of meeting. It is necessary for the invited member to present himself and to deposit the invitation stick upon the floor of the inclosure in which the meeting is held; should he be deprived of the privilege of attending, he must return the stick with an explanation accounting for his absence.

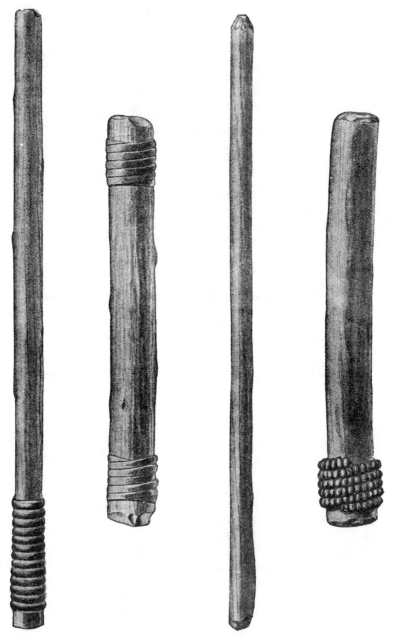

Fig. 474.—Ojibwa invitation sticks.

Fig. 474 exhibits the sticks without coloration.

Another mode of giving invitations for the same ceremony is by sending around a piece of birch bark bearing characters similar to those in Fig. 475, taken from Copway, p. 136.

Fig. 475.—Summons to Midē' ceremony.

The characters, beginning at the left hand, signify as follows: Medicine house; great lodge; wigwam, woods; lake; river; canoe; come; Great Spirit.

Copway remarks as follows:

" In the above, the wigwam and the medicine pale, or worship, represent the depositories of medicine, record, and work. The lodge is represented with men in it; the dots above indicate the number of days.

" The whole story would thus read:

Hark to the words of the Sa-ge-mah'. The Great Medicine Lodge will be ready in eight days. Ye who live in the woods and near the lakes and by streams of water come with your canoes or by land to the worship of the Great Spirit.' "

The above interpretation is too much adapted to the ideas and language of Christianity. The more simple and accurate expression would change the rendition from " worship " and "Great Spirit" to the simple notice about holding a session of the Grand Medicine Society.

Fig. 476, drawn by a Passamaquoddy, shows how the Indians of the tribe would now address the President of the United States, or the governor of Maine for help, and formerly would have made wikhegan for transmittal to a great chief having power over them. They say by this: " You are at the top of the pole, so no one can be higher than you. From this pole you can see the farthest of your country and can see all your children, and when any of your children come to see you they must work hard to get where you are, on top of the high pole. They must climb up this pole to reach you. You must pity them because they come long ways to see you, the man of power on the high pole." This kind of wikhegan the old men called *kinjemeswi waligoh*, homage or salutation to the great chief. It was always in the old time accompanied by a belt of wampum.

Fig. 476.—Passamaquoddy wikhegan.

A highly interesting illustration and account of a diplomatic packet from the pueblo of Tesuque appears in Schoolcraft (*g*), and in the same series (*h*) is a pictograph from the Caroline islands still more in point.

A. W. Howitt (*c*) reports:

Messengers in central Australia were sent to gather people together for dances from distances even up to 100 miles. Such messengers were painted with red ocher and wore a headdress of feathers.

In calling people together for the ceremonies of Wilyaru or Mindari the messengers were painted with diagonal stripes of yellow ocher, and had their beards tied tightly into a point. They carried a token shaped like a Prince of Wales feather, and made of emu feathers tied tightly with string.

The sending of a handful of red ocher tied up in a small bundle signifies the great Mindari or peace festival. In giving notice of the intention to "make some young men" the messenger takes a handful of charcoal and places a piece in the mouth of each person present without saying a word. This is fully understood to mean the "making of young men" at the Wilyaru ceremony.

The following is a description of a Turkish love letter, which was obtained by Lady Mary Wortley Montagu (*a*) in 1717:

I have got for you a Turkish love letter. * * * The translation of it is literally as follows. The first piece you should pull out of the purse is a little pearl, which must be understood in this manner:

Pearl	Fairest of the young.
Clove	You are as slender as the clove.
	You are an unblown rose.
	I have long loved you and you have not known it.
Jonquil	Have pity on my passion.
Paper	I faint every hour.
Pear	Give me some hope.
Soap	I am sick with love.
Coal	May I die and all my years be yours.
A rose	May you be pleased and your sorrows mine.
A straw	Suffer me to be your slave.
Cloth	Your price is not to be found.
Cinnamon	But my fortune is yours.
A match	I burn, I burn! My flame consumes me.
Gold thread	Don't turn away your face from me.
Hair	Crown of my head.
Grape	My two eyes.
Gold wire	I die; come quickly.

And, by way of postscript:

Pepper	Send me an answer.

You see this letter is all in verse, and I can assure you there is as much fancy shown in the choice of them as in the most studied expressions of our letters, there being, I believe, a million of verses designed for this use. There is no color, no flower, no weed, no fruit, herb, pebble, or feather that has not a verse belonging to it; and you may quarrel, reproach, or send letters of passion, friendship, or civility, or even of news without ever inking your fingers.

The use by Turks and Persians of flower letters or communications, the significance of which is formed by the selection and arrangement of flowers, is well known. A missive thus composed of flowers is called sélam, but the details are too contradictory and confused to furnish materials for an accurate dictionary of the flower language, though dictionaries and treatises on it have been published. (See Magnat.) Individual fancy and local convention, it seems, fix the meanings.

A Japanese girl who decides to discourage the further attentions of a lover sends to him, instead of the proverbial "mitten" of New England, a sprig of maple, because the leaf changes its color more markedly than any other. In this connection it is told that the Japanese word for love also means color, which would accentuate the lesson of the changing leaf.

MESSAGE STICKS.

The following extracts are made from Curr's (*a*) Australian Race:

I believe every tribe in Australia has its messenger, whose life, whilst he is in the performance of his duties, is held sacred in peace and war by the neighboring tribes. His duties are to convey the messages which the tribe desires to send to its neighbors, and to make arrangements about places of meeting on occasions of fights or corroborees. In many tribes it is the custom to supply the messenger when he sets out with a little carved stick, which he delivers with his message to the most influential man of the tribe to which he is sent. This carved stick he often carries whilst traveling stuck in the netted band which the blacks wear round the head. I have seen many of them, and been present when they were received and sent, and have some from Queensland in my possession at present. They are often flat, from 4 to 6 inches long, an inch wide, and a third of an inch thick; others are round, of the same length, and as thick as one's middle finger. When flat their edges are often notched, and their surface always more or less carved with indentations, transverse lines, and squares; in fact, with the same sort of figures with which the blacks ornament their weapons throughout the continent; when round, fantastic lines are cut around them or lengthwise. I have one before me at this moment which is a miniature boomerang, carved on both sides, notched at the edges, and colored with red ocher. Any black could fashion sticks of this sort in an hour or two. Some of my correspondents have spoken of them as a sort of writing, but when pressed on the subject have admitted that their surmise, all the circumstances weighed, was not tenable. The flat sticks especially have that sort of regularity and repetition of pattern which wall papers exhibit. That they do not serve the purpose of writing or hieroglyphics I have no hesitation in asserting; and I may remark that in all cases which have come under my notice the messenger delivered his message before he presented the carved stick. That done the recipient would attempt to explain to those about him how the stick portrayed the message. Still this eminently childish proceeding leads one to consider whether the most savage mind does not contain the germ of writing. Bernal Diaz del Castillo, in his Discovery and Conquest of New Spain, relates that, when his country sent verbal messages by Mexican bearers to distant tribes, the messengers who had seen the Spaniards write always asked to be supplied with a letter, which, of course, neither they nor the people to whom they were sent could read.

Fig. 477 reproduces the illustration of the message sticks published in the work above mentioned.

Vol. I, p. 306.—In the Majanna tribe messengers are sent with a notched or carved stick, and the bearer has to explain its meaning. If it be a challenge to fight, and the challenge is accepted, another stick is returned.

Vol. II, p. 183.—The bearer of an important communication from one party to another often carries a message stick with him, the notches and lines on which he refers to whilst delivering his message. This custom, which prevails from the north coast to the south, is a very curious one. No black fellow ever pretends to be able to understand a message from a notched stick, but always looks upon it as confirmatory of the message it accompanies.

Vol. II, p. 427.—Message sticks are in use, the marks carved on them being a guaranty of the messenger, the same as a ring with us in former times.

Vol. III, p. 263.—Message sticks are used by the Maranoa river tribe. An informant has in his possession a reed necklace attached to a piece of flat wood about 5 inches long; on the wood are carved straight and curved lines, and this piece of wood was sent by one portion of the tribe to another by a messenger, the two parties being about 60 miles apart. The interpretation of the carving was: "My wife has been stolen; we shall have to fight; bring your spears and boomerangs." The straight lines, it was explained, meant spears and the curved ones boomerangs; but the stealing of the wife seems to have been left to the messenger to tell.

A. W. Howitt (a) gives a further account on this topic:

The messenger carries with him as the emblems of his missions a complete set of male attire, together with the sacred humming instrument, which is wrapped in a skin and carefully concealed from women and children. It is, therefore, in such cases, the totem which assembles the whole community.

In the Adjadura tribe of South Australia the ceremonies are ordered to be held by the headman of the whole tribe by his messenger, who carries a message stick marked in such a manner that it serves to illustrate his message; together with this there is also sent a sacred humming instrument.

Drs. Houzé and Jacques (a) give a different view of the significance of the marks on message sticks:

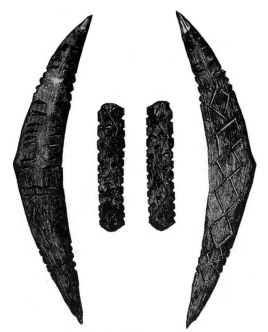

FIG. 477.—Australian message sticks.

It proves very difficult to discover the signification of the notched message sticks. The Europeans have not succeeded in deciphering them. Some marks may represent a whole history. The following anecdote on this subject is reported by M. Cauvin (according to J. M. Davis, Aborigines of Victoria, v. I, p. 356, note): A European, having formed the project of establishing a new station, started from Edward river with a herd of cattle and some Indians. When, all being arranged, the colonist was on the point of returning home, one of the young blacks requested him to take a letter to his father, and, on the consent of his patron, he gave him a stick about a foot long covered with notches and signs. On arriving home the colonist went to the camp of the blacks and delivered the letter to the father of his young follower, who, calling around him the whole encampment, to the great surprise of the European, read from this stick a daily account of the doings of the company from the departure from Edward river until the arrival at the new station, describing the country which they had traversed and the places where they had camped each night.

The Queenslanders did not give Drs. Houzé and Jacques such a long translation of their message sticks, but they informed them that one of the sticks related to the crossing from Australia into America, which is recounted by Tambo, the author of the message. An illustration of it is presented on p. 93 of the above cited work of Houzé and Jacques, but is not sufficiently distinct for reproduction.

WEST AFRICAN AROKO.

G. W. Bloxam (*b*) says of the aroko, or symbolic letters, used by the tribe of Jebu, in West Africa, describing Fig. 478:

This is a message from a native general of the Jebu force to a native prince abroad. It consists of six cowries. Six in the Jebu language is E-fà, which is de-

rived from the verb fà, to draw. They are arranged two and two, face to face, on a long string;
the pairs of cowries set face to face indicate friendly
feeling and good fellowship; the number expresses
a desire to draw close to the person to whom the
message is sent [note the rebus]; while the long
string indicates considerable distance or a long
road. This is the message: "Although the road
between us be very long, yet I draw you to myself

FIG. 478.—West African aroko.

and set my face towards you. So I desire you to set your face towards me and draw to me."

On p. 298 he adds:

Among the Jebu in West Africa odd numbers in their message are of evil import, while even numbers express good will. Thus a single cowrie may be sent as an un-favorable answer to a request or message.

The same author writes, on p. 297, describing Fig. 479:

It is a message from His Majesty Awnjale, the King of Jebu, to his nephew abroad; and here we find other substances besides cowries included in the aroko. Taking

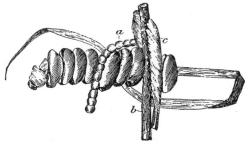

FIG. 479.—West African aroko.

the various articles in order, commencing from the knot, we observe four cowries facing in the same direction, with their backs to the knot; this signifies agreement. Next a piece of spice, *a*, which produces when burnt a sweet odor and is never un-pleasant; then come three cowries facing in the same direction; then a piece of mat, *b;* then a piece of feather, *c;* and, lastly, a single cowrie turned in the same direction as all the others. The interpretation is:

"Your ways agree with mine very much. Your ways are pleasing to me and I like them.

"Deceive me not, because the spice would yield nothing else but a sweet and genuine odor unto God.

"I shall never deal doubly with you all my life long.

"The weight of your words to me is beyond all description.

"As it is on the same family mat we have been sitting and lying down together, I send to you.

"I am, therefore, anxiously awaiting and hoping to hear from you."

The following account of "African Symbolic Messages," condensed from the paper of the Rev. C. A. Gollmer, which appeared in Jour. Anthrop. Inst. of Gr. Bn. and I., XIV, p. 169, et. seq., is highly interesting as showing the ideography attached to the material objects transmitted. The step in evolution by which the graphic delineation of those objects was substituted for their actual presence was probably delayed only by the absence of convenient material, such as birch bark, parchment, or other portable rudimentary form of paper on which to draw or paint, or at least by the want of a simple invention for the application of such material:

The natives in the Yoruba country, West Africa, in the absence of writing, and as a substitute for it, send to one another messages by means of a variety of tangible objects, such as shells, feathers, pepper, corn, stone, coal, sticks, powder, shot, razors, etc., through which they convey their ideas, feelings, and wishes, good and bad, and that in an unmistakable manner. The object transmitted is seen, the import of it known and the message verbally delivered by the messenger sent, and repeated by one or more other persons accompanying the messenger for the purpose as the importance of the message is considered to require.

Cowry shells in the symbolic language are used to convey, by their number and the way in which they are strung, a variety of ideas. One cowry may indicate "defiance and failure;" thus: A cowry (having a small hole made at the back part, so as to be able to pass a string through it and the front opening) strung on a short bit of grass fiber or cord, and sent to a person known as a rival, or one aiming at injuring the other, the message is: "As one finger can not take up a cowry (more than one are required), so you one I defy; you will not be able to hurt me, your evil intentions will come to nothing."

Two cowries may indicate "relationship and meeting;"·thus: Two cowries strung together, face to face, and sent to an absent brother or sister, the message is: "We are children of one mother, were nursed by the same breasts."

Two cowries may indicate "separation and enmity;" thus: Two cowries strung back to back and sent to a person gone away, the message is: "You and I are now separated."

Two cowries and a feather may indicate "speedy meeting;" thus: Two cowries strung face to face, with a small feather (of a chicken or other bird) tied between the two cowries, and sent to a friend at a distance, the message is: "I want to see you, as the bird (represented by the feather) flies straight and quickly, so come as quickly as you can."

The following fivefold painful symbolic message was sent by D., whilst in captivity at Dahomey, to his wife, who happened to be staying with Mr. Gollmer, at Badagry, at the time. The symbols were a stone, a coal, a pepper, corn, and a rag. During the attack of the King of Dahomey, with his great army of Amazons and other soldiers, upon Abeokuta in March, 1852, D., one of the native Christians and defenders of his town, home, and family, was taken captive and carried to Dahomey, where he suffered much for a long time. Whilst waiting for weeks to know the result his wife received the symbolic letter which conveyed the following message:

The stone indicated "health" (the stone was a small, common one from the street); thus the message was: "As the stone is hard, so my body is hardy, strong—i. e., well."

The coal indicated "gloom" (the coal was a small piece of charcoal); thus the message was: "As the coal is black, so are my prospects dark and gloomy."

The pepper indicated "heat" (the pepper was of the hot cayenne sort); thus the message was: "As the pepper is hot so is my mind heated, burning on account of the gloomy prospect—i. e., not knowing what day I may be sold or killed."

The corn indicated "leanness" (the corn was a few parched grains of maize or Indian corn); thus the message was: "As the corn is dried up by parching, so my body is dried up or become lean through the heat of my affliction and suffering."

The rag indicated "worn out;" thus (the rag was a small piece of worn and torn native cloth, in which the articles were wrapped) the message was: "As the rag is, so is my cloth cover—i. e., native dress, worn and torn to a rag."

A tooth brush may indicate "remembrance;" thus: It is a well-known fact that the Africans in general can boast of a finer and whiter set of teeth than most other nations. And those Europeans who lived long among them know from constant observation how much attention they pay to their teeth, not only every morning, but often during the day. The tooth brush made use of is simply a piece of wood about 6 to 9 inches long, and of the thickness of a finger. One end of the stick, wetted with the saliva, is rubbed to and fro against the teeth, which end after awhile becomes soft. This sort of tooth brush is frequently given to friends as an acceptable present, and now and then it is made use of as a symbolic letter, and in such a case the message is: "As I remember my teeth the first thing in the morning, and often during the day, so I remember and think of you as soon as I get up, and often afterwards."

Sugar may indicate "peace and love;" in the midst of a war this good disposition was made known from one party to another by the following symbol: A loaf of white sugar was sent by messengers from the native church at A. to the native church at I., and the message was: "As the sugar is white, so there is no blackness (i. e., enmity) in our hearts towards you; our hearts are white (i. e., pure and free from it). And as the sugar is sweet, so there is no bitterness among us against you; we are sweet (i. e., at peace with you) and love you."

A fagot may indicate "fire and destruction;" when a fagot (i. e., a small bundle of bamboo poles, burnt on one end) is found fastened to the bamboo fence inclosing a compound, or premises, it conveys the message: "Your house will be burnt down"—i. e., destroyed.

Powder and shot are often made use of and sent as a symbolic letter; the message is to either an individual or a people, viz: "As we can not settle the quarrel, we must fight it out" (i. e., "we shall shoot you, or make war upon you").

A razor may indicate "murder." A person suspected and accused of having by some means or other been the cause of death of a member of a family, the representative of that family will demand satisfaction by sending the symbolic objects, viz, a razor or knife, which is laid outside the door of the house of the accused offender and guilty party, and the message is well understood to be: "You have killed or caused the death of N., you must kill yourself to avenge his death."

The following examples indicate a still further step in evolution by which the names of the objects or of the numbers are of the same sound as words in the language the significance of which constitutes the real message. This objective rebus corresponds with the pictorial rebus so common in Mexican pictographs, and which is well known to have borne a chief part in the development of Egyptain and other ancient forms of writing.

Three cowries with some pepper may indicate "deceit;" thus: Three cowries strung with their faces all looking one way (as mentioned before) with an alligator pepper tied to the cowries. Eru is the name of the pepper in the native language, which in English means "deceit." The message may be either a "caution not to betray one another," or, more frequently, an accusation of having deceived and defrauded the company.

Six cowries may indicate "attachment and affection;" thus: Efa in the native language means "six" (cowries implied); it also means "drawn," from the verb fa, to draw. Mora is always implied as connected with Efa; this means "stick to you," from the verb mo, to stick to, and the noun ara, body—i. e. you. Six cowries strung (as before mentioned) and sent to a person or persons, the message is: "I am drawn (i. e. attached) to you, I love you," which may be the message a young man sends to a young woman with a desire to form an engagement.

Rev. Richard Taylor (b) says:

The Maori used a kind of hieroglyphical or symbolical way of communication; a chief, inviting another to join in a war party, sent a tattooed potato and a fig of tobacco bound up together, which was interpreted to mean that the enemy was a Maori and not European by the tattoo, and by the tobacco that it represented smoke; he therefore roasted the one and eat it, and smoked the other, to show he accepted the invitation, and would join him with his guns and powder. Another sent a waterproof coat with the sleeves made of patchwork, red, blue, yellow, and green, intimating that they must wait until all the tribes were united before their force would be waterproof, i. e., able to encounter the European. Another chief sent a large pipe, which would hold a pound of tobacco, which was lighted in a large assembly, the emissary taking the first whiff, and then passing it around; whoever smoked it showed that he joined in the war.

SECTION 5.

CLAIM OR DEMAND.

Stephen Powers (b) states that the Nishinam of California have the following mode of collecting debts:

When an Indian owes another, it is held to be in bad taste, if not positively insulting, for the creditor to dun the debtor, as the brutal Saxon does, so he devises a more subtle method. He prepares a certain number of little sticks, according to the amount of the debt, and paints a ring around the end of each. These he carries and tosses into the delinquent's wigwam without a word and goes his way; whereupon the other generally takes the hint, pays the debt, and destroys the sticks.

The San Francisco (California) Western Lancet, XI, 1882, p. 443, thus reports:

When a patient has neglected to remunerate the shaman [of the Wikchumni tribe of the Mariposan linguistic stock] for his services, the latter prepares short sticks of woo l, with bands of colored porcupine quills wrapped around them at one end only, and every time he passes the delinquent's lodge a certain number of them are thrown in as a reminder of the indebtedness.

G. W. Bloxam (c) decribes Fig. 480 thus:

Among the Jebu of West Africa two cowries facing one another signify two blood relations; two cowries, however, back to back may be sent as a message of reproof for nonpayment of debt, meaning: "You have given me the back altogether; after we have come to an arrangement about the debt you have owed me, I will also turn my back against you."

FIG. 480.—Jebu complaint.

The same authority, p. 299, describes Fig. 481:

It consists of two cowries face to face, followed by one above facing upwards, and is a message from a creditor to a bad debtor, meaning: "After you have owed me a debt you kicked against me; I also will throw you off, because I did not know that you could have treated me thus."

FIG. 481.—Jebu complaint.

Prof. Anton Schrifner (a) describing Fig. 482, says:

On this plank the cuts marked b signify the number of reindeer required. Opposite these cuts are placed the hand marks, a, of various Samoyeds of whom the reindeer

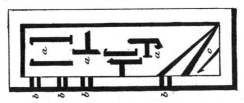

FIG. 482.—Samoyed requisition.

are demanded. At the bottom is found the official mark, c, of the Samoyed chief who forwarded this board to the various Samoyed settlements in place of a written communication.

CHAPTER XIII.

TOTEMS, TITLES, AND NAMES.

The employment of pictographs to designate tribes, groups within tribes, and individual persons has been the most frequent of all the uses to which they have been applied. Indeed, the constant need that devices to represent the terms styled by grammarians proper names should be readily understood for identification has, more than any other cause, maintained and advanced pictography as an art, and in some parts of the world has evolved from it syllabaries and afterwards alphabets. From the same origin came heraldry, which in time designated with absolute accuracy persons and families for the benefit of letterless people. Trade-marks have the same history.

From the earliest times men have used emblems to indicate their tribes or clans. Homer makes no clear allusion to their manifestation at the poetic siege of Troy; but even if his Greeks did not bear them, other nations of the period did. The earlier Egyptians carried images of bulls and crocodiles into battle, probably at first with religious sentiments. Each of the twelve tribes of Israel had a special ensign of its own, which is now generally considered to have been totemic. The subjects of Semiramis adopted doves and pigeons as their token in deference to their queen, whose name meant "dove."

At later dates Athens chose an owl for her sign, as a compliment to Minerva; Corinth, a winged horse, in memory of Pegasus and his fountain; Carthage, a horse's head, in homage to Neptune; Persia, the sun, because its people worshiped fire; Rome, an eagle, in deference to Jupiter. These objects appear to have been carved in wood or metal. There is no evidence of anything resembling modern flags, except, perhaps, in parts of Asia, until the Romans began to use something like them about the time of Cæsar. But these small signs had no national or public character so as to be comparable with the eagles on the Roman standard; nor was any floating banner associated with ruling power until Constantine gave a religious meaning to the labarum.

Emblems also were often adopted by political and religious parties, e. g., the cornstalks and slings of the Mazarinists and anti-Mazarinists during the Fronde, the caps and hats in the Swedish diet in 1788, the scarf of the Armagnacs, and the cross of the Burgundians. The topic of emblems is further discussed in Chapter XVIII.

As with increased culture clans and tribes have become nations, so there has been an evolution by which the ensigns of bands and orders have been discontinued and replaced by the emblems of nationalities. Frederic Marshall (*a*) well says: "Images of animals, badges, war cries, cockades, liveries, coats of arms, tokens, tattooing, are all replaced practically by national ensigns." This change is toward the higher and nobler significance and employment, all members of the community being protected and designated by the simple exhibition of a single emblem.

This chapter is naturally divided into (1) Pictorial tribal designations, (2) Gentile and clan designations, (3) Significance of tattoo, (4) Designations of individuals.

SECTION 1.

PICTORIAL TRIBAL DESIGNATIONS.

Capt. de Lamothe Cadillac (*a*) writing in the year 1696 of the Algonquians of the Great Lake region near Mackinac, etc., describes the emblems on their canoes as follows: "On y voit la natte de guerre le corbeau, l'ours ou quelque autre animal * * * estant l'esprit qui doit conduire cette enterprise."

This, however, was a mistake as applicable to the time when it was written. The animals used as emblems may originally have been regarded as supernatural totemic beings, but had probably become tribal designations.

IROQUOIAN TRIBAL DESIGNATIONS.

Bacqueville de la Potherie (*c*) says that a treaty with the French in Canada, about 1700, was "sealed" with the "proper arms," pictorially drawn, of the Indian tribes which were parties to it. The following is a copy of the original statement in its archaic form:

Monsieur de Callieres, de Champigni, & de Vaudreüil, en signerent le Traité, que chaque Nation scella de ses propres armes. Les Tsonnontouans & les Onnontaguez designerent une araignée, le Goyogouin un calumet, les Onneyouts un morceau de bois en fourche, une pierre au milieu, un Onnontagué mit un Ours pour les Aniez, quoi qu'ils ne vinrent pas. Le Rat mit un Castor, les Abenaguis un Chevreüil, les Outaouaks un Liévre, ainsi des autres.

From this it appears that—

The Seneca and Onondaga tribes were represented by a "spider." [This was doubtless a branching tree, so badly drawn as to be mistaken for a spider.]

The Cayuga tribe, by a calumet.

The Oneida tribe, by a forked stick with a stone in the fork. [The forked stick was really designed for the fork of a tree.]

The Mohawk tribe, by a bear.

Le Rat, who was a representative Huron of Mackinaw, by a beaver.

The Abnaki, by a deer.

The Ottowa, by a hare.

Several other accounts of the tribal signs of the Iroquois are published, often with illustrations, e. g., in Documents relating to the Colonial History of New York (*a*), with the following remarks:

When they go to war, and wish to inform those of the party who may pass their path, they make a representation of the animal of their tribe, with a hatchet in his dexter paw; sometimes a saber or a club; and if there be a number of tribes together of the same party, each draws the animal of his tribe, and their number, all on a tree, from which they remove the bark. The animal of the tribe which heads the expedition is always the foremost.

Another account of interest, which does not appear to have been published, was traced and contributed by Mr. William Young, of Philadelphia. It is a deed from the representatives of the Six Nations (the Tuscaroras then being admitted) to the King of Great Britain, dated November 4, 1768, and recorded at the recorder's office, Philadelphia, in Deed Book I, vol. 5, p. 241. Nearly all of these accounts and illustrations are confused and imperfect. An instructive blunder occurs in the translated signature representing the Mohawk tribe in the above mentioned deed. It is called "The Steel," which could hardly have been an ancient tribal name, but after study it was remembered that the Mohawks have sometimes been called by a name properly translated the "Flint people." By some confusion about flint and steel, which were still used in the middle of the last century to produce sparks of fire, perhaps assisted by the pantomime of striking those objects together, the one intended to be indicated, viz, the flint, was understood to be the other, the steel, and so these words were written under the figure, which was so roughly drawn that it might have been taken for a piece of flint or of steel or, indeed, anything else.

EASTERN ALGONQUIAN TRIBAL DESIGNATIONS.

The illustrations in Fig. 483 were drawn in 1888 by a Passamaquoddy Indian, in Maine, near the Canada border. The Passamaquoddy, Penobscot, and Amalecite are tribal divisions of the Abnaki, who formerly were also called Tarrateens by the more southern New England tribes and Owenunga by the Iroquois. The Micmacs are congeners of the Abnaki, but not classed in their tribal divisions. All the four tribes belong to the Algonquian linguistic stock.

Fig. 483 *a* is the tribal emblem of the Passamaquoddy. It shows two Indians in a canoe, both using paddles and not poles, following a fish, the pollock. The variation which will appear in the represented use of poles and paddles in the marks of the Algonquian tribes in Maine, Nova Scotia, New Brunswick, etc., is said to have originated in the differing character of the waters, shoal or deep, sluggish or rapid, of the regions of the four bodies of Indians whose totems are indicated as next follows, thus requiring the use of pole and paddle, respectively, in a greater or less degree. The animals figured are in all cases repeated consistently by each one of the several delineators, and in all cases there is some device to show a difference between the four canoes, either in their structure or in their mode of propulsion, but these devices are not always consistent. It is therefore probable that the several animals designated constitute the true and ancient totemic emblems, and that the accompaniment of the canoes is a modern differentiation.

b The Maresquite or Amalecite emblem. Two Indians in a canoe, both with poles, following a muskrat.

c The Micmac emblem. Two Indians, both with paddles, in a canoe built with high middle parts familarly called "humpback," following a deer.

d The Penobscot emblem. Two Indians in a canoe, one with a paddle and the other with a pole, following an otter.

In Margry (*a*) is an account, written about 1722, of the "Principal divisions of the Sioux and their distinctive marks," thus translated:

There are from twenty to twenty-six villages of Scioux and they comprise the nations of the prairies:

(1) The Ouatabatonha, or Scioux des Rivières, living on the St. Croix river or Lake de la Folle-Avoine which is below, and 15 leagues from the Serpent river. Their distinctive sign is a bear wounded in the neck.

FIG. 483.—Eastern Algonquian tribal designations.

(2) The Menesouhatoba, or Scioux des Lacs, having for their mark a bear wounded in the neck.

(3) The Matatoba, or Scioux des Prairies, having for their mark a fox with an arrow in its mouth.

(4) The Hictoba, or Scioux de la Chasse, having for their symbol the elk.

(5) The Titoba, or Scioux des Prairies, whose emblem is the deer. It bears a bow on its horns.

We have as yet had no commerce save with five nations. The Titoba live 80 leagues west of Sault Saint-Antoine.

The above early, though meager, notice will serve as an introduction to the following series of pictorial tribal signs, all drawn by Sioux Indians, and many of them representing tribal divisions of the Siouan linguistic stock. The history and authority of the several "Winter Counts" mentioned are referred to supra, chapter x, section 2. Red-Cloud's census and the Oglala roster are also described below. Explanations of some figures are added which have no reference to the present topic, but which seemed necessary and could not be separated and transferred to more appropriate division without undue multiplication of figures and text.

Fig. 484.—Dakota and Crow, Cloud-Shield's Winter Count, 1819–'20.
In an engagement between the Dakotas and the Crows both sides
expended all of their arrows, and then threw dirt at each other. A

Crow is represented on the right, and
is distinguished by the manner in
which the hair is worn. Hidatsa
and Absaroka are represented with
striped or spotted hair, which denotes
the red clay they apply to it.

The custom which prevails among
these tribes, and is said to have originated with the Crows, is to wear a
wig of horse hair attached to the
occiput, thus resembling the natural
growth, but much increased in length.

FIG. 484.—Absaroka.

These wigs are made in strands having the thickness of a finger, varying
from eight to fifteen in number, and held apart and in place by means of
thin cross strands, thus resembling coarse network. At every intersection of strands of hair and crossties, lumps of pine gum are attached
to prevent disarrangement and as in itself ornamental, and to these
lumps dry vermilion clay is applied by the richer classes and red ocher
or powdered clay by the poorer people.

Pictures drawn by some of the northern tribes of the Dakota show
the characteristic and distinctive features for a Crow Indian to be the
distribution of the red war paint which covers the forehead.

Fig. 485.—Cloud-Shield's Winter Count, 1830–'31. The Crows were
approaching a village at a time when there was a great deal of snow

on the ground and intended to surprise it, but, some herders
discovering them, the Dakotas went out, laid in wait for
the Crows, surprised them, and killed many. A Crow's
head is represented in the figure.

The Crow is designated not only by the arrangement of
back hair, before mentioned, but by a topknot of hair extending upward from the forehead, brushed upward and
slightly backward. See also the seated figure in the record of Running
Antelope, in Fig. 820, infra.

FIG. 485.—Ab-
saroka.

Fig. 486.—The Dakotas surrounded and killed ten
Crows. Cloud-Shield's Winter Count, 1857–'58.

The hair is somewhat shortened and not intentionally
foreshortened, which was beyond the artist's skill.

FIG. 486.—Absaroka.

Fig. 487.—The Dakotas killed a Crow and his squaw who were found on a trail. Cloud-Shield's Winter Count, 1839–'40.

This is a front view. The union line signifies husband and wife.

FIG. 487.—Absaroka.

ARAPAHO.

Fig. 488.—Arapaho, in the Dakota language, magpiyato, blue cloud, is here shown by a circular cloud, drawn in blue in the original, inclosing the head of a man. Red-Cloud's census.

FIG. 488.—Arapaho.

ARIKARA OR REE.

Fig. 489 is the tribal sign of the Arikara, made by the Dakota, taken from the Winter Count of Battiste Good for the year 1823–'24, which he calls "General-——-first-appeared-and-the-Dakotas-aided-in-an-attack-on-the-Rees winter," also "Much corn winter."

The gun and the arrow in contact with the ear of corn show that both whites and Indians fought the Rees. The ear of corn signifies "Ree" or Arikara Indians, who are designated in gesture language as "corn shellers."

FIG. 489.—Arikara.

Fig. 490.—A Dakota kills one Ree. The-Flame's Winter Count, 1874–'75. Here the ear of corn, the conventional sign for Arikara, has become abbreviated.

FIG. 490.—Arikara.

ASSINIBOIN.

Fig. 491 is the tribal designation for Assiniboin or Hohe made by the Dakota, as taken from the Winter Count of Battiste Good for the year 1709–'10.

The Hohe means the voice, or, as some say, the voice of the musk ox, and the device is the outline of the vocal organs, according to the Dakota concept, and represents the upper lip and roof of the mouth, the tongue, the lower lip, and chin and neck. The view is lateral, and resembles the sectional aspect of the mouth and tongue.

FIG. 491.—Assiniboin.

Fig. 492.—A Brulé, who had left the village the night before, was found dead in the morning outside the village, and the dogs were eating his body. Cloud-Shield's Winter Count, 1822–'23.

The black spot on the upper part of the thigh shows he was a Brulé.

FIG. 492.—Brulé.

Fig. 493.—A Brulé was found dead under a tree, which had fallen on him. Cloud-Shield's Winter Count, 1808–'10.

Again the burnt thigh is suggested by the black spot.

The significance of these two figures is explained by the gesture sign for Brulé as follows: Rub the upper and outer part of the right thigh in a small circle with the open right hand, fingers pointing downward. These Indians were once caught in a prairie fire, many burned to death, and others badly burned about the thighs; hence the name Si-caⁿ-gu, burnt thigh, and the sign. According to the Brulé chronology, this fire occurred in 1763, which they call "The-people-were-burned winter."

FIG. 493.—Brulé.

CHEYENNE.

Fig. 494.—The Cheyenne who boasted that he was bullet and arrow proof was killed by white soldiers, near Fort Robinson, Nebraska, in the intrenchments behind which the Cheyennes were defending themselves after they had escaped from the fort. Cloud-Shield's Winter Count, 1878–'79.

The marks on the arm constitute the tribal pictographic emblem. It is explained by the gesture sign as follows: Pass the ulnar side of the extended index finger repeatedly across extended finger and back of the left hand. Fig. 495 illustrates this gesture sign. Frequently, however, the index is drawn across the wrist or forearm, or the extended index, palm upward, is drawn across the forefinger of the left hand (palm inward), several times, left hand stationary, right hand is drawn toward the body until the index is drawn clear off; then repeat. Some Cheyennes believe this to have reference to the former custom of cutting the arms as offerings to spirits, while others think it refers to a more ancient custom of cutting

FIG. 494.—Cheyenne.

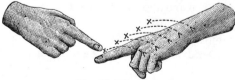

FIG. 495.—Cheyenne.

off the enemy's fingers for necklaces, and sometimes to cutting off the whole hand or forearm as a trophy to be displayed as scalps more generally are.

Fig. 496 is from the Winter Count of Battiste Good for the year 1785–'86. In that record this is the only instance where the short vertical lines below the arrow signify Cheyenne. In all others those marks are numerical and denote the number of persons killed. That these short lines here signify Cheyenne is explained by the foregoing remarks.

FIG. 496.—Cheyenne.

Fig. 497.—Picket-Pin went against the Cheyennes. A picket-pin is represented in front of him and is connected with his mouth by the usual line. Cloud-Shield's Winter Count, 1790–'91.

The black band across his face denotes that he was brave and had killed enemies. The cross is the symbol for Cheyenne. This mark stands for the scars on their arms or stripes on their sleeves, and also to the gesture sign for this tribe. The cross is, therefore, the conventionalized form both for the emblem and the gesture.

FIG. 497.—Cheyenne.

DAKOTA OR SIOUX.

Fig. 498.—Standing-Bull, the great grandfather of the present Standing-Bull, discovered the Black Hills. American-Horse's Winter Count, 1775–'76. He carried home with him a pine tree of a species he had never seen before. In this count the Dakotas are usually distinguished by the braided scalp lock and the feather they wear at the crown of the head, or by the manner in which they brush back and tie the hair with ornamented strips. Many illustrations are given in the present paper in which this arrangement of the hair is shown more distinctly.

FIG. 498.—Dakota.

With regard to the designation of this tribe by paint it seems that pictures made by the northern Dakotas represent themselves as distinguished from other Indians by being painted red from below the eyes to the end of the chin. But this is probably rather a special war painting than a tribal design.

HIDATSA, GROS VENTRE, OR MINITARI.

Fig. 499 shows the tribal designation of the Gros Ventres by the Dakotas, on the authority of Battiste Good, 1789-'90.

FIG. 499.—Hidatsa.

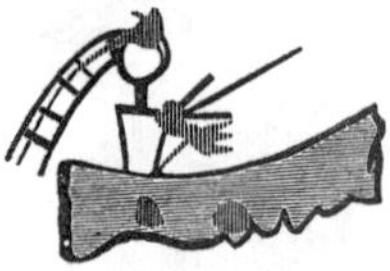

Two Gros Ventres were killed on the ice by the Dakotas. The two are designated by two spots of blood on the ice, and killed is expressed by a blood-tipped arrow against the figure of the man above. The long hair, with a red forehead, denotes the Gros Ventre. In other Dakota records the same style of painting the forehead red designates the Arikara and Absaroka Indians. The horizontal band, which is blue in the original, signifies ice.

KAIOWA.

Fig. 500 shows the tribal designation of the Kaiowa by the Dakota, taken from the Winter Count of Battiste Good, 1814-'15. He calls the winter "Smashed-a-Kaiowa's-head-in winter." The tomahawk with which it was done is in contact with the Kaiowa's head.

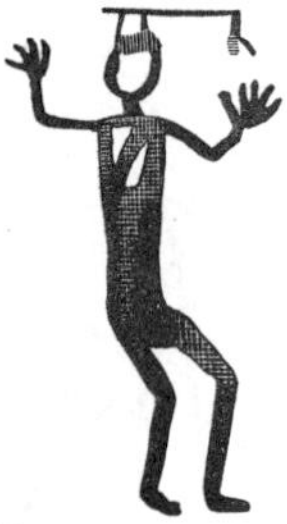

FIG. 500.—Kaiowa.

The sign for Kaiowa is sometimes made by passing one or both hands, naturally extended, in short horizontal circles on either side of the head, together with a shaking motion, the conception being "rattle-brained" or "crazy heads." The picture is drawn to represent the man in the attitude of making this gesture, and not the involuntary raising of the hands upon receiving the blow, such attitudes not appearing in Battiste Good's system.

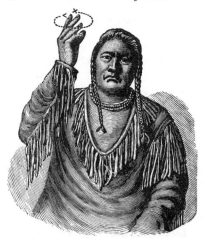

FIG. 501.—Kaiowa.

This gesture is illustrated in Fig. 501.

MANDAN.

Fig. 502.—Two Mandans killed by Minneconjous. The peculiar arrangement of the hair distinguishes the tribe. The-Flame's Winter Count, 1789–'90.

FIG. 502.—Mandan.

MANDAN AND ARIKARA.

Fig. 503.—The Mandans and Rees made a charge on a Dakota village. An eagle's tail, which is worn on the head, stands for Mandan and Ree. American-Horse's Winter Count, 1783–'84.

The mark on the tipi, which represents a village, is not, as it at first sight appears, a hatchet, but a conventional sign for "it hit." See Fig. 987 and accompanying remarks.

FIG. 503.—Mandan and Arikara.

OJIBWA.

Carver (*a*), writing in 1776–'78, tells that an Ojibwa drew the designation of his own tribe as a deer. The honest captain of provincial troops may have mistaken a clan mark to be a tribal mark, but the account is mentioned for what it is worth, and the context serves to support the statement.

OMAHA.

Fig. 504 is the tribal designation of the Omahas by the Dakotas, taken from the Winter Count of Battiste Good, for the year 1744–'45. The pictograph is a human head with cropped hair and red cheeks. It is a front view. This tribe cuts the hair short and uses red paint upon the cheeks very extensively. This character is of frequent occurrence in Battiste Good's count.

FIG. 504.—Omaha.

Fig. 505.—The Dakotas killed an Omaha in the night. Cloud Shield's Winter Count, 1806–'07.

This is a side view of the same. The illustration does not show the color of the cheeks.

FIG. 505.—Omaha.

Fig. 506.—The Dakotas and Omahas made peace. Cloud-Shield's Winter Count, 1791–'92.

The Omaha is on the right and the Dakota on the left.

FIG. 506.—Omaha.

FIG. 507.—Pawnee.

Fig. 507 is the tribal designation of the Pawnee by the Dakotas, taken from Battiste Good's Winter Count for the year 1704–'05.

He says: The lower part of the legs are ornamented with slight projections resembling the husks on the bottom of an ear of corn.

FIG. 508.—Pawnee.

Fig. 508.—Brulés kill a number of Pawnees. The-Flame's Winter Count, 1873–'74.

This is the abbreviated or conventionalized form of the one preceding.

FIG. 509.—Pawnee.

Fig. 509.—They killed many Pawnees on the Republican river. Cloud-Shield's Winter Count, 1873–'74.

Here the arrangement of the hair makes the distinction.

In this connection it is useful to quote Dunbar (a):

The tribal mark of the Pawnees in their pictographic or historic painting was the scalp lock dressed to stand nearly erect or curving slightly backwards, somewhat like a horn. This, in order that it should retain its position, was filled with vermillion or other pigment, and sometimes lengthened by means of a tuft of horse hair skillfully appended so as to form a trail back over the shoulders. This usage was undoubtedly the origin of the name Pawnee. * * * It is most probably derived from *pá-rik-ĭ*, a horn, and seems to have been once used by the Pawnees themselves to designate their peculiar scalp lock. From the fact that this was the most noticeable feature in their costume, the name came naturally to be the denominative term of the tribe.

FIG. 510.—Ponka.

Fig. 510.—The Ponkas came and attacked a village, notwithstanding peace had just been made with them. American-Horse's Winter Count, 1778–'79.

Some elk hair which is used to form a ridge about 8 inches long and 2 in breadth, worn from the forehead to the back of the neck, and a feather, represent Ponka. Horse tracks are used for horses. Attack is indicated by marks which represent bullet marks, and which convey the idea that the bullet struck. The marks are derived from the gesture-sign "it struck." See Chapter XVIII, section 4.

Fig. 511.—An Indian woman, who had been un-
faithful to a white man to whom she was married,
was killed by an Indian named Ponka. American-
Horse's Winter Count, 1804–'05.

The emblem for Ponka is the straight elk hair
ridge.

FIG. 511.—Ponka.

Fig. 512.—A Ponka, who was captured when a boy
by the Oglalas, was killed while outside the village
by a war party of Ponkas. American-Horse's Winter Count, 1793–'94.

The artificial headdress, consisting of a ridge of
elk hair, is again portrayed.

FIG. 512.—Ponka.

SHOSHONI.

Dr. George Gibbs (*b*) describes a pictograph made by one of the
Indian tribes of Oregon and Washington, upon which "the figure of a
man with a long queue or scalp lock reached to his heels denoted a Shoshoni, that tribe being in the habit of braiding horse or other hair into
their own in that manner."

This may be correct regarding the Shoshoni Indians among the
extreme northwestern tribes, but the mark of identification could not be
based upon the custom of braiding with their own hair that of animals, to
increase the length and appearance of the queue, as this custom also prevails among the Absaroka, Hidatsa, and Arikaa Indians, respectively,
as before mentioned in this work.

Tanner's Narrative (*e*) gives additional information on this topic
regarding the absence of any tribal sign in connection with a human
figure.

The men of the same tribe are extensively acquainted with the totems which belong to each, and if on any record of this kind the figure of a man appears without
any designatory mark, it is immediately understood that he is a Sioux or at least a
stranger. Indeed, in most instances the figures of men are not used at all, merely
the totem or surname, being given. * * * It may be observed that the Algonkins believe all other Indians to have totems, though from the necessity they are
in general under of remaining ignorant of those hostile bands, the omission of the
totem in their picture writing serves to designate an enemy. Thus, those bands of
Ojibbeways who border on the country of the Dahcotah or Sioux, always understand the figure of a man without totem to mean one of that people.

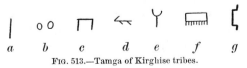

FIG. 513.—Tamga of Kirghise tribes.

In Sketches of Northwestern Mongolia, (*a*) are the tamga or seals of
Kirghise tribes, of which Fig. 513 is a copy.

The explanation given is as follows: *a*. Kipchaktamga: letter alip. *b*. Arguin tamga: eyes. *c*. Naiman tamga: posts (of door). *d*. Kongrat, Kirei, tamga: vine. *e*. Nak tamga: prop. *f*. Tarakti tamga: comb. *g*. Tyulimgut tamga: pike.

SECTION 2.

GENTILE AND CLAN DESIGNATIONS.

The clan and totemic system formerly called the gentile system undoubtedly prevailed anciently in Europe and Asia, but first became understood by observations of its existence in actual force among the aborigines of America and Australia, and typical representations of it are still found among them. In Australia it is called kobong. An animal or a plant, or sometimes a heavenly body was mythologically at first and at last sociologically connected with all persons of a certain stock, who believe, or once believed, that it was their tutelar god and they bear its name.

Each clan or gens took as a badge or objective totem the representation of the tutelar daimon from which it was named. As most Indian tribes were zootheistic, the object of their devotion was generally an animal—e. g., an eagle, a panther, a buffalo, a bear, a deer, a raccoon, a tortoise, a snake, or a fish, but sometimes was one of the winds, a celestial body, or other impressive object or phenomenon.

American Indians once generally observed a prohibition against killing the animal connected with their totem or eating any part of it. For instance, most of the southern Indians abstained from killing the wolf; the Navajo do not kill bears; the Osage never killed the beaver until the skins became valuable for sale. Afterward some of the animals previously held sacred were killed; but apologies were made to them at the time, and in almost all cases the prohibition or taboo survived with regard to certain parts of those animals which were not to be eaten on the principle of synecdoche, the temptation to use the food being too strong to permit entire abstinence. The Cherokee forbade the use of the tongues of the deer and bear for food. They cut these members out and cast them into the fire sacramentally. A practice still exists among the Ojibwa as follows: There is a formal restriction against members of the bear clan eating the animal, yet by a subdivision within the same clan an arrangement is made so that sub-clans may among them eat the whole animal. When a bear is killed, the head and paws are eaten by those who form one branch of the bear totem, and the remainder is reserved for the others. Other Indian tribes have invented a differentiation in which some clansmen may eat the ham and not the shoulder of certain animals, and others the shoulder and not the ham.

It follows, therefore, that sometimes the whole animal is designated as a clan totem, and also that sometimes only parts of it is selected.

Many of the devices given in this paper under the heading of personal
names have this origin.   The following figures show a selection of parts
of animals that may further illustrate the subject.   It must, however,
be borne in mind that some of the cases may be connected with indi-

FIG. 514.—Dakota gentile designations.

vidual visions or with personal adventures and not directly with the
clan system.   In the absence of detailed information in each instance
discrimination is impossible.

Schoolcraft says that the Ojibwa always placed the totemic or clan pictorial mark upon the *adjedatig* or grave-post, thereby sinking the personal name which is not generally indicative of the totem. The same practice is found in other tribes. The Pueblos depict the gentile or totemic pictorial sign upon their various styles of ceramic work.

Fig. 514, gives examples taken from Dakota drawings, which appear to be pictured totemic marks of gentes or clans. If not in every instance veritable examples, they illustrate the mode of their representation as distinct from the mere personal designations mentioned below, and yet without positive information in each case, it is not possible to decide on their correct assignment to this section of the present chapter.

FIG. 515.—Kwakiutl carvings.

a. Bear-Back.   Red-Cloud's Census.

This and the six following figures exhibit respectively the portions of the bear, viz, the back or chine, the ears, the head, the paw, the brains, and the nostrils or muzzle, which are probably the subject of taboo and are the sign of a clan or subclan.

b. Bear's-Ears, a Brulé, was killed in an Oglala village by the Crows. American-Horse's Winter Count, 1785–'86.

c. Bear's-Ears was killed in a fight with the Rees.   Cloud-Shield's Winter Count, 1793–'94.

This is another and more graphic delineation of the animal's ears.

d. Bear-Head. Red-Cloud's Census.

e. Bear-Paw. Red-Cloud's Census. The paws of the bear are considered to be a delicacy.

f. Bear-Brains. Red-Cloud's Census.

g. Bear-Nostrils. Red-Cloud's Census.

h. Hump. Red-Cloud's Census. The hump of the buffalo has been often praised as a delicious dish.

i. Elk-Head. Red-Cloud's Census.

Fig. 515 represents carved uprights in a house of the Kwakiutl Indians, British Columbia, taken from a work of Dr. Franz Boas (*b*).

The author says that these uprights are always carved according to the crest of the gens of the house owner, and represent men standing on the heads of animals. This use of the term "crest" is not heraldically correct, as literally it would require the men to be standing on the coverings of their own heads, but the idea is plain, the word being used for a device similar in nature and significance to the crest in heraldry, and it was adopted by the ancestors of the Kwakiutl gentes in relation to certain exploits that they had made. Both human figures show painting and probably also tattooing on their faces.

The character on the left hand also shows a design on the breast. That on the right hand presents a curious artifice of carving by which the legs and an arm are exhibited while preserving the solidity of the upright.

SECTION 3.

SIGNIFICANCE OF TATTOO.

Tattooing proper is a permanent marking of the skin accomplished by the introduction of coloring matter under the cutaneous epidermis. In popular expression and often in literature it includes penetration of the skin by cuts, gashes, or sometimes burns, without the insertion of coloring matter, the cicatrix being generally whiter than the sound skin of the people, most frequently of the dark races, among whom the practice is found. This form of figuration is distinguished as scarification and some examples of it are given below. The two varieties of tattoo may, however, for the purpose of this paper, be considered together and also in relation to painting the human body, which in its early use differs from them only in duration.

Mr. Herbert Spencer (*a*) considers all forms of tattoo to be originally tribal marks, and draws from that assumption additional evidence for his favorite theory of the deification of a dead tribal chief. Miss A. W. Buckland (*a*), in her essay on tattooing, follows in the same track, although recognizing modern deviations from the rule. A valuable article in the literature of the subject entitled "Tattooing among civilized people," by Dr. Robert Fletcher should be consulted. Also A tatuagem em Portugal, by Rocha Peixoto.

Dr. C. N. Starcke (*a*) lays down the law still more distinctly, thus:

The tattoo-marks make it possible to discover the remote connection between clans, and this token has such a powerful influence on the mind that there is no feud between tribes which are tattooed in the same way. * * * Tattooing may also lead to the formation of a group within the tribe.

Prof. Frederick Starr (*a*) makes these remarks:

As a sign of war prowess the gash of the Kaffir warrior may be described. After an act of bravery the priest cuts a deep gash in the hero's thigh. This heals blue and is a prized honor. To realize the value of a tribal mark think for a moment of the savage man's relation to the world outside. He is a very Ishmaelite. So long as he remains on his own tribal territory he is safe; when on the land of another tribe his life is the legitimate prey of the first man he meets. To men in such social relations the tribal mark is the only safety at home; without it he would be slain unrecognized by his own tribesmen. There must have been a time when the old Hebrews knew all about this matter of tribe marks. By this custom only can we fully understand the story of Cain (Gen. IV, 14, 15), who fears to be sent from his own territory lest he be slain by the first stranger he meets, but is protected by the tribal mark of those among whom he is to wander being put upon him. But in scarring, as in so many other cases, the original idea is often lost and the mark becomes merely ornamental. This is particularly true among women. Among men it more frequently retains its tribal significance.

After careful study of the topic, less positive and conclusive authority is found for this explanation of tattooing than was expected, considering its general admission.

The great antiquity of tattooing is shown by reference to it in the Old Testament, and in Herodotus, Xenophon, Tacitus, Ammianus, and Herodian. The publications on the topic are so numerous that the notes now to be presented are by no means exhaustive. They mainly refer to the Indian tribes of North America with only such comparatively recent reports from other lands as seem to afford elucidation.

TATTOO IN NORTH AMERICA.

G. Holm (*b*) says of the Greenland Innuit that geometric figures consisting of streaks and points, are used in tattooing on the breasts, arms, and legs of the females.

H. H. Bancroft (*b*) says:

The Eskimo females tattoo lines on their chins; the plebeian female of certain bands has one vertical line in the center and one parallel to it on either side The higher classes mark two vertical lines from each corner of the mouth. * * * Young Kadiak wives tattoo the breast and adorn the face with black lines. The Kuskoquim women sew into their chin two parallel blue lines.

William H. Gilder (*a*) reports:

The Esquimau wife has her face tattooed with lampblack and is regarded as a matron in society. * * * The forehead is decorated with the letter V in double lines, the angle very acute, passing down between the eyes almost to the bridge of the nose, and sloping gracefully to the right and left before reaching the roots of the hair. Each cheek is adorned with an egg-shaped pattern, commencing near the wing of the nose and sloping upward toward the corner of the eye; these lines are also double. The most ornamented part, however, is the chin, which receives a gridiron pattern; the lines double from the edge of the lower lip, and reaching to the throat toward the corners of the mouth, sloping outward to the angle of the lower jaw. This is all that is required by custom, but some of the belles do not stop here. * * * None of the men are tattooed.

An early notice of tattooing in the territory now occupied by the United States, mentioned in Hakluyt (*d*), is in the visit of the Florida chief, Satouriona, in 1564, to Réné Laudonnière. His tattooed figure was drawn by Le Moyne, Tabulæ VIII, IX.

Capt. John Smith (*a*) is made to say of the Virginia Indians:

They adorne themselues most with copper beads and paintings. Their women, some haue their legs, hands, breasts and face cunningly imbrodered with divers workes, as beasts, serpents, artificially wrought into their flesh with blacke spots.

Thomas Hariot (*a*), in Pl. XXIII, here reproduced as Fig. 516, Discoveries of 1585, discussing "The Marckes of sundrye of the Chief mene of Virginia," says:

The inhabitats of all the cuntrie for the most parte haue marks rased on their backs, wherby yt may be knowen what Princes subiects they bee, or of what place

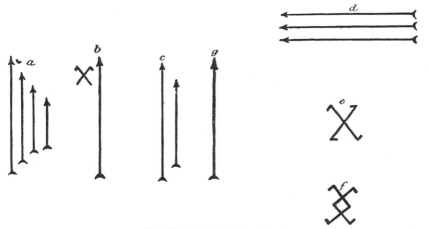

FIG. 516.—Virginian tattoo designs.

they haue their originall. For which cause we haue set downe those marks in this figure, and haue annexed the names of the places, that they might more easelye be discerned. Which industrie hath god indued them withal although they be verye simple, and rude. And to confesse a truthe I cannot remember, that euer I saw a better or quietter people than they.

The marks which I observed amonge them, are heere put downe in order folowinge.

The marke which is expressed by A. belongeth tho Wingino, the cheefe lorde of Roanoac.

That which hath B. is the marke of Wingino his sisters husbande.

Those which be noted with the letters of C. and D. belonge vnto diverse chefe lordes in Secotan.

Those which haue the letters E. F. G. are certaine cheefe men of Pomeiooc, and Aquascogoc.

Frère Gabriel Sagard (*b*) says (about 1636) of the Hurons that they tattooed by scratching with a bone of bird or fish, a black powder being applied to the bleeding wounds. The operation was not completed at once, but required several renewals. The object was to show bravery by supporting great pain as well as to terrify enemies.

In the Jesuit Relation for 1641, p. 75, it is said of the Neuter Nation that on their bodies from head to foot they marked a thousand diverse figures with charcoal pricked into the flesh on which beforehand they have traced lines for them.

Lemoyne D'Iberville, in 1649, Margry (b), remarked among the Bayogoulas that some of the young women had their faces and breasts pricked and marked with black.

In the Jesuit Relation for 1663, p. 28, there is an account that the head chief of the Iroquois, called by the French Nero, had killed sixty enemies with his own hand, the marks of which he bears printed on his thigh, which, therefore, appears covered over with black characters.

Joutel, in Margry (c), speaks of tattooing among the Texas Indians in 1687. Some women make a streak from the top of the forehead to chin, some make a triangle at the corners of their eyes, others on the breast and shoulders, others prick the lips. The marks are indelible.

Bacqueville de la Potherie (b) says of the Iroquois:

They paint several colors on the face, as black, white, yellow, blue, and vermillion. Men paint snakes from the forehead to the nose, but they prick the greater part of the body with a needle to draw blood. Bruised gunpowder makes the first coat to receive the other colors, of which they make such figures as they desire and they are never effaced.

M. Bossu (a) says of tatooing among the Osages in 1756:

It is a kind of knighthood to which they are only entitled by great actions; they suffer with pleasure in order to pass for men of courage.

If one of them should get himself marked without having previously distinguished himself in battle he would be degraded, and looked upon as a coward, unworthy of an honor. * * *

I saw an Indian, who, though he had never signalized himself in defense of the nation, got a mark made on his body in order to deceive those who only judged from appearance. The council agreed that, to obviate such an abuse, which would confound brave men with cowards, he who had wrongfully adorned himself with the figure of a club on his skin, without ever having struck a blow at war, should have the mark torn off; that is, the place should be flayed, and that the same should be done to all who would offend in the same case.

The Indian women are allowed to make marks all over their body, without any bad consequences; they endure it firmly, like the men, in order to please them, and to appear handsomer to them.

James Adair (a) says of the Chikasas in 1720:

They readily know achievements in war by the blue marks over their breasts and arms, they being as legible as our alphabetical characters are to us. Their ink is made of the root of pitch pine, which sticks to the inside of a greased earthen pot; then delineating the parts, they break through the skin with gairfish teeth, and rub over them that dark composition, to register them among the brave, and the impression is lasting. I have been told by the Chikasah that they formerly erased any false marks their warriors proudly and privately gave themselves, in order to engage them to give real proofs of their martial virtue, being surrounded by the French and their red allies; and that they degraded them in a public manner, by stretching the marked parts, and rubbing them with the juice of green corn, which in a great degree took out the impression.

Sir Alex. Mackenzie (b) tells that the Slave and Dog Rib Indians of the Athabaskan stock practiced tatooing. The men had two double lines, either black or blue, tattooed upon each cheek from the ear to the nose.

In James's Long (c) it is reported that—

The Omahas are often neatly tattooed in straight lines, and in angles on the breast, neck, and arms. The daughters of chiefs and those of wealthy Indians generally are denoted by a small round spot tattooed on the forehead. The process of tattooing is performed by persons who make it a business of profit.

Rev. J. Owen Dorsey (a) says:

In order that the ghost may travel the ghost-road in safety it is necessary for each Dakota, during his life, to be tattooed either in the middle of the forehead or on the wrists. In that event his spirit will go directly to the "Many Lodges."

The female Midē′ of the Ojibwa frequently tattoo the temples, forehead, or cheeks of sufferers from headache or toothache, which varieties of pain are believed to be caused by some malevolent manido or spirit. By this operation such demons are expelled, the ceremony being also accompanied by songs and gesticulations of exorcism. Relief is sometimes actually obtained through the counterirritant action of the tattooing, which is effected by using a small bunch of needles, though formerly several spicules of bone were tied together or used singly.

One old Ojibwa woman who was observed in 1887 had a round spot over each temple, made there to cure headache. The spots were of a bluish-black color, and about five-eighths of an inch in diameter. Another had a similar spot upon the nasal eminence, and a line of small dots running from the nostrils, horizontally outward over either cheek, two-thirds of the distance to the ears.

The men of the Wichita wore tattoo lines from the lips downward, and it is a significant fact that their tribal sign means "tattooed people," the same expression being used to designate them in the language of several neighboring tribes. This would imply that tattooing was not common in that region. The Kaiowa women, however, frequently had small circles tattooed on their foreheads, and the Sixtown Choctaws still are distinguished by perpendicular lines tatooed on the chin.

Mr. John Murdoch (b) reports of the Eskimo:

The custom of tattooing is almost universal among the women, but the marks are confined almost exclusively to the chin, and form a very simple pattern. This consists of one, three, five, or perhaps as many as seven vertical lines from the under lip to the tip of the chin, slightly radiating when there are more than one. When there is a single line, which is rather rare, it is generally broad, and the middle line is sometimes broader than the others. The women, as a rule, are not tattooed until they reach a marriageable age, though there were a few little girls in the two villages who had a single line on the chin. I remember seeing but one married woman in either village who was not tattooed, and she had come from a distant settlement, from Point Hope, as well as we could understand.

Tattooing on a man is a mark of distinction. Those men who are, or have been, captains of whaling umiaks that have taken whales have marks to indicate this tattooed somewhere on their persons, sometimes forming a definite tally. For instance, Añoru had a broad band across each cheek from the corners of the mouth, made up of many indistinct lines, which was said to indicate "many whales." Amaiyuna had the "flukes" of seven whales in a line across his chest, and Mŭ'ñialu had a couple of small marks on one forearm. Niăksára, the wife of Añoru, also had a little mark tattooed in each corner of her mouth, which she said were "whale marks," indicating that she was the wife of a successful whaleman. Such marks, according to Petitot (Monographie, etc., p. 15), are a part of the usual pattern in the Mackenzie district—"deux traits aux commissures de la bouche." One or two men at Nuwŭk had each a narrow line across the face over the bridge of the nose, which were probably also "whale marks," though we never could get a definite answer concerning them.

The tattooing is done with a needle and thread, smeared with soot or gunpowder, giving a peculiar pitted appearance to the lines. It is rather a painful operation, producing considerable inflammation and swelling, which lasts several days. The practice of tattooing the women is almost universal among the Eskimo from Greenland to Kadiak, including the Eskimo of Siberia, the only exception being the natives of Smith sound, though the custom is falling into disuse among the Eskimo who have much intercourse with the whites.

The simple pattern of straight, slightly diverging lines on the chin seems to prevail from the Mackenzie district to Kadiak, and similar chin lines appear always to form part of the more elaborate patterns, sometimes extending to the arms and other parts of the body, in fashion among the eastern Eskimo and those of Siberia, St. Lawrence island, and the Diomedes.

TATTOO ON THE PACIFIC COAST.

During the summer of 1884 Dr. Hoffman met, at Port Townsend, Washington, a party of Haida Indians from Queen Charlottes island, who were encamped there for a short time. Most of them were tattooed after the manner of the Haidas, the breast, back, forearm, and legs bearing partial or complete designs of animate forms relating to totems or myths. Some of the persons had been tattooed only in part, the figures upon the forearms, for instance, being incomplete, because the operation at a previous "potlatch" or festival had to be suspended on account of the great length of time required, or on account of an extra inflammatory condition of the affected parts.

Among this party of Haidas was Makdē'gos, the tattooer of the tribe, whose work is truly remarkable. The designs made by him are symmetrical, while the lines are uniform in width and regular and graceful in every respect. In persons tattooed upon the breast or back the part operated upon is first divided into halves by an imaginary vertical line upon the breast through the middle of the sternum and upon the back along the middle of the vertebral column. Such designs are drawn double, facing outward from this imaginary line. One side is first drawn and completed, while the other is merely a reverse transfer, made immediately afterwards or at such future time as the operation of tattooing may be renewed.

The colors are black and red, the former consisting of finely powdered charcoal, gunpowder, or India ink, while the latter is Chinese vermilion. The operation was formerly performed with sharp thorns, spines of certain fishes, or spicules of bone; but recently a small bunch of needles is used, which serves the purpose to better effect.

As is well known, the black pigments, when picked into the human skin, become rather bluish, which tint, when beneath the yellowish tinge of the Indian's cuticle, appears of an olive or sometimes a greenish-blue shade. The colors, immediately after being tattooed upon the skin, retain more or less of the blue-black shade; but by absorption of the pigment and the persistence of the coloring matter of the pigmentary membrane the greenish tint soon appears, becoming gradually less conspicuous as time progresses, so that in some of the oldest tattooed Indians the designs are greatly weakened in coloration.

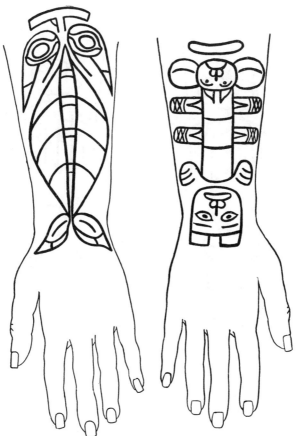

Fig. 517.—Haida tattoo, sculpin and dragon fly.

Upon the bodies of some persons examined the results of ulceration are conspicuous. This destruction of tissue is the result of inflammation caused by the tattooing and the introduction under the skin of so great a quantity of irritating foreign matter that, instead of designs in color, there are distinct, sharply defined figures in white or nearly white cicatrices, the pigmentary membrane having been totally destroyed by the ulceration.

The figures represented upon the several Indians met with, as above-mentioned, were not all of totemic signification, one arm, for instance, bearing the figure of the totem of which the person is a member, while the other arm presents the outline of a mythic being, as shown in Fig. 517, copied from the arms of a woman. The left device is taken from the left forearm, and represents kul, the skulpin, a totemic animal, whereas the right hand device, taken from the right arm of the same subject, represents mamathlóna, the dragon fly, a mythic insect.

In Fig. 518 two forms of the thunderbird are presented, copied from

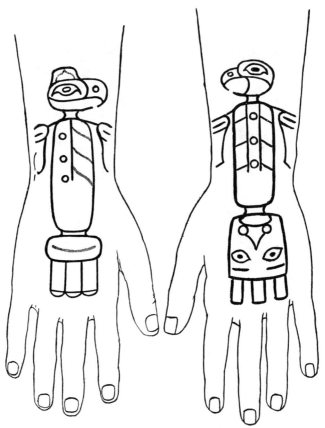

FIG. 518.—Haida tattoo, thunder-bird.

the right and left forearms and hands, respectively, of a Haida woman. The right hand device is complete, but that on the left, copied from the opposite forearm and hand, is incomplete, and it was expected that the design would be entirely finished at the "potlatch" which was to be held in the autumn of 1884. In the completed design the transverse curve in the body of the tail was red, as also the three diagonal lines upon the body of the bird running outward from the central vertical toward the radial side of the hand. The brace-shaped lines within the head ornament had also been tattooed in red.

In some instances the totem and mythic character are shown upon the same member, as is represented in Fig. 519. This tattooing was copied from the left arm of a woman, the complete figure upon the forearm and hand being that of a thunder bird, while the four heads upon the fingers represent that of the tshimō's, a mythic animal. The thunderbird had been tattooed upon the arms a number of years before the heads were added, probably because the protracted and painful operation of tattooing so large a figure deterred the sufferer from further

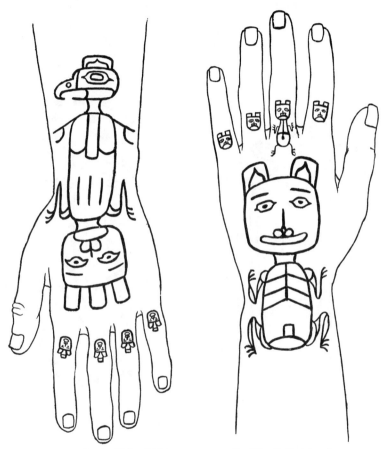

Fig. 519.—Haida tattoo, thunder-bird and tshimō's.　　　Fig. 520.—Haida tattoo, bear.

sitting. Sometimes, however, such postponement or noncompletion of an operation is the result of inability on the part of the subject to defray the expense.

Another instance of the interrupted condition of tattooed designs is presented in Fig. 520. The figure upon the forearm and hand is that of the bear totem, and was made first. At a subsequent festival the bear heads were tattooed upon the fingers, and, last of all, the body was tattooed upon the middle finger, leaving three yet to be completed.

Fig. 521 shows tattoo designs upon the leg.   These represent mēt, the mountain goat.

It is seldom that double designs occur on the extremities, such being reserved for the breast and back, but an instance was noted, represented in Fig. 522, which is a representation of hélinga, the thunderbird, and was on the left arm of a man.

One of the most conspicuous examples of the art observed among the party of traveling Haidas mentioned, was that of a double raven tattooed upon the breast of Makdē′gos, copied here as Fig. 523.

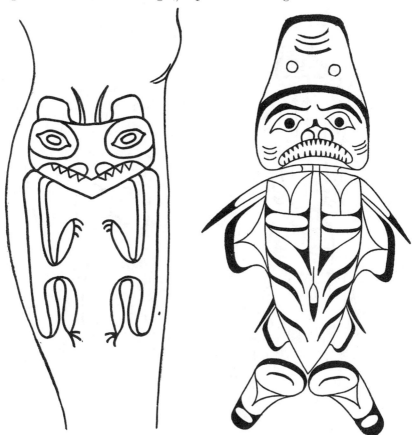

FIG. 521.—Haida tattoo, mountain goat.   FIG. 524.—Haida tattoo, dogfish.

Upon the back of this Indian is also the figure of kahátta, the dog-fish, Fig. 524.   In addition to these marks he bears also upon his extremities totemic and mythic animals.

Sometimes the simple outline designs employed in tattooing are painted upon property belonging to various persons, such as boats, housefronts, etc.   In such instances colors are employed that could not be used in tattooing.   One fine example of such is presented in Pl. XXIV and another of more elaborate design in Pl. XXV.

Plate XXIV.

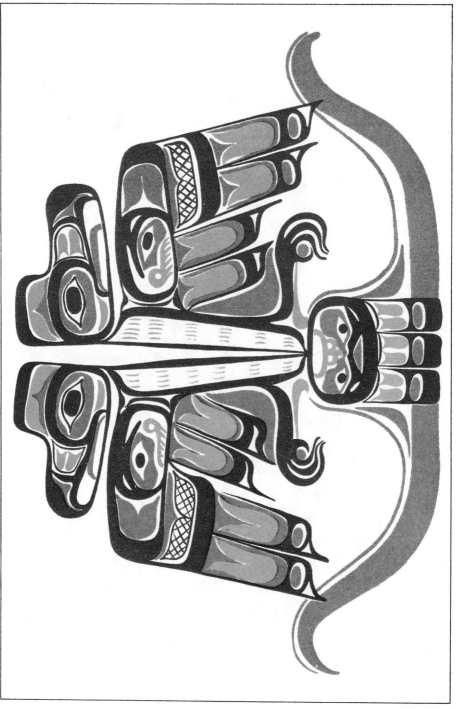

HAIDA DOUBLE THUNDERBIRD.

Plate XXV.

HAIDA DOG-FISH.

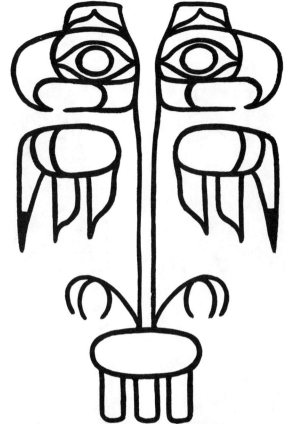

Fig. 522.—Haida tattoo, double thunder-bird.

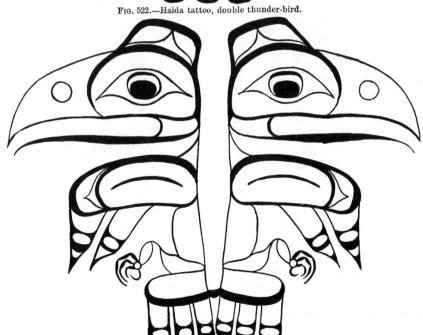

Fig. 523.—Haida tattoo. double raven.

Mr. James G. Swan made a valuable contribution on tattoo marks of the Haida Indians of Queen Charlotte islands, British Columbia, and the Prince of Wales archipelago, Alaska, published in the Fourth

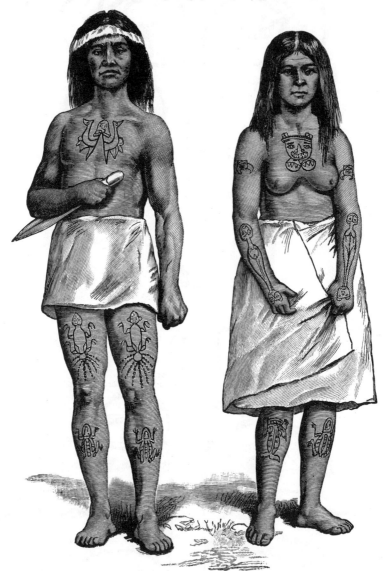

FIG. 525.—Tattooed Haidas.

Annual Report of the Bureau of Ethnology, which, much condensed, is reproduced as follows:

Among all the tribes or bands belonging to the Haida family, the practice of tattooing the person in some manner is common; but the most marked are the Haidas proper, or those living on Queen Charlotte islands, and the Kaiganis, of Prince of Wales archipelago, Alaska.

I am of the opinion, judging from my own observation of over twenty years among the coast tribes, that but few females can be found among the Indians, not only on Vancouvers island, but all along the coast to the Columbia river, and perhaps even to California, that are *not* marked with some device tattooed on their hands, arms, or ankles, either dots or straight lines; but of all of the tribes mentioned, the Haidas stand preeminent for tattooing, and seem to be excelled only by the natives of the Fiji islands or the King's Mills group in the south seas. The

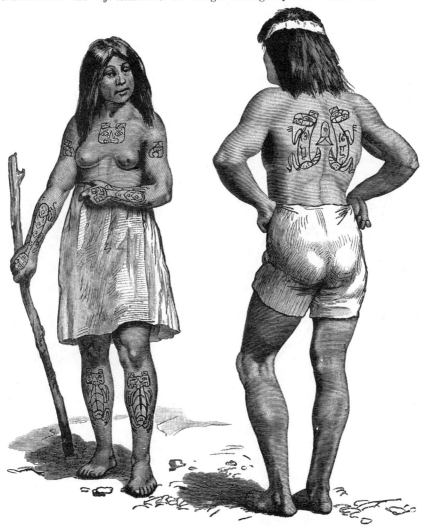

Fɪɢ. 526.—Tattooed Haidas.

tattoo marks of the Haidas are heraldic designs or the family totem, or crests of the wearers, and are similar to the carvings depicted on the pillars and monuments around the homes of the chiefs, which casual observers have thought were idols.

These designs are invariably placed on the men between the shoulders just below the back of the neck, on the breast, on the front part of both thighs, and on the legs below the knee. On the women they are marked on the breast, on both shoulders, on both forearms, from the elbow down over the back of the hands to the knuckles, and on both legs below the knee to the ankle.

Almost all of the Indian women of the northwest coast have tattoo marks on their hands and arms, and some on the face; but as a general thing these marks are mere dots or straight lines having no particular significance. With the Haidas, however, every mark has its meaning; those on the hands and arms of the women indicate the family name, whether they belong to the bear, beaver, wolf, or eagle totems, or any of the family of fishes. As one of them quaintly remarked to me, "If you were tattooed with the design of a swan, the Indians would know your family name."

In order to illustrate this tattooing as correctly as possible I inclose herewith sketches of the tattoo marks on two women and their husbands, taken by me at Port Townsend.

The man on the left hand of Fig. 525 is a tattooed Haida. On his breast is the cod (kahatta), split from the head to the tail and laid open; on each thigh is the octopus (noo), and below each knee is the frog (flkamkostan).

FIG. 527.—Two forms of skulpin, Haida.

The woman in the same figure has on her breast the head and fore-paws of the beaver (tsching); on each shoulder is the head of the eagle or thunder-bird (skamskwin); on each arm, extending to and covering the back of the hand, is the halibut (hargo); on the right leg is the skulpin (kull); on the left leg is the frog (flkamkostan).

The woman in Fig. 526 has a bear's head (hoorts) on her breast. On each shoulder is the eagle's head, and on her arms and legs are figures of the bear.

The back of the man in the same figure has the wolf (wasko), split in halves and tattooed between his shoulders, which is shown enlarged in Fig. 531. Wasko is a mythological being of the wolf species, similar to the chu-chu-hmexl of the Makah Indians, an antediluvian demon supposed to live in the mountains.

The skulpin, on the right leg of the woman in Fig. 525, is shown enlarged in Fig. 527; the frog on the left leg in Fig. 528. The codfish on the man in Fig. 525 is shown enlarged in Fig. 529; the octopus or squid in Fig. 530.

As the Haidas, both men and women, are very light-colored, some of the latter—full blooded Indians, too—having their skins as fair as Europeans, the tattoo marks show very distinct.

FIG. 528.—Frog, Haida.

FIG. 529.—Cod, Haida.

The same author continues:

This tattooing is not all done at one time, nor is it everyone who can tattoo. Certain ones, almost always men, have a natural gift which enables them to excel in this kind of work. One of the young chiefs, named Geneskelos, was the best designer I knew, and ranked among his tribe as a tattooer.

He told me the plan he adopted was first to draw the design carefully on the person with some dark pigment, then prick it in with needles, and then rub over the wound with some more coloring matter till it acquired the proper hue. He had a variety of instruments composed of needles tied neatly to sticks. His favorite one was a flat strip of ivory or bone, to which he had firmly tied five or six needles, with their points projecting beyond the end just far enough to raise the skin without inflicting a dangerous wound, but these needle points stuck out quite sufficiently to

FIG. 530.—Squid, Haida.

FIG. 531.—Wolf, Haida.

make the operation very painful, and although he applied some substance to deaden the sensation of the skin, yet the effect was on some to make them quite sick for a few days; consequently, the whole process of tattooing was not done at one time. As this tattooing is a mark of honor, it is generally done at or just prior to a Tomanawos performance and at the time of raising the heraldic columns in front of the chief's houses. The tattooing is done in open lodge and is witnessed by the company assembled. Sometimes it takes several years before all the tattooing is done, but when completed and the person well ornamented, then they are happy and can take their seats among the elders.

Other notices about the tattooing of the Indians of the Pacific slope of North America are subjoined.

Stephen Powers (c) says the Karok (California) squaws tattoo in blue three narrow fern leaves perpendicularly on the chin, one falling from each corner of the mouth and one in the middle.

The same author reports, page 76:

Nearly every (Hupâ, California) man has ten lines tattooed across the inside of the left arm about halfway between the wrist and the elbow; and in measuring shell money he takes the string in his right hand, draws one end over his left thumb nail, and if the other end reaches to the uppermost of the tattoo lines the five shells are worth $25 in gold, or $5 a shell. Of course, it is only one in ten thousand that is long enough to reach this high value.

Also on page 96:

The Pátawăt (California) squaws tattoo in blue three narrow pinnate leaves perpendicularly on their chins, and also lines of small dots on the backs of their hands.

On page 148, of the Kástel Pomo:

The women of this and other tribes of the Coast range frequently tattoo a rude representation of a tree or other object covering nearly the whole abdomen and breast.

Of the Wintūns he says, page 233: "The squaws all tattoo three narrow lines, one falling from each corner of the mouth and one between."

The same author says, on page 109:

The Mattoal, of California, differ from other tribes in that the men tattoo. Their distinctive mark is a round blue spot in the center of the forehead. The women tattoo pretty much all over their faces.

In respect to this matter of tattooing there is a theory entertained by some old pioneers which may be worth the mention. They hold that the reason why the women alone tattoo in all other tribes is that in case they are taken captives their own people may be able to recognize them when there comes an opportunity of ransom. There are two facts which give some color of probability to this reasoning. One is that the California Indians are rent into such infinitesimal divisions, any one of which may be arrayed in deadly feud against another at any moment, that the slight differences in their dialects would not suffice to distinguish the captive squaws. The second is that the squaws almost never attempt any ornamental tattooing, but adhere closely to the plain regulation mark of the tribe.

Blue marks tattooed upon a Mohave woman's chin denote that she is married. See Whipple (f).

Mr. Gatschet reports that very few Klamath men now tattoo their faces, but such as are still observed have but a single line of black running from the middle of the lower lip to the chin. Half-breed girls appear to have but one perpendicular line tattooed down over the chin while the full-blood women have four perpendicular lines on the chin.

In Bancroft's Native Races (c), it is stated that the Modoc women tattoo three blue lines, extending perpendicularly from the center and corners of the lower lip to the chin.

The same author on pages 117 and 127 of the same volume says:

The Chippewas have tattooed cheeks and foreheads. Both sexes have blue or black bars or from one to four straight lines to distinguish the tribe to which they belong. They tattoo by entering an awl or needle under the skin and drawing it out, immediately rubbing powdered charcoal into the wounds. * * * On the Yukon river among the Kutchins, the men draw a black stripe down the forehead and the nose, frequently crossing the forehead and cheeks with red lines and streaking the chin alternately with red and black, and the women tattoo the chin with a black pigment.

Stephen Powers, in Overland Monthly, XII, 537, 1874, says of the Normocs:

I saw a squaw who had executed on her cheeks the only representation of a living object which I ever saw done in tattooing. It was a couple of bird's wings, one on each cheek, done in blue, bottom-edge up, the butt of the wing at the corner of the mouth, and the tip near the ear. It was quite well wrought, both in correctness of form and in delicateness of execution, not only separate feathers but even the filaments of the vane, being finely pricked in.

Dr. Franz Boas (c) says:

Tattooings are found on arms, breast, back, legs, and feet among the Haida; on arms and feet among the Tshimshian, Kwakiutl and Bilqula; on breast and arms among the Nootka; on the jaw among the Coast Salish women.

Among the Nootka scars may frequently be seen running at regular intervals from the shoulder down the breast to the belly, and in the same way down the legs and arms. * * *

Members of tribes practicing the Hamats'a ceremonies show remarkable scars produced by biting. At certain festivals it is the duty of the Hamats'a to bite a piece of flesh out of the arms, leg, or breast of a man.

TATTOO IN SOUTH AMERICA.

Dr. im Thurn (c) says:

Tattooing or any other permanent interference with the surface of the skin by way of ornament is practiced only to a very limited extent by the Indians; is used, in fact, only to produce the small distinctive tribal mark which many of them bear at the corners of their mouths or on their arms. It is true that an adult Indian is hardly to be found on whose thighs and arms, or on other parts of whose body are not a greater or less number of indelibly incised straight lines; but these are scars originally made for surgical, not ornamental purposes.

Herndon and Gibbon (a), p. 319, report:

Following the example of the other nations of Brazil (who tattoo themselves with thorns, or pierce their nose, the lips, and the ears,) and obeying an ancient law which commands these different tortures, this baptism of blood, * * * the Mahués have preserved * * * the great festival of the Tocandeira.

Paul Marcoy (b) says of the Passés, Yuris, Barrés, and Chumanas, of Brazil, that they mark their faces (in tattoo) with the totem or emblem of the nation to which they belong. It is possible at a few steps distant to distinguish one nation from another.

EXTRA-LIMITAL TATTOO.

Ancient monarchs adopted special marks to distinguish slaves; likewise for vengeance as an indelible and humiliating brand, a certain tattoo denounced him who had fallen into disgrace with a sovereign. Two monks having censured the iconoclastic frenzy of the emperor

Theophilus, he ordered to be imprinted on their foreheads eleven iambic verses; Philip of Macedon, from whom a soldier had solicited the possession of a man saved by him from shipwreck, ordered that on his forehead should be drawn signs indicative of his base greed; Caligula, without any object, commanded the tattooing of the Roman nobles.

In the period of the decline of Rome, tattooing was extensively practiced. Regulative laws prescribed the adopted symbols which were a proof of enlistment in the ranks and on which the military oath was taken. The purpose of this ordinance, which continued in force for a long time, was similar to that which authorized the marking of the slaves, since, the spirit of the people having become degenerated, the army was composed of mercenaries who, if they should run away, must be recognized, pursued, and captured. Until recently the practice,

Fig. 532.—Australian grave and carved trees.

though more as a mark of manhood, was followed by the soldiers of the Piedmontese army.

Élisée Reclus (a) says:

Tattooing was in Polynesia widespread, and so highly developed that the artistic designs covering the body served also to clothe it. In certain islands the operation lasted so long that it had to be begun before the children were six years old, and the pattern was largely left to the skill and cunning of the professional tattooers. Still traditional motives recurred in the ornamental devices of the several tribes, who could usually be recognized by their special tracings, curved or parallel lines, diamond forms and the like. The artists were grouped in schools like the old masters in Europe, and they worked not by incision as in most Melanesian islands, but by punctures with a small comb-like instrument slightly tapped with a mallet. The pigment used in the painful and even dangerous operation was usually the fine charcoal yielded by the nut of Aleurites triloba, an oleaginous plant used for illuminating purposes throughout eastern Polynesia.

The following is from Rev. Richard Taylor (c) about the New Zealanders, Te Ika a Maui:

Before they went to fight, the youth were accustomed to mark their countenances with charcoal in different lines, and their traditions state that this was the beginning of the tattoo, for their wars became so continuous, that to save the trouble of thus constantly painting the face, they made the lines permanent by the moko; it is, however, a question whether it did not arise from a different cause; formerly the grand mass of men who went to fight were the black slaves, and when they fought side by side with their lighter colored masters, the latter on those occasions used charcoal to make it appear they were all one.

Fig. 533.—New Zealand tattooed head and chin mark.

Whilst the males had every part of the face tattooed, and the thighs as well, the females had chiefly the chin and the lips, although occasionally they also had their thighs and breasts, with a few smaller marks on different parts of the body as well. There were regular rules for tattooing, and the artist always went systematically to work, beginning at one spot and gradually proceeding to another, each particular part having its distinguishing name.

Fig. 532 is an illustration from the same work, facing page 378. It shows the " grave of an Australian native, with his name, rank, tribe, etc., cut in hieroglyphics on the trees," which " hieroglyphics " are supposed to be connected with his tattoo marks.

Fig. 534.—Tattoo design on bone, New Zealand.

Fig. 533 is a copy of a tattooed head carved by Hongi, and also of the tattooing on a woman's chin, taken from the work last cited.

The accompanying illustration, Fig. 534, is taken from a bone obtained from a mound in New Zealand, by Prof. I. C. Russell, formerly of the U. S. Geological Survey. He says that the Maori formerly tattooed the bones of enemies, though the custom now seems to have been abandoned. The work consists of sharp, shallow lines, as if made with a sharp-pointed steel instrument, into which some blackish pigment has been rubbed, filling up some of the markings, while in others scarcely a trace remains.

In connection with the use of the tattoo marks as reproduced on artificial objects see Fig. 734.

Fig. 535 is a copy of a photograph obtained in New Zealand by Prof. Russell. It shows tattooing upon the chin.

Prof. Russell, in his sketch of New Zealand, published in the Am. Naturalist, XIII, 72, Feb., 1879, remarks, that the desire of the Maori for ornament is so great that they covered their features with tattooing,

FIG. 535.—Tattooed woman, New Zealand.

transferring indelibly to their faces complicated patterns of curved and spiral lines, similar to the designs with which they decorated their canoes and their houses.

E. J. Wakefield (a) reports of a man observed in New Zealand that he was a tangata tabu or sacred personage, and consequently was not adorned with tatu. He adds, p. 155, that the deeds of the natives are signed with elaborate drawings of the moko or tatu on the chiefs' faces.

Dr. George Turner (b) says:

Herodotus found among the Thracians that the man who was not tattooed was not respected. It was the same in Samoa. Until a young man was tattooed he was considered in his minority. He could not think of marriage, and he was constantly exposed to taunts and ridicule, as being poor and of low birth, and as having no right to speak in the society of men. But as soon as he was tattooed he passed into his majority, and considered himself entitled to the respect and privileges of mature years. When a youth, therefore, reached the age of 16, he and his friends were all anxiety that he should be tattooed. He was then on the outlook for the tattooing of some young chief with whom he might unite. On these occasions six or a dozen young men would be tattooed at one time, and for these there might be four or five tattooers employed. Tattooing is still kept up to some extent and is a regular profession, just as house-building, and well paid. The custom is traced to mythologic times and has its presiding deities.

In Révue d'Ethnographie (a) (translated) it is published that—

Tattoo marks of Papuan men in New Guinea can be worn on the chest only when the man has killed an enemy. · Fig. 26, p. 101, shows the marks upon the chest of Waara, who had killed five men.

Tattoo marks upon parts other than the chest of the bodies of men and women do not seem to have significance. They are made according to the fancy of the designer. Frequently the professional tattooers have styles of their own, which, being popular and generally applied, become customary to a tribe.

The illustration above mentioned is reproduced as Fig. 536.

FIG. 536.—Tattoo on Papuan chief.

In the same article, p. 112, is the following, referring to Fig. 537:

Among the Papuans of New Guinea tattooing the chest of females denotes that they are married, though all other parts of the body, including the face and legs, may be tattooed long before; indeed the tattooing of girls may begin at 5 years of age. Fig. 39, p. 112, gives an illustration of a married woman. * * * The different forms of tattoo depend upon the style of the several artists. Family marks are not recognizable, but exist.

De Clercq (a) gives further particulars about tattooing among the Papuans of New Guinea. Among the Sègèt it is only on women. They call it "fadjan," and the figures consist of two rows of little circles, on each side of the abdomen toward the region of the arm-pit, with a few cross strokes on the outer edge; it is done by pricking with a needle and afterwards the spots are fumigated with the smoke of burning resin. It is said to be intended as an ornament instead of dress, and that young girls do it because young men like to see it.

At Roembati tattooing is called "gomanroeri" and at Sĕkar "béti." They do it there with bones of fish, with which they prick many holes in the skin until the blood flows, and then smear on it in spots the soot from pans and pots, which, after the staunching of the blood, leaves an ineffaceable bluish spot or streak.   Besides the breast and upper arm they also tattoo in the same way the calf of the leg, and in some cases the forehead, as a mere ornamentation, both of men and women—children only in very exceptional cases.

The Bonggose and Sirito are much tattooed over the breast and shoulder.   At Saoekorèm, a Doré settlement, a few women were seen tattooed on the breast and in the face.   At Doré it is called "pa," and

FIG. 537.—Tattooed Paupan woman.

is done with thorns, and charcoal is rubbed over the bloody spots; only here and at Mansinam is it a sign of mourning; everywhere else it merely serves as ornamentation.

At Ansoes it does not occur much, and is principally in the face; it is there called "toi." It is found somewhat more commonly on Noord-Japèn, and then on shoulder and upper arm. In Tarfia, Tana-mérah, and Humboldt bay but few persons were tattooed, mostly on the forehead.

The tattooing is always the work of women, generally members of the family, both on men and on women.   First the figure is drawn with charcoal, and if it suits the taste then begins the pricking with the thorn of a citrus or a fine bone of some animal.   It is very painful and only a small spot can be pricked at one time, so long as the tattooee can stand it.   If the pain is too violent, the wounds are gently pressed with a certain leaf that has been warmed, in order to soothe the pain, and the work is continued only after three or four days.   No special names are given to the figures; those are chosen which suit the taste.   Children are never tattooed at the wish of the parents; it is entirely a matter of individual choice.

Mr. Forbes, in Journ. Anthrop. Inst. G. B. and I., August, 1883, p. 10, says that in Timor Laut, an island of the Malay archipelago—

Both sexes tattoo a few simple devices, circles, stars, and pointed crosses, on the breast, on the brow, on the cheek, and on the wrists, and scar themselves on the arms and shoulders with red-hot stones, in imitation of immense smallpox marks, in order to ward off that disease.   *   *   *   I have, however, seen no one variolamarked, nor can I learn of any epidemic of this disease among them.

Prof. Brauns, of Halle, reports, Science, III, No. 50, p. 69, that among the Ainos of Yazo the women tattoo their chins to imitate the beards of the men.

Carl Bock (*a*) says:

All the married women here are tattooed on the hands and feet and sometimes on the thighs. The decoration is one of the privileges of matrimony and is not permitted to unmarried girls.

In Myths and Songs from the South Pacific, London, 1876, p. 94, it is said that in Mangaia, of the Hervey group, the tattoo is in imitation of the stripes on the two kinds of fish, avini and paoro, the color of which is blue. The legend of this is kept in the song of Iná.

Elisée Reclus (*b*) says:

Most of the Dayaks tattoo the arms, hands, feet, and thighs; occasionally also breast and temples. The designs, generally of a beautiful blue color on the coppery ground of the body, display great taste, and are nearly always disposed in odd numbers, which, as among so many other peoples, are supposed to be lucky.

In L'Anthropologie (*a*), 1890, T. I, No. 6, p. 693, it is thus reported:

Tradition tells that the Giao chi, the alleged ancestors of the Annamites, were fishermen and in danger from marine monsters. To prevent disasters from the genii of the waters the king directed the people to tattoo their bodies with the forms of the marine monsters, and afterwards the dragons, crocodiles, etc., ceased their persecution. The custom became universal, and even the kings tattooed a dragon on their thighs as a sign of power and nobility. The same idea was in the painting of eyes, etc., on the prows of Annamite boats, which strongly resembled the sea monsters.

Mr. O'Reilly, the professional tattooer of New York, in a letter, says that he is familiar with the tattoo system of Burmah, and that, besides the ruling principle of ordeal, the Burmese use special tattoo marks to charm and to bring love. They also believe that tattooing the whole person renders the skin impenetrable to weapons.

In Zeitschrift für Ethnologie (*a*) it is recounted of the Badagas in the Nilgiri mountains, India:

All the women are tattooed on the forehead. The following [Fig. 538] *a* is the most usual form:

Besides this there occur the following (same Fig., *b*, *c*, *d*, and *e*):

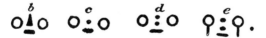

Besides the forehead, the tattooing of which is obligatory for women, other parts of the body are often tattooed thus (same Fig., *f*)

FIG. 538.—Badaga tattoo marks.

on each shoulder. Other forms not infrequently found are variously grouped dots, also those shown in the same Fig., *g*, on the forearm and the back of the hand.

Nordenskiöld (*a*) gives the following account of tattooing among the Chukchis of Siberia:

It is principally the women that tattoo. The operation is performed by means of pins and soot; perhaps also graphite is employed, which the Chukchis gather. The tattooing of the women seems to be the same along the whole Chukchi coast from Cape Shelagskoy to Bering strait. The usual mode of tattooing is found represented in Nordenskiöld's "Voyage of the Vega around Asia and Europe," second part, p. 104. Still the tattooing on the cheek is not rarely more compound than is there shown. The picture given below [Fig. 539] represents a design of tattooing on the cheek.

Girls under nine or ten years are never tattooed. On reaching that age they gradually receive the two streaks running from the point of the nose to the root of the hair; next follow the vertical chin streaks and lastly the tattooing on the cheeks, of which the anterior arches are first formed and the posterior part of the design last. The last named in fact is the part of the design which is oftenest wanting.

The accompanying picture (the left hand of the same Fig.) represents the tattooing of the arms of a woman from the town of T'ápka. The design of the tattooing extends from the shoulder joint, where the upper triple ring is situated, to the hand joint at the bottom. As appears from the drawing, the tattooing on the right an left arm is different.

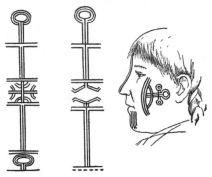

FIG. 539.—Chukchi tattoo marks.

The men at the winter station of the Vega tattooed themselves only with two short horizontal streaks across the root of the nose. Some of the men at Rerkaypiya (C. North), on the other hand, had a cross tattooed on each cheek bone; others had merely painted similar ones with red mold. Some Chukchis at the latter place had also the upper lip tattooed.

The Chukchi designs are much simpler than those of the Eskimo.

Dr. Bazin, in "Étude sur le Tatouage dans la Régence de Tunis," in L'Anthropologie (*b*), tells that the practice of tattooing is very widespread and elaborate in Tunisia, but chiefly among the natives of Arab race, who are nomads, workmen in the towns, and laborers, and also among the fellahs. The Berbers, on the contrary, who have remained mountaineers, the merchants of the coast towns, and the rich proprietors are little or not at all tattooed. In regard to the last class this proves that tattooing has become nothing but an ornament, since the members of this class are clothed in such a way that the legs and arms are completely covered, so that it would be useless to draw figures which would be invisible or almost entirely hidden. He adds that the notables "du Tinge" do not disfigure themselves by incisions. The distinctive sign of the lower classes is the presence of three incisions on the temples, three on the cheeks, and three also on the lower part of the face.

Notes on East-Equatorial Africa, in Bull. Soc. d'Anthro. de Bruxelles (a) contains the following memoranda: Tattooing is done by traveling artists. Perhaps at first it showed tribal characteristics, but now it is difficult to distinguish more than fancy. The exception is that Wawenba alone tattoo the face. The local fetiches bear marks of tattoo.

Gordon Cumming (a) says:

One of the "generals" of Mosielely, King of the Bakatlas group of the Bechuana tribe, had killed about twenty men in battle with his own hand, and bore a mark of honor for every man. This mark was a line tattooed on his ribs.

David Greig Rutherford (a) makes remarks on the people of Batanga, West Tropical Africa, from which the following is extracted:

Tattooing evidently originated in certain marks being applied to the face and other parts of the body in order to distinguish the members of one tribe from those of another. The same marks would be used for both sexes, but as the tendency to ornamentation became developed, they would be apt to observe some artistic method in making them. Among the Dualles the custom at one time appears to have obtained with both sexes, with a preponderance, however, in the practice of it on the side of the women. The men did not always see the force of giving themselves needless pain, but the women, with a shrewd idea that it added to their charms, persisted in having it done. The men (and it is significant that in places where the men have ceased to tattoo themselves they continue to do it for the women) tattooed their children at an early age, but as the girls approached a marriageable age they added, on their own account, various ornamentations to those already existing. As an example that tattooing in its later stages is regarded as an increase of beauty, I may mention an instance given me by the wife of a missionary here. A woman belonging to some neighboring tribe having come to stay at the mission, was presented with a dress of some showy material as an inducement to her to discard the loin cloth she had been in the habit of wearing and as an introduction to the habits of civilized life. She objected to wear the dress, however, upon the ground that if she did so she would thereby hide her beauty. It appears certain that the unmarried woman who is most finely tattooed wins most admiration from the men.

Oscar Peschel (a) describes tattooing as another substitute for raiment and remarks: "That it actually takes away from the impression of nudity is declared by all who have seen fully tattooed Albanese." As bearing in the same direction Mr. Darwin, in "Voyage of the Beagle," may be quoted, who, when at New Zealand, speaking of the clean, tidy, and healthy appearance of the young women who acted as servants within the houses, remarks: "The wives of the missionaries tried to persuade them not to be tattooed, but a famous operator having arrived from the south they said: 'We really must have a few lines on our lips, else when we grow old our lips will shrivel, and we shall be so very ugly.'"

In September, 1891, a Zulu, claiming to be a son of the late Cetewayo, gave to a reporter of the Memphis Avalanche the following account:

When some one expressed a doubt of his coming from Zululand he promptly rolled up his sleeve and showed on his right arm the brand of the tribe. The brand is just below the elbow-joint, and it is of a bright red color, showing conclusively that it had been burned into the flesh. The design is very much on the principle of a double heart with a cross running through the center. The same design has been branded over his left eye in a somewhat smaller shape. When questioned about these brands he said:

"In our country all the men have to have the brand of their tribe burned into their skin so that they can never desert us, and no matter where they are found, you can always tell a Zulu by the brand. Always look for it just over the left eye and on the inside of the right arm. Does it hurt? Oh, no; you see they just take the skin together in their fingers and when the brand is red hot touch it once to the skin and it is all done, and the brand can never wear away."

SCARIFICATION.

The following notes regarding scarification are presented:
Edward M. Curr (*b*), p. 94, says:

The principal and most general ornament throughout Australia consists of a number of scars raised on the skin. They are made by deep incisions with a flint or shell, which are kept powdered with charcoal or ashes. The wounds thus made remain open for about three months, and, when covered with skin, scars sometimes almost as thick and long as one's middle finger remain raised above the natural surface of the skin. The incisions are made in rows on various parts of the body, principally on the chest, back, and on the upper muscle of the arm, and less frequently on the thighs and stomach. The breasts of the female are often surrounded with smaller scars. In some tribes dots cut in the skin take the place of scars. The operation is a very painful one, and is often carried out amidst yells of torture. Both sexes are marked in this manner, but the male more extensively than the female.

In the same volume, p. 338, is the following:

When, as often happens, a young man and girl of the Whajook tribe in Australia elope and remain away from the tribe for a time, it is not unusual for them to scar each other in the interim as a memorial of their illicit loves; a singular proceeding when one remembers the agony caused by the operation and the length of time required to get over it. This proceeding is a great aggravation of the original offense in the eyes of husbands.

In Vol. II, p. 414, the same author says:

Men of the Cape river tribe scar their backs and shoulders in this way. Scars are made generally on the left thigh both of the men and women, continues Mr. Chatfield, but occasionally on the right, for the purpose of denoting the particular class to which they belong; but as such a practice would conflict with the custom prevalent throughout the continent as far as known, which is to make these marks for ornament alone, the statement cannot be received without further evidence.

Thomas Worsnop, in the Prehistoric Arts of the Aborigines of Australia, says:

This practice of tattooing by scarification was common all over the continent, varying in character amongst the respective tribes, each having its own distinctive marks, although all patterned upon one monotonous idea.

This is far from evidence of distinct tribal marks, the slight varieties of which may be only local or tribal fashions.

Alfred C. Haddon (*a*), p. 366, says:

Tattooing is unknown, but the body used to be ornamented with raised cicatrices. * * * The Torres strait islanders are distinguished by a large, complicated, oval scar, only slightly raised and of neat construction. This, which I have been told has some connection with a turtle, occupies the right shoulder and is occasionally repeated on the left. I suspect that a young man was not allowed to bear a cicatrice until he had killed his first turtle or dugong.

The same author, op. cit., says of the Mabuiag of Torres straits:

The people were formerly divided up into a number of clans. * * * A man belonging to one clan could not wear the badge of the totem of another clan. * * * All the totems appear to have been animals—as the crocodile, snake, turtle, dugong, dog, cassowary, shark, sting-ray, kingfish, etc.

The same writer, in Notes on Mr. Beardsmore's paper, in Jour. Anthrop. Inst. of Gr. Br. and I. (a), says:

A large number of the women of Mowat, New Guinea, have a ∧-shaped scar above the breasts. * * * Maino of Tud told me that it was cut when the brother leaves the father's house and goes to live with the men; and another informant's story was that it was made when a brother harpooned his first dugong or turtle. Maino (who, by the by, married a Mowat woman) said that a mark on the cheek recorded the brother's prowess.

D'Albertis (c) tells that the people of New Guinea produced scars "by making an incision in the skin and then for a lengthened period irritating it with lime and soot. * * * They use some scars as a sign that they have traveled, and tattoo an additional figure above the right breast on the accomplishment of every additional journey. * * * In Yuli island women have nearly the whole body covered with marks. Children are seldom tattooed; slaves never. Men are hardly ever tattooed, though they have frequently marks on the chest and shoulders; rarely on the face. Tribes and families are recognized by tattoo marks."

Mr. Griffith, in his paper on Sierra Leone, in Jour. Anthrop. Inst. of Gr. Br. and I. (b), says:

The girls are cut on their backs and loins in such a manner as to leave raised scars, which project above the surface of the skin about one-eighth of an inch. They then receive Boondoo names, and after recovery from the painful operation are released from Boondoo with great ceremony and gesticulation by some who personate Boondoo devils. They are then publicly pronounced marriageable.

Dr. Holub (b), speaking of three cuts on the breast of a Koranna of Central South Africa, says:

They have among themselves a kind of freemasonry. Some of them have on their chest three cuts. When they were asked what was the reason of it they generally refused to answer, but after gaining their confidence they confessed that they belonged to something like a secret society, and they said, "I can go through all the valleys inhabited by Korannas and Griquas, and wherever I go when I open my coat and show these three cuts I am sure to be well received."

Mr. H. H. Johnston (a) tells us that scarification is practiced right along the course of the Congo up to the Stanley falls. The marks thus made are tribal. Thus the Bateke are always distinguished by five or six striated lines across the cheek bones, while the Bayansi scar their foreheads with a horizontal or vertical band.

E. Brussaux, in L'Anthropologie (c), reports that scarifications in Congo, which are chiefly on the back, are made for therapeutic reasons.

Julian Thomas (*a*) gives the following description of a New Hebrides woman:

She had a pattern traced over her throat and breast like a scarf. It was done with a shark's tooth when a child. The women's skins are blistered up into flowers and ferns. The skin is cut and earth and ashes placed inside the gashes, and the flesh grows into these forms. Of course they do not cover up these beauties by clothing.

According to Mr. Man, Journ. Anthrop. Inst. of Gr. Br. and I. (*c*), the Andamanese, who also tattoo by means of gashing, do so first by way of ornament, and, secondly, to prove the courage of the individual operated upon and his or her power of enduring pain.

SUMMARY OF STUDIES ON TATTOOING.

Many notes on the topic are omitted, especially those relating mainly to the methods of and the instruments used in the operation. But from those presented above it appears that tattooing still is or very recently was used in various parts of the world for many purposes besides the specific object of designating a tribe, clan, or family, and also apart from the general intent of personal ornament. The most notable of those purposes are as follows: 1, to distinguish between free and slave without reference to the tribe of the latter; 2, to distinguish between a high and low status in the same tribe; 3, as a certificate of bravery exhibited by supporting the ordeal of pain; 4, as marks of personal prowess, particularly, 5, as a record of achievements in war; 6, to show religious symbols; 7, as a therapeutic remedy for disease, and 8, as a prophylactic against disease; 9, as a brand of disgrace; 10, as a token of a woman's marriage, or, sometimes, 11, of her marriageable condition; 12, identification of the person, not as tribesman or clansman, but as an individual; 13, to charm the other sex magically; 14 to inspire fear in the enemy; 15, to magically render the skin impenetrable by weapons; 16, to bring good fortune; and 17, as the device of a secret society.

The use of tattoo marks as certificates and records of prowess in war is considered to be of special importance in any discussion of their origin. A warrior returns from the field stained with blood from an honorable wound, the scars of which he afterwards proudly displays. It would be strictly in the line of ideography to make artificial scars or to paint the semblance of wounds on the person as designations of honor, and from such origin quite as well as from a totemic representation all other forms and uses may have been evolved. For instance, the vigor of manhood being thus signified, the similar use would show the maturity of women. Yet some of the practices of tattoo may have originated independently of either totem or glory mark. The mere idea of decoration as shown in what civilized people call deformations of nose, lip, ear, teeth, and in fact all parts of the body, is sufficient to account for the inception of any form of tattoo. Primitive man never seemed to be content to leave the surface of his body in its natural condition, and from recognition of that discontent studies of clothing and of ornament should take their point of departure.

In this paper many examples are presented of the use, especially by the North American Indians, of tribal signs carved or painted on rock, tree, bark, skin, and other materials, and suggestion is made of an interesting connection between these designs and those of heraldry in Europe. It would, therefore, seem natural that the same Indians who probably for ages used such totemic and tribal devices should paint or tattoo them on their own persons, and the meagerness of the evidence that they actually did so is surprising. Undoubtedly the statement has been made in a general way by some of the earlier explorers and travelers, but when analyzed it is frequently little more than a vague expression of opinion, perhaps based on a preconceived theory. Nearly all the Indian tribes have peculiarities of arrangement of the hair and of some article of apparel and accouterment by which they can always be distinguished. These are not totemic, nor are they by design expressions of a tribal character. They come under the heading of fashion, and such fashions in clothing and in arrangement of the hair still exist among civilized peoples, so that the people of one nation or province can at once be distinguished from others. Very little appears from the account of actual observers to show that the character of the tattoo marks of the North American Indians, perhaps excluding those of the northwest coast, was more than a tribal fashion. Such styles or fashions with no intent or deliberate purpose that they should serve as tribal signs prevail to-day in Africa and in some other regions, and have been introduced by the professional artists who had several styles. Besides the necessary influence of a school of artists, it is obvious that people living together would contract and maintain the same custom and fashion in their cutaneous decoration.

SECTION 4.

DESIGNATIONS OF INDIVIDUALS.

These are divided into: (1) Insignia or tokens of authority. (2) Signs of individual achievements. (3) Property marks. (4) Personal names.

INSIGNIA OR TOKENS OF AUTHORITY.

Champlain (*e*) says of the Iroquois in 1609:

Those who wore three large "pannaches" [plumes] were the chiefs, and the three chiefs delineated have their plumes much larger than those of their companions who were simple warriors.

In Travels of Lewis and Clarke (*a*) it is said:

Among the Teton Sioux the interior police of a village is confided to two or three officers who are named by the chief for the purpose of preserving order, and remain in power some days, at least till the chief appoints a successor; they seem to be a sort of constable or sentinel, since they are always on the watch to keep tranquility during the day and guarding the camp in the night. * * * Their distinguishing mark is a collection of two or three raven skins fixed to the girdle behind the back in such a way that the tails stick out horizontally from the body. On the head too is a raven skin split into two parts and tied so as to let the beak project from the forehead.

In James's Long (d) it is reported that-

Among the Omaha on all occasions of public rejoicings, festivals, dances, or general hunts, a certain number of resolute warriors are previously appointed to preserve order and keep the peace. In token of their office they paint themselves entirely black; usually wear the crow, and arm themselves with a whip or war-club with which they punish on the spot those who misbehave, and are at once both judges and executioners.

Prince Maximilian of Wied (a) says:

In every numerous war party there are four leaders (partisans, karokkanakah) sometimes seven, but only four are reckoned as the real partisans; the others are called bad partisans (karokkanakah-chakohosch, literally, partisans galeux). All partisans carry on their backs a medicine pipe in a case which other warriors dare not have. To become a chief (Numakschi) a man must have been a partisan and then kill an enemy when he is not a partisan. If he follows another partisan for the second time he must have first discovered the enemy, have killed one and then possessed the hide of a white buffalo cow complete with the horns to pretend to the title of chief (Numakschi). * * * All the warriors wear small war pipes round their necks, which are often very elegantly ornamented with porcupine quills.

Pls. XXVI and XXVII are illustrations specially relating to insignia of office selected from an important and unique pictorial roster of the heads of Oglala families, eighty-four in number, in the band of Chief Big-Road, which were obtained by Rev. S. D. Hinman at Standing Rock Agency, Dakota, in 1883, from the United States Indian agent, Maj. McLaughlin, to whom the original had been delivered by Chief Big-Road when brought to that agency and required to give an account of his followers. Other selections from this Oglala Roster appear under the headings of Ideography, Personal names, Comparisons, Customs, Gestures, Religion, and Conventionalizing.

Chief Big Road and his people belong to the northern Oglala, and at the time mentioned had been lately associated with Sitting-Bull in various depredations and hostilities against settlers and the United States authorities. The translations of the names have been verified and the Oglala name attached. At the date of the roster Chief Big-Road was above 50 years old, and was as ignorant and uncompromising a savage in mind and appearance, as one could well find.

The drawings in the original are on a single sheet of foolscap paper, made with black and colored pencils, and a few characters are in yellow-ocher waters color paint. They were made for the occasion with the materials procured at the agency.

Pl. XXVI exhibits the five principal chiefs with their insignia. Each

Plate XXVI.

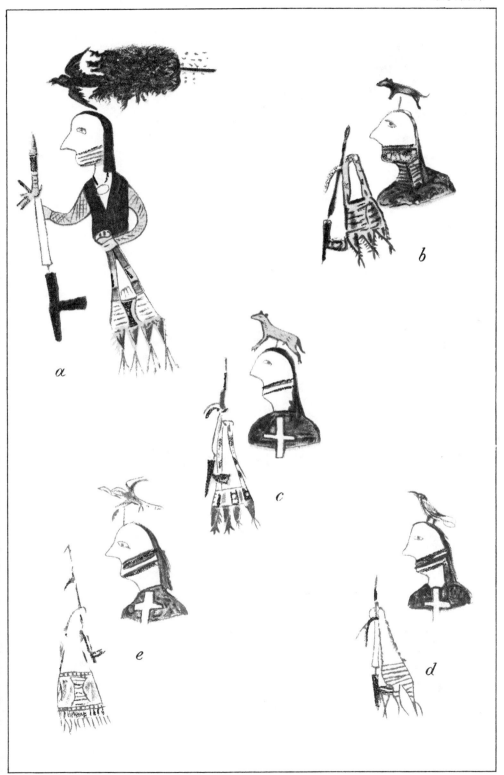

a

b

c

d

e

OGLALA CHIEFS.

Plate XXVII.

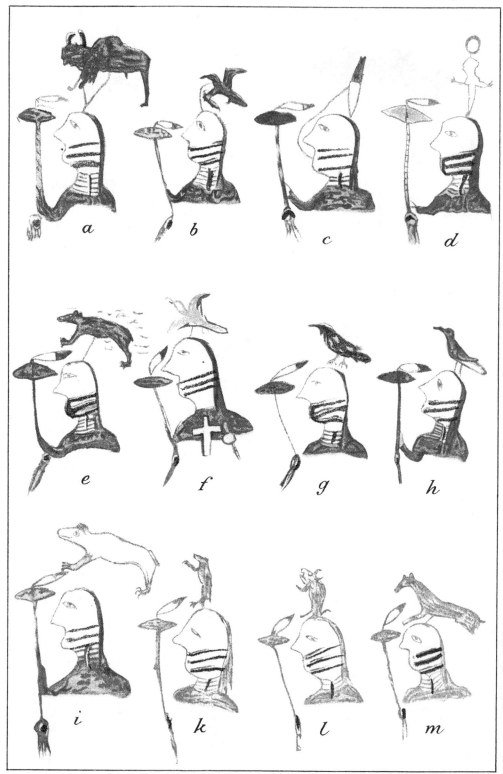

OGLALA SUB-CHIEFS.

has before him a decorated pipe and pouch, the design of each being distinct from the others. The use of pipes as insignia for leaders is frequently mentioned in this work. The five chiefs do not have the war club, their rank being shown by pipe and pouch. Each of the five chiefs has at least three transverse bands on the cheek, with differentiations of the pattern.

Pl. XXVII shows the subchiefs of the band. The three red bands are the sign that they are Akicita-itacanpi, which means head soldiers—captains in war, and captains of police in civil administration. Each of them is decorated with three red transverse bands on the cheek and carries a war club held vertically before the person.

The other male figures not represented in the plates have in general each but a single red band on the cheek; others, two bands, red and blue. These are merely ornamental and without significance.

It will be noticed that in this series the device indicating the name is not generally connected by lines with the mouth but only when there is a natural connection with it. It appears attached by a line to the crown of the head, but sometimes without any connecting line.

Pl. XXVI shows the five principal chiefs of the Oglala in 1883, who are severally designated as follows:

a. Cankutanka, Big-Road. Big-Road is often called Good-Road because a road that is big or broad and well traveled is good. The tracks on both sides of the line indicating a mere path show that the road is big. The bird flying through the dusk indicates the rapidity of travel which the good road allows. This is the same chief as the following:

Fig. 540, Big-Road as appearing in Red-Cloud's Census, No. 96. The broad and big road is indicated by the artist of that series as having distinctly marked sides and horsetracks between these roadsides. In this instance as in several others it is obvious that the ideographic device was not fixed but elastic and subject to variation, the intention being solely to preserve the idea.

FIG. 540.—Big-Road.

b. Sunka-kuciyela, Low-Dog. The dog figure is represented as "low" by the shortness of the legs as compared with the next figure of Long-Dog.

c. Sunka-hanska, Long-Dog. This term "long" is in the pictography of the Siouan tribes, but is differently translated as tall. There is a marked variation in the length of the legs between this and the next foregoing.

d. Kangi-maza, Iron-Crow. The term "iron" is explained above. The color blue is always used in Dakotan pictography for the word translated as iron.

e. Cetan-cigala, Little-Hawk.

Pl. XXVII shows the subchiefs or partisans of the Oglala at the time of the roster in 1883.

a. Represents Tatanka-he-luta, Red-horn-Bull.   The bull's horns have been made bloody by goring.

b. Represents Cetan-watakpe, Charging-Hawk.   This subchief also appears with a slightly different form of "charging" in Red-Cloud's Census, in which the bird is represented head downward.

Fig. 541.—Charging-Hawk, from Red-Cloud's Census, No. 142.   On careful examination the bird is seen to be not erect, as at first appears, but is swooping down.

FIG. 541.— Charging-
Hawk.

c. Represents Wiyaka-aopazan, Wears-the-Feather.   The feather in its conventional form is presented twice, once connected by a line with the mouth and also over the war club as in common with other pictures of this series.   The same person is represented next below.

Fig. 542.—Feather-on-his-Head, from Red-Cloud's Census, No. 86.   In this case the feather droops while it is erect in the figure next above.   No significance is indicated in the slight variation.

FIG. 542.—Feather-
on-his-Head.

d. Represents Pankeskahoksila, Shell-Boy.   The shell is the circular object over the head of the small human figure, which is without the proper number of legs, showing perhaps that he can not march, and his open, weaponless hands say that he is not a warrior, i. e., he is a boy.   The object, now translated shell, was originally a large excrescence on the trunk of a tree which was often cut away by the Dakotas, hollowed out and used as a bowl.

e. Mato-niyanpi, The-Bear-spares-him.   The bear passing through the marks of several tracks indicates an incident not explained, in which the subchief was in danger.

f. Represents Cetan-maza, Iron-Hawk.   The bird is colored blue, as before explained.

g. Represents Kangi-luta, Red-Crow.

h. Represents Situpi-ska, White-Tail.   The bird is probably one of the hawks, as is more distinctly indicated in the representation of the same name as follows:

Fig. 543.—White-Tail; from Red-Cloud's Census, No. 190. This is inserted for convenient comparison with the foregoing, being a slightly variant device for the same person.

FIG. 543.—White-Tail.

i. Represents Mato-ska, White-Bear.

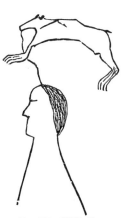

Fig. 544.—White-Bear; from Red-Cloud's Census, No. 252. This is inserted here for comparison of the drawings. The characteristics of the animal appear in both.

FIG. 544.—White-Bear.

k. Represents Mato-najin, Standing-Grizzly-Bear. The differentiations of these and other similar positions of the same object remind one of the heraldic devices "statant," "regardant," "passant," and the like.

Fig. 545.—Standing-Bear; from Red-Cloud's Census, No. 140. This is probably the same man as in the last-mentioned figure, though the fancy of the artist has blazoned the bear as demi. This was, however, for convenience and without special significance, as the fore-quarters are not indicated in the name. But that might well have been done if the device were strictly totemic and connected with the taboo. Some of the bear gens are only allowed to eat the fore quarters of the animal, others the hind quarters.

FIG. 545.—Standing-Bear.

l. Represents Tatanka-najin, Standing-Buffalo-Bull.

m. Represents Tasunke-inyanke, His-Running-Horse. This man was probably the owner of a well known racing pony.

Fig. 546.—A Minneconjou Dakota, named Red-Fish's-Son, danced the calumet dance. The-Swan's Winter Count, 1856–'57.

Maj. Bush says: "A Minneconjou, Red-Fish's-Son, The-Ass, danced the Four-Horn calumet."

The peculiarly ornamented pipe, frequently portrayed and mentioned in the parts of the paper relative to the Dakotas, is, at least for the time of the duration of the ceremonies, the sign of the person who leads them.

FIG. 546.—Four-Horn calumet.

In connection with the display of pipes as insignia of authority and rank, Figs. 547 and 548 are introduced here.

Fig. 547, drawn and explained by an Oglala Dakota, exhibits four erect pipes, to show that he had led four war parties.

FIG. 547.—Two-Strike as partisan.

Fig. 548 is a copy of a drawing made by Lean-Wolf, when second chief of the Hidatsa, to represent himself. The horns on his head-dress show that he is a chief. The eagle feathers on his war bonnet, arranged in the special manner portrayed, also show high distinction as a warrior. His authority as "partisan," or leader of a war party, is represented by the elevated pipe. His name is also added, with the usual line drawn from the head. He explained the outline character of the wolf, having a white body with the mouth unfinished, to show that it was hollow, nothing there; i. e., lean. The animal's tail is drawn in detail and dark, to distinguish it from the body.

The character for "partisan" is also shown in Lone-Dog's Winter Count for the year 1842–'43.

Fig. 549 gives three examples, actual size, of a large number of similar designs scratched on the rocks of Kejimkoojik lake, Nova Scotia. They were at first considered to be connected with the ceremonial or mystery lodges, many sketches of which appear on the same rocks, and examples of which are given in Figs. 717 and 718. Undoubtedly there is some connection between the designs, but those now under consideration are recognized by the Indians of the general locality as the elaborate forms of head dress sometimes so extended as to become masks, which are still worn by a few of the Micmac and Abnaki women. Those women are or were of special authority and held positions in social and religious

Fig. 548.—Lean-Wolf as partisan.

ceremonies. Their ornamental head coverings therefore were insignia of their rank. The modern specimens seen by the present writer are elaborately wrought with beads, quills, and embroidery on fine cloth, velvet or satin, but were originally of skin. The patterns still used show some fantastic connection with those of the rock drawings of this class, and again the latter reproduce some of the tracings on the ground plans of the mystery lodges before mentioned. The feathery branches of trees appearing on both of the two classes of illustrations are in the

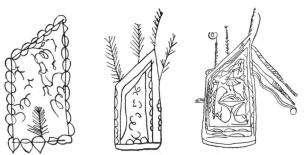

549.—Micmac head dress in pictographs.

modern head coverings actual feathers. The first of the three figures shows the branch or feather inside of the pattern, and the other two have them outside, in which variation the bushes or branches of the medicine lodges show a similar proportion. The third sketch, in addition to the exterior feathers, shows flags or streamers, which in the ceremonial head gear in present use is imitated by ribbons.

If there had been any doubt remaining of the interpretation of this class of drawing it would be removed by the presence of a number of contiguous and obviously contemporary sketches of which Fig. 550 is an example. Here the female chieftain or, perhaps, priestess appears in a ceremonial robe, with her head completely covered by one of these capote masks. The researches made not only establish the significance of this puzzling class of designs, but also show that their authors were of the Abnaki or Micmac branches of the Algonquian linguistic family.

The two lower drawings in Fig. 551 were printed from the Kejim-koojik slate rocks, Nova Scotia, and are recognized by Micmacs of that peninsula as copies of insignia which they say their chiefs used to wear. the Roman Catholic Church, though the figuration of the cross is by no

FIG. 550.—Micmac chieftainess in pictograph.

The designs show some marks suggesting the artistic devices used in means conclusive of European origin. The use of gorgets and other ornaments bearing special designs, as insignia of rank and authority, was well established, and it is quite possible that some of the Micmac designs were affected by the influence of the early missionaries, who indeed may have issued to the chiefs of their flock medals which adopted the general aboriginal style, but were redeemed by Christian symbols. There is no intrinsic evidence to decide whether these particular drawings were or were not made before the arrival of the earliest French missionaries.

The upper right-hand drawing of the three trees with peculiar devices near their several roots was also printed from one of the Kejimkoojik rocks. It became intelligible to the present writer after examination of a silver disk in the possession of Mrs. W. Wallace Brown, of Calais, Maine, which, not long before, had been owned by the head chief of the Passamaquoddy tribe, whose title had been modernized into "governor."

FIG. 551.—Insignia traced on rocks, Nova Scotia.

The disk, which is copied in the upper left-hand corner, was probably not of Indian workmanship, but appeared to have been ordered from a silversmith to be made from a Passamaquoddy design. It was known to represent the three superior officers of the tribe mentioned and had been worn by a former governor as a prized sign of his rank. The mid-

Fig. 552.—Chilkat ceremonial shirt.

dle device is for the governor and the right and left for the officers next in rank to him. The devices at the roots of the trees of the drawing before mentioned are noticeably similar. They may have been made, as were most of the other characters on the Kejimkoojik rocks, by the Micmacs, in which case it would seem that they designated their chiefs by emblems similar to those used by their congeners of the Passamaquoddy tribe or some member of the last named tribe may have drawn the emblem on the rocks in the Micmac territory. In any case there is encouragement in the attempt to decipher petroglyphs from the fact that the tree drawing in Nova Scotia, which seemed without significance, was readily elucidated by a metal inscription found in Maine, the interpretation being verified through living Indians, not only in the two geographic divisions mentioned, but also by the Amalecites in New Brunswick.

Father P. J. De Smet (b), referring to the Piegan and Blackfeet or Satsika, describes the great Tail-Bearer:

His tail, composed of buffalo and horse hair, is about 7 or 8 feet long, and instead of wearing it behind, according to the usual fashion, it is fastened above his forehead

FIG. 553.—Chilkat ceremonial cloak.

and there formed into a spiral coil resembling a rhinoceros's horn. Such a tail among the Blackfeet is a mark of greater distinction and bravery—in all probability the larger the tail the braver the person.

The following description of a Chilkat ceremonial shirt, with the illustration reproduced in Fig. 552, is taken from Niblack (c):

The upper character in the figure represents the sea lion, and that below is a rear view of the same shirt ornamented with a design of wasko, a mythological animal of the wolf species. The edges and arm holes are bordered with red cloth and the whole garment is neatly made.

The same authority describes a Chilkat cloak, with the illustration reproduced as Fig. 553, as follows:

It represents a cloak with a neck opening, ornamented in red cloth with the totemic design of the Orca or Killer. It is in the form of a truncated cone, with no openings for the arms.

The same author gives description accompanying Pl. x, Figs. 33 and 34, of ceremonial blankets and coats. The first-mentioned drawing is reproduced here as Fig. 554:

It is worn by Indians of rank and wealth on the northwest coast, commonly called a "Chilkat blanket," because the best specimens come from the Chilkat country,

FIG. 554.—Chilkat ceremonial blanket.

although other tribes are more or less expert in weaving them. The warp is composed of twisted cord or twine of cedar bark fiber, and the woof of worsted spun from the wool of the mountain goat. Brown, yellow, black, and white are the colors used, and these are skillfully wrought into a pattern representing the totem or a totemic legend of the owner.

The design on the blanket shown represents Hoorts, the bear.

FIG. 555.—Chilkat ceremonial coat.

Fig. 555 is described thus: "A ceremonial shirt or coat of similar workmanship as the blanket just described, is trimmed on the collar and cuffs with sea-otter fur."

In the Verhandl. der Berliner Gesellsch. für Anthrop. (*a*) is the illustration from which Fig. 556 is reproduced. It shows a group of Bella Coola Indians, which is made interesting by the elaborate ceremonial coat worn by the middle figure in the foreground.

FIG. 556.—Bella Coola Indians.

Dr. S. Habel (*c*) gives the following description of Fig. 557, which reproduces only the upper part of the sculpture:

The design represents in low relief an erect human figure in profile, with the head and shoulders slightly inclined forward. The body is apparently naked, excepting

FIG. 557.—Guatemala priest.

those portions which are concealed by elaborate ornaments, the most prominent of which is a crab covering the head. Since there is every reason to believe the figure to represent a priest, the crab may be taken as the emblem of priestly rank.

Pls. LXV and LXVI of the Codex Mendoza, in Vol. I of Lord Kingsborough's Antiquities of Mexico, exhibit the devices and insignia of the soldiers who advanced step by step to higher command, according to their military achievements. The chief criterion, indeed the only one mentioned for these steps and promotions, was the number of prisoners severally taken by the soldiers in war. From the large number of degrees in rank and titles of valor expressed in the above-mentioned plates, a number have been selected and copies of them, exact in drawing, size, and coloration,* are presented here in Pls. xxviii and xxix. The quaint text relating to them is in Kingsborough (p).

Pl. xxviii.—a represents a young man who if he took any prisoners was presented with a square mantle bearing a device of flowers as a sign of valor. He holds a prisoner by the hair. b: This brave man has been presented with a device of arms, which he wears, and with a square orange-colored mantle with a scarlet fringe besides, as a sign of valor, on account of his having taken prisoner two of the enemy, one of whom he holds by the hair. c: This brave man, whose title is that of Quachie, and device of arms such as he wears, bears proof that he has captured five prisoners in war, besides having taken many other prisoners from the enemy in other wars. He also is drawn holding a prisoner. d: This brave man, whose title is Tlacatecatl and device the robe which he wears, with his braided hair and the insignia of a rich plume, declares by his presence that he has obtained the title of a valiant and distinguished person, by merit surpassing that of the others who are represented behind him.

In Pl. xxix.—a: An Alfaqui or superior officer, who merits further promotion and to whom has been presented as a reward for his valor, on account of his having taken three prisoners in war, the device and arms which he wears. He grasps a prisoner by the hair. b: The same Alfaqui, who, as a sign of valor on account of his having captured four of the enemy, has been presented with the device of arms which he wears. He holds a prisoner as before.

Each one of the remaining figures in the plate of Kingsborough declares the titles which officers gained and acquired in the exercise of arms, by which they rose to higher rank, the kings of Mexico creating them captains and generals of their forces or as officers of dispatch [similar to aids-de-camp] to execute their orders, whether they related to the affairs of their own kingdom or to those of the other vassal states, who promptly obeyed without in any manner deviating from the commands which they had received. The two selected are shown in the present Pl. xxix, viz: c, Ezguaguacatl, an officer of dispatch, and d, Tocinltecatl, a man of distinguished courage in war and one of the officers who filled the post of generals of the Mexican armies.

Wiener (b), p. 763, says:

Passing in review the numerous delineations of men on the different tissues in the Peruvian graves, it is to be remarked that a chief is always recognized by a panache, which for the decurion has two plumes, for the centurion four, for the chief of a thousand men six, and the colors of these plumes indicate civil or military functions.

*Reproduced in black and white in the present edition.

Plate XXVIII.

a

c

b

d

MEXICAN MILITARY INSIGNIA.

Plate XXIX.

a

b

c

d

MEXICAN MILITARY INSIGNIA.

A. W. Howitt (c) says:

Messengers in central Australia sent to form a Pinya to avenge a death wear a kind of net on the head and a white frontlet in which is stuck a feather. The messenger is painted with yellow ochre and pipeclay and bears a bunch of emu feathers stuck in his girdle at the back, at the spine. He carries part of the deceased's beard or some balls of pipeclay from the head of one of those mourning for him. These are shown at the destination of the messenger and are at once understood.

The same author, p. 78, reports:

A third party which the Dieri sent out was the dreaded Pinya. It was the avenger of the dead, of those who were believed to have been done to death by sorcery.

The appearance at a camp of one or more men marked each with a white band round the head, with diagonal white and red stripes across the breast and stomach, and with the point of the beard tied up and tipped with human hair, is the sign of a Pinya being about. These men do not converse on ordinary matters, and their appearance is a warning to the camp to listen attentively and to reply truly to such questions as may be put concerning the whereabouts of the condemned man. Knowing the remorseless spirit of the Pinya, any and every question is answered in terror.

FIG. 558—Mark of exploit. Dakota.   FIG. 559.—Killed with fist. Dakota.

SIGNS OF INDIVIDUAL ACHIEVEMENTS.

Prince Maximilian of Wied, (b) gives an account explanatory of Figs. 558 and 559:

The Sioux highly prize personal bravery, and therefore constantly wear the marks of distinction which they have received for their exploits; among these are, especially, tufts of human hair attached to the arms and legs, and feathers on their heads. He who, in the sight of the adversaries, touches a slain or living enemy places a feather horizontally in his hair for this exploit.

They look upon this as a very distinguished act, for many are killed in the attempt before the object is attained. He who kills an enemy by a blow with his fist sticks a feather upright in his hair.

If the enemy is killed with a musket a small piece of wood is put in the hair, which is intended to represent a ramrod. If a warrior is distinguished by many deeds he has a right to wear the great feather-cap with ox-horns. This cap, composed of eagle feathers, which are fastened to a long strip of red cloth hanging down the back, is highly valued by all the tribes on the Missouri. * * * Whoever first discovers the enemy and gives notice to his comrades of their approach is allowed to wear a small feather which is stripped except towards the top.

The following scheme, used by the Dakotas, is taken from Mrs. Eastman's Dahcotah. Colors are not given, but red undoubtedly predominates, as is known from personal observation.

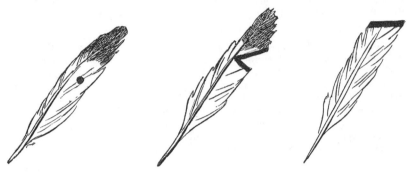

FIG. 560.—Killed an enemy.   FIG. 561.—Cut throat and scalped.   FIG. 562.—Cut enemy's throat.
Dakota.   Dakota.   Dakota.

A spot upon the larger web denotes that the wearer has killed an enemy. Fig. 560.

Fig. 561 denotes that the wearer has cut the throat of his enemy and taken his scalp.

FIG. 563.—Third to strike. Dakota.   FIG. 564.—Fourth to strike. Dakota.

Fig. 562 denotes that the wearer has cut the throat of his enemy.

Fig. 563 denotes that the wearer was the third that touched the body of his enemy after he was killed.

FIG. 565.—Fifth to strike. Dakota.   FIG. 566.—Many wounds. Dakota.

Fig. 564 denotes that the wearer was the fourth that touched the body of his enemy after he was killed.

Fig. 565 denotes that the wearer was the fifth that touched the body of his enemy after he was killed.

Fig. 566 denotes that the wearer has been wounded in many places by the enemy.

The following variations in the scheme were noticed in 1883 among the Mdewakantanwan Dakotas, near Fort Snelling, Minnesota.

Feathers of the eagle are used as among the other bands of Dakotas.

A plain feather is used to signify that the wearer has killed an enemy, without regard to the manner in which he was slain.

When the end is clipped transversely, and the edge colored red, it signifies that the throat of the enemy was cut.

A black feather denotes that an Ojibwa woman was killed. Enemies are considered as Objibwas, that being the tribe with which the Mdewakantanwan Dakotas have been most in collision.

When a warrior has been wounded a red spot is painted upon the broad side of a feather. If the wearer has been shot in the body, arms, or legs, a red spot is painted upon his clothing or blanket, immediately over the locality of the wound. These red spots are sometimes worked in porcupine quills, or in cotton fiber as now obtained from the traders.

Belden (a) says:

Among the Sioux an eagle's feather with a red spot painted on it, worn by a warrior in the village, denotes that on the last war-path he killed an enemy, and for every additional enemy he has slain he carries another feather painted with an additional red spot about the size of a silver quarter.

A red hand painted on a warrior's blanket denotes that he has been wounded by the enemy, and a black one that he has been unfortunate in some way.

Boller (a) in Among the Indians, p. 284, describes a Sioux as wearing a number of small wood shavings stained with vermilion in his hair, each the symbol of a wound received.

Lynd (c) gives a device differing from all the foregoing, with an explanation:

To the human body the Dakotas give four spirits. The first is supposed to be a spirit of the body, and dies with the body. The second is a spirit which always remains with or near the body. Another is the soul which accounts for the deeds of the body, and is supposed by some to go to the south, by others to the west, after the death of the body. The fourth always lingers with the small bundle of the hair of the deceased kept by the relatives until they have a chance to throw it into the enemy's country, when it becomes a roving, restless spirit, bringing death and disease to the enemy whose country it is in.

From this belief arose the practice of wearing four scalp-feathers for each enemy slain in battle, one for each soul.

It should be noted that all the foregoing signs of individual achievements are given by the several authorities as used by the same body of Indians, the Dakota or Sioux. This, however, is a large body, divided into tribes, and it is possible that a different scheme was used in the several tribes. But the accounts are so conflicting that error in either observation or description or both is to be suspected.

Rev. J. Owen Dorsey (b) explains the devices on the shield of a Teton Dakota:

* * * The three pipes on the shield, in a colored sketch prepared by Bushotter, denote that on so many expeditions he carried a war pipe. The red stripes declare how many of the enemy were wounded by him, and the human heads show the number of foes that he killed. The half moon means that he shouted at his foes on a certain night. Once he threw aside his arms and engaged in a hand-to-hand struggle with a foe; this is shown by the human hand. The horse tracks indicate that he ran off with so many horses. If his name was Black Hawk, for instance, a black hawk was painted in the middle of his shield.

Irving (a), in Astoria, says of the Arikara:

He who has killed an enemy in his own land is entitled to drag at his heels a fox skin attached to each moccasin; and he who has slain a grizzly bear wears a necklace of his claws, the most glorious trophy that a hunter can exhibit.

Prince Maximilian, of Wied (c), thus reports on the designations of the Mandans connected with the present topic:

The Mandans wear the large horned feather cap; this is a cap consisting of strips of white ermine with pieces of red cloth hanging down behind as far as the calves of the legs, to which is attached an upright row of black and white eagle feathers, beginning at the head and reaching to the whole length. Only distinguished warriors who have performed many exploits may wear this headdress.

If the Mandans give away one or more of these headdresses, which they estimate very highly, they are immediately considered men of great importance. * * * On their buffalo robes they often represent this feather cap under the image of a sun. Very celebrated and eminent warriors, when most highly decorated, wear in their hair various pieces of wood as signals of their wounds and heroic deeds. Thus Mato-Topé had fastened transversely in his hair a wooden knife painted red and about the length of a hand, because he had killed a Cheyenne chief with his knife; then six wooden sticks, painted red, blue, and yellow, with a brass nail at one end, indicating so many musket wounds which he had received. For an arrow wound he fastened in his hair the wing feather of a wild turkey; at the back of his head he wore a large bunch of owl's feathers, dyed yellow, with red tips, as the badge of the Meniss-Ochata (the dog band). The half of his face was painted red and the other yellow; his body was painted reddish-brown, with narrow stripes, which were produced by taking off the color with the tip of the finger wetted. On his arms, from the shoulder downwards, he had seventeen yellow stripes, which indicated his warlike deeds, and on his breast the figure of a hand, of a yellow color, as a sign that he had captured some prisoners.

* * * A Mandan may have performed many exploits and yet not be allowed to wear tufts of hair on his clothes, unless he carries a medicine pipe and has been the leader of a war party. When a young man who has never performed an exploit is the first to kill an enemy on a warlike expedition he paints a spiral line round his arm, of whatever color he pleases, and he may then wear a whole wolf's tail at the ankle or heel of one foot. If he has first killed and touched the enemy he paints a line running obliquely round the arm and another crossing it in the opposite direction, with three transverse stripes. On killing the second enemy he paints his left leg (that is, the leggin) a reddish-brown. If he kills the second enemy before another is killed by his comrades he may wear two entire wolves' tails at his heels. On his third exploit he paints two longitudinal stripes on his arms and three transverse stripes. This is the exploit that is esteemed the highest; after the third exploit no more marks are made. If he kills an enemy after others of the party have done the same he may wear on his heel one wolf's tail, the tip of which is cut off.

The Hidatsa scheme of designating achievements was obtained by Dr. Hoffman, at Fort Berthold, North Dakota, during 1881, and now follows:

A feather, to the tip of which is attached a tuft of down or several strands of horse hair, dyed red, denotes that the wearer has killed an enemy and that he was the first to touch or strike him with the coup stick. Fig. 567 *a*.

A feather bearing one red bar made with vermillion, signifies the wearer to have been the second person to strike the fallen enemy with the coup stick. Same Fig. *b*.

A feather bearing two red bars signifies that the wearer was the third person to strike the body. Same Fig. *c*.

A feather with three bars signifies that the wearer was the fourth to

FIG. 567.—Marks of exploits, Hidatsa.

strike the fallen enemy. Fig. 568 *a*. Beyond this number honors are not counted.

A red feather denotes that the wearer was wounded in an encounter with an enemy. Fig. 568 *b*.

A narrow strip of rawhide or buckskin is wrapped from end to end with porcupine quills dyed red, though sometimes a few white ones are inserted to break the monotony of color. This strip is attached to the inner surface of the rib or shaft of the quill by means of very thin fibers of sinew, and signifies that the wearer killed a woman belonging to a hostile tribe. It is shown in Fig. 568 *c*. In very fine specimens the quills are directly applied to the shaft without resorting to the strap of leather.

FIG. 568.—Marks of exploits, Hidatsa.

Similar marks denoting exploits are used by the Hidatsa, Mandan, and Arikara Indians. The Hidatsa claim to have been the originators of the devices.

The following characters are marked upon robes and blankets, usually in red or blue colors, and often upon the boat paddles. Frequently an Indian has them painted upon his thighs, though this is generally resorted to only on festal occasions or for dancing.

FIG. 569.—Successful defense. Hidatsa, etc.

Fig. 569 denotes that the wearer successfully defended himself against the enemy by throwing up a ridge of earth or sand to protect the body. The manner of depicting this mark upon the person or clothing is shown in Pl. XXX upon the shirt of the third figure in the lower row.

FIG. 570.—Two successful defenses. Hidatsa, etc.

Fig. 570 signifies that the wearer has upon two different occasions defended himself by hiding his body within low earthworks. The character is merely a compound of two of the preceding marks placed together. Both of the devices shown in Figs. 569 and 570 are displayed on the clothing in Fig. 575, drawn by a Hidatsa.

FIG. 571.—Captured a horse. Hidatsa, etc.

Fig. 571 signifies that the one who carries this mark upon his blanket, leggings, boat paddle, or any other property, or upon his person, has distinguished himself by capturing a horse belonging to a hostile tribe. This character appears upon the garments and legs of several of the human figures 'in Pl. XXX, drawn by a Hidatsa, at Fort Berthold, North Dakota.

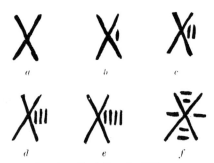

FIG. 572.—Exploit marks, Hidatsa.

In Fig. 572, *a* signifies among the Hidatsa and Mandans that the wearer was the first person to strike a fallen enemy with a coup stick. It signifies among the Arikara simply that the wearer killed an enemy.

b represents among the Hidatsa and Mandans the second person to strike a fallen enemy. It represents among the Arikara the first person to strike the fallen enemy.

c denotes the third person to strike the enemy, according to the Hidatsa and Mandan; the second person to strike him according to the Arikara.

d shows among the Hidatsa and Mandan the fourth person to strike the fallen enemy. This is the highest and last number; the fifth person to risk the danger is considered brave for venturing so near the ground held by the enemy, but has no right to wear a mark therefor.

The same mark among the Arikara represents the person to be the third to strike the enemy.

e, according to the Arikara, represents the fourth person to strike the enemy.

According to the Hidatsa, the wearer of the mark *f* had figured in four encounters; in those recorded by the marks in each of the two lateral spaces he was the second to strike the fallen enemy, and the marks in the upper and lower spaces signify that he was the third person upon two other occasions.

The marks at *c*, in Fig. 572, may be compared with Fig. 573. The head of the victim in this instance is a white man. Such drawings are not made upon the person or clothing of the hero, but upon buffalo robes or other sub stances used for record of biographical events.

FIG. 573.—Record of exploits.

The marks at *d*, in Fig. 572, are drawn on records in the mode shown in Fig. 574.

FIG. 574.—Record of exploits.

Illustrations of the actual mode of wearing several of the above devices appear in Fig. 575, drawn by a Hidatsa.

FIG. 575.—Exploit marks as worn.

The mark of a black hand, sometimes made by the impress of an actually blackened palm or drawn of natural size, or less, signifies that the person authorized to wear the mark has killed an enemy.

Fig. 576, drawn by a Hidatsa, means that the owner of the robe or record on which it appears had taken a scalp. Fig. 577, also drawn by a Hidatsa, means that the bearer struck the enemy in the order above mentioned and took his scalp and his gun.

The drawing reproduced on Pl. XXX was made by a Hidatsa at Fort Berthold, North Dakota. It represents several dancing figures, upon which the several marks of personal achievements can be recognized. The fourth figure of the upper row shows the wearer to have been the second person to strike an enemy upon four different occasions. Upon the right-hand figure of the lower row two distinct marks will be observed; that upon the wearer's left leg indicating him to have been the second to strike an enemy upon two different occasions; and the mark upon the right leg, that he was twice the second person to strike enemies, and twice the third person to perform that exploit.

FIG. 576.—Scalp taken.   FIG. 577.—Scalp and gun taken.

Miss Agnes Crane (a), in an article on Ancient Mexican Heraldry, seems to assert that the evidence of emblems in the western hemisphere as boastful records of individual achievements is confined to Mexico. The present section may supply the evidence lacking.

The following information regarding Winnebago devices of the character now under consideration was given by St. Cyr, a mixed blood Winnebago, in April, 1886.

To show that the wearer killed a man, strike the muddy hand upon the body or horse. Clay of any kind is used. When 20 men have been killed, an otter skin is worn on the back. A skunk skin worn on the calf signifies a man killed.

Scented grass worn on the neck or the wrist shows that a prisoner had been captured and tied with grass in the absence of other cords.

To show that the wearer had been wounded, cover the part of the body with white clay, and indicate the spot with red paint.

Paul Kane (a) says that among the Cree Indians red earth was spotted on a leg to indicate that the wearer had been wounded.

HIDATSA DANCERS BEARING EXPLOIT MARKS.

Prof. Dall (*b*) tells of the Sitka-Kwan:

They perforate their noses, wearing a ring adorned with feathers. They make a succession of perforations all around the edge of the ears, which are ornamented with scarlet thread, shark's teeth, or pieces of shell. Each hole is usually the record of a deed performed or a feast given by the person so adorned.

PROPERTY MARKS.

This topic, upon which much interesting material has been collected in many geographic and ethnologic divisions of the earth, can not include objectively or pictorially many genuine and distinctive illustrations from the North American Indians. The reason for this paucity is that the individual Indian had very little property. Nearly everything which could be classed as personal property belonged to his tribe or, more generally, to his clan or gens. Yet articles of a man's personal manufacture, such as arrows, were often marked in such a manner as to be distinguished. Those marks, many examples of which are upon arrows in the U. S. National Museum, are not of sufficient general interest to be reproduced here. They are not valuable unless they are connected with the makers or owners by a concurrence of the devices with the signs adopted by persons or by classes, the evidence of which can not now except in rare instances be procured. Most of the devices mentioned seem to have degenerated into mere ornamentation, which might be expected, because the arrows are not of great antiquity, and during recent years the records which could have been used for their identification have decayed as authorities even when they have remained in the immediate family, having escaped sale and robbery.

As a general rule neither a man nor a family, in the modern sense, had any property in land, which belonged to a much larger sociologic division, but on their arrival in California Europeans noticed among the Indians there a device to assert rights in realty by the use of distinctive marks. It is not clear whether these marks were merely personal or were tribal or gentile.

According to Mr. A. F. Coronel, of Los Angeles, California, the Serrano Indians in that vicinity formerly practiced a method of marking trees to indicate the corner boundaries of patches of land. The Indians owning areas of territory of whatever size would cut lines upon the bark of the tree corresponding to lines drawn on their own faces, i. e., lines running outward and downward over the cheeks, or perhaps over the chin only, tattooed in color. These lines were made on the trees on the side facing the property, and were understandingly recognized by the whole tribe. This custom still prevailed when Mr. Coronel first located in southern California about the year 1843.

Among the Arikara Indians a custom prevails of drawing upon the blade of a canoe or bull-boat paddle such designs as are worn by the chief and owner to suggest his personal exploits. This has to great extent been adopted by the Hidatsa and Mandans. The marks are chiefly horseshoes and crosses, as in Fig. 578, referring to the capture of the enemy's ponies and to coups in warfare. The entire tribe being inti-

mately acquainted with the courage and actions of all its members, imposition and fraud in the delineation of any character

FIG. 578.—Boat paddle. Arikara.

are not attempted, as such would surely be detected, and the impostor would be ridiculed if not ostracised.

The brands upon cattle in Texas and other regions of the United States where ranches are common illustrate the modern use of property marks. A collection of these brands made by the writer compares unfavorably for individuality and ideography with the genuine marks of Indians for similar purposes.

The following translation from Kunst and Witz der Neger in Das Ausland (a), describing Fig. 579, is inserted for comparison:

> Whenever a pumpkin of surprisingly fine appearance is growing, which promises to furnish a desirable water vase, the proprietor hurries to distinguish it by cutting into it some special mark with his knife, and probably superstitious feelings may coöperate in this act. I have reproduced herewith the best types of such property marks which I have been able to discover.

Sir John Lubbock (a) tells that many of the arrows found at Nydam, Slesvick, had owner's marks on them, now reproduced in Fig. 580 as a and c, resembling those on the modern Esquimaux arrows shown in the same figure as b.

Prof. Anton Schiefner (b) gives a remarkable parallel between the Runic alphabet and the property marks of the Finns, Lapps, and Samoyeds.

Fig. 579.—African property mark.

PERSONAL NAMES.

The names of Indians as formerly adopted by or bestowed among themselves were generally connotive. They very often refer to some animal and predicate an attribute or position of that animal. On account of their sometimes objective and sometimes ideographic nature, they almost invariably admit of being expressed in sign language; and for the same reason they can readily be portrayed in pictographs. The device generally adopted by the Dakotan tribes to signify that an object drawn in connection with a human figure was a totemic or a personal name of the individual, is to connect that object with the figure by a line drawn to the head or, more frequently, to the

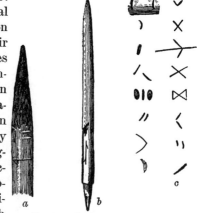

FIG. 580.—Owner's marks, Slesvick.

mouth of the latter. The same tribes make a distinction to manifest that the gesture sign for an object gestured is intended to be the name of a person and not introduced for any other purpose by passing the index forward from the mouth in a direct line after the conclusion of the sign for the object. This signifies "that is his name," the name of the person referred to.

As a general rule, Indians were named in early infancy according to a tribal system, but in later life each generally acquired a new name, or perhaps several names in succession, from some special exploits or adventures. Frequently a sobriquet is given which is not complimentary. All of the names subsequently acquired as well as the original names are so connected with material objects or with substantive actions as to be expressible in a graphic picture and also in a pictorial sign. In the want of alphabet or syllabary they used the same expedient to distinguish the European invaders. A Virginian was styled Assarigoa, "Big Knife." The authorities of Massachusetts were called by the Iroquois, Kinshon, "a fish," doubtless in allusion to the cod industry and the fact that a wooden codfish then hung, as it did long afterwards, in the state house at Boston, as an emblem of the colony and state.

The determination to use names of this connotive character is shown by the objective translation, whenever possible, of such European names as it became necessary for them to introduce frequently into their speech. William Penn was called Onas, that being the word for feather-quill in the Mohawk dialect. The name of the second French governor of Canada was De Montmagny, erroneously translated to be "great mountain," which words were correctly translated by the Iroquois into Onontio, and this expression becoming associated with the title has been applied to all successive Canadian governors, though the origin having been generally forgotten, it has been considered to be a metaphorical compliment.

The persistence of titles is shown by the fact that the Abnaki of New Brunswick to-day call Queen Victoria, "King James," with a feminine addition.

Gov. Fletcher was named by the Iroquois Cajenquiragoe, "the great swift arrow," not because of his speedy arrival at a critical time, as has been supposed, but because they had somehow been informed of the etymology of his name, "arrow-maker" (Fr. fléchier). A notable example of the adoption of a graphic illustration from a similarity in the sound of the name to known English words is given in the present paper, in Fig. 919, where Gen. Maynadier is represented as "many deer."

While, as before said, some tribes give names to children from considerations of birth and kinship according to a fixed rule, others conferred them after solemn deliberation. Even these were not necessarily permanent. A diminutive form is frequently bestowed by the affection of the parent. On initiation into one of the cult associations a name is generally received. Until this is established a warrior is liable to change his name after every fight or hunt. He will sometimes only acknowledge the name he has himself assumed, perhaps from a dream or vision, though he may be habitually called by an entirely different name. From that reason the same man is sometimes known under several different epithets. Personal peculiarity, deformity, or accident is sure to fix a name against which it is vain to struggle. Girls do not often change names bestowed in their childhood. The same precise name is often given to different individuals in the same tribe, but not so frequently in the same band, whereby the inconvenience would be increased. For this reason it is often necessary to specify the band, sometimes also the father. For instance, when the writer asked an Indian who Black-Stone, a chief mentioned in the Lone-Dog winter counts, was, the Indian asked, first, what tribe was he; then, what band; then, who was his father; and, except in the case of very noted persons, the identity is not proved without an answer to these questions. A striking instance of this plurality of names among the Dakotas was connected with the name Sitting-Bull, belonging to the leader of the hostile band, while one of that name was almost equally noted as being the head soldier of the friendly Dakotas at Red-Cloud Agency.

The northeastern tribes sometimes formally resurrected the name of the dead and also revived it by adoption. See Jes. Rel., 1639, p. 45, and 1642, p. 53.

Among the peculiarities connected with Indian personal names, far too many for discussion here, is their avoidance of them in direct address, terms of kinship or relative age taking their place. Maj. J. W. Powell states that at one time he had the Kaibab Indians, a small tribe of northern Arizona, traveling with him. The young chief was called by white men "Frank." For several weeks he refused to give his Indian name and Maj. Powell endeavored to discover it by noticing the term by which he was addressed by the other Indians, but invariably some kinship term was employed. One day in a quarrel his wife called him Chuarumpik ("Yucca-heart"). Subsequently Maj. Powell questioned the young chief about the matter, who explained and apologized for the great insult which his wife had given him and said that she was excused by great provocation. The insult consisted in calling the man by his real name.

Everard F. im Thurn (g) gives the following account of the name-system of the Indians of Guiana, which might have been written with equal truth about some tribes of North America:

The system under which the Indians have their personal names is intricate and difficult to explain. In the first place, a name, which may be called the proper name, is always given to a young child soon after birth. It is said to be proper that the peaiman, or medicine-man, should choose and give this name, but, at any rate now, the naming seems more often left to the parents. The word selected is generally the name of some plant, bird, or other natural object. But these names seem of little use, in that owners have a very strong objection to telling or using them, apparently on the ground that the name is part of the man, and that he who knows the name has part of the owner of that name in his power.

One Indian, therefore, generally addresses another only according to the relationship of the caller and the called, as brother, sister, father, mother, and so on. These terms, therefore, practically form the names actually used by Indians amongst themselves. But an Indian is just as unwilling to tell his proper name to a white man as to an Indian, and, of course, between the Indian and the white man there is no relationship the term for wh ch can serve as a proper name. An Indian, therefore, when he has to do with a European, asks the latter to give him a name, and if one is given to him always afterwards uses this. The names given in this way are generally simple enough—John, Peter, Thomas, and so on.

The original of Fig. 581 was made in 1873 by Running Antelope, chief of the Uncapapa Dakota, in the style of a signature instead of being attached to his head by a line as is the usual method of the tribe in designating personal names.

FIG. 581.—Signature of Running Antelope, Dakota.

Fig. 582 presents a curious comparison with Figs. 548 and 903 showing the manner in which the wolf, proverbially a lean animal, was delineated by Germans in the thirteenth and fourteenth centuries. It is taken from Rudolf Cronau (*b*), whose remarks are translated and condensed as follows:

a. The oldest representation known to me of the "wolf" occurs on a Gothic sword of the thirteenth century, in the Historical Museum of Dresden.

b. Is more primitive, from a sword of the last half of the fourteenth century, in the "Berliner Zeughause;" also similar to *c*, of the same period, from a specimen in the Züricher Zeughaus.

d and *e.* Signatures on two specimens in the collection in Feste Coburg; *e* is a rare representation of the figure of the wolf of 1490, in the Germanic Museum at Nürnberg, and still more intricate (verzwickter) is the drawing *f* on a Dresden specimen of the year 1559.

FIG. 582.—Solinger sword-makers' marks.

A large proportion of the pictographs of several names next to be presented are from Red-Cloud's Census, the history of which is as follows:

A pictorial census was prepared in 1884 under the direction of Red-Cloud, chief of the Dakota at Pine Ridge Agency, Dakota Territory. The 289 persons enumerated, many of whom were heads of families, were the adherents of Red-Cloud and did not represent all the Indians

at that agency. Owing to a disagreement the agent refused to acknowledge that chief as head of the Indians at the agency, and named another
as the official chief. Many of the Indians exhibited their allegiance to
Red-Cloud by having their names attached in their own pictorial style
to a document showing their votes and number. This filled seven
sheets of ordinary manila paper and was sent to Washington. While
in the custody of Dr. T. A. Bland, of that city, it was loaned by him to
the Bureau of Ethnology to be copied by photography. The different
sheets were apparently drawn by different persons, as the drawings of
human heads vary enough to indicate individuality. This arrangement seems to imply seven bands or, perhaps, gentes.

Dr. V. T. McGillicuddy, who at the time was Indian agent at Pine
Ridge Agency, Dakota, in correspondence gives the impression that the
several pictographs representing names were attached as signatures
by the several individuals to a subscription list for Dr. Bland, before
mentioned, who was the editor of The Council Fire, in support of that
publication and with an agreement that each should give 25 cents.
The document in that view would be a subscription list, but the sub-
scribers were, in fact, the adherents of Red-Cloud. Whatever was the
motive for this collection of pictured names, its interest consists in
the mode of their portrayal, together with the assurance that they were
the spontaneous and genuine work of the Indians concerned.

In addition to the personal names which immediately follow, a considerable number of the 289 pictographic names appear elsewhere in
this paper under the various heads of Tribal Designations, Ideography,
Conventionalizing, Customs, special Comparison, etc.

Interspersed among the personal names taken from the above mentioned list are others selected from the Oglala Roster, the origin of
which is explained above, and the several winter counts of The-Flame,
The-Swan, American-Horse, and Cloud-Shield, mentioned, respectively,
in Chap. x, Sec. 2. The authority is in each case attached to the pictograph with the translation of the Indian name, and in some cases with
the name in the original.

Rev. J. Owen Dorsey, in Vol. xxxiv of the Proceedings of the American Association for the Advancement of Science and in the American
Anthropologist for July, 1890, gives valuable notes on the subject of
Indian personal names and also has made oral suggestions to the present
writer. Some of those may be considered with reference to the list
now presented. He thinks that the frequent use of color names is
from a mythical or symbolic significance attributed to the colors.
Also the word translated "iron," or "metal," is connected with the
color blue, the object called iron being always painted blue when
colors are used, and that color is mystically connected with the water
powers of the Dakotan mythology. The frequent use of the terms
"Little" and "Big," with or without graphic differentiation, may be
as the terms young and old, junior and senior, are employed by civilized people, but the expressions in other cases may refer to the size

of the animals seen in the visions of fasting which have determined the names.

Explanations on parts of the pictographs not strictly connected with the personal name are annexed for the reason before indicated and the objects connected by the names are to some extent arranged in classes.

OBJECTIVE.

In the figures immediately following the delineation is objective. It is sometimes interesting to note the different modes of representing the same object or concept.

Fig. 583.—High-Back-Bone, a very brave Og-lala, was killed by the Shoshoni. They also shot another man, who died after he reached home. American-Horse's Winter Count, 1870–'71.

FIG. 583.

Fig. 584.—High-Back-Bone was killed in a fight with the Snakes (Shoshoni). Cloud-Shield's Winter Count, 1870–'71. White-Cow-Killer calls it "High-Back-Bone-killed-by-Snake-Indians winter."

FIG. 584.

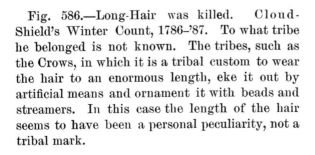

Fig. 585.—A Minneconjou Dakota named Broken-Back was killed by the Crow Indians at Black Hills. Swan's Winter Count, 1848–'49.

FIG. 585.

Fig. 586.—Long-Hair was killed. Cloud-Shield's Winter Count, 1786–'87. To what tribe he belonged is not known. The tribes, such as the Crows, in which it is a tribal custom to wear the hair to an enormous length, eke it out by artificial means and ornament it with beads and streamers. In this case the length of the hair seems to have been a personal peculiarity, not a tribal mark.

FIG. 586.

Fig. 587.—They killed the long-haired man in a fight with the Cheyennes while on an expedition to avenge the death of The-Man-Who-Owns-The-Flute, who was killed by the Cheyennes the year before. American-Horse's Winter Count, 1796–'97. This may be the same man who is referred to in the last preceding figure, as the expression "killed," given in translation by the interpreters, does not always mean wounded to death, but severely wounded—Hibernicé "kilt." Here the scalp shows the length of the hair, and the victim is called a Cheyenne.

FIG. 587.

Fig. 588.—The Stabber. Cloud-Shield's Winter Count, 1783–'84. The man's name is suggested by the spear in the body over his head, which is connected with his mouth by a line.

FIG. 588.

Fig. 589.—Stabber. Red-Cloud's Census. This figure is substantially the same as the preceding, though more rude.

FIG. 589.

Fig. 590.—Red-Shirt. Red-Cloud's Census. This and the following figure exhibit the name, the first showing only the garment and the second exhibiting it as worn.

FIG. 590.

Fig. 591.—Red-Shirt, a Dakota, was killed by the Crows while looking for his ponies near Old Woman's fork. American-Horse's Winter Count, 1810–'11. The bow over the head and the absence of scalp-lock signifies death by the arrow of enemies.

FIG. 591.

Fig. 592.—Chief Red-Cloud. Red-Cloud's Census. This and the next figure give two modes of expressing the name of the celebrated chief, Red-Cloud.

FIG. 592.

Fig. 593.—Three-Stars (General Crook) took Red-Cloud's young men to help him fight the Cheyennes. Cloud-Shield's Winter Count, 1876–'77.

FIG. 593.

Fig. 594.—Caught-the-Enemy. Red-Cloud's Census. The enemy seems to be caught by his hair.

FIG. 594.

Fig. 595.—Black-Rock was killed by the Crows. His brother, whose name he had taken, was killed by the Crows three years before. American-Horse's Winter Count, 1809–'10.

FIG. 595.

FIG. 596.

Fig. 596.—Bird, a white trader, was burned to death by the Cheyennes. Cloud-Shield's Winter Count, 1864–'65. He is surrounded by flames in the picture. His name was probably Bird, which was pictorially represented as usual.

FIG. 597.

Fig. 597.—Red-Lake's house, which he had recently built, was destroyed by fire, and he was killed by the accidental explosion of some powder. American-Horse's Winter Count, 1831–'32. This figure is introduced here in connection with the simple fire on the one preceding to show the artistic portrayal separately of a steady flame and of an explosion.

FIG. 598.

Fig. 598.—Two-Face, an Oglala, was badly burnt by the explosion of his powder horn. American-Horse's Winter Count, 1860–'61. Here is another view of the explosion of gunpowder.

FIG. 599.

Fig. 599.—A Two-Kettle Dakota, named The-Breast, died. Swan's Winter Count, 1836–'37.

Mato Sapa says: A Two-Kettle, named The-Breast, died. This is the same character as is given elsewhere for abundance, plenty of buffalo. But here it has a wholly personal application.

FIG. 600.

Fig. 600.—Left-Handed-Big-Nose was killed by the Shoshoni. American-Horse's Winter Count, 1839–'40. His left arm is represented extended, and his nose is grotesquely conspicuous.

FIG. 601.

Fig. 601.—Roman-Nose. Red-Cloud's Census. The large and aquiline nose is exhibited, which was very liberally translated "Roman Nose," and the term became the popular name of a celebrated chief of the Dakotas.

Fig. 602.—Torn-Belly. Red-Cloud's Census.

FIG. 602.

Fig. 603.—Spotted-Face. Red-Cloud's Census.

FIG. 603.

Fig. 604.—Licks - with - his - tongue. Red-Cloud's Census. The tongue is exaggerated as well as protruded, and without explanation might be mistaken for a large object bitten off for eating in a gluttonous manner.

FIG. 604.

Fig. 605.—Knock-a-hole-in-the-head. Red-Cloud's Census.

FIG. 605.

Fig. 606.—Broken-Leg-Duck, an Oglala, went to a Crow village to steal horses and was killed. American-Horse's Winter Count, 1786–'87. A line connects the bird, one of whose legs is out of order, with the mouth of the man's head, which is without scalplock.

FIG. 606.

Fig. 607.—Antelope-Dung broke his neck while surrounding buffalo. American-Horse's Winter Count, 1853–'54.

FIG. 607.

FIG. 608.

Fig. 608.—Antelope-Dung broke his neck while running antelope. Cloud-Shield's Winter Count, 1853–'54. His head is the only part of his body that is shown, and it is bleeding copiously. Without the preceding figure this one would not be intelligible.

FIG. 609.

Fig. 609.—Broken-Arrow fell from his horse while running buffalo and broke his neck. American-Horse's Winter Count, 1859–'60.

FIG. 610.

Fig. 610.—Sits-like-a-Woman. Red-Cloud's Census. This person is also portrayed in a recent Dakota record, where the character is represented by the "woman seated" only. The name of this man is not "Sits-like-a-Woman," but High-Wolf—shunkmanitu (wolf), wankantuya (up above). This is an instance of giving one name in a pictograph as if the correct or official name and retaining another by which the man is known in camp to his companions.

FIG. 611.

Fig. 611.—The-Man-Who-Owns-the-Flute was killed by the Cheyennes. American-Horse's Winter Count, 1795–'96. His flute is represented in front of him with sounds coming from it. A bullet mark is on his neck. In reference to this character, see Chap. xx, Sec. 2.

Fig. 612.—Smoking-Bear. Red-Cloud's Census. The bear does not appear to be smoking the pipe, but the smoke of the latter is mounting to the animal's neck, so the bear is smoking in a passive sense.

FIG. 612.

Fig. 613.—Biting-Bear. Red-Cloud's Census. The bear seems to be biting at the bark on the limb of a tree, which shows the marks of his claws. This animal, as is well known, eats the bark of certain trees.

FIG. 613.

METAPHORIC.

Fig. 614.—Wolf-Ear. Red-Cloud's Census. The designation of the ear of a wolf probably refers to size, and is substantially the same as big-ear.

FIG. 614.

Fig. 615.—Fighting-Cuss. Red-Cloud's Census. This warrior appears, while only armed with a lance, to be successfully fighting an enemy who has a gun.

FIG. 615.

Fig. 616.—Man-with-hearts. Red-Cloud's Census. There is no information as to the significance of this drawing, but it is conjectured that the warrior had eaten the heart of one or more enemies, as was frequently done. This was not cannibalism, but a superstitious and sometimes ceremonial performance, by which the eater acquired the qualities of the victim, and in this case would be supposed to have more than one heart, i. e., the courage attributed to those hearts.

FIG. 616.

Fig. 617.—Takes-the-Gun. Red-Cloud's Census. It appears from the name that the man is not handling his own gun, but is on the point of grasping and taking away the weapon of another person.

FIG. 617.

Fig. 618.—Jola, Whistler. The Oglala Roster. This is one of the instances where the usual rule in the Oglala Roster, of representing the name above the head, is abandoned, because it is essential to connect it with the mouth to express the whistle. Without this arrangement the musical instrument would not be suggested.

FIG. 618.

Fig. 619.—American-Horse's Winter Count for 1872–'73 gives the pictograph of Whistler, also named Little-Bull. Both of his names appear; that of Whistler is expressed by the sounds blown from the mouth. He whistles without an instrument.

FIG. 619.

Fig. 620.—Ceji, Tongue. The Oglala Roster. This man was not necessarily an orator, but probably the nickname was given in derision as orally "tonguey" might be. Again the line is from the crown of the head to the protruded tongue.

FIG. 620.

Fig. 621.—Canku-sapa, Black-Road. The Oglala Roster. This road, on which horse tracks are shown, is distinguished from that of the head chief Big-Road (*a*, on Pl. XXVI) as being much more narrow and obscure, therefore black.

FIG. 621.

ANIMALS.

The following figures are selected from a large number to show the variety of animals, and the differentiation by marks and attitudes found necessary to present the names. A similar multiplication of the animals by different coloration is exhibited, but can not be repeated in the text figures.

Fig. 622.—Bob-tail-Horse. Red-Cloud's Census. The translation of the Indian's name is rather liberal, but the device is graphic.

FIG. 622.

Fig. 623.—Two-Eagles. Red-Cloud's Census.

FIG. 623.

Fig. 624.—Minneconjou Dakota chief, named Swan, died. The-Swan's Winter Count, 1866–'67. This bird is supposed to be swimming on the water, its legs not being visible.

FIG. 624.

Fig. 625.—Bear - Looks - Back. Red-Cloud's Census.

FIG. 625.

FIG. 626.

Fig. 626.—Mouse.   Red-Cloud's Census.

FIG. 627.

Fig. 627.—Badger, a Dakota, was killed by enemies, as shown by the absence of his scalp. Cloud-Shield's Winter Count, 1796–'97.

FIG. 628.

Fig. 628.—Spider was killed (stabbed) in a fight with the Pawnees. American-Horse's Winter Count, 1861–'62.   An immense effusion of blood is depicted flowing from the wound.

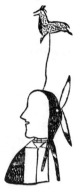

FIG. 629.

Fig. 629.—Spotted-Elk.   Red-Cloud's Census.

Fig. 630.—Spotted-Horse. Red-Cloud's Census.

FIG. 630

Fig. 631.—White-Goose was killed in an attack made by some enemies. Cloud-Shield's Winter Count, 1789–'90. White - Cow - Killer calls it, "Goose-Feather-killed winter."

FIG. 631.

Fig. 632.—Maka-gleska, Spotted-Skunk. The Oglala Roster. The special characteristic of the animal is suggested.

FIG. 632.

Fig. 633.—Hoka-qin, Carried-the-Badger. The Oglala Roster. The design explains itself. The animal is exaggerated in size and some of its features are accentuated.

FIG. 633.

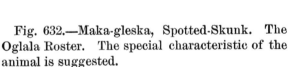

FIG. 634.

Fig. 634.—Kangi-topa, Four-Crows. The Oglala Roster. The four crows are cawing forth such explanation as they can give of the reasons, probably coming from visions, why they were used to form a name for an Oglala.

VEGETABLE.

The products of the vegetable kingdom are not often used by the Dakotas in their personal designations. The three following figures, however, are examples of such use.

FIG. 635.

Fig. 635.—Tree-in-the-Face. Red-Cloud's Census. This man probably painted a tree on his face.

FIG. 636.

Fig. 636.—Leaves. Red-Cloud's Census. This and the following figure represent two different men of the same name and the devices are distinctly individual.

FIG. 637.

Fig. 637.—Leaves. Red-Cloud's Census.

With regard to the errors arising from bad translation, an example may be given, relating to a name the explanation of which has often been asked. A former chief of the Oglala was called "Old-man-afraid-of-his-Horses," by the whites, and his son is known as "Young-man-afraid-of-his-Horses." A common interpretation about "afraid-of-his-horses" is that the man valued his horses so much that he was afraid of losing them. The representative of the name, however, stated to the writer that the correct name was Ta-shunka Kokipapi, and that the true meaning was "He-whose-horse-they-fear"; literally "His-horse-they-fear-it."

A large number of pictorially rendered Indian names attached to deeds and treaties have been published, e. g., in Documents relating to the Colonial History of New York (b). Few of them are of interest, and they generally suggest the assistance of practiced penmen. In the collections mentioned some of the Dutch marks are in the same general style as those of the Indians.

Mr. P. W. Norris, late of the Bureau of Ethnology, had a buffalo robe containing a record of exploits, which was drawn by Black-Crow, a Da-

FIG. 638.—Loud-Talker.

kota warrior. The successful warrior is represented in each instance upright, the accompanying figure being always in a recumbent posture, representing the enemy who was slain. The peculiar feature of these pictographs is that instead of depicting the victim's personal name with a connecting line, the object denoting his name is placed above the head of the victor in each instance, and a line connects the character with his mouth. The latter thus seems to proclaim the name of his victim. A pipe is also figured between the victor and the vanquished, showing that he is entitled to smoke a pipe of celebration.

A copy of the whole record was shown to the Mdewakantanwan Dakotas, near Fort Snelling, Minnesota, in 1883, and the character reproduced in Fig. 638, about which there was the most doubt, was explained as signifying "many tongues," or Loud-Talker.

The circle at the end of the line running from the mouth contains a number of lanceolate forms, one-half of each of which is black, the other white. They have the appearance of feathers, but also may represent tongues and signify voice, sound issuing from the mouth, and correspond in some respect to those drawn by the Mexicans with that significance, of which examples are given in this work, Chap. xx, Sec. 2. The considerable number of these tongue-like figures suggests intensity and denotes loud voice, or, as given literally, "loud talker," that being the name of the victim.

It is, however, to be noted that "Shield," an Oglala Dakota, contends that the character signifies Feather-Shield, the name of a warrior formerly living at the Pine Ridge Agency, Dakota.

Designation of an object, as a name, by means of a connecting line is mentioned in Kingsborough (*a*). Pedro de Alvarado, one of the companions of Cortez, was red-headed. Designating him, the Mexicans called him Tonatihu, the "Sun," and in their picture-writing his name was represented by their conventional character for the sun attached to his person by a line.

FIG. 639.—Mexican names.

Other examples are now presented both of the linear connection and of the iconographic figuration by the old Mexicans.

In Kingsborough (*b*) is a pictograph of Chimalpopoca, which name signifies a smoking shield, here reproduced as Fig. 639 (*a*). The smoking shield is connected with the head by a line, and the form of smoke should be noticed in comparison with the representation of flame and of voice by the same pictors.

The same authority and volume, p. 135 (illustration in Vol. I, Pt. 4, Pl. v), gives the name and illustration (reproduced in the same Fig., *b*) of Ytzcohuatl, the signification of which name is a serpent armed with knives. The knives refer to the Itzli stone.

In the same volume, p. 137, is the name Face of Water, with the corresponding illustration in Vol. I, Pt. 4, Pl. 12 (here Pl. XII *c*). The drops of water are falling profusely from the face.